Cultural Entrepreneurship in Theory,
Pedagogy and Practice

Olaf Kuhlke
Annick Schramme
Rene Kooyman (Ed)

D1524771

CREATING CULTURAL CAPITAL

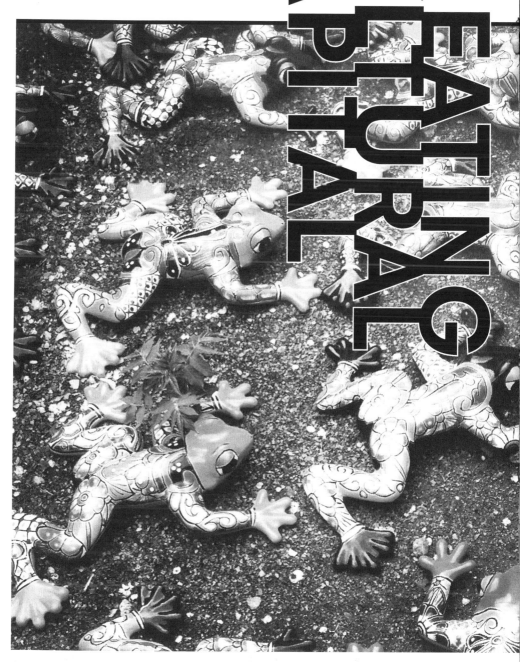

Pioneering Minds
Worldwide

CONTENTS

INTRODUCTION AND READING GUIDE

I A GLOBAL PERSPECTIVE

II THEORY

III PEDAGOGY

IV CASES

CONTENTS

V PRACTICE

CONTENTS

EXPANDING THE GLOBAL VISION

Olaf Kuhlke
Annick Schramme
Rene Kooyman

CULTURAL ENTREPRENEURSHIP AS AN ACADEMIC DISCIPLINE AND PROFESSIONAL PRACTICE
EMBRACING NEW THEORIES, EXPLORING NEW PEDAGOGIES AND FOSTERING NEW SKILLS

Introduction: The Rise of the Creative Economy

For well over a decade now, regional, national and international reports have carefully documented the rise of the creative economy, particularly in the Western Hemisphere (Bakhshi, Freeman, & Higgs, 2013; Dos Santos-Dulsenberg, 2009, Harris, Collins, & Cheek, 2013; Reis et al., 2008; Restrepo & Marquez, 2013). As the most current UNCTAD Creative Economy Report (2013) points out, culture is now *'a driver [emphasis in the original document] of economic development, led by the growth of the creative economy in general and the cultural and creative industries in particular, recognized not only for their economic value but also increasingly for their role in producing new creative ideas or technologies, and their non-monetized social benefits'* (Programme, 2013). As a consequence scholars and policy makers alike have paid close attention to scalable, specific strategies and policy instruments that boost both public and private investment in cultural activities and creative occupations, specifically in urban areas (Connell, 2013; Florida, 2010; Hagoort, 2003; Haselbach, Gerecht, & Hempel, 2010; Henry & de Bruin, 2011; Howkins, 2002; Kooyman, 2011; Kunzmann, 1995; Oakley, 2004; Reis et al., 2008). Creative place making, or the purposeful selection, clustering and use of creative activities to stimulate economic and social development in strategically urban areas, has become an important tool to boost the cultural vibrancy of cities (Markussen & Gadwa, 2010; Schramme, Kooyman & Hagoort, 2014).

Parallel to this extensive interest in the creative economy and its growth trajectory and potential, and ever since the publication of Richard Floridas' seminal work on what he referred to as *'the creative class'* (Florida, 2002) countless scholars have not only sought to define, delineate and measure the impact of cultural and creative industries on national economies and global trade, but have tried to define what creative activities are, what occupations should be considered as part of the creative economy, and what people do to self-identify as *'creative'* (Bakhshi et al., 2013; Howkins, 2002; Oakley, 2004; Reis et al., 2008). To this date, there is no concise definition and delineation of the creative economy, and taxonomies that seek to group occupations into *'creative'* versus *'non-creative'*, differ not only from country to country, but often from region to region *within* countries – and are inherently difficult to construct (Harris et al., 2013). Thus, what we are left with is an increasing body of data, analysis and policy documentation that has documented the economic impact of a variety of creative activities worldwide, yet we are missing a common ground to define and delineate these activities. Given the different ways in which nations collect and classify economic data, this is perhaps not surprising, and may never allow for an exact analysis of global comparative patterns in the creative sector.

Yet, what this work has in common is that is has begun to map a shift in our post-industrial service industry-based economy (Florida, 2012). Knowledge-based, highly-skilled creative workforce is rapidly growing, both in specific countries and globally (Calabrò & Wijngaarde, 2013; Restrepo & Marquez, 2013). As statistics in most reports have shown, this global trend continued even through recent global recession and financial crisis of 2008 and 2009 (Duisenberg, 2008, 2010). In the United States, a similar trend has now been documented, and a systematic framework for categorizing the creative economy has been developed (Harris et al., 2013). Global drivers of this growth are small and medium sized enterprises (SMEs) and even 'nano' enterprises, which points to the increasing significance of entrepreneurship and start-ups in driving the growth of the creative economy (Connell, 2013; Hayter & Pierce, 2011; Kooyman, 2011). Simultaneously, in a lot of European countries, we observe a contin-uous decrease of public funding of arts and culture, forcing art museums, theatres and a variety of other *public* cultural institutions to be more entrepreneurial in looking for other financial resources like *private* funding and donations (Cronshaw & Tullin, 2012; Klamer, 1996). This has also been true for decades in the United States as well, where public, not-for-profit, or donor-based institution that might received little or no public funding, have been looking for ways to increase revenue by exploring for-profit strategies (Brooks, 2001; Gómez-Peña, 2004; Himmelstein & Zaid, 1984).

The Emergence of Cultural Entrepreneurship

As key observers and analysts of societal trends, and as innovators of that are tasked with preparing the next generation of the work force, universities, colleges and think tanks across the globe have increasingly sought to offer courses and programs to pre-pare students for the creative economy of the future, and especially for careers as entre-preneurs. Also on a political level there is a call for more entrepreneurial skills within arts education programs in order to make the CCIs more resilient, to let them grow and to make them more profitable. A strategic framework for European cooperation in education and training is in place until 2020. One of the four strategic objectives is 'enhancing creativity and innovation, including entrepreneurship, at all levels of edu-cation and training'. The specific aims of the Program Creative Europe are also clear: to help the cultural and creative sectors seize the opportunities of the digital age and globalisation; to enable the sectors to reach their economic potential, contributing to sustainable and inclusive growth, jobs, and social cohesion; and to give Europe's culture and media sectors access to new international opportunities, markets, and audiences. At the political level governments in all continents are realizing that the cultural and creative sectors are fundamental for advancing prosperity, inclusive-ness and sustainability.

In addition, educational training for the creative industries has been developed by and proliferated within corporate environments, and such disruptive innovation has in turn impacted the way colleges and universities teach, and students learn about the creative economy. IDEO (stands for?), for example, has been a leader in working with academic institutions, such as Stanford University, in creating learning experiences directed at innovative design solutions, and their work has not only been developed in collaboration with universities, but has been implemented in corporate training worldwide, *and* in academic curricula (Kelley, 2007; Kelley & Kelley, 2013).

In consequence, what has gradually emerged over the past two decades is a focus on combining traditional instruction in the arts, art history, cultural studies and other humanities disciplines with business school and economics training. Business schools are now often offering entrepreneurship and management training with exercises fundamentally rooted and applied in the liberal arts (H. M. Neck & Greene, 2011; H. M. Neck, Greene, & Brush, 2014). In contrast to this, we have seen the emergence of new programs outside of business schools that address both economics and entrepreneurship, and this movement originated in Europe, and later gradually arrived in the United States, where the integration of business and entrepreneurship skills into arts, humanities and social sciences programs is still very much in its infancy (in contrast to strong collaborations between the sciences and management programs). This allows arts students and students from the human sciences to get additional professional skills that make them more resilient in the corporate world.

In Europe, courses and full programs began to emerge in the late 1980s and early 1990s, and have generally been offered under the subject of arts management and cultural economics, highlighting the need to inject a more business-driven approach to the organization and operation of artistic institutions, both large and small (Hagoort & Kooyman, 2009; Hagoort & Shawky, 1993; Klamer, 1996). Some of these programs directed at creative and cultural industries are housed in business and management schools, training students in specific areas of the creative economy, such as fashion, or music, but primarily providing an established business school education with an industry-specific focus on the new and emerging creative economy. In contrast, numerous alternative programs have been created that are cross-collegiate initiatives, or are even housed in fine arts or liberal arts colleges.

Some good practices of educational programs, which are used here as exemplary, but are by no means as an exhaustive representation of the diversity of programs. At the European continent we find *Antwerp University (Belgium),* which developed since the end of the nineties a successful graduate program in cultural management, with a special focus on cultural entrepreneurship since 2008. In 2013, the Antwerp Management School started a tailor-made master class *'creative jumpers',* with a program especially designed for creative entrepreneurs who want to make a *'jump ahead'* in their careers and in the further development of their business. In the Netherlands the *Erasmus University (Rotterdam)* developed a program, not in cultural management but in cultural economics, and a graduate program in cultural economics and entrepreneurship, looking at regional, national and global trends in creative industries, and preparing analysts of this phenomenon for the future. Similarly broad, the *Universität Passau* in Germany, in its International Cultural and Business Studies (*Kulturwirtschaft*) degree, along with a variety of other German programs, is combining cultural and area studies with business and language curricula. In a more industry-oriented approach, *Goldsmith's College* in London began offering a graduate program in cultural entrepreneurship, focusing on career pathways in computing, design, fashion, media and communications, music or theatre and performance. Even more specialized, *Saimaa University of Applied Sciences* in Finland offers a specialized Master's degree in cultural entrepreneurship that is focused on jewellery production and marketing.

INTRODUCTION

In the United States, in contrast, there are also selective programs training students for the creative and cultural industries, and many colleges only offer selective course work rather than certificates or degrees. For example, *Wake Forest University* began a concentration in Entrepreneurship in the Liberal Arts that now has morphed into a new minor entitled Entrepreneurship and Social Enterprise, broadly introducing liberal arts students to entrepreneurship. *Queens College* of the City University of New York offers a minor in Business and Liberal Arts (BALA). Since 2013, the University of Minnesota Duluth now also offers a full Bachelor of Arts program in Cultural Entrepreneurship. More oriented towards professional training, the *Cooperstown Graduate Program* in Museum Studies offers an Institute for Cultural Entrepreneurship, an annual boot camp for mid-career professionals, and several other institutions including Simon Fraser University, the University of British Columbia, Boston University, Carnegie Mellon University and Harvard University are offering individual courses on the subject.

At the centrepiece of these programs across the globe is the discussion of the creative economies, their characteristics and local peculiarities; and a desire to create post-secondary training for a future workforce that possesses both creative, cultural or artistic skills *and* considerable business acumen. A relatively recent development of business training for creative industries has been the gradual shift from an almost exclusive focus on management to the potential of entrepreneurship, or more precisely, *cultural entrepreneurship.*

Cultural Entrepreneurship as a Leading Paradigm for the Future of the Creative Industries

If you searched for the concept of *cultural entrepreneurship* in scholarly articles, archives, or in the popular media, you likely would have ended up with only a handful of references (Acheson, Maule, & Filleul, 1996; Paul DiMaggio, 1991; P. DiMaggio, Social, & Organizations, 1990; Hagoort & Shawky, 1993), as little as ten years ago. While economists have certainly studied the economic impact of art since the 1960s, and continue to do so with great interest (Andersson & Andersson; Baumol & Bowen, 1966; Grampp, 1989; Kneafsey, Ilbery, & Jenkins, 2001; Peacock, Rizzo, & Brosio, 1994), the last decade has witnessed an explosion of interest in, and a multitude of definitions of *cultural entrepreneurship* as an applied academic field or discipline, a pedagogical approach and/or practical training for the creative industries (Hagoort, 2007; Klamer, 2011; Louise, 2003; Lounsbury & Glynn, 2001; Nijboer, 2006; Rea, 2008; Scott, 2012; Sorin & Sessions, 2015; Swedberg, 2006; Wilson & Stokes, 2002; Wry, Lounsbury, & Glynn, 2011; Zimmermann, Schulz, & Ernst).

This book is a collection of essays and academic contributions that want to reflect on the education principles and programs in cultural entrepreneurship. Which knowledge, skills and attitudes are required to become a cultural entrepreneur? And how can we teach students with a different disciplinary background these entrepreneurial skills, which are characterized by risk-taking, dealing with uncertainty and unpredictability in a digitalized and globalized environment? Several articles seek also to address the shift within arts management programs from – and productive tension between – arts and cultural management skills to cultural entrepreneurship. It moves the focus of creative industry education from the business operation and oversight to the ideation and start-up of cultural non-profit and for-profit businesses. Furthermore, this book seeks to set apart cultural entrepreneurship as an interdisciplinary teaching approach, therefore separating it from the literature on teaching entrepreneurship that has been generated by traditional business scholars (who increasingly begin entrepreneurship training with and culturally-grounded learning approaches and anthropological research techniques)(H. Neck, 2011; H. M. Neck & Greene, 2011; H. M. Neck et al., 2014).

With this volume, we provide a comprehensive global overview of scholarship that explores the theoretical roots, pedagogical approaches, and practical training in and for cultural entrepreneurship. This is, first and foremost, a teaching-focused book. Teaching cultural entrepreneurship gives a lot of opportunities to explore new teaching methods that are focused on a close cooperation with the working field, the use of digital tools, the development of intercultural competencies, the cross fertilization between different disciplines, the linking of theoretical insights with practical skills and to development a high degree of self reflection. We wanted to bring together a group of scholars from four different continents that illustrate the various theoretical concepts that today inform the creation of new cultural and creative businesses, and we intended to show how entrepreneurship is taught across the globe, via experiments, simulations, case studies, and internships; in single courses, certificate programs, or entire undergraduate (Bachelor of Arts) as well as graduate (Masters and PhD) programs. The book provides also a comparative perspective on how cultural entrepreneurship is taught in different parts all over the world.

The title of our book 'Creating Cultural Capital. Cultural entrepreneurship in Theory, Pedagogy and Practice', is intended as a call to develop entrepreneurial skills for the creative and cultural sectors, in order to contribute to economic development, but we also want to emphasize the cultural value of this sector for society. In addition to economic value, the creative sector also has tremendous social value, especially through the stimulation of various art forms and the preservation of cultural heritage.

The added value that the creative industries represent is underestimated and underemployed by other sectors. For professionals and emerging talent it is crucial that the necessary knowledge and skills be developed, to enable them to positively put a spotlight on the under-recognised added value and unique identity of the creative industry.

For the purpose of this book, we draw from numerous definitions of cultural entrepreneurship (Anheier & Isar, 2008; Hagoort, 2007; Klamer, 2011; Lounsbury & Glynn, 2001; Swedberg, 2006). We understand it as a body of theory and practices intended to create cultural change. Innovative thinkers and visionaries organize cultural, financial, social and human capital, to generate revenue from a cultural activity and/or creatively preserve the intrinsic value of cultural artifacts, practices and traditions. The ultimate outcome of such thinking and practice are economically sustainable cultural enterprises that enhance livelihoods and create cultural value and wealth for both creative producers and consumers of cultural services and products.

INTRODUCTION

CREATING CULTURAL CAPITAL
A READING GUIDE

The discussions presented here are divided in five different chapters, covering an introduction from the global perspective, theoretical approaches, the pedagogical dimension, an overview of significant cases, and the practicalities of teaching cultural entrepreneurship.

PART I **THE GLOBAL PERSPECTIVE**

In the first section we offer a glimpse at the present *State of Affairs* at the global level. **Dennis Cheek** starts by noting that Entrepreneurship appears in many guises around the globe. It is not limited to profit-maximizing entrepreneurship, yet covers both commercial and non-profit social entrepreneurship (including social enterprises and social businesses), and cultural entrepreneurship. He draws upon diverse bodies of relevant literature across several disciplines and forms of entrepreneurship research to draw some preliminary lessons for the further legitimization of cultural entrepreneurship and the improvement of cultural entrepreneurship education.

For centuries, as **Jerry C Y Liu** notes, Europe and its cultural modernity has long been a model for Asian countries to follow. However, there is a growing approval in East Asian countries to devise localized discourses. Different models of practice in arts management, cultural policy and cultural industries have emerged after the 1990s in the Far East. Different theoretical roots and approaches in curriculum design and competence building, as well as practical application of teaching and learning have been developed. A re-articulation of traditional cultural value and meaning, combined with modern institutional efficiency, entrepreneurial innovation and creativity in cultural management and administration is presented.

Marcin Poprawski discusses the recent developments in Central Europe. After 25 years of dynamic change initiated by the fall of communist regimes, a very multi-dimensional, experimental cultural entrepreneurship playground surfaces. Entrepreneurial styles, competencies, values, theories and practices, are vastly reoriented in this part of the world. The article will try to answer essential research questions like: what is the impact of teaching cultural management and entrepreneurship skills on practice of cultural organizations? Who are and where can we find mentors and career models for the next generation cultural entrepreneurs; individuals ready to risk, fail and professionally be reborn in the creative sector. And how should we stimulate trans-generational transmission of values and sense-making in the cultural sector in Central Europe?

PART II **DIFFERENT THEORETICAL APPROACHES**

The second chapter offers the *theoretical perspectives* that lay underneath the actual developments. **Walter van Andel** an **Annick Schramme** offer an exploration into the specific entrepreneurial behaviours that creative entrepreneurs typically follow. They discuss the practical application of such knowledge in the field of education and guidance. One of the key assumptions commonly used in published research on entrepreneurship in general is that it is the task of the entrepreneur to discover and exploit opportunities, which is coined in literature the '*causation logic*'. However, not all entrepreneurs follow this logic in reality. On the contrary. They identify the '*effectuation logic*', that does not assume that opportunities await to be discovered, but that opportunities arise when they are created by an entrepreneur and its partners. They indicate that the latter logic has a natural fit with the standard manner of working in the creative industries.

Entrepreneurship education at the undergraduate level is most often situated in business schools. Frequently their pedagogy involves case methodology and a capstone course in entrepreneurship towards the end of the curriculum. *Aparna Katre* states that there is little emphasis on the development of skills to deal with the wicked nature of societal problems. She contends that such education develops the hard business skills and the soft skills necessary to create sustained social, cultural and environmental values. She explores how entrepreneurship education, with rigorous course work in humanities disciplines and which embeds design thinking, prepares individuals for social innovation.

Arts and cultural management programs have typically focused on the management of organizations. Arts and cultural entrepreneurship adds a new dimension. It needs an emphasis on the freelance, self-employed, and micro-level landscape that has not heretofore been a priority. The local level is an especially important context for arts and cultural entrepreneurs *Margaret Jane Wyszomirski* and *Shoshanah Goldberg Miller* have become increasingly aware of the size and significance of this aspect of the creative economy. In arts and culture enterprises, some follow a growth path and grow from a micro-enterprise, into an emerging organization, and eventually become an established arts or cultural organization. Others aim to stay small and either work in collective or cooperative small groups while defining success as the ability to balance artistic creativity with economic sustainability. From this viewpoint, being more business-like is the Promethean Fire - the utility that will solve all problems. But the embers of business-like practice cannot be fanned into arts and cultural entrepreneurship flames, unless they are adapted to creative entrepreneurship.

Manuel Montoya criticizes the current state of debate regarding the global creative and cultural enterprise (CCE). He places the concept of poetics as an essential component of CCE. Poetics can be broadly defined as qualities or features that emphasize beauty, imagination, or elevated thoughts; '*words when words are insufficient.*' We have to mobilize the need for social innovation, while also attending to the artistic and cultural forces endemic to economic identity. Why does CCE distinguish itself from social entrepreneurship? How will educators preserve higher order concepts that can apply broadly to the practitioners, students, and policy makers, as these terms become subject to disciplinary boundaries? He outlines a set of basic learning outcomes that can be utilized in both traditional academic teaching and community outreach, using poetics as a core concept in the study and practice of cultural and creative enterprise.

In business schools, research and pedagogy in entrepreneurship focus on new venture creation and management. Developing individuals to think like an entrepreneur and adopt an '*entrepreneurial identity*' enables them to more effectively build and grow

businesses and enjoy financial success. *Erin Bass, Ivana Milosevic,* and *Dale Eesley* state that the assumption that all entrepreneurs desire financial success, may not hold across non-business entrepreneurs. Often, the '*artist identity*' stands in stark contrast to the '*entrepreneurial identity*'. Artists create to satisfy an artistic need, rather than a market opportunity. Given the continuing decay of artistic endeavours, due to the lack of

INTRODUCTION

financial support, we ask: can these identities be reconciled so that the artist can be a successful entrepreneur? They turn to identity theory, for insight into the differences in identities of entrepreneurs and artists.

Rene Kooyman and **Ruben Jacobs** offer a plea for a radicle re-thinking of art management education. For the past decade the sector of Cultural and Creative Industries (CCIs) has gained a growing interest, both within the political arena and amongst policy developers. Within the sector, however, we can identify two different positions. On the one hand find Art Managers, holding managerial responsibilities within cultural and art organizations. And there is a more frequently found second profile: the Cultural and Creative Entrepreneur. The largest part of the Cultural and Creative Industries consists of very small, independent entrepreneurial initiatives. This Cultural Ant works within a continuous, fast changing environment, characterized by uncertainty. They challenge the educational dilemma's, facing the support of these small-scale entrepreneurs. They offer five fundamental dilemmas that we have to address.

PART III **PEDAGOGY**

When discussing the educational dimension, we cannot avoid reflecting upon the different *Pedagogical Approaches.*

Richard Strasser starts off with the music industry. Creating value in music education has become of paramount interest to faculty, students and employers. As questions about the validity of higher education continue, especially in relation to the creative industries, institutions are struggling to meet stakeholders' expectations. Strasser examines the creation of an innovative graduate music industry program, designed to address the needs of three major stakeholders. He proposes three guiding principles, in order to meet academic, student and business needs.

During the last decades, public and private universities in Europe have started to design and offer undergraduate and master's degrees, as well as specialized courses, workshops and seminars. According to **Irene Popoli** these initiatives focus on cultural management and entrepreneurship, with the explicit purpose of forming a class of knowledgeable, skilled professionals to operate specifically within the cultural industry. What appears to be still missing from the existing academic training is the preparation of cultural managers with specific social skills necessary in the digital age. The professional ability to guarantee administrative efficiency, cultural excellence, and social impact equally, is crucial for the fulfilment of political expectations; and this cannot be achieved today without a full set of digital and social media skills.

Majda Tafra, Ana Skledar, and **Ines Jemrić** offer us a glimpse of the discussions in Central Europe; Croatia. They analyse the Impact of Blended Learning on Students' Skills and Competencies. Blended learning is broad by definition, but always includes a combination of face-to-face and online activities. The digital transformation usually takes time because the innovation lies not only in the technology to be used, but also in the methods of instruction. Teachers need to be learning alongside their students and students. Though often being digital natives; they need additional training as well. The desired outcome would be a flex model of blended learning which includes face-to-face lectures complemented by online activities.

INTRODUCTION

Bruno Verbergt and *Laila De Bruyne* confront two different positions; the arts manager and the cultural entrepreneur. Both positions hold consequences for management education in the fields of arts and culture. A comparative study gives an insight into the distinctive qualities of an arts management master program compared to a general management program, and how such a degree can meet the labour market needs of the arts and culture industries. A simultaneous look at general management and the arts is essential to the success of an arts management education program. Arts managers and cultural entrepreneurs need to be acquainted with both banks of the river, as well as with the techniques needed to build solid, beautiful and '*challenging*' bridges.

The need for entrepreneurial skills development has become a significant issue for both cultural policy makers and the educational community. Yet, while artists and entrepreneurs have long been compared, the distance between them often seems abysmal. *Valérie Ballereau, Christine Sinapi, Olivier Toutain,* and *Edwin Juno-Delgado* study the perception of entrepreneurial self-efficacy among students in the cultural and creative industry. They offer a plea on entrepreneurial educational experiences, built on the hybridization of the artistic and entrepreneurial worlds.

What is it that we talk about, when we talk about entrepreneurship? *Melanie Levick-Parkin* explores the attitudes to creative entrepreneurship of students and staff engaged in creative education on a graphic design programme at a university in the UK. In line with the UK governments' drive of the employability agenda, many creative and design programmes now include elements or modules explicitly focusing on entrepreneurship or enterprise. Art and Design has well established and successful pedagogic methods and strategies for encouraging creative behaviour. Creative disciplines also have their own specific value systems that motivate them to engage in entrepreneurship. Can we identify links between art and design pedagogy, and general advice on teaching of entrepreneurial behaviour?

Oluwayemisi Adebola Oyekunle explores entrepreneurial education in the creative industries in South Africa. Traditional entrepreneurship training is concerned with providing knowledge, yet he signals a lack of understanding and research about the processes of creative entrepreneurship. He offers an attempt to gain a clearer understanding of creative entrepreneurship as a whole, and skill developments needed to successfully overcome the over-supply of university graduates in a very difficult employment market. He questions the relevance and effectiveness of entrepreneurship education, and inadequacy with the development in entrepreneurial activities. He proposes a six phase conceptual framework of entrepreneurial training to help creative discipline students develop a vision for a business.

Brea M. Heidelberg finishes the chapter by discussing Transition Courses in the Arts Management Curriculum. She concentrates on the position of a recent graduate, trying to navigate in the job market. While the global economy, and the United States economy in particular, is on the rebound the competition is stiff. Job seekers who complete an undergraduate degree spend a considerable amount of time and money building their skill sets and resumes. But are academic programs truly preparing students for a successful job search upon graduation? Are we equipping students with a strong foundation upon which they can build their careers? She offers us to join her concern that students lack the professional writing and technical skills required to successfully enter a competitive job market.

INTRODUCTION

PART IV **CASES**

We tend to treat the Cultural and Creative Economy as one, coherent sector. However, in reality it is a multi-layered concept, covering very different practices (Hagoort & Kooyman (Ed), 2010). A number of these practices are problematized in this chapter.

Ira Levine and *Jeremy Shtern* discuss the curriculum design, theoretical roots and pedagogical approaches in Toronto. They present a reflexive case study, which discusses the theory and methodology behind the intellectual and pedagogical structure of the Ryerson School of Creative Industries. Ryerson's mix of academic programs traverses the gamut of the Creative Industries. From publishing and digital journalism to TV production, fashion and interior design, dance and film, the University's diverse media, design and artistic units are represented in the B.A. in Creative Industries. Challenges, both theoretical and practical, implicated in the development of an innovative academic program.

Paola Dubini describes how cultural entrepreneurship is taught at the Bocconi University in Milan, as the result of the development of educational and research activities in the field of arts management and cultural policy. The evolution of the schools' positioning in these domains is described, by highlighting the history, philosophy and unique characteristics of the first program launched. In addition, the process of legitimization of the leading business school in Italy among practitioners in the arts is treated. It offers two principle activities; Liberal Arts for managers, and the creation of Managers for the arts.

A new approach to teach and learn cultural entrepreneurship at the Erasmus University in Rotterdam is treated by *Marilena Vecco.* Entrepreneurship has become a strong field of interest in the educational area. The subject is taught in several education sectors, ranging from business entrepreneurship to social entrepreneurship. Among them also cultural entrepreneurship is increasingly gaining popularity as university degrees all around the world. Why and how can we improve the traditionally taught entrepreneurship? Marilena Vecco discusses three years of observation and experiences, focusing on the innovative approach adopted in comparison to more traditional ways of teaching and learning entrepreneurship.

Jeannette Guillemin and *Wendy Swart Grossman* discuss the creation of a Cultural Entrepreneurship course, firmly rooted in real world experiences and taught in Boston University's graduate Arts Administration program. The article outlines four core components: Self-Reflection, Assessment, Spotlight and Action, and provides examples of interactive activities and case studies.

In addition, *Dany Jacobs* and *Tamara Rookus* offer us an insight at the experiences with a practice-oriented minor at ArtEZ institute of the Arts in the Netherlands. They present hands-on experience within minor on creative entrepreneurship during the last four years. Students learn what entrepreneurship means within the field of the arts (including applied arts such as product and graphic design) by following an artist they admire, and in doing this trying to understand what their business model looks like. They explain the concepts behind the curriculum development, the structure of the program, and offer a first reflection regarding the results.

INTRODUCTION

In the neighboring country, Germany, the Masters course Strategies for European Cultural Heritage is an innovative extra-occupational program of study offered by the European University Viadrina in Frankfurt. It is a course addressed to conservators and other professionals who wish to become more successful on the cultural heritage market. **Paul Zalewski** and **Izabella Parowicz** discuss the curriculum design of the course, with special emphasis on how a targeted approach can help turn professional conservators into cultural entrepreneurs.

Ana Maria de Mattos Guimarães and **Cristiane Schnack** presents an ongoing experience at Unisinos, a traditional 30.000-student University in Brazil, with the implementation of its School of Creative Industries. The School is structured around communication, design and languages. Education is based on four aspects: centrality of Culture, Creativity, Innovation, and Entrepreneurship. The implementation of the School has brought a call to its 13 undergraduate courses for changing the existing curricula.

PART V **THE PRACTICE**

All theoretical and pedagogical arguments aside, it is the reality that counts. Chapter five offers an overview of a number of practical cases. The examples presented here are offering an overview of 'how things are done'. This last chapter offers a most concrete description of *practical experiences*.

Robert Davis, Julia Calver, and **Steven Parker** start off by disrupting disciplines in order to meet the challenge of an industry-ready agenda for the freelance creative practitioner. They argue that for higher education, to actively promote and prepare students to undertake a freelance career, a more innovative approach than the existing rhetoric around employability and entrepreneurship may be required.

Rosa Perez Monclus, Roberta Comunian and **Nick Wilson** reflect on extra-curricular opportunities, that creative graduates voluntarily engage with, when studying cultural entrepreneurship and enhancing their profile. It highlights the role of universities in creating platforms for graduates to avail themselves of such learning beyond their specific degree. In particular, they present a university-wide project-based competition, established by the Kings' Cultural Institute at Kings' College London; the Kings' College Challenge (KCC).

Additional experiences are based on new teaching and learning approaches to cultural entrepreneurship for heritage conservation training programs in Brazil. **Karla Penna, Jorge Tinoco** and **Elisabeth Taylor** investigate training programs established at world heritage sites in Latin America, with a particular focus on a postgraduate program developed by the Centre for Advanced Studies in Integrated Conservation (CECI) in Brazil.

Stephen B. Preece is applying lean start-ups principles to Cultural Entrepreneurship. Despite roots in Silicon Valley (dominated by engineers and software developers), lean start-up principles have been successfully applied to multiple fields and disciplines, generating a methodology that can provide guidance to new ventures across sectors and industries, holding a promise for the field of arts entrepreneurship. However,

INTRODUCTION

the unique challenges associated with new arts ventures arguably require special consideration in the application of lean start-up principles for them to be successfully applied.

Moving to Chile, **Guillermo Olivares Concha** describes the Creative Industries Node, an entrepreneurial support project funded by the National Agency for Entrepreneurship and Innovation (CORFO) in Chile and run by the Universidad San Sebastian Business School in the city of Valdivia. An intensive training program for professional cultural entrepreneurship has been developed, *Innovuss*; a community based training program, focussing on sectorial innovation for active creative entrepreneurs in the Southern region of Chile.

Elonahas Lubyte discusses the training in environment observation and assessment of artists-to-be in Lithuania. The article focusses on the possibilities of applying the method of PEST (political, economic, social, technological) macro-environmental research, when training the skills of environment observation and assessment of artists-to-be.

When discussing the Cultural and Creative Industries we cannot surpass the crafts sector. **Isaac Bongani Mahlangu** discusses Product Development training, as a tool for empowerment in crafts in South Africa. The craft sector has been identified as one of the eight key priority sectors to grow the economy and create employment in South Africa. It is a sector dominated by women, and thus makes them visible producers in the value chain. The indigenous knowledge transfer and the general low cost of some raw materials, and the potential of entering into existing local markets are characteristics that have stimulated the identification of crafts production in the region.

EXPANDING THE GLOBAL VISION

We started this book at the global level. We have noted that the Cultural and Creative Industries have become part of our every-day life; it is part of our evolving Creative Economy.

The Creative Economy has been playing a catalytic role by dealing with the interface among arts, culture, technology, social innovation and business. **Edna dos Santos Duisenberg** has been the initiator of the world-spanning *Creative Economy Reports*, published by the five core-institutions of the United Nations. Strategies focusing on the creative economy are being implemented as a pragmatic way to revitalize not only economic growth and the cultural and social life of cities, but also have been used as an attractive path offering new prospects for the youth, particularly in the post-crisis period.

The Creative Economy offers a development opportunity and a policy challenge. Edna dos Santos -Duisenberg iterates that Education has become a fundamental right. Knowledge and access to information and communication are at the core of human progress and well-being. The challenge is, however, to shape policies and build the capacities needed to explore the wide range of opportunities the creative sector can offer.

The United Nations Institute for Training and Research (UNITAR) has the mission to deliver innovative training and conduct research on knowledge systems to increase the capacity of its beneficiaries to respond to global challenges. UNITAR, as the UN umbrella for research and training, designed its *Creative Economy Initiative*, proposing a series of capacity-building activities to the UN Member States. The objective is to develop a learning approach to enhance knowledge, build skills and develop capacities to harness the potential of the creative economy to promote inclusive socio-economic transformations.

About the Authors

Prof Dr Olaf Kuhlke is Associate Dean of the College of Liberal Arts at the University of Minnesota Duluth, USA, where he is also an Associate Professor of Geography. He is the Founding Director of the B.A. Program in Cultural Entrepreneurship.

Olaf received his license at Philipps-Universität Marburg, Germany, and his PhD at the Kent State University, Ohio. His scholarly work focuses on the various scales of the geography of movement. He has conducted research on the ritualistic practices of walking, modern-day parades and music festivals, the representation of landscapes in popular music, and also has an interest in international migration.

—

okuhlke@d.umn.edu

Prof Dr Annick Schramme is professor and academic coordinator of the master in Cultural Management at the University of Antwerp (Faculty of Applied Economics). She is also Academic Director of the Competence Centre Creative Industries and the master class Creative Jumpers at the Antwerp Management School.

References

Acheson, K., Maule, C. J., & Filleul, E. (1996). Cultural entrepreneurship and the Banff television festival. *Journal of Cultural Economics, 20*(4), 321-339.

Andersson, Å. E., & Andersson, D. E. *The Economics of Experiences, the Arts and Entertainment:* Edward Elgar Publishing.

Anheier, H. K., & Isar, Y. R. (2008). *Cultures and Globalization: The Cultural Economy.* SAGE Publications.

Bakhshi, H., Freeman, A., & Higgs, P. (2013). *Mapping the UK's Creative Industries.* London, UK: Nesta Foundation.

Baumol, W. J., & Bowen, W. G. (1966). *Performing Arts: The Economic Dilemma; a Study of Problems Common to Theater, Opera, Music, and Dance:* Twentieth Century Fund.

Brooks, A. C. (2001). Who opposes public arts funding? *Public Choice, 108*(3-4), 355-367.

Calabrò, A., & Wijngaarde, I. (2013). *Creative Industries for Youth: Unleashing Potential and Growth.* Vienna.

Connell, S. (2013). *Korea's Creative Economy Agenda.* Honolulu: East-West Center.

Cronshaw, S., & Tullin, P. (2012). *Intelligent Naivety: Commercial Opportunities for Museums and Culture Institutions* Retrieved from: http://www.slideshare.net/culturelabel/culturelabel-intelligent-naivety

DiMaggio, P. (1991). Cultural entrepreneurship in nineteenth-century Boston. *Rethinking popular culture: Contemporary perspectives in cultural studies, 374.*

DiMaggio, P., Social, Y. U. I. f., & Organizations, P. S. P. o. N.-P. (1990). *Class Authority and Cultural Entrepreneurship: The Problem of Chicago:* Program on Non-Profit Organizations, Institution for Social and Policy Studies, Yale University.

Dos Santos-Duisenberg, E. (2009). The creative economy: Beyond economics. *After the crunch,* 24-25.

Duisenberg, E. D. S. (Ed.). (2008). *Creative Economy Report 2008: the challenge of assessing the creative economy: towards informed policy-making.* Geneva: United Nations Conference on Trade and Development.

INTRODUCTION

Duisenberg, E. D. S. (Ed.). (2010). *Creative Economy Report 2010: Creative Economy: A Feasible Development Option.* Geneva: United Nations Conference on Trade and Development.

Florida, R. (2002). *The Rise of the Creative Class: and how it's transforming work, leisure, community and everyday life.* New York: Basic Books.

Florida, R. (2010). *Who's Your City?: How the Creative Economy Is Making Where to Live the Most Important Decision of Your Life.* Toronto, Ontario: Random House of Canada.

Florida, R. (2012). *The Rise of the Creative Class Revisited.* New York: Basic Books.

Gómez-Peña, G. (2004). An open letter to the national arts community. *Contemporary Theatre Review, 14*(2), 88-93. doi: 10.1080/10267160410004968

Grampp, W. D. (1989). *Pricing the priceless: art, artists, and economics:* Basic Books.

Hagoort, G. (2003). *Art management: Entrepreneurial style:* Eburon Uitgeverij BV.

Hagoort, G. (2007). *Cultural Entrepreneurship: On the freedom to create art and the freedom of enterprise.* Utrecht: HKU Utrecht School of the Arts.

Hagoort, G., & Kooyman, R. (2009). *Creative Industries: Colourful Fabric in Multiple Dimensions:* Eburon Uitgeverij BV.

Hagoort, G., & Shawky, A. (1993). *Cultural entrepreneurship: an introduction to arts management:* Phaedon.

Harris, C., Collins, M., & Cheek, D. (2013). A*merica's Creative Economy: A Study of Recent Conceptions, Definitions, and Approaches to Measurements across the USA.* Oklahoma City: National Creativity Network.

Haselbach, D., Gerecht, C., & Hempel, L. (2010). *Kulturwirtschaft in Duesseldorf: Entwicklungen und Potentiale.* Berlin: ICG culturplan.

Hayter, C., & Pierce, S. C. (2011). *Arts and the Economy: Using Arts and Culture to Stimulate State Economic Development.* Washington, D.C.

Henry, C., & de Bruin, A. (2011). *Entrepreneurship and the Creative Economy: Process, Practice and Policy.* Cheltenham, United Kingdom: Edward Elgar Publishing Limited.

Himmelstein, J. L., & Zaid, M. (1984). American Conservatism and Government Funding of the Social Sciences and Arts. *Sociological Inquiry, 54*(2), 171-187.

Howkins, J. (2002). *The creative economy: How people make money from ideas:* Penguin UK.

Kelley, T. (2007). *The art of innovation: lessons in creativity from IDEO, America's leading design firm:* Crown Business.

Kelley, T., & Kelley, D. (2013). *Creative confidence: Unleashing the creative potential within us all:* Crown Business.

Over the last years she published about creative industries, fashion management, cultural entrepreneurship, arts policy, international cultural policy and heritage management. Besides, she is member of several boards of cultural organizations and advisory committees in Flanders and the Netherlands. Since 2013 she is the president of ENCATC, the International Network on Cultural Management and Policy Education.

—

annick.schramme @uantwerpen.be

Drs Rene Kooyman DEA MUAD graduated with a major in Urban and Regional Planning. He received a Diplôme Educations Approfondies in Economics and Sociology from the University of Geneva, Switzerland. Rene Kooyman has been Project Manager for the EU EACEA Research Project on the Entrepreneurial Dimensions of Cultural and Creative Industries. He has been responsible for the EU INTERREG Creative Urban Renewal Project (CURE). At the moment he is an Associated Fellow at the United Nations Institute of Training and Research (UNITAR) in Geneva.

—

www.rkooyman.com

—

rkooyman@rkooyman.com

Klamer, A. (1996). *The value of culture: On the relationship between economics and arts:* Amsterdam University Press.

Klamer, A. (2011). Cultural entrepreneurship. *The Review of Austrian Economics, 24*(2), 141-156.

Kneafsey, M., Ilbery, B., & Jenkins, T. (2001). Exploring the Dimensions of Culture Economies in Rural West Wales. *Sociologia Ruralis, 41*(3), 296-310.

Kooyman, R. (Ed.). (2011). *The entrepreneurial dimension of the cultural and creative industries.* Utrecht: Hogeschool vor den Kunsten (HKU).

Kunzmann, K. R. (1995). Strategien zur Förderung regionaler Kulturwirtschaft *Kultur und Wirtschaft* (pp. 324-342). Berlin: Springer.

Louise, D. (2003). Encouraging Cultural Entrepreneurship. *Arts Professional(42)*, 7.

Lounsbury, M., & Glynn, M. A. (2001). Cultural entrepreneurship: Stories, legitimacy, and the acquisition of resources. *Strategic management journal, 22* (6-7), 545-564.

Markusen, A., & Gadwa, A. (2010). *Creative placemaking:* National Endowment for the Arts Washington, DC.

Neck, H. (2011). Cognitive ambidexterity: The underlying mental model of the entrepreneurial leader. *The New Entrepreneurial Leader: Developing Leaders Who Shape Social and Economic Opportunity, edited by D. Greenberg, K. McKone-Sweet, and HJ Wilson*, 24-42.

Neck, H. M., & Greene, P. G. (2011). Entrepreneurship education: known worlds and new frontiers. *Journal of Small Business Management, 49*(1), 55-70.

Neck, H. M., Greene, P. G., & Brush, C. G. (2014). *Teaching entrepreneurship: A practice-based approach:* Edward Elgar Publishing.

Nijboer, J. (2006). Cultural entrepreneurship in libraries. *New library world, 107*(9/10), 434-443.

Oakley, K. (2004). Not So Cool Britannia The Role of the Creative Industries in Economic Development. *International journal of cultural studies, 7*(1), 67-77.

Peacock, A. T., Rizzo, I., & Brosio, G. (1994). *Cultural Economics And Cultural Policies:* Springer Netherlands.

Programme, U. N. D. (2013). *Creative Economy Report 2013: Special Report Widening Local Development Pathways.* New York: UNESCO.

Project, N. E. L. (2012). The Low-Wage Recovery and Growing Inequality. New York.

Rea, C. G. (2008). Comedy and Cultural Entrepreneurship in Xu Zhuodai's Huaji Shanghai. *Modern Chinese Literature and Culture*, 40-91.

Reis, A. C. F., Chengyu, X., Piedras Faria, E., Ramanathan, S., Davis, A. M., Dos Santos-Duisenberg, E.,... Solanas, F. (2008). Creative Economy as a Development Strategy.

INTRODUCTION

Restrepo, F. B., & Marquez, I. D. (2013). *The Orange Economy: An Infinite Opportunity.* Washington, DC: Inter-American Development Bank.

Schramme, A., Kooyman, R. (ed), Hagoort, G. (2014). *Beyond Frames. Dynamics between the Creative Industries, Knowledge Institutions and the Urban Context.* Eburon Academic Press, Delft. ISBN 978-90-5972-884-4

Scott, M. (2012). Cultural entrepreneurs, cultural entrepreneurship: Music producers mobilising and converting Bourdieu's alternative capitals. *Poetics, 40*(3), 237-255.

Sorin, G., & Sessions, L. A. (2015). *Case Studies in Cultural Entrepreneurship: How to Create Relevant and Sustainable Institutions:* Rowman & Littlefield Publishers.

Swedberg, R. (2006). The cultural entrepreneur and the creative industries: beginning in Vienna. *Journal of Cultural Economics, 30*(4), 243-261.

Wilson, N., & Stokes, D. (2002). Cultural entrepreneurs and creating exchange. *Journal of Research in Marketing and Entrepreneurship, 4*(1), 37-52.

Wry, T., Lounsbury, M., & Glynn, M. A. (2011). Legitimating nascent collective identities: Coordinating cultural entrepreneurship. *Organization Science, 22* (2), 449-463.

Zimmermann, O., Schulz, G., & Ernst, S. Zukunft Kulturwirtschaft: Zwischen Kuenstlertum und Kreativwirtschaft. Essen: Klartext Verlag.

INTRODUCTION

A GLOBAL PERSPECTIVE

Dennis Cheek

LEGITIMIZATION STRATEGIES ACROSS THE VARIOUS GUISES OF ENTREPRENEURSHIP
IMPLICATIONS FOR CULTURAL ENTREPRENEURSHIP EDUCATORS

A GLOBAL PERSPECTIVE

Abstract

Entrepreneurship appears in many guises around the globe, including but not limited to profit-maximizing entrepreneurship, commercial and non-profit social entrepreneurship (including social enterprises and social businesses), and cultural entrepreneurship. More basic forms have existed in prior centuries and cultures, but without the engagement of large-scale research and institutions of higher education.

All forms of contemporary entrepreneurship have developed over several decades from fledgling efforts into large-scale social and cultural phenomena. All forms face the challenges of ongoing legitimization of their place and importance within societies in three specific arenas: political challenges, academic challenges, and market challenges. This article draws upon diverse bodies of relevant literature across several disciplines and forms of entrepreneurship research to draw some preliminary lessons for the further legitimization of cultural entrepreneurship and the improvement of cultural entrepreneurship education.

Legitimacy

Legitimacy is a *sine qua non* attribution desired by cultural entrepreneurship organizations, academic institutions and their subunits (research centres, schools, and departments), the professoriate and (often) individual practitioners, students pursuing degrees and certificates at all levels, and alumni of these learning institutions. Exactly what constitutes *cultural entrepreneurship* is very much in the eyes of the beholder. For the purposes of this article we will adopt the view expressed by Tom Aageson, founding and current Executive Director of the Global Centre for Cultural Entrepreneurship in Santa Fe, New Mexico that:

> *'The cultural entrepreneur creates a vision for a cultural enterprise that bridges a market need with cultural traditions, cultural experiences and cultural innovation, enhancing the livelihoods of cultural creators and workers while at the same time enriching the consumer. The cultural entrepreneur holds the passion to muster the resources and the people to make the enterprise a sustainable reality.'*
> *(Aageson, 2008: 98).*

Legitimacy has been defined as '*a generalized perception or assumption that the actions of an entity are desirable, proper or appropriate within some socially constructed system of norms, values, beliefs, and definitions*' (Demil & Bensédrine, 2005: 58). Different forms of legitimacy have been recognized including regulative, normative, cultural, and historical (Coskuner-Balli, 2013: 205), all of which strongly invoke societal dimensions and require the creation and maintenance of broad-based positive recognition of an entity and its effects within a wider milieu. The construct of legitimacy is undoubtedly itself undergoing further transformation in response to the waning appeal of traditional national, ideological, political, philosophical, cultural, and religious foundations which formed the basis of early modernity and which have been challenged by global issues such as the recurrent financial crises, youth demonstrations, and massed societal revolts against political structures that have characterized the tumultuous first decade of the new millennium (Mascareño and Araujo, 2012).

The processes by which legitimization is achieved has been the subject of considerable study across time, geographies, disciplines, and the types of institutions, groups, or individuals selected for scrutiny. It seems potentially instructive for cultural entrepreneurs to consider a portion of this research literature that has specifically examined the process(es) of legitimization among a collection of contemporary and admittedly inchoate global movements over the past several decades that fall under the general umbrella of 'entrepreneurship.' Traditional conceptions of entrepreneurship have historically, for example, included: 1) high growth ventures, 2) innovative ventures, 3) recognition and exploitation of opportunities, and 4) creation of new organizations (Lundmark and Westelius, 2014: 587). In more recent years these traditional conceptions have been greatly expanded by emphasizing more of the social and cultural dimensions of entrepreneurial foci, actions, and activities with considerable disagreements and divergent assessments of progress across the various guises of entrepreneurship (e.g., Katz, 2008; Klein, Mahoney, McGahan, and Pitelis, 2010; Hervieux, Gedajlovic, and Turcotte, 2010).

The Concept of Entrepreneurship

The concept of entrepreneurship itself has been a venue for social innovation as it continues to be expanded, refined, redefined, and subjected to the widely perceived contradictory notions of demonstrating both social and economic value (Lisetchi and Brancu, 2014). Accompanying these various trends has been an increased desire and movement towards more valid and reliable methods of measuring the impact of these efforts in varied domains (e.g., Kroeger and Weber, 2014; Morris, Webb, Fu and Singhal, 2013). While the definitions, limitations, boundaries, meanings, purposes, players, and outcomes associated with these various guises of entrepreneurship remain contested, it is clear that all have their antecedents in the ancient world, even if never framed in the manner of contemporary discourse (e.g., Ilchman, Katz & Queen II, 1998; Constantelos, 1991; Landes, Mokyr, & Baumol, 2012).

The universe of activities that fall under the general rubric of entrepreneurship are almost too numerous to mention. Research literature has focused for several decades on attempting to sort out, defend, and delineate these various concepts. It seems reasonable to move beyond these types of discussions and employ cluster concepts moving up to a higher level of abstraction in order to advance more productive discourse and hopefully bring better conceptual coherency to research, education, and teaching among the different types of entrepreneurship. Choi and Majumdar (2014) recently made such an argument for the cluster comprising 'social entrepreneurship,' arguing that this cluster includes the sub-concepts of social value creation, the social entrepreneur, the social entrepreneurship organization, market orientation, and social innovations. A different view on the various forms of social enterprise and their interrelationships can be found in Gawell (2014).

A GLOBAL PERSPECTIVE

For our purposes we will consider the chief manifestations of contemporary entrepreneurship to consist of the following three broad categories aggregated on the basis of their *principal* objective(s):

1.   commercial, profit-maximizing enterprises (**CPME**),
2.   commercial or non-commercial activities focused principally on entrepreneurial ameliorative interventions and desired social outcomes (**EISO**), and
3.   commercial or non-commercial activities focused primarily on entrepreneurial enhancement of cultural resources within society (**EECR**).

Each of these forms of entrepreneurship has associated with it loosely-coupled regional, national, and global systems of individual actors, funding sources, advocates, institutions, organizations, educational and training opportunities, conferences, political supporters, etc. Each category has nested within it many variations across geographies, cultures, disciplines, industries, institutions, legal structures, goals, and actions; often overlapping in lower-priority functions with one or both of the other three broad categories – an issue that will not detain us here.

Legitimacy Mechanisms

There are both *'push'* and *'pull'* aspects to achieving and maintaining legitimacy. While legitimacy is ultimately attributed to an entity for its actions in the wider world by others outside of its direct sphere of influence, there are explicit and implicit socio-political actions that such entities take to precipitate such attribution(s). Lefebvre and Redien-Collot (2012) studied a new French business school created from the merger and conversion of several prior institutions that chose to focus exclusively on entrepreneurship and its quest for legitimacy as a business school over a six-year process from 2004 to 2010. Drawing upon prior work by a range of scholars of legitimacy, Lefebvre and Redien-Collot defined three distinct types of legitimacy that the school sought to achieve/receive over this period:

1.   academic *('the level of conformity to social norms and values, and to the rules and regulations of authority institutions,'* p. 487),
2.   market *('the level of conformity of pedagogical content and skill development to the needs of the market and firms,'* p. 487), and
3.   political *('the level of conformity to local development requirements in terms of start-ups and new jobs creation, growth and internationalization,'* p. 488).

Five main phases were identified in the school's quest for legitimacy, each lasting 12-18 months in duration and focused on one specific form of legitimacy, with the other two types serving at that point as constraints that drove further innovations. The five phases were in order:

a.   political – strategic repositioning of the former historic entities into a new business school that would focus on entrepreneurship,
b.   academic - creating the initial Master's degree curriculum,
c.   market – focused on graduates' employment success and on fund raising from market players,
d.   academic – improving teaching quality, launching interdisciplinary research, and achieving national and international accreditations, and

e. political – consolidating its legitimacy in this sphere through highly visible part-
    nerships going well beyond academic institutions and launching innovative edu-
    cational projects.

It has been noted by other researchers *that 'need and legitimacy in the industry can
precede academic legitimacy'* and that academic journals are generally more open to
innovations and fundamentally new scholarship than universities, which by their very
nature as institutions are more conservative (Coskuner-Balli, 2013: 206).

This new business school and the broader field of CPME entrepreneurship education,
has sought to meet various criteria typically associated with the attribution of academic legitimacy, e.g., 1) the discipline's centrality, 2) the discipline's maturity,
3) the discipline's expansion, 4) its institutional power, 5) theoretical and methodological distinctiveness, 6) research capabilities, and 7) perceived values. They noted
that *'building legitimacy in higher education is also about conveying a quality message
relative to pedagogical contents and processes, pedagogical methods and teams, in an
attempt to improve both the organization's market position and its ability to have an
impact on society, culture, and educational policies.'* (Lefebvre and Redien-Collot, 2012: 483).

Twin Processes of Subversion and Resistance

Central to the advance of any form of entrepreneurship is the creation of the *'new'*,
a process in entrepreneurship whose parallels to the world of the arts has not escaped
researchers. Both entrepreneurs and artists are actively engaged in the twin processes
of subversion and resistance in their search for novel ideas in the arts, business, and
society – the latter either directly the target in the form of social and cultural enterprises or always an important corollary to any desired *'successful'* venture. Creators of
all stripes seek to change the status quo, often in radical ways. Yet success in any avenue
of human creative or innovative activity requires that the new advance achieve recognition
by society for its intrinsic value to a wider audience beyond the creator. The creator's
dilemma is to push the envelope within the broader community or society but not so
much that the innovation (and often its creator) becomes an outcast from the wider
society, within which acceptance and proper function is sought. All art, businesses,
cultural enterprises, and social enterprises must find an audience beyond the one to
ultimately embrace the many if they are to be deemed a success, and thus have conferred
upon them by others a form of legitimacy. We need much more attention to *'subversion
and resistance as a promising but so far neglected avenue of research in entrepreneurial
studies'* (Bureau and Zander, 2014).

The very process by which nascent entrepreneurs of varying types are accepted into the
community of their peers; a group within which they must both *'fit it'* and *'stand out'*,
is another understudied aspect of both legitimization and entrepreneurship research
across CPME, EISO, and EECR forms. Pierre Bourdieu's concept of *habitus* as applied
to the study of newcomers' use of cultural and symbolic capital to attain legitimacy
is but one example of a fruitful avenue to explore (De Clercq and Voronov, 2009; cf.
Araujo, 2012). This very process of *both fitting in and standing out* serves as a useful
constraint that drives innovation since unbridled resources and degrees of freedom
rarely seems to result in breakthrough solutions; rather they emerge when constraints
are real, needs are present, and resources are limited, or as De Clercq and Voronov
(2009: 396) express it, *'entrepreneurial action operates within a social reality that sets
limits on the choice of action possibilities.'*

A GLOBAL PERSPECTIVE

Beyond the individual level, it also appears that this insider-outsider tension adheres to the research exercise itself. A study of entrepreneurship articles published in leading management journals detected the highly permeable nature of entrepreneurship and its engagement and connection with the wider management literature and the literature of distinct subfields. However, that same engagement may have also hindered the further development of entrepreneurship theory the authors speculate as the desire to become an insider, overwhelmed the necessary outsider orientation that stimulates the creation of new theories and research questions (Busenitz, et al., 2003). This particular aspect of legitimization (theory-building stage as a discipline) may well be hindered by the very process within academia that is used to reward tenure, promotion, and merit pay as the *worth and relevance in turn depend on collegial and administrative appraisal of the legitimacy and value of the individual's targeted field of study*' (Busenitz, et al., 2003: 286). It is much more difficult to accurately discern and confer academic legitimacy if the young professor's research veers too much off the well-worn academic research tracks laid down by others within the department, college, and the wider academic milieu of which they are a part. This speaks to the need for stronger institutional support for new forms of inquiry, new types of questions, and reinforces the critical role that foundations, government funding agencies, and external figures with critical social, reputational, and political capital can play in encouraging such behaviours.

Metaphors and Rhetorical Strategies

Metaphorical and analogical thinking have both played and continue to play important roles in the legitimization of entrepreneurship. Academics have noted the many ways in which governments, funders, and famous entrepreneurs have presented entrepreneurship (in all its varied guises) as an *elixir* that is fundamental to a healthy society and that if regularly administered in appropriate doses will cure many of the seemingly persistent problems of modern society such as war, poverty, inequality, intolerance, and violence by revitalizing communities, guaranteeing economic success, and ameliorating problems at their source (Lundmark and Westelius, 2014; Perren and Jennings, 2005). A more productive analogy than that of an elixir might be that of a mutagen which serves as a source of variation using a biological metaphor that may over time prove fecundate with new varieties of entrepreneurial activity that add value in the world (Lundmark and Westelius, 2014).

The study of the types and uses of metaphors within EECR forms of entrepreneurship as part of the research agenda should be approached within the larger framework of research that takes up the role and power of rhetorical strategy as part of legitimization efforts. We earlier mentioned the creator's dilemma of seeking to introduce the new into the socially-normed and already legitimated *old* (i.e., tradition or custom). Case studies of social entrepreneurs have delineated a complex set of meta-narratives within given communities that are somewhat unconsciously invoked within a framework that artfully portrays the innovator as a protagonist of these narratives whose actions will ensure that the narrative is realized with an effective approach and associated positive outcomes. Those who challenge the innovator are portrayed in the role of antagonists that impede the realization of the meta-narrative by their continuing reliance on the wrong approach with their ineffective outcomes (Ruebottom, 2013).

An important arena that should never be ignored is that of the political arena, especially as it exerts direct influence on cultural entrepreneurship activities and institutions in the form of laws, regulations, and the regulatory regime. The increased activity of governments at all levels in the '*business*' of higher education has brought often reluctant academics into the halls of political power seeking to influence legislation, regulations, and funding schemes towards perceived favourable outcomes (or at least minimizing non-favourable ones). Institutional entrepreneurs can be effective players in these worlds by making use of both legitimization and pressure strategies. The former strategy consists of convincing or influencing other stakeholders to adopt your platform for change, seeing it as useful to the wider society and integral in some manner to one or more of their own objectives or beliefs. Pressure strategies consist of galvanizing wider communities with whom you have strong affinities to advocate on your behalf with policy makers bringing the debate into a much wider circle of influence and allowing partisans in concert with your goals and views to describe the many ways in which positive action taken by policy makers can benefit them as constituents (Demil and Bensédrine, 2005).

Curricular, Pedagogical, and Research Concerns

There has been considerable discussion about the degree to which entrepreneurship education and research in entrepreneurship in CPME, EISO, and EECR forms (see above) is useful to policy makers, practitioners, students, and the wider society (combining aspects of both political and market legitimacies) (Zahra and Wright, 2011). Commissions and committees of various kinds, chaired by eminent academics, continue to generate and deliver policy documents to political bodies only to watch many of their careful articulations dissolve in the cauldron of political debates. Debates also continue among practitioners and academics about whether fruitful practices, orientations, dispositions, and skills useful to entrepreneurs can be taught or acquired in academic settings (an aspect of market legitimacy).

In thinking specifically about creative and cultural entrepreneurship, market legitimacy is seemingly enhanced by forming powerful and purposeful collaborations with a broad range of cultural entrepreneurship institutions and individuals outside of the academy in addition to the usual university to university partnerships, if the paucity of research literature on this point is accurate (e.g., Castro-Spila and Unceta,2014; Comunian and Gilmore, 2014; Lefebvre and Redien-Collot, 2012; Moerbeek, 2014). The debate about market relevance is not unique to cultural entrepreneurship but can be found in varying degrees of intensity across almost all fields of human endeavour where formal educational programs exist. One aspect of verifying relevance is to create a validated competency framework for graduates of programs that delineates skills, dispositions, and knowledge that are widely endorsed by potential employers of such graduates. Researchers have only recently produced the first defensible articulation of a competency-based approach to CPME entrepreneurship education along with associated assessment tools (Morris, Webb, Fu and Singhal, 2013), more than 65 years after the first CPME-oriented entrepreneurship course was offered at a research university (Katz, 2003). Wisdom suggests that cultural entrepreneurship educators neither claim too much, nor claim too little about the impact of current approaches and endeavours. While some rudimentary attempts at specifying and measuring competencies for EECR forms of entrepreneurship exist, we cannot yet claim that these formulations are either widely held or sufficiently validated to ensure their widespread adoption and application.

A GLOBAL PERSPECTIVE

Criticism on entrepreneurial Research

There has been considerable criticism around much of the academic research produced to date regarding entrepreneurship, a body of literature that is global in scope, ever increasing in size, and broadly available like never before. Specific criticisms include: 1) the self-referencing behaviour of entrepreneurship education and entrepreneurship education research, 2) its insularity in regards to serious engagement with other fields, 3) the narrowness of topical research driven largely by readily obtainable secondary databases, 4) the control that a few highly cited journals in any given field now exert on all research campuses - especially through the tenure and promotion process, 5) the fact that 'real entrepreneurs' and the contexts within which they work are largely ignored by researchers, and 6) the continuing issues related to disciplinary boundaries, definitions, and concepts (Busenitz, et al., 2003; Cajaiba-Santana, 2014; Katz, 2003; Nicholls, 2010; Meyer, 2011). Some scholars have argued that more radical critique of all existing conceptions and research paradigms are required, if true progress is to be made and these fields are to be emancipated from larger power structures and strictures (Dey and Steyaert, 2012). Others have articulated some specific directions for future research including: 1) better and fuller indicators of entrepreneurial activities, 2) more micro-studies of entrepreneurs in action, 3) closer attention to the contextual nature of entrepreneurial activity, 4) employment of a much wider set of methods, especially those from mixed-methods and qualitative methods, and 5) connecting research questions more to the concerns of policy makers (Zahra and Wright, 2011; Klein, Mahoney, McGahan, and Pitelis, 2010; Pilegaard, Moroz and Neergaard, 2010).

The rhetoric around entrepreneurship has frequently portrayed the entrepreneur or the 'creative' as a lone wolf, other-worldly hero who bravely faces the unknown, does the unthinkable, achieves the impossible, and is, in the best of all possible worlds, celebrated as a global cultural icon (Seitz, 2003; Nicholls, 2010). It can be argued that without a larger society and set of social and other associations, a 'genius' simply cannot exist; most fundamentally because such 'genius' has to be recognized by other human beings, not simply articulated and endorsed by the genius himself/herself. The work for which genius is recognized and the attribution attached is a result not only of the individual with their efforts and insights, which is surely important, but also by a combination of political forces, social forces and cultural forces or resources (Seitz, 2003: 386).

Most entrepreneurial activity, however, is not the province of geniuses but rather more common folk. This fact only reinforces the importance of the provision of fecund environments where entrepreneurial dispositions are cultivated, aspirations are nourished, nascent positive experiences are guided, and fledgling serious explorations are encouraged.

Informed observers, not surprisingly, have noted the critical role that institutions play in establishing appropriate conditions for entrepreneurial actions to occur, i.e., 'crescive entrepreneurship' (Dorado and Ventresca, 2013). The importance of creating environments where reflective practitioners come into regular and intimate contact with students within the context of real-world problems and active problem solving is a critical ingredient to activating robust entrepreneurial behaviours on collegiate campuses (Castro-Spila and Unceta, 2014; Comunian and Gilmore, 2014; Kuhlke, 2014; Moerbeek, 2014). Academic institutions themselves, as part of their legitimization efforts, need to employ heuristic devices such as Hindle's Bridge as a diagnostic tool to 'structurally measure a community's ability to facilitate entrepreneurial outcomes' (Pilegaard, Moroz, and Neergaard, 2010: 59) to better understand whether their pedagogical, programmatic, and support mechanisms are functioning as intended. Simultaneously data collected can help strengthen their case for the impact of their institutional value-add to their students and the wider society (market legitimacy). In a similar manner, cultural entrepreneurship programs would do well to ensure that students are globally competent as the more fluent and conversant they are with other languages and cultures, the more likely it becomes that they can be positively influenced by their growing acquaintance with divergent ideas and conceptions that can renew their own approach to existing cultural activities and recognizing or conceiving emergent possibilities (Kuhlke, 2014).

Entrepreneurship in CPME, EISO, and EECR forms can learn much from one another's efforts at achieving and maintaining legitimization within the wider society. Sometimes in their attempts to garner appropriate political, market, and academic legitimacies, proponents within one or more of these forms have sought to denigrate the work of practitioners and professors within the other forms. It is hoped that this article in some small measure might encourage more cross-border talk, lead to preliminary collaborative work on some issues common to all three forms, and cultivate a wider understanding that the boundaries among these three major forms are indeed porous in the 'real world' that we all inhabit and seek to positively transform through our continued entrepreneurial and educational endeavours.

About the Author

Prof Dr Dennis Cheek is Executive Director, National Creativity Network (USA); Co-chair, Global Creativity United; Visiting Professor, IESEG School of Management (FR); Visiting Scholar, Centre for Economics and Entrepreneurship Education, Lerner College of Business and Economics, University of Delaware (USA); Visiting Professor of Entrepreneurship, Universities Ciputra (Indonesia); Senior Fellow, Wachman Centre, Foreign Policy Research Institute (USA). Dennis Cheek received a Ph.D. in Curriculum & Instruction/Science Education at the Penn State University, and a PhD at University of Durham.

—

Dennis@national-creativitynetwork.com

—

ststoday@gmail.com

References

Aageson, Thomas H. (2008). Cultural entrepreneurs: Producing cultural value and wealth. In: *The Cultural Economy. The Cultures and Globalization Series, Volume 2*. Helmut K. Anheier, Vudhishthir Raj Isar, Eds. Thousand Oaks, CA: SAGE Publishing, pp. 92-107.

Araujo, Kathya (2012). The belief in legitimacy: Social experiences and the relationships of individuals to norms. In: *Legitimization in World Society*. Aldo Mascareño, Kathyn Araujo, Eds. Burlington, VT: Ashgate Publishing, pp. 157-176.

Bureau, Sylvain, Ivo Zander (2013). Entrepreneurship as an art of subversion. In: *Scandinavian Journal of Management*, 30: 124-133.

Busenitz, Lowell W., G. Page West III, Dean Shepherd, Teresa Nelson, Gaylen N. Chandler, Andrew Zacharakis (2003). Entrepreneurship research in emergence: Past trends and future directions. In: *Journal of Management*, 29(3): 285-308.

Cajaiba-Santana, Giovany (2014). Social innovation: Moving the field forward. A conceptual framework. In: *Technological Forecasting & Social Change*, 82: 42-51.

Castro-Spila, Javier, Alfonso Unceta (2014). The relational university social innovation and entrepreneurial skills in creative industries. In: *Beyond Frames: Dynamics between the Creative Industries, Knowledge Institutions and the Urban Context*. Eds. Annick Schramme, Rene Kooyman, Giep Hagoort. Delft, The Netherlands: Eburon Academic Publishers, pp. 192-200.

Choi, Nia, Satyajit Majumdar (2014). Social entrepreneurship as an essentially contested concept: Opening a new avenue for systematic future research. *Journal of Business Venturing*, 29: 363-376.

A GLOBAL PERSPECTIVE

Comunian, Roberta, Abigail Gilmore (2014). From knowledge sharing to co-creation: Paths and spaces for engagement between higher education and the creative and cultural industries. In: *Beyond Frames: Dynamics between the Creative Industries, Knowledge Institutions and the Urban Context*. Annick Schramme, Giep Hagoort, Rene Kooyman (Ed). Delft, The Netherlands: Eburon Academic Publishers, pp. 217-225.

Constantelos, Demetrios J. (1991). *Byzantine Philanthropy and Social Welfare*. Athens, Greece: Aristide D. Caratzas Publishers, 2ⁿᵈ edition.

De Clercq, Dirk, Maxim Voronov (2009). Toward a practice perspective of entrepreneurship: Entrepreneurial legitimacy as habitus. In: *International Small Business Journal*, 27(4): 395-419.

Demil, Benoît, Jabril Bensédrine (2005). Processes of legitimization and pressure toward regulation: Corporate conformity and strategic behavior. In: *International Studies of Management & Organization*, 35(2): 56-77.

Dey, Pascal, Chris Steyaert (2012). Social entrepreneurship: Critique and the radical enactment of the social. In: *Social Enterprise Journal*, 8(2): 90-107.

Dorado, Silvia, Marc J. Ventresca (2013). Crescive entrepreneurship in complex social problems: Institutional conditions for entrepreneurial engagement. In: *Journal of Business Venturing*, 28: 69-82.

Gawell, Malin (2014). Soci(et)al entrepreneurship and different forms of social enterprise. In: *Social Entrepreneurship: Leveraging Economic, Political, and Cultural Dimensions*. Anders Lundstrom, Chunyan Zhou, Yvonne von Friedrichs, Elizabeth Sundin, Eds. NY: Springer, pp. 23-42.

Hervieux, Chantal, Eric Gedajlovic, Marie-France B. Turcotte (2010). The legitimization of social entrepreneurship. In: *Journal of Enterprising Communities: People and Places in the Global Economy*, 4(1): 37-67.

Ilchman, Warren F., Stanley N. Katz, Edward L. Queen II, Eds. (1998). *Philanthropy in the World's Traditions*. Bloomington, IN: Indiana University Press.

Katz, Jerome A. (2003). The chronology and intellectual trajectory of American entrepreneurship education, 1876-1999. In: *Journal of Business Venturing*, 18: 283-300.

Katz, Jerome A. (2008). Fully mature but not fully legitimate: A different perspective on the state of entrepreneurship education. In: *Journal of Small Business Management*, 46(4): 550-566.

Klein, Peter G., Joseph T. Mahoney, Anita M. McGahan, Christos N. Pitelis (2010). Toward a theory of public entrepreneurship. In: *European Management Review*, 7: 1-15.

Kroeger, Arne, Christiana Weber (2014). Developing a conceptual framework for comparing social value creation. In: *Academy of Management Review*, 39(4): 513-540.

Kuhlke, Olaf (2014). Developing cultural and creative industry (CCI) competencies in North American knowledge institutions: Making the case for a B.A. program in cultural entrepreneurship. In: *Beyond Frames: Dynamics between the Creative Industries, Knowledge Institutions and the Urban Context*. Annick Schramme, Giep Hagoort, Rene Kooyman (Ed). Delft, The Netherlands: Eburon Academic Publishers, pp. 242-250.

Landes, David S., Joel Mokyr, William J. Baumol, Eds. (2012). *The Invention of Enterprise: Entrepreneurship from Ancient Mesopotamia to Modern Times.* Princeton, NJ: Princeton University Press.

Lefebvre, Miruna Radu, Renaud Redien-Collot (2012). Achieving legitimacy in entrepreneurship education: A case study. In: *Journal of Enterprising Culture*, 20(4): 481-500.

Lisetchi, Mihai, Laura Brancu (2014). The entrepreneurship concept as a subject of social innovation. In: *Procedia – Social and Behavioral Sciences*, 124: 87-92.

Lundmark, Erik, Alf Westelius (2014). Entrepreneurship as elixir and mutagen. In: *Entrepreneurship Theory & Practice*, 38(3): 575-600.

Mascareño, Aldo, Kathyn Araujo (2012). On legitimacy once again: New challenges in world society. In: *Legitimization in World Society*. Aldo Mascareño, Kathyn Araujo, Eds. Burlington, VT: Ashgate Publishing, pp. 1-21.

Meyer, G. Dale (2011). The reinvention of academic entrepreneurship. In: *Journal of Small Business Management*, 49(1): 1-8.

Moerbeek, Arjan (2014). Towards a learning environment for the creative industry. In: *Beyond Frames: Dynamics between the Creative Industries, Knowledge Institutions and the Urban Context*. Annick Schramme, Giep Hagoort, Rene Kooyman (Ed). Delft, The Netherlands: Eburon Academic Publishers, pp. 234-241.

Morris, Michael H., Justin W. Webb, Jun Fu, Sujata Singhal (2013). A competency-based perspective on entrepreneurship education: Conceptual and empirical insights. In: *Journal of Small Business Management*, 51(3): 352-369.

Nicholls, Alex (2010). The legitimacy of social entrepreneurship: Reflexive isomorphism in a pre-paradigmatic field. In: *Entrepreneurship Theory & Practice*, 34(4): 611-633.

Perren, Lew, Peter L. Jennings (2005). Government discourses on entrepreneurship: Issues of legitimization, subjugation, and power. In: *Entrepreneurship Theory & Practice*, 29(2): 173-184.

Pilegaard, Morten, Peter W. Moroz, Helle Neergaard (2010). An auto-ethnographic perspective on academic entrepreneurship: Implications for research in the social sciences and humanities. In: *Academy of Management Perspectives*, 24(1): 46-61.

Ruebottom, Trish (2013). The microstructures of rhetorical strategy in social entrepreneurship: Building legitimacy through heroes and villains. In: *Journal of Business Venturing*, 28: 98-116.

Seitz, Jay A. (2003). The political economy of creativity. In: *Creativity Research Journal*, 15(4): 385-392.

Zahra, Shaker A., Mike Wright (2011). Entrepreneurship's next act. In: *Academy of Management Perspectives*, 25(4): 67-83.

A GLOBAL PERSPECTIVE

Jerry C Y Liu

REORIENT A PARADIGM SHIFT OF TEACHING IN ARTS MANAGEMENT AND CULTURAL POLICY IN TAIWAN

Abstract

For centuries, Europe and its cultural modernity has long been a model for Asian countries to follow. However, sharing pressures for East Asian countries to devise localized discourses and models of practice in arts management, cultural policy and cultural industries have emerged after the 1990s. This article takes the Graduate School of Arts Management and Cultural Policy (AMCP) at the National Taiwan University of Arts (NTUA) as a case study, to argue for the ReOrient-approach of teaching and learning in arts management and cultural policy. By using the ReOrient as a method and rationale, this article sketches the theoretical roots and approaches in curriculum design and competence building, as well as practical application of teaching and learning. The ReOrient of cultural governance signifies a re-articulation of traditional cultural value and meaning with modern institutional efficiency, entrepreneurial innovation and creativity in cultural management and administration.

Introduction: Network Governance of Arts Management and Cultural Policy

Arts management and cultural policy studies can no longer be considered as a separated field, and be insulated from political economy and the society in the global age. There has always been interconnectivity between culture, society and political economy. In respect of cultural politics, arts management and cultural policy involves cultural powers, institutions, regulations, the function of state cultural diplomacy and strategy, through which states and cities exercise their cultural soft power and assert their domestic cultural sovereignty, identity and international cultural influences (Nye, 2004; Chartrand, 1992; Liu, 2013a; Liu, 2013b; Hu, 2005).

In the aspect of cultural economics, it concerns the booming global creative and cultural industries, a growing creative economy, and the innovative dimension of cross-national cultural entrepreneurship and organization culture (du Gay and Pryke, 2002; Cunningham, 2012 [2002]; Cunningham, Banks, and Potts, 2008; Garnham, 2012 [1987]; Hesmondhalgh and Pratt, 2005; Hesmondhalgh, 2007). And it involves controversial issues of the promotion of cultural diversity through a free cultural market (free movement and consumption of cultural goods, services, and development of creative and cultural industries, with a strong support of the WTO) on the one hand, and that of safeguarding national cultural diversity (especially via the newly enforced provision of the UNESCO Cultural Convention, which allows national protection measures) on the other hand (Throsby, 2010; Voon, 2006; Singh, 2008). In cultural sociology, arts management and cultural policy involves debates between the homogenizing and diverging social traditions, cultural values, sentiments of aestheticism, the consolidation of historical roots and local sense of belonging, the discourse and counter-discourse of social-cultural representation and resistance, formation of cultural public sphere, as well as the empowerment and disturbance of cultural participation (Habermas, 1989; Kymlicka, 1995; Stevenson, 2003; Mulcahy, 2006; Liu, 2011b).

A GLOBAL PERSPECTIVE

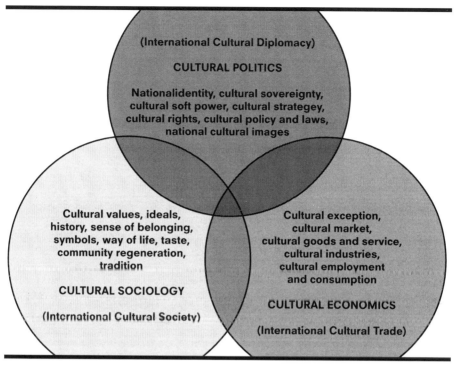

Figure 1 The Interconnectivity of Culture and Political Economy

Starting with the explained framework of interconnectivity among culture, society and political economy, one spontaneously goes on to identify the stakeholders (or agents) in the network (or in P. Bourdieu (1984[1979]), a realist power-interest competing '*field*') of arts-cultural governance. Such networked stakeholders and agents include:

1. government cultural apparatuses, organizations and public cultural institutions (museums, galleries etc.) at the international, national, regional and local levels;
2. agents in cultural economics such as creative and cultural industries, business enterprise sponsors, private donors and art-cultural foundations;
3. agents in civil society such as performance art groups, private (not-for-profit) art-cultural institutions, galleries, social/cultural organizations and local communities, professional associations of arts-cultural practitioners and academic institutions;
4. mass media and individuals and communities on the internet.

Mapping the interconnected relations among the agents, one looks into the mutual understanding of position and mode of interaction; the rule and logic in the field; the interpenetrating connectivity among official, non-official, thematic and general sub-networks; the flow and exchanges of persons, cultural goods, (social, economic and cultural) capital, service, ideas, and values; and importantly, the dominated power relations, or the cooperative, collaborative, dependent or competitive relations among agents in the art-cultural governance network (Rhodes, 1999a, 1999b; Liu, 2012, 2013).

A GLOBAL PERSPECTIVE

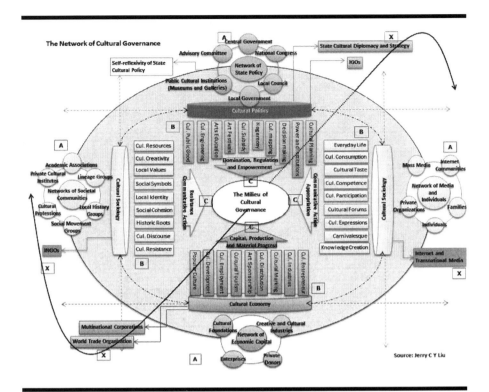

Figure 2 The Network of Cultural Governance

Methodological Framework: Cultural Glocalization and *ReOrient* as a Method of Teaching

Contemporary discourses and mechanical design of cultural governance, administration and arts management (from that of centralised-decentralised-deconcentrated model in France; independent NEA of the US and one-arm length policy of DCMS-Arts Council in the UK; to that of multiculturalist model in Australia and Canada) are founded on specific historical conditions and cultural values of the West) (Owen-Vandersluis, 2003; Miller & Yúdice, 2002; Gattinger, Saint-Pierre & Gagnon, 2008). Yet, building on similar colonized experiences and the successful stories of cultural industries in Europe after the 1950s, cultural management and policy in East Asia are very much influenced by European models. And in international cultural organizations (e.g. the UNESCO), agendas for the pursuit of universal cultural rights, intercultural dialogue, and cultural diversity have often been the overtone.

However, there has been calls for critical reflections of European impacts on Asian minds. The Graduate School of Arts Management and Cultural Policy (AMCP) at the National Taiwan University of Arts (NTUA) is thinking of East Asia. In line with E. Said (1978), G. Frank (1998), K. Chen (2005), J. Liu (2011a, 2014) and B. Wong (1997), we argue for the *ReOrient* of arts management and cultural policy in Taiwan. We ask the question that is it possible for one to envision a localized or indigenous discourse of arts management and cultural policy teaching in Taiwan and East Asia. If so, what is its content and method? If so, have to start thinking of the method and methodology of teaching by taking into account of the Asian ideas and values such as benevolence, virtuous rule, harmony, loyalty and reciprocity, and Oriental sentiments of aestheticism, rather than following the *'universal values'* like free expression of culture, cultural democracy, cultural diversity, cultural citizenship and cultural rights. (Liu, 2011, 2014)

ReOrient as the Contents of Cultural Governance and Entrepreneurship

In practice, the *ReOrient* stands for a re-articulation of traditional cultural value and meaning with modern institutional efficiency, innovation and creativity in cultural entrepreneurship in art-cultural administration. Taking cultural governance teaching as an instance, culture has been at the centre of traditional Chinese statecraft. Even in the 2010s, there are very clear influences of Confucian ethics and cultural values on the administration and management of traditional Chinese state bureaucracy. Morality and virtue was closely associated with the legitimacy of state (bureaucracy) activities. Such a self-restraining feature was/is reflected on Chinese/Taiwanese states' idealistic governing principle, which Confucius termed *weizheng yide*, *'to rule by virtue'*, or *renzhi* the *'rule of benevolence'* (Liu, 2008, 2009, 2014; Yu, 1992; Jin and Liu, 2000). By reinterpreting the traditional Chinese concept and scholarship of *jingshi* (literarily *'managing the world'*), our teaching explores how *'Oriental'* it could possibly be in the sphere East Asian cultural policy discourses and practices. We also test the limits of such Oriental cultural logics against cultural consumerism in modern Taiwanese society.

In the understanding of cultural rights and citizenship, varied modes of cultural logics in the East and West are integrated into a four-faceted analytical framework:

1. culture as the inherent value and meaning;
2. culture as the external practice of behaving and institution;
3. culture as the intersubjectivity of meaning and practice; and
4. culture as the interconnectivity of everyday life and political economy.

Western concept of cultural rights of various attributes (rights of cultural identity, rights to free expression of arts, information, participate in cultural policy, cultural consumption, cultural representation and cultural development etc.) may be designated to the interconnected spectrum of the four analytical cultural facets. Yet the underlying philosophy for the intersubjectivity of meanings and interconnectivity of cultural life may well be grasped in Oriental interpretation of *taiji* and the mutual balancing *yin* and *yang* forces and the attainment of its cultural harmony (Liu, 2015).

Rationale for Curriculum Design and Competence Building

The AMCP at NTUA was founded on the 1st August 2006. The School remains the only institution in Taiwan, which offers a doctoral program of arts management and cultural policy studies. Annually, the School registers 5 PhD and 10 MA research students at an average acceptance rate of 20%-25%. The AMCP engages in serious basic research and teaching in collaboration with the governmental, non-governmental and not-for-profit cultural institutions as well as cultural entrepreneurship, in the field of arts management and cultural policy studies.

A GLOBAL PERSPECTIVE

As the only doctoral research program of cultural policy studies in Taiwan, the AMCP recognizes that art and culture are import indicators which reflect social spirit and material dimension. However, the profundity of contemporary arts-cultural development depends on a visionary cultural policy and effective arts management. The former is based on the investigation of the trend of culture, authentication of theory and thought, analysis of policy and regulations; whilst the latter is rooted in the reflections of art and history, practical training of entrepreneurial marketing and management, stimulation of creativity and design. In order to match the tendency and needs of a free environment of art-cultural expression under the framework of the local and the global, AMCP formulates a program combining the theoretical and the practical. The program is designed to inspire research students to identify problems, comprehend cultural phenomena, start interpretation, utilize rational criticism, and finally provide profound insights through solid research as the foundation of thought and action.

Arts management and cultural policy are the two axes of AMCP, and for core fields of MA and PhD programs respectively. The two programs are the two sides of a coin which helps research students obtain a more comprehensive prospect in the field of arts-cultural management and governance. The AMCP positions itself as a modern educational and research institute, emphasizing the power of action and critical subjectivity. It sets its goals to reflect upon Taiwanese/Chinese cultural traditions and values, and reformulate local cultural discourses in the wake of a globalizing modernity. As an acronym, AMCP also invokes its long-term objectives: traits of Aesthetics, Motivation, Creativity, and Prospects.

Differing from programs of cultural entrepreneurship (which mostly take the name of Creative and Cultural Industries in Taiwan) under the Business School or Design, AMCP under the Faculty of Humanities in the National Taiwan University of Arts is taking a critical and cultural/artistic approach, which emphasizes the 'centrality of culture' (Hall, 1997) in management and governance. Without losing its humanistic and *ReOrient* concerns, it seeks critical, yet compatible, strategies to incorporate the capitalist ethos or entrepreneurial spirit of profit-making, risk-taking and creativity in the newly emerging global cultural entrepreneurship.

A. THEORIES, METHODS AND METHODOLOGY	B. CULTURAL POLICIES AND GOVERNANCE
1. Research Methods and Methodology 2. Arts and Cultural Theories 3. Arts and Cultural Sociology 4. Independent Study 5. Seminars: Contemporary	1. Cultural Policy: Theory and Practice 2. Critics of Cultural Policy 3. Cultural Laws and Regulations 4. European/Asian Cultural Policies
C. ARTS MANAGEMENT RESOURCES	D. MUSEUMS AND CULTURAL
1. Seminars: Arts Management 2. Arts Management: Theory and Practice 3. Design of Exhibition 4. Operation of Arts Institutions	1. Arts and Cultural Economics 2. Cultural Heritage Management 3. Creative and Cultural Industries 4. Cultural Tourism

Figure 3 Four main fields and Course lists

A GLOBAL PERSPECTIVE

Training mainly for prospective governmental cultural policy makers, administrators, as well as not-for-profit cultural sector managers, the program assigned a high artistic, cultural working ethic and professional prospect for art-cultural managers, governors, and even cultural entrepreneurs in Taiwan. State civil servants, who engage in the governance of culture and discourse-making in cultural policy area, need to take into full account of an accommodating cultural milieu and a wider network of governance for various cultural agents. In accordance with our education rationale and long-term objectives, the School designs its curriculum to provide courses in four main fields.

Six sets of core competences (Figure 4) are placed at the centre of the courses in order to foster the well-rounded research students in arts management and cultural policy. And the core competences and indicators (emphasizing the capabilities of research, specialized knowledge, humanism and critical thinking, communication, team works and leadership, sentiments in arts and aesthetics, and building up of local concerns with global visions) are incorporated in the course and teaching designs. These are also used in the assessment of study results.

A. RESERCH METHODOLOGY AND THESIS WRITING	B. APPLICATION OF SPECIALISED KNOWLEDGE IN ARTS MANAGEMENT AND CULTURAL POLICY	C. THEORY, DISCOURSE FORUMATIONS AND CRITICAL THINKINGS IN HUMANISM	A GLOBAL PERSPECTIVE
Competence Indicators - Abilities to collect, analyse and interpret data - Insights in identifying research questions (Problematic) - Capabilities in planning and designing research - Abilities to apply theories and research methods to thesis - Capabilities of making theoretical induction and deduction - Understanding the philosophy and meta-theory behind research methods	**Competence Indicators** - Obtaining specialised Knowledge of Arts Management and Cultural Policy - Familialrising with the operations and mechanisms of cultural institutions - Legislation of arts and cultural laws - Grasping the tendencies and issues of international cultural policies - Capabilties in designing and operatiing arts-cultural projects, programs and policy	**Competence Indicators** - Knowledge of cultural, social and arts theories - Understanding cultural discourses in the East and West academic traditions - Understanding the essence and spirits of Humanism - Capabilities of critical thinking and reflection	
D. COMMUNICATION, COORDINATION, TEAM WORKS AND LEADERSHIP IN MANAGEMENT	E. COMPOSITIONS AND SENTIMENTS IN ARTS, HUMANITIES AND AESTHETICS	F. LOCAL CONCERNS AND GLOBAL VISIONS	
Competence Indicators - Capabilities in making effective communication - Positive attitudes in cooperation and communication - Integrating an individual to organizations - Playing an adequate role in the team - Characters, confidence and skills to lead in arts and cultural institutions	**Competence Indicators** - Taste and sentiments for aesthetics, arts and culture - Abilities to appreciate, understand and analyse culture - Knowledge for arts and culture	**Competence Indicators** - Understaning the development of arts and culture - Knowing issues of regional culture - Visions and abilities for international cultural exchanges - Grasping the tendency of cultural globalization	

Figure 4 Core Competences and Teaching Design of AMPC

ReOrient: Arts Management and Cultural Policy Teaching in Practice

The AMPC not only combines the university museum, centres of performance and exhibition and various teaching resources, but also integrates liberal institutes and experts to develop various courses which focus on arts-cultural management, domestic and international cultural policy, regulations and analyses of global cultural phenomena. It explores the managing condition of art market, arts-cultural institutes, cultural enterprises and public sectors, and strengthen students' critical mind with arts and cultural theories and contemporary issues of arts. Five specific of features can be identified in terms of teaching and learning:

1. **Interdisciplinary Teaching and Joint Knowledge Production.** Cultural policy and arts management is such a broad study area that it requires necessarily collaborative teaching and knowledge creation of experts from varied disciplines. These range from cultural anthropology, arts and cultural history, aesthetics, philosophy, cultural study, sociology, public policy, political economy, business management, entrepreneurships, legal study, area study, and international study. Interdisciplinary dialogues among teachers and students have fostered a critical and favourable learning environment for the School, but truth claiming across various disciplines has never been easy. Despite intensive interdisciplinary dialogues, knowledge creation and common grounds building among cultural studies, aesthetics, management, entrepreneurships, economics and policy process studies gain but limited progress. Apart from individual publishing efforts, collaborative research works among teaching staffs and research students only start to translate into localized practical knowledge in joint edited book forms during the past 5 years (see: Lai, 2011; Lioa, 2010; Liu, 2015; Liu, 2013).

2. **Critical Debates and Integrated Approach of Theory and Practice.** Training leaders in cultural policy and practitioners in arts management requires also a combined approach of theoretical and practical. Many teaching faculty in AMCP have worked in private, public and not-for-profit cultural institutions, and are experienced in exhibition curating with for instance Taipei Modern Museum of Fine Arts, National Palace Museum, Taiwan History Museum, galleries and art auction companies. Others have played a (consulting or planning) role in the process of state or city cultural policy making and implementation. Many have hosted applied research projects with governmental and non-governmental cultural institutions, important projects include the drafting and consulting of state Cultural Basic Law, Museum Law, National Cultural White Paper; hosting state survey project of National Statistics of Cultural Participations and Consumption. All the engagements in research projects and practical cultural affairs have been transformed into materials of the day-to-day based teaching, research, and academic reflection.

3. **Certificated Training Programs of Cultural Practitioners and Civil Servants.** In collaboration with the Ministry of Culture, AMPC designs for a 20-credited-hour Certificated Training Program for Practitioners of Public Museums, and a Certificated Training Programs of Cultural Administration for civil servants who wish to convert their expertise to public cultural sectors. And in cooperation with the Taiwan Association of Project Management, AMPC also organized a Certificate Program for Art Project Management. The graduate school

is supported by various subsidies and funding schemes from the Ministry of Education and was the first to create an Art Project Management Research and Development Centre, a Museum Management Research and Development Centre, and a Taiwan Research Centre of Cultural Policy at a university. The Research Centres are established in response to the interdependency between cultural policy, arts and museum management, in hope that under ever-changing waves of time, cultural institutions can further develop its knowledge in the field of cultural policy and management, in order to build a communicational platform for practitioners in Taiwan and abroad to engage in dialogue, to exchange professional knowledge that leads to a better tomorrow.

4. **Fostering Experiences of Practicality: Internship and Visits to Cultural Institutions and Enterprises.** The University's art museum and exhibition centre are precious teaching resources for the study of cultural management and cultural policy. The Graduate School uses them as experimental bases. The AMCP also brings in experts from contracted strategic partners such as the National Palace Museum, Museums of Fine Arts, National History Museum, City Cultural Bureaus, Arts Foundations, cultural and creative parks, curating companies, designing companies, galleries and art auction Companies in Taiwan to receive and train our research students through practitioners' work of daily routine and via specific art projects. Students are requested to do their internship during the summer or winter vacations. Every semester, excursions, on-site surveys and teachings for controversial cultural issues (from aboriginal groups' minority rights, regeneration of local artist community, ethos of profit making in art market and creative park, to that of city cultural policy decision-making), as well as visits to cultural institutions are planned and led by teaching faculty in various courses to provide students with experiences of cultural practicality.

5. **Public Forums and Symposium for Positive Social Engagements.** In order to promote academic exchanges in arts management and cultural policy, the School organizes annual national or international conferences on cultural governance. Themes for 2012-2015 International Symposiums on Cultural Trajectories are 'The Imagination and Manifestation on Cultural Governance', 'The Dynamics and Counter-Dynamics of Cultural Governance', 'Cultural Governance: Who Benefits' (the 2014 symposium focuses particularly on the conflicting or compatible relations between art-culture and economy, and the entrepreneurial dimension in the private and public cultural sectors)[1], 'Cultural Governance: What's Next?'. By these conferences, AMCP intends to bring together discussions and dialogues of cultural policy and cultural governance among different agents. In collaboration with major museums in Taiwan, the School also holds important conferences on Museum studies. Cultural institutions in Europe and America, with its development spanning centuries, have now occupied an important role in cultural industry around the world. In comparison, institutions in East Asian region, with its relatively short history and the strong influence of national policy under public management, took a different path in subjects such as management, administration efficiency and social resources. However, they start to gain significant growth in global scope and local touch learning from the experience of western institutions, and look to a potential *ReOrient* discourse of international cultural management and governance.

A GLOBAL PERSPECTIVE

ReOrient Arts Management and Cultural Policy Teaching:
Limits and Problems

Arguing for the *ReOrient* of AMCP is not to be *anti-West* or even necessarily *contra-West*. As Chen (2005) suggests, to a great extent, the West is already inside most of us and becomes part of us.

Taking Taiwan, East Asia, or the Orient as a method, one is to take the *Rest of the West* as new referential points, and see how they may depart fundamentally not only from the West, but also from the traditionalist, nationalist, imperialist, Oriental cultural ideology, and cultural hegemony. Thus, by *ReOrient*, we also mean to reflect, reinterpret, restructure, and realign the concept of the Orient, and look for a *ReOrientation* of the teaching of arts management and cultural policy in East Asia (Liu, 2014).

So far, there are still limits and difficulties in teaching and learning of arts management and cultural policy in Taiwan and the AMCP. These include:

1. Limited success in interdisciplinary dialogues and localized knowledge production and accumulation of arts management and cultural policy studies.
2. A still dominating instrumentalist (utilitarian) view of culture with respect to its relations with the society and political economy: Logics of power, material/economic interest, the use value of culture, are still the mainstream thoughts of the society.
3. Still limited progress in its efforts of bridging idealistic artistic/cultural values with the capitalist ethos or entrepreneurial spirit of profit-making, risk-taking. Less emphasis has been laid on the developing of entrepreneurial capacity in starting or organizing a cultural business or venture in Taiwan and abroad.
4. Ongoing debates among idealism and realism, critical and practical intellectuals in the day-to-day operation of official arts-cultural institutions; varied goals and positions among practitioners from the industry, government office, and research and educational institutions.
5. Still very western dominated theoretical discourses in cultural policy and arts management studies, and limited official participations of Taiwanese cultural institutions in international cultural society.
6. Discrepancies in the definition of the core cultural values in Taiwanese society, and difficulties in re-accommodating the traditional cultural values with the localized modern cultural discourses.

To make sense of the contemporary cultural policy in Taiwan and East Asia, what's needed is probably a '*cultural turn*' or even '*paradigm shift*' of theory and practice in governance. Arguing for the *ReOrient* of cultural management and cultural governance therefore means to shift the underlying logic of governance (policy debate) from that of Machiavellian interest, calculation, wealth, power, modern commercial values, capitalist ethos and business model, to that of culture—inherent value, aesthetics, moral-ethical ideals, and humanistic rationality. (Liu, 2011).

[1]*Retreived from: https://sites.google.com/site/culturalgovernance/home*

There still exist gaps between the *ReOrient* of cultural management and governance as logic/ideal and as reality. Overemphasis on a pro-humanistic cultural logic comes at the cost of the precision of quantitative figures, and the efficiency and efficacy of the states' governing technologies. These are limitations of traditional Oriental cultural statecraft. One way to fill the gaps is to adopt '*critical reflexivity*' as a modern revision, reinterpretation and reapplication of Confucian logics in contemporary cultural management and governance. The *ReOrient* of cultural governance thus signifies a re-articulation of traditional cultural value and meaning with modern institutional efficiency, entrepreneurial innovation and creativity in cultural management and administration. In a way, the East and the West become their mutual remedies in cultural governance (Liu, 2014).

• This article is converted from the two papers delivered in The Asia Pacific Network for Cultural Education and Research (ANCER) Inaugural Meeting from 15-16 May 2012 in LaSalle College of Arts of Singapore, and the 4th Annual ENCATC Research Session on 6 November 2013 in University of Antwerp of Belgium.

About the Author

Dr Jerry C Y Liu is an Associate Professor of Graduate School of Arts Management and Cultural Policy at the National Taiwan University of Arts. He teaches cultural policy studies, contemporary cultural theories, and world history of cultures at the undergraduate, postgraduate and doctoral levels. Liu is the author and editor of The Mapping of Cultural Rights in Taiwan (2015, in Chinese) and Global Cities, Cultural Governance and Cultural Strategies: Art-Cultural Events, Festivals and Cultural Images (2013, in Chinese). His current research focuses on cultural governance and cultural policy, the concept of cultural logic in modern Chinese and European history, as well as the interactivity between culture and political economy in international cultural relations. Liu is invited as the ENCATC International Correspondence Board Member between 2015 and 2017.

References

Althusser, L. (1971). *Lenin and Philosophy and Other Essays*. London: New Left Books.

Bennett, T. (2001). Intellectuals, Culture, Policy: The Practical and the Critical. In: *Toby Miller (Ed.). A Companion to Cultural Studies* (pp. 357-374). London, Blackwell Publishers Ltd.

Bourdieu, P. (1984 [1979]). *Distinction: A Social Critique of the Judgment of Taste. R Nice (Trans.).* London: Routledge.

Chartrand, H. H. (1992). International Cultural Affairs: A 14 Country Survey. In: *Journal of Arts Management, Law & Society* 22(2), 134-154.

Chen K. (2005). Asia as a Method. In: *Taiwan Society Research Quarterly*, 57, 139-218. (In Chinese)

Cunningham, S. 2012 [2002]. 'From Cultural to Creative Industries: Theory, Industry, and Policy Implication.' (pp. 206-218) In: *Moeran, Brian and Alačovska, Ana. (Eds.).* 2012. Creative Industries: Critical Readings (Volume 1) Concepts. London and New York: Berg.

Cunningham, S., Banks, J. and Potts, J. 2008. 'Cultural Economy: The Shape of the Field.' (pp. 15-26) In *Helmut Anheier and Yudhishthir Raj Isar (Eds.). The Cultural Economy. The Cultures and Globalization Series 2*. London, Thousand Oaks, New Delhi, and Singapore: Sage.

du Gay, P. and Pryke, M. (2002). 'Cultural Economy: An Introduction.' (pp. 1-19) In: *Paul du Gay and Michael Pryke (eds.) Cultural Economy: Cultural Analysis and Commercial Life*. London, Thousand Oaks and New Delhi: Sage.

Foucault, M. (1991). Governmentality. In G. Burchill, C. Gordon and P. Miller (Eds.). *The Foucault Effect: Studies in Governmentality* (pp. 87-104). Chicago: University of Chicago Press.

Frank, A. G. (1998). *ReOrient: Global Economy in the Asian Age. California: University of California Press.*

A GLOBAL PERSPECTIVE

Garnham, Nicholas. (2012 [1987]). 'Concepts of Culture: Public Policy and the Cultural Industries.' (pp. 161-176) In Moeran, Brian and Alačovska, Ana. (Eds.). 2012. In: *Creative Industries: Critical Readings (Volume 1) Concepts.* London and New York: Berg.

Gattinger, M., Saint-Pierre, D. &, Gagnon, A. C. (2008). Toward Subnational Comparative Cultural Policy Analysis. In: *The Journal of Arts Management, Law, and Society*, 38(3), 167-186.

Gramsci, A. (1971). *Selection from the Prison Notebooks. Quentin Hoare and Geoffrey Nowell Smith (Eds. and Trans).* New York: Lawrence & Wishart.

Habermas, J. (1989). *The Structural Transformation of the Public Sphere: An Inquiry into a Category of Bourgeois Society.* Cambridge: Polity Press.

Hall, S. (1997). The Centrality of Culture: Notes on the Cultural Revolutions of Our Time. In: *K. Thompson (Ed.). Media and Cultural Regulation* (pp. 207–38). London, Sage.

Hesmondhalgh, D. (2007). *The Cultural Industries (2nd Edition)*. Los Angeles, London, New Delhi and Singapore: Sage.

Hesmondhalgh, D. and Pratt, A. C. (2005). 'Cultural Industries and Cultural Policy'. In: *International Journal of Cultural Policy.* 11(1), 1-13.

Hu Huiling. (2005). *The Development of Cultural Industries and National Cultural Security*. Guangzhou: Guangdong People's Publisher, 2005. (In Chinese)

Jin Guantao and Liu Qingfeng. (2000). *The Origins of Modern Chinese Thought—The Evolution of Chinese Political Culture from the Perspective of Ultrastable Structure (Vol. I).* Hong Kong, Hong Kong Chinese University. (In Chinese)

Kymlicka, W. (1995). *Multicultural Citizenship*. New York: Oxford University Press.

Lai, Y. Y. (2011a). *Contemporary Arts Management. Taipei, Artist.* (In Chinese)

Lai, Y. Y. (2011b). *Reflexive Exhibition and Discourse Practice*. Taipei, Feyen. (In Chinese)

Liao, H. T. (2010). *The Tension of Arts: Politics of Culture and Arts in Taiwan.* Taipei, Artco Books. (In Chinese)

Liu C. (2007). Cultural Globalization: An Indigenized and Integrative Mode of Thinking and Practice. In: *Studies in International Cultures,* 3(1), 1-30. (In Chinese)

Liu C. (2012). *Soft Power and the Art-Cultural Governance Network in Taiwan: The Field of Performance Art Governance (2000-2010).* Research Project Sponsored by the National Science Council. (In Chinese)

Liu C. (2015). Cultural Basic Laws: In Pursuit of Citizens' Participation of Cultural Life as the Basic Cultural Rights in Taiwan. In: *Jerry C Y Liu, Yuhsing Chang and Huangding Liao (Eds.).* In: *The Mapping of Cultural Rights in Taiwan.* Taipei, Chuliu. (In Chinese)

He has been the consulting member of the Special Unit for the drafting of Culture Basic Law, and the consultant of the Global Outreach Office of Ministry of Culture in Taiwan. Liu is the initiator of the Taiwan Association of Cultural Policy Study, and Taiwan Research Centre for Cultural Policy. He now acts as a Contract Columnist for the United Daily News in Taiwan.

—

jerryliu@ntua.edu.tw

A GLOBAL PERSPECTIVE

Liu, C. (2013a). Glocal Culture: The Configuration of City Cultural Governance and Cultural Strategies. In *Jerry C. Y. Liu (Ed.). Global Cities Cultural Governance and Cultural Strategies: Art-Cultural Events, Festivals and Cultural Images* (pp. 3-36). Taipei, Chuliu. (In Chinese)

Liu, J. C. Y. (2008). Does Culture Matter? The Logics and Counter-logics of Culture in State Finance, Taxation and Tributary Trade Policies during the Ming Times c. 1300-1600. In: *The Icfai Journal of History and Culture*, 2(1), 24-60.

Liu, J. C. Y. (2009). *Cultural Logics for the Regime of Useful Knowledge during the Ming and Early Qing China.* History of Technology, 29, 29-56.

Liu, J. C. Y. (2011a). Discourses and Networks of Cultural Governance in Europe: A Critical Review. In: *Intergrams*, 11(2), 1-15. (In Chinese)

Liu, J. C. Y. (2011b). *Soft Power: The International Art-Cultural Exchanges of the EU (2001-2010).* Research Project of The National Taiwan University of Arts.

Liu, J. C. Y. (2013b). 'Sino-African Cultural Relations: Soft Power, Cultural Statecraft and International Cultural Governance'. In Stephan Chan (Ed.). In: *The Morality of China in Africa: The Middle Kingdom and the Dark Continent.* London, Zed Books Ltd.

Liu, J. C. Y. (2014). ReOrienting Cultural Policy: Cultural Statecraft and Cultural Governance in Taiwan and China. In: *Lorraine Lim and Hye Kyung Lee (Eds.). Cultural Policies in East Asia: Dynamics between the State, Arts and Creative Industries* (pp. 120-138). London: Palgrave-Macmillan.

McGuigan, J. (1996). *Culture and the Public Sphere.* London and New York: Routledge.

McGuigan, J. (2004). *Rethinking Cultural Policy.* Berkshire, Open University Press, 2004.

Miller, T. & Yúdice, G. (2002). *Cultural Policy.* London: Sage.

Mulcahy, K. V. (2006). *Cultural Policy: Definitions and Theoretical Approaches.* In: The Journal of Arts Management, Law, and Society, 35(4), 319-330.

Nye, J. S. (2004) *Soft Power: The Means to Success in World Politics.* New York: Public Affairs.

Owen-Vandersluis, S. (2003). In: *Ethics and Cultural Policy in a Global Economy.* New York: Palgrave MacMillan.

Rhodes, R. A. W. (1999a). *Control and Power in Central-Local Government Relations* (2nd Ed.). London: Ashgate Publishing Ltd.

Rhodes, R. A. W. (1999b). Governance and Network. In: *G. Stoker (Ed.), The New Management of British Local Government* (pp. xii-xxvi). London: Macmillan Press Ltd.

Said, E. W. (1978). *Orientalism. Western Conceptions of the Orient.* London: Penguin Books.

Singh, J. P. (2008). Agents of Policy Learning and Change: U.S. and EU Perspectives on Cultural Trade Policy. In: *The Journal of Arts Management, Law, and Society,* 38(2), 141-159.

Stevenson, N. (2003). *Cultural Citizenship: Cosmopolitan Questions.* Maidenhead: Open University Press.

A GLOBAL PERSPECTIVE

Throsby, D. (2010). *The Economics of Cultural Policy.* Cambridge: Cambridge University Press.

Tomlinson, J. (1999). *Globalization and Culture.* Cambridge: Polity Press.

Voon, T. (2006). UNESCO and the WTO: a Clash of Cultures?. In: *International and Comparative Law Quarterly*, 55, pp 635-651. doi:10.1093/iclq/lei108.

Wong, R. Bin. (1997). *China Transformed: Historical Change and the Limits of European Experience.* Ithaca and London. Cornell University Press.

Yu Yingshi. (1992). *Observing the Modern Meaning of Chinese Culture from the Value System.* Taipei: Times Culture. (In Chinese)

A GLOBAL PERSPECTIVE

Marcin Poprawski

CULTURAL ENTREPRENEURSHIP TEACHING & LEARNING MODELS IN CENTRAL EUROPE

Abstract

Central Europe, after 25 years period of dynamic change initiated by the fall of communist regimes, is a very multi-dimensional, experimental cultural entrepreneurship playground. Entrepreneurial styles, competencies, values, theories and practices, are vastly reoriented in this part of the world.

The purpose of the article is to identify, compare and discuss structure, essence and quality of a cultural entrepreneurship and cultural management teaching projects and talent development practices in Poland, former East Germany, Czech Republic and Hungary.

An overview of the present situation, conditions and impacts of training and teaching managerial competencies in public, private and civil parts of cultural sector is offered. The selection is based on the analysis of past and existing activities in this field, taking a comparative approach with a selection of most inspiring cases.

The article will try to answer essential research questions like: what is the impact of teaching cultural management and entrepreneurship skills on practice of cultural organizations? Who are and where can we find mentors and career models for the next generation cultural entrepreneurs; individuals ready to risk, fail and professionally be reborn in the creative sector. How should we stimulate trans-generational transmission of values and sense-making in cultural sector?

Introduction

A potential clear view of an entrepreneurial teaching panorama in Central Europe is disturbed by a simple fact that the linguistic expressions of an '*entrepreneurship in culture*' or a '*cultural entrepreneur*' is not a main object of interest when considering cultural sector jobs market. Post-communist countries in Europe were, and mostly still are, public sector oriented cultural spheres. The majority of funds are spent on cultural domains as: theatre, orchestras, cinema, libraries, museums, cultural and art education activities, coming from public sources. The cultural landscapes in former Eastern Bloc countries were and still are dominated by public institutions based on subsidies. Cultural policy academics from Central and Eastern Europe, point out that a badge of being a cultural entrepreneur keeps some negative connotations in artists, critics and intellectuals circles originating in communism times (Dragićević - Šešić 2007). It brings a notion of individuals who are managing entertainment businesses and cheap art productions, commercial cabarets, circus, popular entertainment TV or kitschy music genres, and have much more in common with non-ambitious leisure economy, than serious art initiatives or innovative projects in the arts.

This stereotype is challenged by new media formats, cultural globalization trends, and local cultural tourism initiatives of a very talented generation of creative individuals. Fortunately, recent years bring more positive perceptions of cultural entrepreneurs, as

A GLOBAL PERSPECTIVE

those who are bridging free market of aesthetic needs, successful audience development practices, innovative solutions for serious art productions and branded institutions. But this is a rather fresh trend of last decade, including follow-up of recent narrations on creative economy (UNCTAD, 2010) and creative and cultural industries, where cultural entrepreneurship is one of the key terms (HKU, 2010).

That is why public institutions, being major players in the labour market of cultural production and (public) services, were not looking in last 25 years for cultural entrepreneurs as much as for cultural managers and cultural administrators.

Cultural management is perceived in Central and Eastern Europe as a more neutral, flexible term, bringing less profit-oriented sense of cultural activity than entrepreneurship. A paradox is that not all cultural entrepreneurship term users and critics, are aware that, *'entrepreneur'* came to English language from French, originally applied to the director or manager of a public musical institution (Bilton and Cummings, 2014). Cultural management, than, as a field of practice and knowledge on all multi-dimensional organizational activities and processes in, and around cultural sector, fits to all types of organizational actors, including the major cultural infrastructures; the public, mostly municipal cultural institutions. Cultural management is at the end a dominant professional education domain, in a field of cultural organizations of a different - public, private and civil - kind. Cultural entrepreneurship in education processes is than understood more as an approach or a special skill within a general framework of cultural management.

Both variety of motivations for learning or teaching and, above all some essential terminological problems with cultural entrepreneurs, leads to the conclusion, that a reasonable overview of professional programs of cultural entrepreneurship and cultural management in Central Europe, will have to be based not only on a sort of desk research – collecting a spectrum of data from institutions or web databases. It will need a qualitative perspective of experts and experienced members of teachers and learners communities. In our study we used questionnaires, addressing twenty-four selected, well-informed professionals in Poland, former East Germany, Czech Republic and Hungary.

Teaching Cultural Entrepreneurship and Management Education in Central Europe

A qualitative overview starts from a digest of data on most recognized teaching programs in four selected territories. The majority of highlighted programs are combining several disciplines, such as management, cultural studies, economy, arts, and other fields of interests proper to entrepreneurial and managerial jobs in particular parts of a broad cultural sector.

Poland. Our sample of Education in Poland consists of cultural management programs that contain a component of cultural entrepreneurship topics or module. Cultural management studies are injected into BA, MA, or postgraduate programs of cultural studies, cultural theories, urban studies, humanities focused on culture offered by biggest public universities, like Warsaw University, Adam Mickiewicz University in

Poznan[1] or prestigious university of economics[2] like SGH in Warsaw. Recent studies in cultural management are offered in Cracow by Jagiellonian University – Management Studies Faculty – Institute of Culture. Where other universities are offering some modules, courses, this institution is combining humanities and management studies on culture within all levels of studies from BA, MA, postgraduate, till PhD.

Among main competitors private universities are to be mentioned, above all SWPS – University of Social Sciences and Humanities, part of the Human Touch Group Schools, located in Warsaw and Poznan (School of Form Design School), with an offer of creative, innovative teaching from kindergarten till PhD program, offering as well an entrepreneurial teaching in the arts.

Only few public art schools have cultural management programs, mostly in a post-graduate form, like Academy of Arts in Szczecin or Academy of Fine Arts in Warsaw. This last offer is focused mostly to provide a fine-arts professionals career toolkit of how to survive in art market. The Theatre Academy in Warsaw is providing studies on theatre production and recently Warsaw Film School has offered cultural management BA studies.

The majority of schools prefer to call organizational components of the arts – '*animation*' than management, as this is perceived as a more appropriate name to culture non-profit sector and social interactions with the public. Another group of studies are programs on demand of biggest governmental agencies, like the Collegium Civitas in Warsaw, the International Cultural Centre, the National Cultural Centre in Warsaw, the Małopolska Region Cultural Institute in Cracow.

In general BA and MA studies offered by public higher education systems are for free. It usually works with groups of no more than 50 students each year. Art schools programs are less numbered. Postgraduate studies for professionals and all programs provided by private schools are paid by students. Training and studies offered by NGO's or regional governments are usually free of charge, as they are mostly EU funds supported

The Czech Republic. Cultural entrepreneurship in Czech Republic is also rather a branch of cultural management, than a separate, spotted area of education activities. There are two main streams of managerial education in culture offered by public schools. One is that offered by top academic brands in performance studies, like DAMU in Prague and JAMU in Brno. Both schools are providing BA, MA, PhD study programs in theatre production, theatre management, music management, and some postgraduate work-shops for non-academy student-professionals. DAMU, within its film and television faculty, is also offering film production studies on all three levels, from BA till PhD. Programs are subsidized and as a rule free of charge for BA, MA, and PhD students. Small groups of carefully selected students have individualized training, focused supervision and tutoring.

A GLOBAL PERSPECTIVE

---

[1] *This is the case of programs offered also by UMCS in Lublin, UKSW in Warsaw, Wroclaw University, KUL Catholic University in Lublin, University of Lodz, Silesian University in Katowice, University in Gdansk.*

[2] *Programs operated by universities of economics or business schools – SGH in Warsaw, UEP in Cracow, AGH in Cracow, private Kozminski University or University of Economics in Cracow and University of Economics in Katowice.*

JAMU and DAMU management programs are practice oriented and based on entrepreneurial skills development, including organizing a real theatre festival as a students' teamwork with theatre management and theatre production programs. Topics highlighted are among others: management, theatre, marketing, fundraising, budget management, institutional management, leadership, artistic projects cooperation and leadership.

The second, rather detached from the first stream is that of universities of economics, with a Prague university as a fore player. Some top offers in the cultural management topics ranged from BA till PhD, are provided by subsided state universities like Masaryk University in Brno, with Arts Management program in the structure of the Faculty of Arts and Humanities; as well as University of Economics in Prague, Arts Management curricula offered by Faculty of Business and Administration. The first one offers Management as a theoretical, philosophical field. The last one has a more business entrepreneurial style, and a special focus on tangible heritage and museums. A competitive offer is that of a private school focused on public administration - CEVRO Institute, School of Political Studies in Prague, with its MA, Master in Public Administration, which is planned for future culture and education administration leaders.

These options are supplemented by various online arts management courses of a long-life-learning type (like those offered by www.culturematters.cz). Art Management training is also available for cultural sector professionals due to a cooperation of public universities with NGOs, it is one offered by Faculty of Design of ZCU University of West Bohemia in Plzen. Some new players in the game are Associations and Foundations, absorbing EU and governmental funds for workshops in the field of cultural entrepreneurship, and struggle for professionalization of cultural sector staff in Czech Republic.

Hungary. An overview of options for cultural entrepreneurship education brings several offers from both private and public sector, but rather not directly within regular BA or MA long term studies.

A private University of Applied Sciences - Budapesti Kommunikációs és Üzleti Főiskola - offers 3 semester postgraduate program in Art & Business Manager accessible to cultural sector employees and freelancers for artists and public administration staff. It is not subsidized, has a business recognition, and teaches mostly art, management, strategic development, marketing skills for the art sector. Another private competitor in this sort of education is EDUTUS Főiskola College having 2 semesters postgraduate studies in cultural management, aiming more at the public sphere, teaching media and cultural economics, cultural entrepreneurships, leadership, communication, cultural project management, cultural marketing, event management, and in general making profit with the arts.

An MA program in Tourism Management is offered by private University of Applied Sciences - Budapesti Kommunikációs és Üzleti Főiskola and is not subsidized. It's 6 plus 1 semester long, aiming at students, with a good business circles reputation[3].

Public universities are offering cultural management related studies, like Cultural Mediation (in Győr, Pécs and Szeged), cultural studies, identity, mass culture, intercultural studies, cultural project management, cultural research with some small components of entrepreneurship for cultural sector. Yet, these do not cover central topics to cultural entrepreneurial skills.

Programs of a 'cultural studies' type - with a managerial component in it - are offered also by public universities (Debrecen; Lajos Kossuth University and Budapest; Eotvos Lorand University). A special place for cultural policy, public management and business entrepreneurship is a private international brand in education that is CEU Central European University in Budapest, aiming at international reknown academics, covering a large number of academic programs, including MA and PhD in Public Policy or Cultural Heritage, as well as business studies including Global Entrepreneurship. In addition we find some initiatives in this top-segment; the Pazmany Peter Catholic University and its Faculty of Humanities and Social Sciences; and MOME Moholy-Nagy University of Art and Design in Budapest, training for entrepreneurship is a systematic aim with special semesters focused on. At least two private institutions have got professional management trainings for music managers: Zeneipari Hivatal (Music Industry Bureau) trains pop-rock music industry managers, and Majdnem Híres Rocksuli (Almost Famous Rock School). Some support for entrepreneurs is provided by the diplomatic branch - Balassi Institute or other bureaucracies: Hungarian Institute for Culture, and National Institute for Community Culture – institutions supported by Ministry of National Resources a government unit, responsible for culture, education and research.

Eastern Germany. The full, educational and life-long learning potential of the new Germany after re-unification of the country is visible via a databases of Kultur Management Network[4], or by Institut für Kulturpolitik der Kulturpolitischen Gesellschaft.[5] This is a set of over 110 offers of studies from BA, and MA to postgraduates and PhD provided currently in all Germany by state, regional, foundation-based or private higher education institutions, including the best known university brands. The range of programs in cultural management - including entrepreneurial curricula - involves topics of arts and management taught from the perspective of applications in the fields of theatre, music industry, visual arts, urban culture, book market, media and culture management, heritage, tourism, public institutions, cities and governments. In addition we find some 60 programs, offered in German by Austrian and Swiss universities, arts schools, economic and applies sciences schools. There are some 35 study programs of cultural managerial interest in former East Germany territories. Nearly half of them in the capital Berlin, completed by former East Bolc locations: Leipzig, Potsdam, Weimar, Dresden, Frankfurt (Oder), Magdeburg, Merseburg, Halle, Görlitz and Cottbus.

A GLOBAL PERSPECTIVE

---

[3]*Teaching: Sustainable Development of Tourism; Tourism Marketing and Communication Theory; Tourism Destination Management; Visitors and Attraction Management; Destination Marketing; Ecotourism; Media Management; Preservation and Management of Heritage Sites; Information Management of World Heritage Sites.*

[4]*http://www.kulturmanagement.net/ausbildung/prm/57/cs__11/chi_ia__1/index.html*

[5]*http://www.studium-kultur.de/datenbank.html*

The Impact of Professional Performance

In our study we asked our experts to estimate the impact of teaching and training cultural management after 1989, and the influence on the quality of cultural organizations performance in Central European countries.

Respondents pointed several remarks on that topic.

1. **Impact on public institutions**. The impact of university-based education programs on institutions and cultural market players still seems rather poor and slow. The fast pace of know-how exchange within cultural staff is more visible, especially in bigger cities. The impact of political influence on public institutions seems often bigger than educational qualifications. Public subsided arts institutions have little opened themselves to educated managers (in terms of graduates profiles after 2000), and employees are considered to be poor in strategic management and in answering current culture users demands.

2. **Training teams.** Ambitious individuals trained in entrepreneurial and competitive skills for culture within postgraduates' studies or workshops, when reintegrated into their workplace organizational culture, crash with a fence of colleagues or leaders resistance when implementing changes needed. Implementing Change needs a collective, team approach.

3. **Growing managerial education**. The market of cultural management study programs and courses is rapidly growing in last few years, workshops and activities are getting more professional and attractive. There are more employees already working in the sector wanting to upgrade their competencies in a professional way.

4. **Translating vocabularies**. Cultural sector got more privatized, but this does not translate into a deep understanding of cultural entrepreneurial risks and advantages. There is a wide misunderstandings and unawareness in art and culture circles, when talking about competition, economy, and markets. There is still an essential need of translation from vocabulary of management or economy into arts or socio-cultural topics.

5. **Training self-made entrepreneurs**. There is a growing number of small enterprises or NGO's educating in the arts offering workshops for kids etc., that are usually conducted by self-made cultural entrepreneurs, passionate of the arts or particular craft, who have not experienced cultural management education. They started from an intuition and observation of the art world, transmitting creative education trends, with more or less success.

6. **Less talk – more action**. Cultural sector debate in cultural education is too often more busy with ideological trends and fashions than supporting concrete needs of communities. There seems to be too much talk and debate on communication and integration and less effort on operational success.

7. **Injecting management to art studies**. More modules and courses on cultural entrepreneurship and management are needed within all humanities, arts and social studies. Having separate study programs on cultural management is not enough for impacting cultural sector.

8. **Flexible careers**. The growth of programs in cultural management is a consequence of illusive hopes of arts and humanities students, thinking that attending program will give them new practical skills that will facilitate applying for a job.

9. **The impact of the EU**. The boom for managerial workshop was related to EU funds stream starting around 2004, when many organizations started to offer subsided workshops. Thousands of new students, mostly postgraduate professionals used a chance to learn new skills in managing cultural field. The problem was that nobody certified, or controlled the content and final quality of this mass of teaching.

10. **Mobility**. Entrepreneurial teaching in cultural sector is not systemically connected to mobility programs. Students are not enough motivated to move abroad or move to another institution or city to learn, share and bring inspirations.

11. **Space for Freelancers**. New graduates are creating spaces for their activity as freelancers, mostly in media industry, popular culture industry and cultural tourism, all which rather opposite to official institutions than in direct cooperation with them.

12. **Professional Associations**. Non-existence of professional association of cultural managers in Poland, Hungary and Czech Republic results in lack of coordination of educational activities in this field. Therefore most of arts management graduates have no opportunity and not enough influence to enforce modern management methods.

Barriers, Challenges, and Achievements

A third issue raised by experts is that of challenges and barriers for cultural entrepreneurs in the post-communist, post-transition environments.

1. We can identify '*forced cultural entrepreneurship*'; people who start a small enterprise instead of being employed in an institution or bigger cultural organization; the so called '*forced*' or '*adaptive*' entrepreneurship (Oakley, 2014). As a consequence there grows a negative climate around cultural entrepreneurship.

2. We find a lack of financial stability of NGO's, due to the present grant system that promotes short projects and not provide operational grants. For creatives, there is no time for entrepreneurial further development within the organization they work for.

3. Limited investment/investors' portfolios in post-communist countries. Individual entrepreneurs, after graduating, are forced to find money for their ideas within a granting system, that is very standardized and is based on fixed public agendas

4. There is also a communication and vocabulary barrier when management professionalization is due. People from the sector do talk to each other, but use separate linguistic niches.

5. Cultural entrepreneurs in Central Europe are less committed to long term planning, and respond easily to commercial popular standards of cultural consumption. An additional discouragement comes from tax systems, making cultural services more expensive, promoting public institutions on the costs of private one.

6. There is also exaggerated mistrust to private players in cultural sector, who, paradoxically, mostly are much better client-friendly professionals than institutions working for the public interest. On the other hand political and peer connections or '*knowing right people*' is very often the only gate to successful public support of cultural projects and institutions.

7. The last barrier mentioned by Central European experts is that Entrepreneurial Education is hardly enough practice oriented, applied managerial teaching for cultural sector. More often, education is based on prejudices that economy in culture means only cheap, popular mass culture oriented services.

A GLOBAL PERSPECTIVE

Careers and Masters

A fourth issue raised is that of a career path for cultural entrepreneurs in Central Europe. The job market for them is rather in progress, developing, growing. It is a potential platform, or a broad space for work that is not ready yet. Some would say that the market from the side of cultural offers in some places, is overcrowded, and that obviously relate to graduates careers, too. There is a limited amount of job posts in institutions, so huge numbers of graduates are landing as entrepreneurs or cultural field freelancers. The major group of successful art entrepreneurs are not those well-educated, but most ambitious and determined. People in post-communist Central Europe seem to invest little for growth. One enters the market often too early and as a consequence creates failure and a less ambitious and quality offering. Another negative scenario mentioned is that of well-trained cultural entrepreneur, becoming a cultural administrator in institution or municipality.

Conclusion

There are hardly any obvious, well-defined roots and grounds of cultural entrepreneurship teaching in post-communist Central European countries. Management curricula for cultural sector are developed as a spontaneous reaction to:

a. current condition of the cultural sector, mostly needs of major employers - cultural public institutions in a process of organizational transition;
b. changing spectrum of cultural practices, clients demands, innovative formats and media of culture, asking for new skills;
c. the existence EU supportive funds for new member states – a stimuli for development of programs, trainings of new soft skills in cultural sector;
d. new fields of academic interests, particular teachers and university departments to develop programs and applied studies in cultural policy, cultural management and entrepreneurship, cultural economy, managing heritage, cultural diplomacy, creative industries, new cultural media.

To map the full potential and disturbing deficits of cultural management teaching and learning processes in this part of the world, one cannot limit research methods to desk researches, content analysis, statistics and experts feedback. The last of these approaches were selected for this text to construct arguments and assess the state of the art in academic and life-long-learning education in cultural sector.

In order to understand the present conditions for cultural entrepreneurship development in Poland, Czech Republic and Hungary, we have to keep in mind that Central Europe is still a battlefield of paradoxes in cultural policy theories and practices, cultural and aesthetics driven ideas, styles, interest and values directly related to organizational, managerial, social, administrative and political aspects of cultural and art activities. It's a real laboratory of 'collective imagination' (Klaić, 2007). With no doubt, Central Europe is a space in which one of most demanding definition of cultural policy gets its proper size - where culture is understood as an activity within society in a form of expression, entrepreneurship and creativity, directed from individual satisfactions to responsibility for social development and the quality of cultural public spheres (Poprawski, 2015). After a 25 years' period of dynamic change initiated by the fall of communist regimes, this part of the world seems to be a very multi-dimensional, experimental cultural entrepreneurship territory. Entrepreneurial styles, competencies, values, theories and practices, studied and trained are vastly reoriented from 1989 on, conditioned or influenced by political, economic, social, cultural and technological factors (Inkei, 2009).

The Cultural sector in Central Europe witnessed at least 3 stages of change since the fall of communism that could be illustrated with a use of three compelling emotions: enthusiasm, frustration and pride. This is in fact a story of a unique and unexpected rebirth of nations in a middle of Europe, liberated after nearly fifty years.
It is wise not to forget that two balanced emotions, that of frustration and the emotion of pride continue to coexist in different parts of the Central European post-communist cultural sector. It is injecting the engines of the four national cultural systems with bad and good fuel in the same time. All that is evident when looking through the spectrum of resources, barriers, challenges and achievements of cultural entrepreneurship education, as presented in this analysis.

- I would like to express my gratitude to my respondents, above all: Prof. Dorota Ilczuk, Dr Janos Szabo, Dr Katarzyna Plebańczyk, Blanka Chladkova, Dr Peter Inkei, Michal Laznovsky, Prof. Slawek Magala, Dr Patrick Föhl, Dr Ulrike Blumenreich, Philipp Dietachmair, Jagoda Komusińska, Dr Marek Chojnacki, Małgorzata Ćwikła, Piotr Knaś, Paweł Gogołek, Maciej Zygmunt, Dr Małgorzata Sternal, Moritz von Rappard, Dr Martin Zierold, Dr Vera Patockova.

About the Author

Dr Marcin Poprawski is Assistant Professor in the Institute of Cultural Studies at the Adam Mickiewicz University in Poznan, coordinator of AMU Culture Observatory, lecturer at the European University Viadrina in Frankfurt/Oder (D), Vice-president of ENCATC European Network based in Brussels and an expert of the Association of Polish Cities. He improved his professional skills during internship in the Centre for Cultural Policy Studies, University of Warwick (UK) and within the project 'Teaching Cultural Policies' held at Central European University in Budapest (H). His research interests include cultural policies, culture-led city development, aesthetics in management, and organizational cultures in cultural and creative sector, intercultural management, cultural branding and music aesthetics.

—

pop@amu.edu.pl

References

Bilton C., Cummings S. (2014). *Handbook of Management and Creativity*, Edward Elgar, Cheltenham.

Dragićević – Šešić M., Stojković B. (2007). *Culture: management, animation, marketing*, CLIO, Belgrade.

HKU, (2010). Rene Kooyman (Ed): *The Entrepreneurial Dimension of the Cultural and Creative Industries*, Hogeschool voor de Kunsten Utrecht, Utrecht.

Klaić D. (2007). *Mobility of imagination*, CEU, Budapest.

Poprawski M. (2015). Cultural Education Organizations and Flexible Individualization of Taste. In: *Journal of Organizational Change Management*, 2015, Vol. 28, Issue 2.

Inkei P. (2009). *Culture and Development 20 years after the fall of communism in Europe*. Article presented at The Culture Watch Europe Conference, 4th - 6th June 2009, Cracow, Poland. Retrieved from: http://www.budobs.org/pdf/Cracow_background_article.pdf, (accessed 27 October 2014).

Oakley K. (2014). *Good work? Rethinking cultural entrepreneurship,* in: C. Bilton, S. Cummings (2014), op. cit., pp. 145-159.

UNCTAD, (2010). *The Creative Economy Report 2010 - Creative economy: A feasible development option*. Geneva

A GLOBAL PERSPECTIVE

THEORY

Walter van Andel
Annick Schramme

EXPLORING ENTREPRENEURIAL ACTIONS OF CREATIVE ENTREPRENEURS AND ITS CONSEQUENCES FOR ENTREPRENEURSHIP EDUCATION

THEORY

Abstract

This article takes on an exploration into the specific entrepreneurial behaviours creative entrepreneurs typically follow, and discusses a practical application of such knowledge in the field of education and guidance. One of the key assumptions commonly used in published research on entrepreneurship in general is that it is the task of the entrepreneur to discover and exploit opportunities, which is coined in literature the '*causation logic*'. However, research has shown that not all entrepreneurs follow this logic in reality. The '*effectuation logic*', does not assume that opportunities await to be discovered, but that opportunities arise when they are created by an entrepreneur and its partners. This article posits and finds indications that the latter logic has a natural fit with the standard manner of working in the creative industries. In a second part, this article focuses on an application of knowledge on specific entrepreneurial behaviour in educational programs for creative entrepreneurs. A single case study – the master class '*Creative Jumpers*' taught at Antwerp Management School (Belgium) – is examined in which the assumption that effectuation logic fits naturally with these entrepreneurs is taken as premise for program design and development.

Introduction: Entrepreneurship

Many scholars have been attempting to make sense of what the concept of entrepreneurship really is. Throughout the years, pioneers such as Cantillon, Schumpeter, Kirzner, Knight, Hayek, Casson, Gartner, Shane and Venkataraman, to name but a few, have made significant contributions to entrepreneurship theory (Stokes, Wilson, & Mador, 2010). Even though Busenitz et al. (2014) find that entrepreneurship research has been gaining legitimacy and has been finding its place within major management In: Journals over the past two decades, there is as of yet still lacking a generally accepted definition of entrepreneurship in the research community (Brixy, Sternberg, & Stüber, 2012; Parker, 2009). However, one can distinguish at least two important meanings. First, entrepreneurship can refer to owning and managing a business on a person's own account and at his or her own risk. Second, entrepreneurship can refer to '*entrepreneurial behaviour*' in the sense of incorporating economic opportunities (Brixy et al., 2012). This second definition is important, as this article takes on an exploration into the specific entrepreneurial actions and behaviours creative entrepreneurs typically follow.

We propose a certain theory on entrepreneurial behaviour, the effectuation theory developed in a traditional business environment. It offers a natural fit with the internal functioning of the creative industries, and can therefore have value in terms of effective educational program design for creative entrepreneurs.

Entrepreneurial Behaviour: Causation and Effectuation Approaches

It is often claimed that it is the task of the entrepreneur to discover and exploit opportunities. For example, Drucker (1998) claims that most opportunities are discovered through a purposeful search process. Here the desired goal or endpoint is the basis that determines the actions to be carried out. In other words, entrepreneurship starts with defining the goal that one wants to achieve. Subsequently, means are sought that help achieving that goal. Consistent with this approach, competitive advantage is conceptualized to be largely determined by competencies related to finding and exploiting opportunities and the resources controlled by the firm. Entrepreneurship in this sense can be seen as a linear process in which the desire of the entrepreneur leads to planned activities revolving conception, and further development toward a (set of) pre-set goal(s). Central to this approach are concepts of intentionality (Katz & Gartner, 1988), opportunity identification and evaluation (Shane & Venkataraman, 2000), planning (Delmar & Shane, 2003), resource acquisition (Katz & Gartner, 1988), and the deliberate exploitation of opportunities (Shane & Venkataraman, 2000) (Fisher, 2012, p.1023). Figure 1 provides a graphic representation of this causation approach (Fisher, 2012; adapted from Shah & Tripsas, 2007). This widely accepted approach makes that the predominant entrepreneurial decision model taught in many (business) schools is a goal driven, deliberate model of decision making referred to by Sarasvathy (2001) as a 'causation logic' (Perry, Chandler, & Markova, 2012).

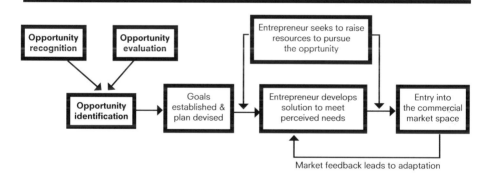

Figure 1 Causation approach to Entrepreneurship Fisher (2012)

However, research has shown that not all entrepreneurs follow this logic in reality. The alternative 'effectuation logic', does not assume that opportunities await to be discovered, but that opportunities arise when they are created by an entrepreneur and its partners (Sarasvathy, 2001). When using effectuation processes, entrepreneurs start not with an envision goal in mind, but rather by focusing on and utilizing the resources they have at their immediate disposal (i.e., who they are, what they know, and who they know). As the desired endpoint is not clearly defined at the beginning, those using effectuation processes remain flexible, take advantage of environmental contingencies as they arise, and learn as they go (Perry et al., 2012). Starting from the resources available; their own traits, tastes, and abilities; the knowledge corridors they are in; and the social networks they are a part of, the entrepreneur (in a multitude of iterations) seeks to achieve – in collaboration with a group of self-selected external partners – small steps forward towards an ex-ante undefined and unpredicted goal

(Sarasvathy, 2001). From this point of view, a different set of ideas and competencies are important in understanding (start-up) entrepreneurship, such as how each party contributes in the process of creating possibilities, handles risks, and deals with surprises and challenges (Read, Song, & Smit, 2009).

Entrepreneurs use both causal and effectual approaches in different combinations at different moments and in different contexts. The use of, or preference for a particular approach is related among others to the expert level of the entrepreneur, the resources available, and the progression the company has made in its life cycle. Effectuation processes are not posited as '*better*' or '*more efficient*' than causation processes in creating firms, markets, or economies (Sarasvathy, 2001).

Research Setup

According to the effectuation logic, the ex-ante information many companies have about the market is both incomplete and overwhelming, with a result that the information seems to be confusing and even contradictory. The market can therefore not clearly be defined, or predicted. Moreover, consumers are unaware of their future needs and preferences, while changes (such as new technologies and practices) can arise constantly. The term effectuation hinges on the notion that entrepreneurs proactively effectuate a transformation (Sarasvathy, 2001, 2009) and attempts to explain how entrepreneurs make decisions in the face of non-existent markets, featured by uncertainty, risk, and unpredictability. This theory postulates that entrepreneurs (collaboratively) create new opportunities outside of a causal framework (Ohlsson-Corboz, 2013).

This environment, which forms the basis for the effectuation logic, is on many accounts similar to the situation which many (aspiring) creative entrepreneurs face. The principles that underlie the effectuation logic, therefore, seem to be adjacent to the way of working in the creative industries, as it is often described. Consequently, it could be argued that the effectuation logic is an approach that many creative entrepreneurs follow intuitively, which forms the main proposition for this article: *the effectuation logic has a natural fit with the usual manner of working for creative entrepreneurs.*

As we believe a deeper knowledge of the way creative entrepreneurs operate within their very specific contexts can bring helpful insights, we will first attempt to find a preliminary validation of this research proposition through a small empirical study. Afterwards, we'll take a next step, and review an entrepreneurship program for creative entrepreneurs in which the proposed natural fit has been applied within the program's development.

In Theory: Entrepreneurship and the Creative Industries

Due to the specific context, many scholars are convinced that entrepreneurship within the creative industries adhere to different circumstances, regularities, and thought processes, both on the producer as on the consumer side. Hearn, Roodhouse, and Blakey (2007) therefore suggest that it would be unwise to adopt uncritically models derived from other industry sectors without considering the particular dynamic of the creative industries. These industries commonly revolve around entrepreneurial, innovative and often unorthodox collaborations, whereby numerous large, small and micro-businesses come together for the duration of a single project, often under a strict finite time frame, then disband and form new partnerships for the next project (Warren &

Fuller, 2009). Furthermore, Caves (2002) identified several distinctive characteristics that point to major risk and uncertainty about the economic outcomes of creative activities. These include a considerable uncertainty about the likely demand for a creative product, an unpredictability in the quality levels consumers see in the outputs, and an unpredictability in the capacity of their producers to continue to extract economic rents. Moreover, Colbert (2009) warns for saturation of the markets, a surplus of supply relative to demand and an almost infinite variety of creative products available.

Overall, these market conditions combined with typical intrinsic characteristics of industry players make creative entrepreneurs behave in a certain, industry-particular way, which can for many cases be generalized in the following process elements (this generalization has been formed by combining research on industry specifics of the creative industries, i.e. Caves, 2002; Jeffcutt & Pratt, 2002; Lampel et al., 2000; Warren & Fuller, 2009, and research on the importance and specific functioning of social networks and social capital for production in the creative industries, i.e. Delmestri, Montanari, & Usai, 2005; Hargadon & Sutton, 1997; Haunschild, 2003; Skilton, 2008; Uzzi, 1997):

Creative entrepreneurs often start their activities based on their strong, intrinsic interests, their corresponding skills and structured within networks they have at their disposal. This forms the basis from which their creative inspiration flourishes, and (vague) ideas come into life.

- To further develop these ideas, they often work in project-based collaborations with open structures. For example in the production stage of a movie, several creative individuals and organizations from different backgrounds come together on the basis of their skills and joint interests.
- These open structures are typically not bounded by solid rules that impose natural limitations, but tend to have a flexible character that leaves room for contingencies and 'out-of-the-box' thinking, which is necessary for the highly unpredictable creative marketplaces.
- The collaborations are further enabled by (informal) commitments of the participants to the project.
- Once the project is finished, the temporary partnership-structure dismantles and new collaborations are formed based on new ideas and interests.

THEORY

Common themes in the inner workings of the creative industries are therefore a high degree of experimentation, many partnerships, open structures and communication, action-oriented way of working, and a holistic view on the total process.

Method

In order to examine our proposition, a multiple case study design has been constructed. In order to examine our proposition, a multiple case study design has been constructed. This design allows the researchers to collect detailed information on both the entrepreneurial practices under scrutiny, and the contextual circumstances as well, which is necessary in the construction of explanatory middle range theory (Fredrickson, 1983). To analyse the proposition, the two opposing theories of entrepreneurial logic (causation and effectuation) have been further operationalized into five dimensions, resulting in a 5x2 matrix (Table 1). These five dimensions were based on the underlying rationality of five guiding principles of effectuation theory. These principles invert key decision-making criteria in common management practices used by expert entrepreneurs. For more information on the five effectuation principles (bird in hand, affordable loss, crazy quilt, lemonade, pilot in the plane), we refer to Sarasvathy (2009). For both of the entrepreneurial logics, indicators have been developed that capture each of the five dimensions for that particular way of reasoning. Using this framework, nine small and medium-sized creative companies from differing creative sectors have been analysed in terms of entrepreneurial growth and corresponding planned actions. Interviews have been held with the companies' CEO or strategic director following a semi-structured interview protocol. Topics discussed were the company's definition of growth and their growth ambitions, thresholds for achieving growth, and planned steps for achieving growth. Besides these interviews, industry specialists have been consulted that have a particular knowledge of entrepreneurship in creative industries from an academic, and/or practitioners' point of view.

THEORY

	CAUSATION	EFFECTUATION
STARTING POINT	Starting point is the achievable goal. Resources are selected based on the chosen goals	Starting point are resources at hand and the effects that can be achieved with these
DECISION CRITERION	Focus lies on maximizing possible profits	Focus lies on what you're willing to lose
CONTINGENCIES	Surprises are negative, they interfere with achieving the predetermined goal	Surprises are opportunities that can help shape goals and directions
PARTNERS	Partners are predetermined with the achievable goal in mind	Partners self-select and help to determine and define goals
MANAGEMENT OF UNCERTAINTY	The future can be managed by accurately predicting it	The future can be managed by focusing on the aspects you can control yourself, through which you can shape your own future

Table 1 Operationalization

During the interviews, the researchers made no particular reference to a certain (effectuation or causation) practice or theory. Directly after each interview, the content was transcribed and analysed using a directed approach to content analysis, which aims to validate or extend conceptually a theoretical framework or theory, in which existing theory or research help focusing the research question, and determining the initial coding scheme (Hsieh & Shannon, 2005). In the analysis, the researchers searched for particular references to actions or thought processes that can be related to one of the options from the operationalization table.

Results

The results of the content analysis of the transcripts found that during the interviews, 34 mentions were found that directly refer to one of the practices from the operationalization table. Table 2 provides an overview of the findings, separated for each of the five dimensions.

As the findings indicate, there is a strong indication that effectuation practices are more utilized in the nine cases studied with 26 occurrences for effectuation practices versus eight occurrences of practices stemming from the causation logic. This means that the proposition that the effectuation logic has a natural fit with the standard manner of working for creative entrepreneurs holds, based on our research pool.

	CAUSATION	EFFECTUATION
STARTING POINT	5	5
DECISION CRITERION	0	5
CONTINGENCIES	0	7
PARTNERS	3	7
MANAGEMENT OF UNCERTAINTY	0	2
TOTAL	8	26

Table 2 Results

In Practice: Creative Entrepreneurship Education

The results give a first indication that effectuation practices are common working principles for creative entrepreneurs. A key value gained from this understanding lies in the translation of these practical insights for among others entrepreneurial educational purposes, as a deeper knowledge of the way creative entrepreneurs operate within their very specific contexts can bring many useful application. In this second part of this article, we will zoom in one of those applications, by focusing on its value for training and guidance purposes.

Entrepreneurship Education

Mwasalwiba (2010) synthesized 108 scientific studies on entrepreneurship education, resulting in a model that gives an overview of the choices to make for educators (Figure 2). In his view, entrepreneurship education should start with a definition of perspective on entrepreneurship (1). Next (2), the perspective chosen leads to specific objectives the program aspires to achieve. Is the goal of the program to learn *about* entrepreneurship, to develop entrepreneurial skills and attitudes (*in*) entrepreneurship? Or, to further develop (the idea of) the company (*for*) entrepreneurship? These choices also determine the program design characteristics, such as target audience, structure (length and timing of the program) and content of the program (3). The final elements in program design are the teaching methods and activities (4) and the manner of evaluation and measurement of the success of the program (5). This meta-study analyses the complexity of teaching entrepreneurship, and offers a logic to configure (and analyse) a program, in which the internal logic between the different building blocks is specifically of interest.

THEORY

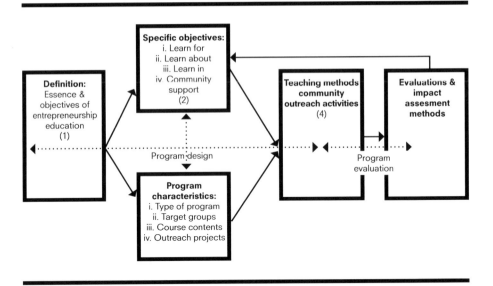

Figure 2 Synthesis on scientific research on entrepreneurial development (Mwasalwiba, 2010, p.23)

THEORY

Application of the Model: the Creative Jumpers Program
Overview of the Creative Jumpers Program

In 2013, Antwerp Management School (Belgium) started a new program specifically targeted at young entrepreneurs from the creative industries: '*Master Class Creative Jumpers*'. In the set-up of this program, knowledge on the effectuation logic was used to design a program that '*fits*' with the natural workings of entrepreneurs within these industries.

The overall program design consisted of five two-day content blocks, with each block consisting of a theoretical class session around a specific theme, and a practical '*lab*' session in which participants directly applied the theoretical knowledge to their own situation. Moreover, a leadership development track was added, focusing on increasing self-awareness on entrepreneurial choices (Figure 3). Each content block is aimed at providing and applying new knowledge and insights which participants use to develop a growth-oriented plan for their creative enterprise. After finishing the in-class content blocks, participants have the opportunity to seek guidance from an external coach to further strengthen their plan. Up to six hours of coaching is permitted per participant. The program ended with an event in which participants pitch their growth plan for a panel of experts. In its first edition, the program attracted 22 participants from different creative sectors.

BLOCK 1	BLOCK 2	BLOCK 3	BLOCK 4	BLOCK 5		
Idea context	Situating your idea	Validating your idea	Financing your idea	Working your idea	Coaching	Pitching
Class + lab sessions	Class + lab sessions	Class + lab sessions	Class + lab sessions	Class + lab sessions		
Personal development track						

Table 3 Creative Jumpers Program Design

Below, a further analysis of the Creative Jumpers program design follows, utilizing the program design elements out of Figure 2.

1. Definition

An entrepreneurship program design starts with a perspective on entrepreneurship. The definition of entrepreneurship as a *process* – which is consistent with effectuation theory – holds that the emphasis is less on the innate or stable personality aspects of a '*potential*' entrepreneur, and more on the behaviour of the entrepreneur: how he/she utilizes his/her capabilities and commitment in its environment (Gartner, 1988; Haase & Lautenschläger, 2011; Honig, Davidsson, & Karlsson, 2005). Therefore, the Creative Jumpers program emphasizes the action-oriented and social aspects of enterprise development, in line with the effectuation theory (Korunka, Frank, Lueger, & Mugler, 2003; Sarasvathy, 2001, 2009; Szerb, 2003). In terms of focus, the program is designed for the level of '*young entrepreneurs*', meaning that all participants are strategic decision-making founders/managers in an existing creative enterprise (Figure 4). As every stage in the entrepreneurial development process requires different impetus, a choice for only including '*young entrepreneurs*' creates common ground for learning and cross-participant sharing (Brixy et al., 2012).

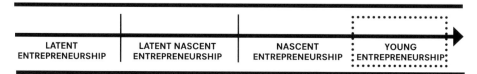

| LATENT ENTREPRENEURSHIP | LATENT NASCENT ENTREPRENEURSHIP | NASCENT ENTREPRENEURSHIP | YOUNG ENTREPRENEURSHIP |

Figure 4 Emphasis in the Creative Jumpers program (cf. Brixy et al., 2012)

2. Specific Objectives and Program Characteristics

As the participants are full-time entrepreneurs, Creative Jumpers is set-up as a part-time entrepreneurship program with five two-day blocks. Since the program aims to impact both knowledge and personal development, blocks are spread out over three months giving room for internalization of the knowledge and personal reflection.

The scope of the program is defined by the question of how the development of young entrepreneurs can be strengthened. In terms of Mwasalwiba (2010), Creative Jumpers is a program '*for*' entrepreneurship. In line with effectuation theory, social skills (know-how) are considered to be important know-how abilities, as entrepreneurship (in an action-oriented and social context) is considered to be a process of working

THEORY

together: building social capital, persuading, participating in (in)formal networks, managing stakeholders, and expanding the circle of trust are skills often mentioned in research (Honig et al., 2005; Szerb, 2003; Taylor, Jones, & Boles, 2004; Vecchio, 2003). Furthermore, theory finds that conviction (know-why) has a number of dimensions that can enhance entrepreneurship. First: self-awareness as an entrepreneur, as entrepreneurs have their own story or personal theory, based on a set of conclusions on vision, collaboration, market definition, and amount of control versus release (Rae & Carswell, 2000). Second: self-efficacy, which is the self-confidence the entrepreneur has in his/her ability to counter difficult situations and challenges (Thompson & Downing, 2007). Third: the motivation to set high goals and a willingness to learn and actively explore are regarded to be important (Haase & Lautenschläger, 2011; Rae & Carswell, 2000).

In the program, emphasis is thus placed on the social aspects of know-how, and some aspects of know-why. Specifically, the leadership development track places high emphasis on these important facets as social capital, political skills, dominant logics, personal thinking patterns and the development of the entrepreneurs' personal leadership claim and story. This aligns with the bird-in-hand principle, in which emphasis is placed on creating small effects with existing means such as the entrepreneurs' personality and preferences, knowledge and abilities, and networks. Besides the underlying personal development track, course content follows five themes, each of which consists of a class session with a goal to inspire and encourage critical and analytic thinking and a lab session in which participants work on internalizing the theory and translating it to their own entrepreneurial practice. By combining theory with practice, the content of the program is action-oriented and works on both the know-why of entrepreneurship as well as the know-how. Afterwards, external coaches can be consulted to further develop entrepreneurial skills, or to simply reflect on the participants' progress as entrepreneurs. The pitch that signals the end of the program is focused on defining and delivering the entrepreneurs' personal story. This story is the basis on which the entrepreneur should be able to convince others of the intricate value of the undertaking, explaining who they are, what they aspire, and why others should participate in this story (cf. the idea of self-selection in effectuation theory).

3. Teaching Methods

Literature states that: '*Entrepreneurial learning primarily consists of* 'learning by doing' *(Smilor, 1997), problem solving and discovery (Young & Sexton, 1997) and feedback and mistakes (Gibb, 1997)England. This paper begins with a review of the present concerns to link training with competitiveness in the United Kingdom and Europe. It notes that many of the issues raised in this respect are over 20 years old. It suggests therefore a new way to approach the problems, namely by considering the learning needs that will reduce the transaction costs of the small firm operating its stakeholder environment. After defining the concept of learning it makes the distinction between contextual learning (via experience and is, therefore, experiential in nature*' (Haase & Lautenschläger, 2011, p.152). In other words, the development process of an entrepreneur is best enhanced by using '*experiences*' of those entrepreneurs in their own context. Honig, Davidsson & Karlsson (2005) arrive at the same conclusion based on the effectuation logic. Young entrepreneurs learn best by adapting the development process to their experiences and progress incrementally. Experimentation and taking small steps are important. Scientific learning or systematic, causal learning have little or no effect. However, this does

THEORY

not indicate that programs should offer experiences 'at random' (Kirschner, Sweller, & Clark, 2006). To enhance entrepreneurial learning, the Creative Jumpers program brings together entrepreneurs from different creative disciplines. In such, the program aims to build a common ground in the fact that they are all young entrepreneurs with similar experience levels, in related disciplines, enabling a high level of transfer of knowledge and ideas facilitating learning from each other's experiences. Furthermore, participants are selected on their openness and willingness to share their experiences and ideas within the classroom settings, which is also emphasized in the rules charter of the program. Autobiographical sharing of experiences, coupled with directly applying new theories and concepts (learning by doing) in the lab sessions leads to an intimate setting in which reflection on entrepreneurship and your own role as entrepreneur is encouraged. By designing a program that provides a guided, challenging, yet safe environment in which experiences and feedback are combined with entrepreneurial development theory, a process is started that enhance the integration of new (personal) thinking patterns and theoretical insights into the entrepreneurs' identity, building a strong foundation of (self-awareness regarding) the entrepreneurs' personal means (bird-in-hand principle).

Conclusion and Discussion

This article serves a dual purpose. On the one hand, it attempts to further investigate the specific entrepreneurial behaviours of creative entrepreneurs. Based on our - albeit limited - research sample, it seems as predicted that the effectuation logic does have natural linkages with the manner in which creative entrepreneurs inherently behave. Even though research on this linkage is still rather underdeveloped, indications are present that these entrepreneurs have a specific set of behaviours that might not be best captured by standard models of entrepreneurship. Many interesting research questions still remain, for instance whether this preliminary finding holds for larger samples, whether there are specific instances in which these entrepreneurs deviate from this observed pattern of behaviour, etc.

The value of the undertaking of this current research lies in the second purpose of this article, which focused on the translation of these practical insights for educational purposes. A deeper knowledge of the way creative entrepreneurs operate within their very specific contexts, gives valuable insights that can be used in training and guidance purposes on the one hand, and in mutual understanding and the creation of common language on the other. This study is a first indication on the proximity between effectuation and creative entrepreneurship, based on a relatively small selection of cases. In further research, the research sample can be extended to further our understanding and to find a stronger base for conclusions. Furthermore, future research can focus not only on relation between effectuation and creative entrepreneurship, but can also investigate if all parts of the effectuation process as described by Sarasvathy (2001) are represented in equal importance, or whether there are specific differences in the case of creative entrepreneurs. Furthermore, the research can be extended by combining the results with intervening factors such as the life stage of the enterprises, creative sectors or clusters.

THEORY

References

Brixy, U., Sternberg, R., & Stüber, H. (2012). The Selectiveness of the Entrepreneurial Process. In: *Journal of Small Business Management*, *50*(1), 105–131. Retrieved from: http://doi.org/10.1111/j.1540-627X.2011.00346.x

Busenitz, L. W., Plummer, L. A., Klotz, A. C., Shahzad, A., & Rhoads, K. (2014, September). Entrepreneurship Research (1985-2009) and the Emergence of Opportunities. *Entrepreneurship: Theory & Practice*, pp. 981–1000.

Caves, R. E. (2002). *Creative industries: Contracts between art and commerce*. Cambridge: Harvard University Press.

Colbert, F. (2009). Beyond branding: Contemporary marketing challenges for arts organizations. *International In: Journal of Arts Management*, *12*(1), 14–21.

Delmar, F., & Shane, S. (2003). Does business planning facilitate the development of new ventures? *Strategic Management In: Journal*, *24*(12), 1165–1185. Retrieved from: http://doi.org/10.1002/smj.349

Delmestri, G., Montanari, F., & Usai, A. (2005). Reputation and Strength of Ties in Predicting Commercial Success and Artistic Merit of Independents in the Italian Feature Film Industry. *In: Journal of Management Studies*, *42*(5), 975–1002. Retrieved from: http://doi.org/10.1111/j.1467-6486.2005.00529.x

Drucker, P. F. (1998). The Discipline of Innovation. In: *Harvard Business Review*, *76*(6), 149–157.

Fisher, G. (2012). Effectuation, Causation, and Bricolage: A Behavioural Comparison of Emerging Theories in Entrepreneurship Research. In: *Entrepreneurship: Theory & Practice*, *36*(5), 1019–1051. Retrieved from: http://doi.org/10.1111/j.1540-6520.2012.00537.x

Fredrickson, J. W. (1983). Strategic Process Research: Questions and Recommendations. In: *Academy of Management Review*, *8*(4), 565–757. Retrieved from: http://doi.org/10.5465/AMR.1983.4284655

Gartner, W. B. (1988). Who is an entrepreneur? is the wrong question. In: *American In: Journal of Small Business*, *12*(4), 11–32.

Gibb, A. A. (1997). Small Firms' Training and Competitiveness. Building Upon the Small business as a Learning Organisation. In: *International Small Business In: Journal*, *15*(3), 13–29. Retrieved from: http://doi.org/10.1177/0266242697153001

Haase, H., & Lautenschläger, A. (2011). The 'Teachability Dilemma' of entrepreneurship. In: *International Entrepreneurship and Management In: Journal*, *7*(2), 145–162. Retrieved from: http://doi.org/10.1007/s11365-010-0150-3

Hargadon, A., & Sutton, R. I. (1997). Technology Brokering and Innovation in a Product Development Firm. *Administrative Science Quarterly*, *42*(4), 716–749.

Haunschild, A. (2003). Managing Employment Relationships in Flexible Labour Markets: The Case of German Repertory Theatres. In: *Human Relations*, *56*(8), 899–929. Retrieved from: http://doi.org/10.1177/00187267030568001

Hearn, G., Roodhouse, S., & Blakey, J. (2007). From value chain to value creating ecology. In: *International In: Journal of Cultural Policy*, *13*(4), 419–436.

About the Authors

Walter van Andel is a PhD researcher on entrepreneurship and creativity at Antwerp Management School and the University of Antwerp, Belgium. His research focusses on business models, innovation and entrepreneurial growth at small and medium-sized creative enterprises. In 2012 he co-authored the book 'Creative Jumpers' in which business models for fast-growing companies in creative industries are examined. Before joining Antwerp Management School, Walter worked as a researcher and consultant in the Netherlands, Mexico and the United States.
—
Walter.vanAndel@ams.ac.be

Prof Dr Annick Schramme is full professor and academic coordinator of the master in Cultural Management at the University of Antwerp (Faculty of Applied Economics). She is also Academic Director of the Competence Centre Creative Industries and the master class Creative Jumpers at the Antwerp Management School. Over the last years she published about creative industries, fashion management, cultural entrepreneurship, arts policy, international cultural policy and heritage management. Besides, she is member of several boards of cultural organizations and governmental advisory committees in Flanders and the Netherlands. Since 2013 she is a member of the Arts Council in the Netherlands and that year she became also the president of ENCATC, the European Network on Cultural Management and Policy Education.

—

*annick.schramme
@uantwerpen.be*

Honig, B., Davidsson, P., & Karlsson, T. (2005). Learning strategies of nascent entrepreneurs. In R. Sanchez & A. Heene, *A Focused Issue on Managing Knowledge Assets and Organizational Learning* (Vol. 2). Amsterdam: Elsevier.

Hsieh, H.-F., & Shannon, S. E. (2005). Three Approaches to Qualitative Content Analysis. In: *Qualitative Health Research*, *15*(9), 1277–1288. Retrieved from: http://doi.org/10.1177/1049732305276687

Jeffcutt, P., & Pratt, A. C. (2002). Managing creativity in the cultural industries. *Creativity & Innovation Management*, pp. 225–233.

Katz, J., & Gartner, W. B. (1988). Properties of Emerging Organizations. *Academy of Management Review*, *13*(3), 429–441. Retrieved from: http://doi.org/10.5465/AMR.1988.4306967

Kirschner, P. A., Sweller, J., & Clark, R. E. (2006). Why Minimal Guidance During Instruction Does Not Work: An Analysis of the Failure of Constructivist, Discovery, Problem-Based, Experiential, and Inquiry-Based Teaching. *Educational Psychologist*, *41*(2), 75–86. Retrieved from: http://doi.org/10.1207/s15326985ep4102_1

Korunka, C., Frank, H., Lueger, M., & Mugler, J. (2003). The Entrepreneurial Personality in the Context of Resources, Environment, and the Startup Process—A Configurational Approach. *Entrepreneurship: Theory & Practice*, *28*(1), 23–42. Retrieved from: http://doi.org/10.1111/1540 8520.00030

Lampel, J., Lant, T., & Shamsie, J. (2000). Balancing act: Learning from organizing practices in cultural industries. *Organization Science*, *11*(3), 263–269. Retrieved from: http://doi.org/10.1287/orsc.11.3.263.12503

Mwasalwiba, E. S. (2010). Entrepreneurship education: a review of its objectives, teaching methods, and impact indicators. *Education + Training*, *52*(1), 20–47. Retrieved from: http://doi.org/10.1108/00400911011017663

Ohlsson-Corboz, A.-V. (2013). Effectual entrepreneurship and the social enterprise: an examination of the fit between the principles of effectuation and the sphere of the social enterprise as a form of new venture. RMIT University.

Parker, S. C. (2009). *The Economics of Entrepreneurship*. Cambridge, UK; New York: Cambridge University Press.

Perry, J. T., Chandler, G. N., & Markova, G. (2012). Entrepreneurial Effectuation: A Review and Suggestions for Future Research. *Entrepreneurship: Theory & Practice*, *36*(4), 837–861. Retrieved from: http://doi.org/10.1111/j.1540-6520.2010.00435.x

Rae, D., & Carswell, M. (2000). Using a life-story approach in researching entrepreneurial learning: the development of a conceptual model and its implications in the design of learning experiences. *Education + Training*, *42*(4/5), 220–228. Retrieved from: http://doi.org/10.1108/00400910010373660

Read, S., Song, M., & Smit, W. (2009). A meta-analytic review of effectuation and venture performance. *In: Journal of Business Venturing*, *24*(6), 573–587. Retrieved from: http://doi.org/10.1016/j.jbusvent.2008.02.005

Sarasvathy, S. D. (2001). Causation and Effectuation: Toward a Theoretical Shift from Economic Inevitability to Entrepreneurial Contingency. *Academy of Management Review*, *26*(2), 243–263. Retrieved from: http://doi.org/10.2307/259121

THEORY

Sarasvathy, S. D. (2009). *Effectuation: elements of entrepreneurial expertise*. Cheltenham: Edward Elgar.

Shah, S. K., & Tripsas, M. (2007). The accidental entrepreneur: the emergent and collective process of user entrepreneurship. *Strategic Entrepreneurship In: Journal, 1*(1-2), 123–140. Retrieved from: http://doi.org/10.1002/sej.15

Shane, S., & Venkataraman, S. (2000). The Promise of Entrepreneurship as a Field of Research. *Academy of Management Review, 25*(1), 217–226. Retrieved from: http://doi.org/10.5465/AMR.2000.2791611

Skilton, P. F. (2008). Similarity, familiarity and access to elite work in Hollywood: Employer and employee characteristics in breakthrough employment. *Human Relations, 61*(12), 1743–1773. Retrieved from: http://doi.org/10.1177/0018726708098084

Smilor, R. W. (1997). Entrepreneurship: Reflections on a subversive activity. *In: Journal of Business Venturing, 12*(5), 341–346. Retrieved from: http://doi.org/10.1016/S0883-9026(97)00008-6

Stokes, D., Wilson, N., & Mador, M. (2010). *Entrepreneurship*. Australia ; United States: Cengage Learning.

Szerb, L. (2003). The Changing Role of Entrepreneur and Entrepreneurship in Network Organisations. In I. Lengyel (Ed.), *Knowledge Transfer, Small and Medium-Sized Enterprises, and Regional Development in Hungary* (pp. 81–95). Szeged: JATEPress.

Taylor, D. W., Jones, O., & Boles, K. (2004). Building social capital through action learning: an insight into the entrepreneur. *Education + Training, 46*(5), 226–235. Retrieved from: http://doi.org/10.1108/00400910410549805

Thompson, J., & Downing, R. (2007). The entrepreneur enabler: identifying and supporting those with potential. *In: Journal of Small Business and Enterprise Development, 14*(3), 528–544. Retrieved from: http://doi.org/10.1108/14626000710773592

Uzzi, B. (1997). Social Structure and Competition in Interfirm Networks: The Paradox of Embeddedness. *Administrative Science Quarterly, 42*(1), 35–67. Retrieved from: http://doi.org/10.2307/2393808

Vecchio, R. P. (2003). Entrepreneurship and leadership: common trends and common threads. *Human Resource Management Review, 13*(2), 303.

Warren, L., & Fuller, T. (2009). Methodological issues arising from research into the emergence of enterprise in the creative industries. Presented at the British Academy of Management Conference, Brighton.

Young, J. E., & Sexton, D. L. (1997). Entrepreneurial learning: A conceptual framework. *In: Journal of Enterprising Culture, 05*(03), 223–248. Retrieved from: http://doi.org/10.1142/S0218495897000144

THEORY

Aparna Katre

ENTREPRENEURSHIP EDUCATION FOR SOCIAL INNOVATION
AN APPROACH BASED IN DESIGN THINKING AND THE HUMANITIES

Abstract

Entrepreneurship education at the undergraduate level is most often situated in business schools. Their pedagogy involves case methodology and a capstone course in entrepreneurship towards the end of the curriculum. There is little emphasis on the development of skills to deal with the wicked nature of societal problems. This article explores how entrepreneurship education, with rigorous course work in humanities disciplines and which embeds design thinking, prepares individuals for social innovation.

We contend that such education develops the hard business skills and the soft skills – to live with uncertainty, ambiguity, communicate effectively across cultural contexts, create opportunities, empathize, design the business, and leverage failures – necessary to create sustained social, cultural and environmental value. We begin by outlining the characteristics of social innovation and the importance of entrepreneurship to promote it, followed by discussion of a model which addresses the lacunae of current entrepreneurship education with regards to social innovation.

Introduction

While the economic development of the past century has led to growth, it has also resulted in issues of social exclusion, inequity, and environmental degradation. These issues cannot be effectively addressed by simply using outdated models of the past: today's problems are complex, highly interconnected, and characterized by ambiguity, and it is not always possible to conclusively formulate the problem and the solution independent of each other. Not only does innovating solutions involve the birth of ideas, their development and, finally, their utilization through products and services (Westley, 2008), but also generating an agreement between multiple agencies on both the issues and the solutions (Hagoort, Thomassen, & Kooyman, 2012).

Design Thinking, which involves an active search for a fit between problems and possible solutions (Buchanan & Margolin, 1995; Cross, 1995; Margolin, 1995), offers an approach to innovating for social change. The search is intended to gain insights, broaden our understanding, and continually refine understanding of the problems while generating insights and remaining alert for emergent solution ideas. Development of these ideas and their provision as products and services requires innovation and risk-taking, i.e. entrepreneurial skills. Educating for this form of innovation requires new pedagogies: in contrast to the past half century, the new generation of entrepreneurship education needs to include humanization (Ipsos Public Affairs, 2014) to make individuals comfortable with ambiguity, uncertainty, and the complexities associated with social innovation.

THEORY

This article presents one such model, where entrepreneurship education grounded in the humanities and which employs Design Thinking. On the one hand, the course work in humanities leads to the development of social, intercultural, and conceptual competencies necessary to be comfortable with the complexities surrounding social innovation; on the other hand entrepreneurship courses directed at solving societal problems enable students to practice innovation and risk-taking.

How is Social Innovation Characterized?

The past century's innovations in the fields of science, technology, and business have solved several of humanity's problems. However, these innovations have also resulted in newer and more complex problems that we now face as a global society (Ehrenfeld, 2009). The crises we face today are much more nuanced, larger in scale and scope, and inextricably linked. Our collective challenge in the 21st century is to create a safe and just space for humanity to thrive. It requires that we address grand challenges such as ending extreme poverty and hunger, achieving universal primary education, and promoting gender equality in inclusive ways while achieving environmental sustainability. Newer approaches (i.e., different from the ones which created these problems) are necessary to address these crises. Rodin, (2013) states that approaches in which the goal is to *make our world more resilient than it is vulnerable, to do what we can to reduce the shocks and disruptions; and most important, to ensure that all people, particularly the poor, can withstand that which we cannot prevent'* are necessary.

Such innovations, also called social innovations, are radical and novel: they challenge the basic routines, resources, and authority flows and beliefs of the social system (Dees & Elias, 1998; Guclu, Dees, & Anderson, 2002; Westley, 2008). Social innovation is different from most other forms of innovation, since social system changes are slow to develop and the results are often only seen in the long-term. The process of social innovation requires intense and extended cross-sector collaboration (Alvord, Brown, & Letts, 2004; Mair & Schoen, 2007; Wei-Skillern, Austin, Leonard, & Stevenson, 2007), and it needs to address the interdependencies of social and planetary boundaries for sustenance (Raworth, 2012).

Social innovation is similar to dealing with wicked problems where innovators have to engage in an iterative process of idea generation until a solution agreeable to all collaborators is developed (Brown & Wyatt, 2010; Sarasvathy & Simon, 2000; York, Sarasvathy, & Larson, 2009). Social innovators need to be comfortable with ambiguity and uncertainty, must have the skills of negotiation and persuasion, and stay focused on the long term sustained change. This requires knowledge of and capabilities drawn from the discipline of Design Thinking (Hagoort et al., 2012) and humanistic approaches.

Entrepreneurship for Social Innovation

Entrepreneurship, defined as bringing unique ideas to fruition by inspiring others' imagination, is a key resource for social innovation. It is about generating and developing creative solutions to everyday problems and creating value for others. Social innovators' motivations originate from the dissatisfaction with a societal situation (Guclu et al., 2002) and they act entrepreneurially to change the status quo. Entrepreneurs do not stop at conceptualizing and designing creative solutions to problems: instead, they take risks throughout the entire lifecycle of creating and developing an enterprise.

THEORY

Their task is to bring their creative ideas to market in the form of products and services, to generate profits, and to scale the enterprise appropriately. Frequently market entry does not return the desired profits, or the products and services do not have the desired uptake, causing financial and reputational losses for the entrepreneur. Consider a typical social innovation lifecycle such as that illustrated in Figure 1. It requires taking risks, often much more complex because it involves agreement amongst diverse and multiple stakeholders (Brush, Greene, Hart, & Haller, 2001). In addition, due to the fact that the non-profit community tends to be less forgiving of failures with market economics, social entrepreneurs as innovators carry a heightened reputational risk, should the endeavour fail.

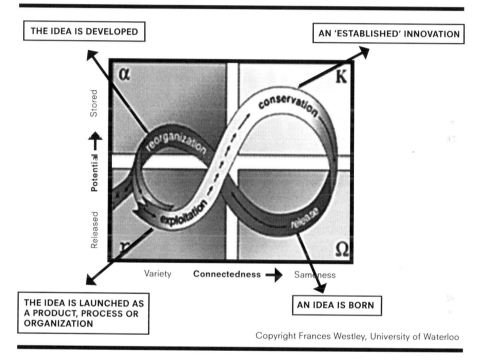

THE IDEA IS DEVELOPED

AN 'ESTABLISHED' INNOVATION

THE IDEA IS LAUNCHED AS A PRODUCT, PROCESS OR ORGANIZATION

AN IDEA IS BORN

Copyright Frances Westley, University of Waterloo

Figure 1 Social Innovation Life-cycle (Westley, 2008)

Social innovation is a collaborative process from the onset: over and above the development of products and services, it requires working together with an ecosystem of actors to produce and maintain alignment of goals (Wei-Skillern et al., 2007). Entrepreneurial approaches employing market mechanisms to generate income must not only compete in the marketplace, they must also align and collaborate with agencies having the common goal of social change. This requires social innovators to swiftly navigate the ambidexterity (Dees & Elias, 1998; Katre, Salipante, Bird, & Perelli, 2012): between competing and collaborating; attending to those stakeholders focused on business performance and also those who prioritize improving the social situation; and have decision processes which are able to balance short-term profit-generation goals with the goal of producing social value, which often happens over the long term.

In summary, educating entrepreneurship for social innovation needs to adopt intensive humanistic approaches to effectively work within an ecosystem of stakeholders, including the beneficiaries of social change. There is an increasing recognition of the inadequacies of traditional entrepreneurship educational programs with pedagogy based in prediction logic only (Neck & Greene, 2011). Several new educational programs have been launched in the past decade (while additional new programs continue to arise), some of which are focused on social innovation. However, majority of these programs are situated in business schools with a minimal emphasis on developing those specific skills necessary for social innovation. The next section outlines a model for entrepreneurship education offered through the B.A. degree in Cultural Entrepreneurship at the University of Minnesota, Duluth. The primary purpose of their entrepreneurship education is social, cultural, or environmental value creation, and the learning equips students with the skills most needed for social innovation.

A Model for Entrepreneurship Education for Social Innovation

There are several ways in which the team innovating for social change can ensure a comprehensive base of skills. Often successful entrepreneurial endeavours are headed by a team of cofounders (Barringer, Jones, & Neubaum, 2005). One may argue that a situation in which the team collectively possesses the totality of skills, with each cofounder specializing in a specific knowledge base, is sufficient for the entrepreneurial endeavour. This model is plausible but requires social innovators to be cognizant of the needs, proactively look for complementary skills in the making of the leadership team, and be able to deploy the right skills for the right job. However, it may be challenging for, say, a technocrat to comprehend the skills of an anthropologist and the complementary role such individuals can play in the entrepreneurial process for social innovation, let alone have the right people in the network to find one. The model outlined in this article systematically develops awareness of, and the basic capabilities pertaining to, the various skills through an integrated experiential learning program. Figure 2 shows the model underlying cultural entrepreneurship education where learning is centred in social, cultural, or environmental problems in the local community (or even a grand challenge) with which students can empathize. At the core of the program is the study of humanities and developing conceptual competencies augmented by entrepreneurship courses. Pedagogically this model assumes that Design Thinking skills are best developed contextually rather than being offered via standalone courses. As a result Design Thinking is integrated into both humanities as well entrepreneurship courses.

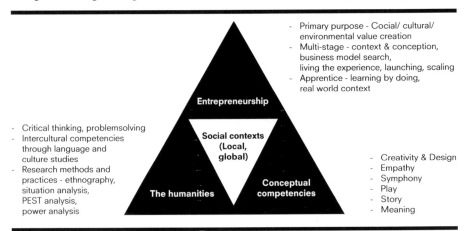

Figure 2 Foundations of the BA Degree in Cultural Entrepreneurship

THEORY

The most significant learning outcome of the program is entrepreneurship for social, cultural, or environmental innovation as a '*method*,' (Neck & Greene, 2011) wherein the measures of success include both kinds of innovation attempts – those which take off successfully and those which turn out not to be viable. Figure 3 outlines typical undergraduate coursework along two main streams: Humanities-related and Entrepreneurship- and Business Management-related. Next, a separate discussion on each component of the model can be presented, starting with Design Thinking, since it forms the fabric which holds both components of the model together.

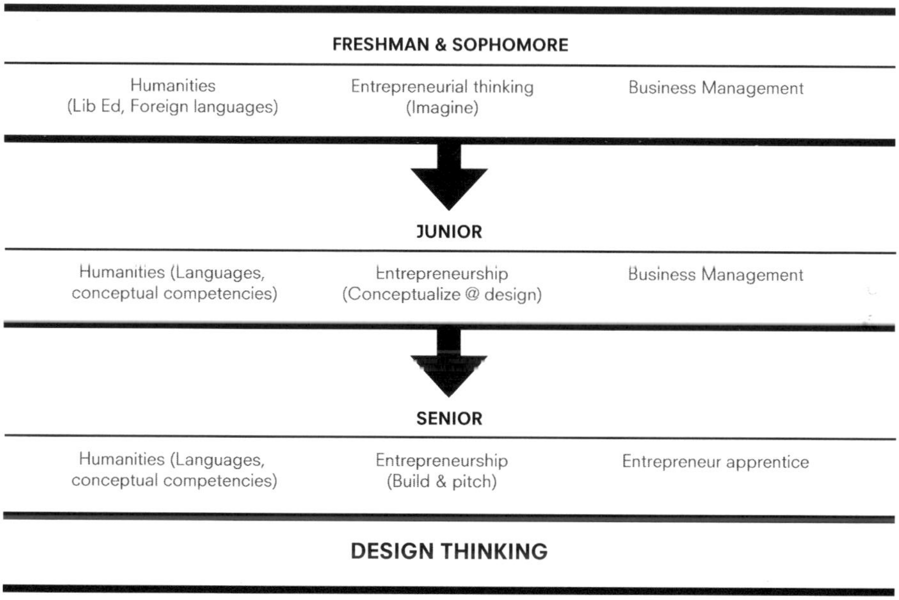

FRESHMAN & SOPHOMORE		
Humanities (Lib Ed, Foreign languages)	Entrepreneurial thinking (Imagine)	Business Management

JUNIOR		
Humanities (Languages, conceptual competencies)	Entrepreneurship (Conceptualize @ design)	Business Management

SENIOR		
Humanities (Languages, conceptual competencies)	Entrepreneurship (Build & pitch)	Entrepreneur apprentice

DESIGN THINKING

THEORY

Figure 3 Typical coursework for the Cultural Entrepreneurship degree

Design Thinking for Social Innovation

Design has been historically thought of as a purposeful behaviour focused on giving form to concepts, giving order to physical things, or the making of objects or intangibles (Alexander, 1973). This discipline of design deals with objects. Contrarily, (Simon, 1996) others view design as a rational set of procedures intended to solve ill-structured problems and accommodate objects which do not figure in this conception. (Dorst & Cross, 2001) (Dorst, 2011), suggest that design is the process of co-evolution of the problem and solution spaces using a repertoire of both creative and analytical practices (Dorst, 2011; Hagoort et al., 2012). The context for social innovation is both a problem (dissatisfaction with a particular societal situation) and a vision of the desired state. The features of both current and future states are subjective interpretations wherein individuals' goals (and the process to achieve the end state) can differ significantly from one individual to the other. The problem-solving process requires accommodating shifts in the understanding of the problem and the solution. Effective solution design requires individuals with different levels of expertise to integrate knowledge from a wide range of domains, and to transcend extreme perspectives and swiftly navigate the paradoxes (Dorst, 2006), in this case of business and social good.

Social Concerns

Consider the case of poverty and the lack of sustainable livelihood for residents in a village which has a rich heritage of ethnic crafts. Craft designers, entrepreneurs, local NGOs, and government and village leaders may all be unhappy with the current situation and interested in developing sources of sustainable income for villagers. However, each may have different perspectives on topics such as the causes of the current situation, how poverty is affecting the lives of the villagers, what the villagers are doing about it, whether change will be adopted by the villagers, and so on. They may also have different views about income generation such as employment, providing subsidies, promoting self-employment, entrepreneurship, and cooperative entrepreneurship. The actors' knowledge and prior experience play a crucial role in informing various dimensions of the current situation, as well as framing the problem and the solution. Similarly, actors from different domains may view the problem differently. For example, engineers may look at it as lack of access to and/or training in modern technology; business people may think of market access as the central issue; and policy makers may think of the lack of sound minimum wage policies as a prime issue.

A process, whereby concerned actors engage in collaborative and cooperative analysis of the situation; which allows actors to get close to the situation, establish a rich understanding of it, gain first-hand experience of the problem, and enable the development and adoption of multiple 'frames' (Dorst, 2006; Dorst, 2011) can lead to articulating a sustainable response. These methods are central to Design Thinking as defined by (Dorst & Cross, 2001), and offer practical approaches necessary for social innovation.

In the various humanities related courses (Figures 2), instruction is focused on the development of skills such as creativity, thoughtful analysis, ingenuity, empathy, collaboration, systems thinking, experimentation, problem-solving and sensitivity to cross-cultural contexts. The courses challenge students to move outside of their existing comfort zones and to recognize the value of that exploration. It helps students understand the importance of diverse ideas, and to convey that understanding to others. Courses such as Cultural Anthropology, American Indian Families and Society, the Geography of Religion, Intercultural Communications, and Women, Race and Class emphasize the development of listening skills, empathy, whole-systems thinking, and collaboration. The instruction creates a lasting, permanent, and integrated connection between the student, their own skills, and the social contexts. As an example the course titled 'creative problem-solving' involves a series of 'different', where students are challenged to identify and change their own cultural, habitual, and normal patterns of behaviour. Beginning with a prompt (e.g. 'Eat something different'), learners recognize their limits and overcome them. They are encouraged to understand that creativity is based on societal norms, and that, by its nature, it will differ from and be discouraged by society. In this course, the persistence of the creative person is developed through practice. Additional Design Thinking practices are discussed in the next two sections.

Humanities Education for Social Innovation

Humanities, the branch of learning concerned with human culture, involves disciplines such as languages, literature, archaeology, cultural studies, history, geography, psychology, sociology, politics, and religious studies. Nussbaum (2012) associates the following attributes with the study of humanities and the arts: the ability to think critically, transcend local loyalties, approach world problems as a *citizen of the world*, and imagine sympathetically the predicament of another person. Humanities education develops skills in individuals which enable them to engage with the world, contextualize information, and communicate effectively across cultures.

To bring about alignment between the goals and actions of multiple actors, social innovators need to collaborate, negotiate competing interests, and work through high-levels of ambiguity. It requires that social innovators understand human relationships, develop an appreciation of diverse points of view, have knowledge of languages and cultures to effectively communicate across these cultures, and know the relevance of contexts while understanding the problem domain and developing solution ideas. These skills are acquired through the study of psychology, anthropology, languages, and literature (Nussbaum, 2012; Small, 2013).

Social innovation requires resilience when those involved need to look at broader interconnections between the components of a whole, and at the impact a solution might have on each component. It also requires the actors to engage in a balanced top-down and bottom-up approach to craft innovative solutions (Westley, 2008). Liberal education is the foundation for these skills. Further analytical tools from applied anthropology, sociology, and politics – such as situational analysis, PEST (political, economic, social, and technological) analysis, social network analysis, and power analysis, among others – are useful in collaborative solution development for complex social issues (Ipsos Public Affairs, 2014). Social innovation requires empathizing with the beneficiaries as well as other agencies in order to generate rich contexts in which to situate the problem. In addition, it requires a playful environment to generate unfathomable and creative responses to the social issue. Such conceptual competencies as empathy, storytelling, play, design, meaning, and symphony (Pink, 2005) are best developed through arts and humanities education.

In the model presented (Figure 3), students study a wide variety of Liberal Education (LE) courses during their Freshman and Sophomore years, which sets these students up to be lifelong learners and globally engaged citizens. It provides the foundation for critical thinking, problem-solving, deductive reasoning, creativity, and written and oral communications. The LE course work is followed by 10 courses across various conceptual competencies and from across humanities disciplines for deeper understanding and application of the foundational skills. In addition, the study of two foreign languages (one up to the advanced level and the other to the beginner level) helps develop language competencies as well as the skills to engage in cross-cultural contexts.

Entrepreneurship Education for Social Innovation

Entrepreneurship education has to teach *hard skills* (those of strategy, finance, human resources, marketing, and operations, among others), as well as *soft skills* (to live with uncertainty, identify or create opportunities, make decisions, empathize, design the business, and leverage failures). Teaching entrepreneurship is about teaching the individual to pursue a life-path, not just a career (Neck & Greene, 2011). Most entrepreneurship education is based on one or a combination of three different approaches.

1. The first advocates that entrepreneurs have specific traits, the presence or absence of which can be diagnosed, but the traits themselves are not teachable. In this approach students see entrepreneurship as a box in which they do or do not fit.
2. The second is a causal process-oriented approach which emphasizes planning and prediction, and which teaches students opportunity evaluation, feasibility analysis, and business planning, thus laying the foundation for linear thinking and emphasizing secondary research.
3. The third is an approach based in cognition, and which teaches how to think entrepreneurially. This pedagogy teaches entrepreneurial decision-making using simulations, case studies, narratives, and exercises directed toward the search for opportunities.

More recently, entrepreneurship has been seen as a *'method'*, consisting of a body of skills and techniques to help students understand, develop, and practice, linking their personal motivations with desired outcomes or their own measures of success. Pedagogically, it means teaching a way to think and act simultaneously by iterating between the two sets: (1) to understand, know, and tell, and (2) use, apply, and act.

This pedagogy is also suited in the context of social innovation, but with a subtle twist: the desired outcomes or measures of success are not those of the individual entrepreneur but, rather, of all key stakeholders. As suggested by (Neck & Greene, 2011), while learning a method it is necessary that novices gain early exposure to venture creation so as to empathize with the entrepreneur.

Internalizing soft skills such as empathy, confidence, and overcoming the fear of failure requires repetition in various contexts. A capstone course at the end is inadequate. Entrepreneurial learning outcomes are achieved when courses are designed to practice these skills along various stages of venture creation – those of pre-conception, conception, design, and building. Such course design provides students with opportunities to experience uncertainties, navigate unknown territories, and learn to live with *'ups and downs'* at each stage as well as to understand the interconnectedness of these stages and develop unique styles to deal with situations. A critical component of the pedagogy is reflective practice embedded in day-to-day instruction.

The model (Figure 3) is designed such that a typical student develops entrepreneurial thinking and action along two parallel tracks:

1. First, students learn the basics of operating a business through a Business Administration Certificate consisting of courses in marketing, finance, human resource management, accounting, and operations, among others. Students take these courses during their Sophomore and Junior years.
2. Second track is a sequence of courses to experience the stages of entrepreneurship starting from Freshman through Senior years.

Pre-conception stage is about developing the ability to identify cultural, social, or environmental issues; navigating various dimensions of these issues; and applying Design Thinking for ideation. In the conception course, students learn the importance of empathizing with customers and beneficiaries, and learn that their search for solution involves pivoting several times as new insights are generated, and until

THEORY

a fit between a problem and its solution is found. Using ethnographic, semi-structured interviews and empathy-map, they generate insights to inform the problem and solution domains. The course for design stage teaches students skills related to experimentation, rapid and frugal prototyping, failing fast and often (but in small scope), and, more importantly, the skill to learn from the failures. During their Senior year, students are encouraged to pursue year-long entrepreneurial apprenticeships with non-profit, businesses, or public-sector enterprises. By integrating various Design Thinking practices, these courses allow students to recognize and develop their own entrepreneurial capabilities for social innovation.

Conclusions

This article set out to explore various dimensions of social innovation and the role of entrepreneurship in promoting it. Recognizing that educating for this kind of entrepreneurship is different, a model which employs Design Thinking and is based in the humanities is presented. The model is one in which students learn Entrepreneurship for Social Innovation as a *method* (not as a linear process), and in which the measures of success consist of entrepreneurial attempts that fail, not just those which appear to take off. While this model has strong theoretical foundations, it is expected that longitudinal control studies measuring the development of core skills over time will validate the contribution of humanities coursework and Design Thinking. Such studies will also help advance theories of entrepreneurship education. Findings from comparative studies which track the creation and success of entrepreneurial ventures for Social Innovation, started by alumni of the program, and those from a control group can make direct pedagogical contributions.

While successful entrepreneurial ventures resulting from the program and/or created by the alumni directly contribute to solving societal issues, failed attempts should also be viewed as contribution: they teach as much, if not more, for subsequent social innovation attempts. Employers of the entrepreneur apprentice benefit from the program as these skills are brought to bear to solve their organizational issues. Entrepreneurship in which the pedagogy is that of a method, whether for social innovation or other purposes, aids the workforce readiness of the students. Having developed hard and soft skills through thinking and acting, students are suited for jobs related to business development as well as new product or service launches, and for intraprenuerial initiatives within private, non-profit, and public sector institutions. Specific cross-cultural, stakeholder management, collaboration, and negotiation skills developed during the practice of Social Innovation make the students ready for jobs in international non-profit organizations and in the corporate social responsibility domains of private enterprises.

THEORY

About the Author

Dr Aparna Katre is the Director and Assistant Professor of Cultural Entrepreneurship for the newly started B.A. in Cultural Entrepreneurship degree program at UMD. Her research interests include start-up stages of social, cultural and environmental mission-based

References

Alexander, C. (1973). *Notes on the synthesis of form* Harvard University Press Cambridge, MA, USA.

Alvord, S. H., Brown, L. D., & Letts, C. W. (2004). Social entrepreneurship and societal transformation. In: *The Journal of Applied Behavioral Science, 40*(3), 260-282.

Barringer, B. R., Jones, F. F., & Neubaum, D. O. (2005). A quantitative content analysis of the characteristics of rapid-growth firms and their founders. In: *Journal of Business Venturing, 20*(5), 663-687.

Brown, T., & Wyatt, J. (2010). *Design thinking for social innovation.* Unpublished manuscript. Retrieved 01/15/2015, Retrieved from: https://open-knowledge.worldbank.org/handle/10986/6068

Brush, C. G., Greene, P. G., Hart, M. M., & Haller, H. S. (2001). From initial idea to unique advantage: The entrepreneurial challenge of constructing a resource base. In: *Academy of Management Executive, 15*(1), 64-78.

Buchanan, R., & Margolin, V. (1995). *Discovering design: Explorations in design studies* University of Chicago Press. Chicago: IL

Cross, N. (1995). *Discovering design ability* University of Chicago Press. Chicago: IL

Dees, J. G., & Elias, J. (1998). The challenges of combining social and commercial enterprise. In: *Business Ethics Quarterly, 8*(1), 165-178.

Dorst, K. (2006). Design problems and design paradoxes. In: *Design Issues, 22*(3), 4-17.

Dorst, K. (2011). The core of 'design thinking' and its application. In: *Design Studies, 32*(6), 521-532.

Dorst, K., & Cross, N. (2001). Creativity in the design process: Co-evolution of problem–solution. In: *Design Studies, 22*(5), 425-437.

Ehrenfeld, J. R. (2009). Sustainability by design: A subversive strategy for transforming our consumer culture. Yale University Press. New York: NY

Guclu, A., Dees, G., & Anderson, B. (2002). *The process of social entrepreneurship: Creating opportunities worthy of serious pursuit.* Center for the advancement of social entrepreneurship, 1-15.

Hagoort, G., Thomassen, A., & Kooyman, R. (Ed) (2012). Pioneering minds worldwide: On the entrepreneurial principles of the cultural and creative industries: Actual insights into cultural and creative entrepreneurship research Eburon Uitgeverij BV.

Ipsos Public Affairs. (2014). *Mobilising the humanities: The development perspective.* British Council. Retrieved from: http://www.britishcouncil.org/sites/britishcouncil.uk2/files/humanities_final_report.pdf

Katre, A., Salipante, P., Bird, B., & Perelli, S. (2012). Balancing competition and collaboration: How early stage social ventures succeed. In J. R. Kickul (Ed.), In: *Patterns in social entrepreneurship research* (pp. 323-383) Edward Elgar Publishing.

Mair, J., & Schoen, O. (2007). Successful social entrepreneurial business models in the context of developing economies: An explorative study. In: *International Journal of Emerging Markets, 2*(1), 54-68.

Margolin, V. (1995). The product milieu and social action.in *Discovering design: Explorations in design studies* University of Chicago Press. Chicago: IL, *p.122*

Neck, H. M., & Greene, P. G. (2011). Entrepreneurship education: Known worlds and new frontiers. In: *Journal of Small Business Management, 49*(1), 55-70.

entrepreneurship with a focus on entrepreneurial strategies and behaviours. She is a Fellow of The Mandel Centre for Non-profit Organization Studies. Before Aparna has worked extensively with Global Information Technology consulting firms, has provided leadership in the areas of strategy, organizational change management, business process improvement, and program management. She has served in the roles of Chief Innovation Officer, Chief Process Officer and held P&L responsibility. She has also led a technology based non-profit organization and was a small business owner prior to taking the current position at the University.
—
aukatre@d.umn.edu

THEORY

Nussbaum, M. C. (2012). *Not for profit: Why democracy needs the humanities* Princeton University Press.

Pink, D. H. (2005). *A whole new mind: Moving from the information age to the conceptual age.* Riverhead Books, Penguin, New York:NY

Raworth, K. (2012). A safe and just space for humanity. *Can we Live within the Doughnut,* Regenerative Organizations online. Retrieved from: http://www.regenerativeorganizations.com/

Rodin, J. (2013). Innovation for the next 100 years, 01/15/2015. Retrieved from: http://www.ssireview.org/articles/entry/innovation_for_the_next_100_years

Sarasvathy, S., & Simon, H. A. (2000). Effectuation, near-decomposability, and the creation and growth of entrepreneurial firms. Article presented at the *First Annual Research Policy Technology Entrepreneurship Conference,*

Simon, H. (1996). *The sciences of the artificial* (3rd ed. ed.). Cambridge: MA: The MIT Press.

Small, H. (2013). *The value of the humanities.* Oxford University Press.

Wei-Skillern, J., Austin, J., Leonard, H., & Stevenson, H. (2007). *Entrepreneurship in the social sector.* Thousand Oaks, CA: Sage Publications.

Westley, F. (2008). *The social innovation dynamic.* Frances Westley, SiG@ Waterloo.

York, J. G., Sarasvathy, S. D., & Larson, A. (2009). The thread of inchoate demand in social entrepreneurship. In: *Values and Opportunities in Social Entrepreneurship,* 141.

THEORY

Margaret Jane Wyszomirski
Shoshanah Goldberg-Miller

ADAPTING THE PROMETHEAN FIRE OF BUSINESS FOR ARTS AND CULTURAL ENTREPRENEURSHIP

THEORY

Abstract

Arts and cultural management programs have typically focused on the management of organizations. Arts and cultural entrepreneurship adds a new dimension. It needs an emphasis on the freelance, self-employed, and micro-level landscape that has not heretofore been a priority. The focus on arts and cultural organization management has occurred across fields as well as across the local, state, and national terrain. However, the local level is an especially important context for arts and cultural entrepreneurs. We have become increasingly aware of the size and significance of this aspect of the creative economy. In arts and culture enterprises, some follow a growth path and grow from a micro-enterprise. Into an emerging organization, and eventually become an established arts or cultural organization. Others aim to stay small and either work in collective or cooperative small groups while defining success as the ability to balance artistic creativity with economic sustainability.

Management reform proponents tend to assert that arts and culture needs to be more business-like, and cultural entrepreneurship can be regarded as a recent example of this belief. From this viewpoint, being more business-like is the Promethean Fire - the utility that will solve all problems. But the embers of business-like practice cannot be fanned into arts and cultural entrepreneurship flames, unless they are adapted, and that adaptation needs to be grounded in different value assumptions and trade-offs between the cultural and economic benefits that guide the creative economy. The risk and uncertainty inherent in creative enterprise means that we need to teach adaptability. Rather than the business approach of best practice, we need to teach our students how to aspire to 'smart practice', which includes flexibility, opportunity spotting. Innovation, and a kind of *creative cost-benefit analysis*.

Introduction

Most artists don't think of themselves as entrepreneurs. Yet many of the skills that they excel at in creating their artwork are similar to the skills that business entrepreneurs use. Most business entrepreneurship programs focus on how to create new ventures and have an exit plan. Artists often create new artworks without a market or business plan, do not culminate with an exit strategy, and look to build a sustainability strategy for their new product. Arts entrepreneurship educational programs tend to focus on the specific management skills and tactics needed in the creative industries. Such programs are less focused on the fact that arts entrepreneurs tend to employ a greater variety of strategies than the typical business program. For example, arts and cultural entre-preneurs not only focus on new venture creation but also frequently engage in social and cultural heritage entrepreneurship. Social entrepreneurship uses the arts as a key resource to achieve social goals. Cultural entrepreneurship uses heritage and cultural diversity as key assets (Aageson, 2008; Kellogg, 2010). Furthermore, arts entrepreneurs commonly engage in creative recombination of business management tactics, skills, and resources as they take into account the influence of disciplinary and locational context.

Indeed we might better understand arts and cultural entrepreneurs, particularly those of the non-profit sector, as engaged in a dual leadership venture: in new product creativity on the artistic side and in entrepreneurial business management on the other. Artists and arts managers are adept at opportunity spotting on the creative side, looking for new ways to work and to create new artworks. Arts entrepreneurship is typically about new artistic products and services. Arts and cultural entrepreneurship can also focus on new venture creation or new revenue streams as well as intrapreneurship within existing organizations. Yet on the management side, artists and arts managers are less facile at seeing or developing opportunities. An arts and cultural entrepreneurship program should help train artists and cultural managers to promote the fruits of their creative impulses, to cultivate partners and networks, and to adapt their innovative skills and habits of mind to the business side.

Arts and cultural entrepreneurship requires both artistic creativity and managerial innovativeness. It is common to worry that business considerations might constrain or direct artistic creativity. This is to confuse purpose with various means of supporting and sustaining the core artistic vision. More clarity is achieved if we accept that the arts and cultural entrepreneurship construct actually operates at five levels: (1) vision, (2) strategy, (3) tactics, (4) the personal level, and (5) the contextual circumstances. The basic value assumptions of arts and cultural entrepreneurship necessitate, at the least, an adaptation of business teaching techniques. Each level requires pedagogical adjustments, and as this field continues to develop and mature, these teaching techniques are likely to become more codified. We have offered an overview of this multi-level construct drawn from the literature to provide definitions of the different levels and examples of approaches used on various levels. We then present a deeper discussion of the strategic level and the urban/city context.

Understanding Arts and Cultural Entrepreneurship

Many arts supporters, both public and private, have called for the cultivation of arts and cultural entrepreneurship as a solution to many funding concerns: as a way of fostering the sustainability of arts, cultural and heritage organizations; as a source of greater independence for individuals in the creative economy; and as a key component of developing creative cities. Additionally, many institutions of higher education have called for the expansion of the curriculum for artists and other cultural professionals into arts and cultural entrepreneurship. Despite these demands, it is broadly recognized that there is little agreement about either the definition of arts and cultural entrepreneurship and its practice or about how it might best be taught (Beckman, 2007; Roberts, 2013).

Many definitions seem to focus on new, microenterprise venturing, portfolio career self-management (sometimes referred to as career transitioning), and being entrepreneurial (Bridgstock, 2012). In a review of the pertinent literature, Wyszomirski and Chang (2014) found that many other meanings were also offered. These included opportunity spotting, marketing, technology adaptation, change management, crafts and rural heritage development, the acquisition of business skills, networking, creative economy partnerships, and even cultural policy entrepreneurship. Some asked whether arts-based social entrepreneurship is another facet of arts and cultural entrepreneurship. Still others contend that non-profit arts and cultural organizations are inherently entrepreneurial because they constantly recombine sources of revenue as

THEORY

part of their business model (Mulcahy, 2003). Conversely, others argue that efforts to cultivate arts and cultural entrepreneurship will result in greater commodification and marketization of the creative sector. Amidst such ambiguity about the definitional starting point of arts and cultural entrepreneurship, how are researchers, educators and practitioners to bring any structure to this subject?

Effective teaching requires students to appreciate the macro and micro views - to understand the holistic view and the relation of more specialized topics to one another, as well as seeing the big picture. Thus, after understanding the larger concept, students then can focus on learning how each level contributes to the effective practice of arts and cultural entrepreneurship and how all of the levels are integrated.

A comprehensive definition of arts and cultural entrepreneurship operates simultaneously at five levels: Goal/Purpose, Strategy, Tactics/Tools, Personal Characteristics, and Contextual Elements.

1. The overall **purpose** of arts and cultural entrepreneurship is to enable cultural workers to achieve greater self-sufficiency and autonomy by cultivating their capacity for adaptability and sustainability and to produce not only economic value through their artworks but also cultural, social and/or community value.
2. This purpose can be advanced through a variety of **strategies**: through new venture creation as independent microenterprises or as organizational projects; as arts based social entrepreneur activities (Neck et al, 2009); through the creation of new artistic products or services; or through promoting policy change through policy entrepreneurship.
3. Any of these strategies can be pursued through a set of **tactics,** which include using a new invention or technology; developing new markets; finding new ways of securing resources or new ways of mixing existing resources (Mollick, 2014); developing new ways of producing or distributing arts or cultural products; developing and exploiting networks (Jackson & Oliver, 2003); cultivating new and varied partnerships; finding ways of cost-savings and/or making do with what they have (bricolage) (Preece, 2014), or cultural policy entrepreneurship that can affect the legal and economic circumstances within artists and arts entrepreneurship operate (Goldberg-Miller, 2015).
4. The ability of an individual to envision and carry out any combination of these strategies and tactics are facilitated or hindered by **personal attributes and skills,** that may occur naturally or that can be learned and refined. Commonly identified characteristics include tolerance of failure, tolerance of risk, persistence, and flexibility. Frequently noted skills include opportunity spotting and sociability that enables network building (Essig, 2013; Pollard & Wilson, 2014). Leading students through leadership self-assessment exercises often is an effective teaching device for understanding this level.
5. These personal qualities also facilitate or hinder an individual's **awareness of context. In**cluding the ability to spot trends and changes; to discern the possible impact of such context developments to produce opportunities, to prompt adaptation, and/or to need recombination.

Much of the research on art and cultural entrepreneurship has focused on the explorations of tactics—on reaching new markets and reaching them in new ways; on using

Internet and social networks to deliver and promote the distribution of the arts via digital technology; on the benefits and processes of cultivating partnerships between arts and cultural organizations as well as non-arts actors; of crowdsourcing methods of fundraising; and of turning bricolage into an innovative production approach. While better understanding of these tactical tools of implementation tell us how arts entrepreneurs can act effectively, they do not help us understand (or teach) how to think entrepreneurially. More specifically, researchers, educators and practitioners need to deepen knowledge of how strategic considerations interact with the skills of opportunity spotting and network building. We also need a better understanding — particularly as it concerns local conditions as well as differences among art forms and creative industries — of how context influences risk management, opportunity spotting, and the composition of networks.

According to this multi-level perspective, arts and cultural entrepreneurship can be regarded as a dynamic system of recombinations that draws upon and integrates elements of all five levels. There are many gaps in our current understanding of how each of these levels work, how they interact, and the impact of both context and personal characteristics on individual arts and cultural entrepreneurs.

The Strategic Level of Arts Entrepreneurship

David Throsby (2001) has been a leading proponent of the dual value of arts and culture, arguing that such a defining characteristic of such activities, products and services is their dual value—meaning both economic value and cultural value. Economic value may lie directly within the income earned from artistic products or indirectly induced through economic development, through cultural tourism, or through the value added to non-arts products and activities through design. In turn, cultural value includes both intrinsic and instrumental components. Intrinsic cultural value is aesthetic and often perceived primarily by individuals. Instrumentally, cultural value can take many forms, such as social change, educational impact, heritage preservation, place branding, or social cohesion and mutual understanding. Furthermore, decisions about the relative mix and importance of such dual value creation are a central concern of shaping the strategic level of arts and cultural entrepreneurship.

It is not rare for analysts of arts and cultural entrepreneurship to focus on one strategy without recognizing that that it is not the only possible strategy. Considerable attention has been focused on the creation of new, artist-based micro-enterprises. This follows from trying to transfer business thinking directly to non-profit arts and from the recent cultural policy focus on finding new ways to support and assist individual artists, as public fellowships for artists have become scarcer. It also relates to recent policy emphasis on arts-driven place making and culture-led urban development. Such an entrepreneurial strategy relies on enhancing business tactics to support artistic creativity and can focus on a goal of sustainability, of growth, or of profitmaking (i.e. in the commercial arts industries).

Alternatively, cultural heritage-driven enterprises could be new or established ventures that seek to employ a range of entrepreneurial tactics not only to financially support crafts and culturally specific activities, but also to pursue a social mission, such as preservation, skill development and survival, group identity, and/or community recognition (Aageson, 2008). This approach is evident in the Louisiana cultural economy report, which builds around heritage resources displayed in architecture,

THEORY

literature, music and culinary arts (Mt. Auburn Assoc., 2005). Cultural heritage entrepreneurship may also consider the generation of financial value as a means to community change by helping to improve family conditions, educational attainment, or social mobility (W. K. Kellogg Foundation, 2010).

This brief discussion of the strategic level of arts entrepreneurship demonstrates both that strategy often involves the key entrepreneurial process of the combination and recombination of pre-existing elements in novel ways that involve a measure of risk (Schumpeter, 1983).

Contextual Circumstances: The Local Level

Teaching arts and cultural entrepreneurship means informing students about the variety and kind of decisions that will need to be made once they are in the field. As burgeoning arts and cultural entrepreneurs contemplate their creative business ideas, it is important that they develop an understanding of the context in which these strategies exist, as well as learning how to design entrepreneurial initiatives (Neck & Greene, 2011). Perspectives on the home city or region's economic framework, issues of place, worker and consumer profiles, and policy frameworks are essential tools in creating a viable business strategy as well as in building a successful and sustainable enterprise. Thus, local context is not a singular concept but rather a compound that includes the particularities of local community context, the urban framework, and considerations of strategic choice. Entrepreneurs must develop an awareness of the contextual circumstances within which they function and develop familiarity with the background of the business' urban or regional general economic condition. The case study method, based on interviews, focus groups, and ethnographic studies can be a particularly effective teaching tool to illuminate and understand the effects of local context.

Many arts and cultural enterprises can be seen as being a part of the social enterprise landscape. In which the business strategy has business as well as social or cultural goals. This context combines the economic and public good or social purpose aspects of business development, fostering an integrated approach that reflects the inherent goals of seemingly dissimilar objectives into a new kind of profit maximization; one which embraces the triple bottom line of economic health, organizational sustainability, and cultural accountability (Matthew, 2008; Wyszomirski, 2014). This kind of blended social purpose and economic vitality gives the arts entrepreneur a powerful platform through which to gain access to the policy agenda on the local level and beyond (Henry, 2007, p. 206).

Through an examination of what differences in customization at the local level mean and why it is important to understand this context, we can provide tools for arts and cultural entrepreneurs to overcome barriers to success. The arts and cultural entrepreneur exists within a network of colleagues, partners and consumers and includes not only the arts-related organizations, but also those in the general business realm. Additionally, these entrepreneurs play an important role as champions not only of the business of art but the societal and heritage value of cultural assets. Interventions, and entities (Kolsteeg, 2013, p. 5). The local framework is an important part of the entity's opportunity landscape, and since many arts and cultural organizations and businesses are located in urban settings, issues within this realm are an essential component of any strategic plan.

While arts and cultural entrepreneurs concern themselves primarily with the creation of new products, channels of distribution, and markets, it is critical to understand the local context in which the entity exists (Schumpeter, 1983). Practitioners in the established business world invariably look at the local level, and they are adept at customization. The local level is an especially important context for arts and cultural entrepreneurs, whether the product or service is being consumed in the place of origin or exported. A vernacular focus links arts and cultural entrepreneurship to the creative city and creative placemaking discourse. Within this dialogue, the outputs of arts and cultural individuals and businesses have been recognized as a powerful segment of the economy, especially in an urban setting (Markusen & Schrock, 2006).

Arts and cultural entrepreneurs exist within a physical and economic environment, as well as being embedded in a social network. In an urban context, these entrepreneurs must recognize the value and essential role that relationships play (Groen et al, 2008). These include collegial exchanges, fostering relationships with consumers, and building bridges within the policy framework in which the entity is found. Customization at this local level incorporates an understanding of environmental factors and network opportunities, each of which provides connections to what Matthew (2008) calls the *'business ecosystem'*. This is especially true in the start-up phase of any cultural entrepreneurship venture. Groen et al (2008) recognize that oftentimes entrepreneurial or start-up ventures exist in an environment where numerous entities are working on the same idea or application simultaneously. They are part of a network landscape, which includes the private sector, advocacy and lobbying groups, government agencies and non-profit organizations. Developing an awareness of those key actors involved in each of these areas is critical for the arts entrepreneur, especially in an urban setting.

As the venture progresses in its lifecycle, arts and cultural entrepreneurship students must learn how to collaborate, develop effective marketing and branding strategies, and adapt to changes in the policy landscape and the economic environment. Customization at the local level involves developing the skills to attract and utilize financial, human capital, and relationship resources in the best interests of the creative economy business or organization. Strategies and tactics for creating, nurturing, and sustaining entrepreneurial entities must take into account the assets available at the local level.

Customization and the Urban Context

What is the urban context and how does it relate to arts and cultural entrepreneurship? Despite the perception that business sectors outside the creative industries have a more cohesive and strategic alliance among various sectors, the cultural economy in today's cities has the opportunity to coalesce, specifically through the shared interests of its entrepreneurial factions (Kolsteeg, 2013). Operating within a socio-economic framework, arts and cultural entrepreneurs often experience a disconnect between the creative content of their output and the managerial constructs within which they must operate in order to create a successful entity (Hong et al, 2012). Arts and cultural entrepreneurs must adapt the substantive roadmap created in the business entrepreneur lexicon, while situating themselves within a policy framework (Mulcahy, 2006). Arts and culture's increasingly integrated place on the economic development agenda will facilitate the allocation of funding resources and the ongoing support by appropriate planning and regulatory frameworks (Markusen, 2014). Local policy entrepreneurs may

THEORY

have identified opportunities for the development of interventions that can benefit the arts and cultural entrepreneur. Developing a relationship with these policy actors will give an organization or business the chance to participate in these strategies. Municipal actors, business leaders, elected officials, and other entrepreneurial colleagues in the creative sector can be a part of the entity's local network (Adam & Kriesi, 2007, p. 144). These considerations are magnified in the urban landscape, as the density of people and place means that a plethora of issues are competing for the attention of workers, consumers and policymakers.

In order to make the most of resources, networks, policy windows and opportunities, arts and cultural entrepreneurs must recognize and utilize assets inherent in creative cities and regions (Scott, 2004). These include place-based assets, people-based resources, and policy-based opportunities. *Place-based assets* include aspects such as location, anchor institutions, and transportation opportunities (Rae, 2007, p. 59). *People-based resources* focus on seeing and developing opportunities through building networks, partnerships, and linkages (Reid et al, 2008). This is true for arts entrepreneurs within the freelance, self-employed, and micro-level landscapes. The development of people skills includes assessing and leveraging resources such as clusters of creative workers (Schoales, 2006), and targeting consumers including residents and visitors. *Policy-based opportunities* point to municipal support, economic development policies fostering creative economy interventions, and the interest and guidance of policy entrepreneurs and policy advocates (McCann, 2013). Policy entrepreneurs in the creative city context can engage in cultural planning, advocate for cultural organizations, and leverage financial support within the non-profit and for-profit arenas (Goldberg-Miller, 2015). Developing and sustaining relationships in the policy realm is an essential and ongoing process, and one that can be fostered through strategic planning and demonstration of smart practice examples within the local entrepreneurial context (Matthew, 2008).

Urban Plan, Cultural Plan

Cities have the capacity to develop the role of arts and culture within the economic development, brand building, tourism, and quality of life agendas by creating cultural plans. A cultural plan is a strategic process for a city's arts and cultural development that takes place first by determining the needs and assets of a city, and subsequently meeting those needs resulting in the development of arts and culture as an economic and public good powerhouse.

The ultimate goal of a cultural plan is to increase awareness of art and culture and identify opportunities in the creative economy within cities and regions. There are many steps cities can take in order to realize the success of these plans. Identifying the wide variety of community stakeholders from the three sectors and bringing them to the table is imperative to this process. Buy-in from policymakers, anchor cultural institutions, arts service organizations, entities in the for-profit and non-profit creative economy, civic and corporate leaders and individual artists can be established through community meetings, focus groups, and interviews with individuals. The process of establishing and implementing a cultural plan can prove to be a boon for arts and cultural entrepreneurs from both the non-profit and for-profit sectors, as the value and scope of the creative economy is brought into a policy framework, providing a platform for relationship building, business development, and effective advocacy.

THEORY

Conclusion

The burgeoning arts and cultural entrepreneurship field can learn from as well as contribute to the business community's smart practices. Knowledge and innovation economies of today are heralded worldwide as important sources for economic development and financial growth, with entrepreneurship and worker mobility serving as hallmarks of this new paradigm (Thrift, 2010). The cultural economy, specifically through the development, growth and sustainability of arts and cultural enterprises, can be an additional engine for this kind of advancement in today's global economy. Arts and cultural entrepreneurs must focus on the contextualization of their strategy, opportunity spotting, and the customization of their product or service to meet the realities at the local level and respond to the changing demands of the urban marketplace.

Arts and cultural entrepreneurship education needs to identify the strengths inherent in the creative economy, such as adaptability. Innovation, and resilience, then blend these with the business community's focus on strategic thinking and customization. The business world and the arena of social change have long possessed the 'fire' of entrepreneurial knowledge and practice. Arts and cultural entrepreneurship educators are sifting through these 'embers', seeking to fan them into new 'flames' that will illuminate the path for entrepreneurs who can foster businesses, microenterprises, and arts and culture organizations that can take their place as economic and social purpose engines within the global business pantheon.

About the Authors

Prof Dr Margaret Jane Wyszomirski is Director of the Graduate program in Arts Policy and Administration at the Ohio State University where she also holds faculty appointments in the Department of Art Education and the John Glenn School of Public Affairs. Professor Wyszomirski's research focuses on arts and cultural policy, international cultural affairs and cultural diplomacy, creative industries and creative cities, professionalism in the arts, and arts leadership and entrepreneurship. She has edited, co-edited, and con-tributed to numerous books on arts and cultural policy. She teaches an undergraduate course on 'Exploring the Creative Sector in the United States' and has taught a graduate seminar on arts and entrepreneurship. She is a member of the editorial board for Artivate:

References

Aageson, Thomas H. (2008). Cultural Entrepreneurs: Producing Cultural Value and Wealth. In: H. Anheier & Y. Isar (Eds.). *The Cultural Economy (The Cultures and Globalization Series).* Thousand Oaks: Sage.

Adam, S., & Kriesi, H. (2007). The network approach. In P. Sabatier (Ed.), *Theories of the policy process* (2nd ed.). Boulder: Westview Press.

Beckman, Gary D. (2007). 'Adventuring' Arts Entrepreneurship Curricula in Higher Education: An Examination of Present Efforts, Obstacles, and Best Practices. In: *Journal of Arts Management, Law, and Society,* 37(2), 87-112.

Bridgstock, Ruth (2012). Not A Dirty Word: Arts Entrepreneurship and Higher Education. *Arts and Humanities in Higher Education,* 12(2-3), 122-137.

Cardamore, M. & Rentschler, R. (2006). Indigenous innovators: The Role of web Marketing for Cultural Micro-enterprises. In: *International Journal of Non-profit Voluntary Sector Marketing*, 11(4), 347-360.

Essig, L. (2013). Teaching Habits of Mind for Arts Entrepreneurship. In: *Artivate: A Journal of Entrepreneurship in the Arts,* 1(2), 65-77.

Goldberg-Miller, S.B.D. (Winter 2015). Creative Toronto: Harnessing the Economic Development Power of Arts & Culture. In: *Artivate: A Journal of Entrepreneurship in the Arts,* 4(1), 25-48.

Groen, A., Wakkee, I., & De Weerd-Nederhof, P. (2008). Managing Tensions in a High-tech Start-up: An Innovation Journey in Social System Perspective. In: *International Small Business Journal,* 26(1), 57-81.

Henry, C. (Ed.). (2007). *Entrepreneurship in the Creative Industries: An International Perspective.* Edward Elgar: Northampton.

THEORY

Hong, C., Essig, L., & Bridgstock, R. (2012). The enterprising artist and the arts entrepreneur: Emergent pedagogies for new disciplinary habits of mind. In N. Chick, A. Haynie, & R. Gurung (Eds.). In: *Exploring More Signature Pedagogies: Approaches to Teaching Disciplinary Habits of Mind.* Sterling: Stylus.

Jackson, J. & Oliver, T. (2003). Personal networks theory and the arts: A literature review with special reference to entrepreneurial popular musicians. In: *Journal of Arts Management Law & Society*, 33(3), 240-256.

Kolsteeg, J. (2013). Situated Cultural Entrepreneurship. In: *Artivate: A Journal of Entrepreneurship in the Arts.* 2(3), 3–13.

Markusen, A. (2014). Creative cities: A 10-year research agenda. In: *Journal of Urban Affairs, 36*(S2), 567-589.

Markusen, A., & Schrock, S. (2006). The artistic dividend: urban artistic specialization and economic development implications. **Urban Studies, 43**(10), 1661-1686.

Mathew, P. (2008). Social Enterprises in the Competitive Era. In: *Economic and Political Weekly*, 43(38), 22-24.

McCann, E. (2013). Policy Boosterism, Policy Mobilities, and the Extrospective City. In: *Urban Geography, 34*(1), 5-29.

Millick, E. (2014). The Dynamics of Crowdfunding: An exploratory study. In: *Journal of Business Venturing*, (29)1, 1-16.

Mt. Auburn Associates. (2005). *Louisiana: Where Culture Means Business.* Office of the Lt. Governor, Division of Culture, Recreation, and Tourism, Office of Cultural Development: Baton Rouge.

Mulcahy, Kevin. (2003). Entrepreneurship or Cultural Darwinism? Privatization and American Cultural Patronage. In: *Journal of Arts Management, Law and Society,* 33(3), 165-184.

Mulcahy, K.V. (2006). Cultural policy. In B. G. Peters and J. Pierre (Eds.) In: *Handbook of public policy.* London: Sage.

Neck, H. Brush, C. & Allen, E. (2009). The landscape of social entrepreneurship. In: *Business Horizons.* 52(1), 13-19.

Neck, H. & Greene, P. (2011). Entrepreneurship education: Known worlds and new frontiers. In: *Journal of Small Business Management,* 49(1), 55-70.

Phillips, R. (2011). *Arts Entrepreneurship and Economic Development: Can Every City be 'Austintatious'?.* Indianapolis: Networks Financial Institute.

Pollard, V. & Wilson, E. (2014). The 'Entrepreneurial Mindset' in creative and performing arts higher education in Australia. In: *Artivate: A Journal of Entrepreneurship in the Arts*, (3)1, 3-22.

Preece, S. (2014). Social Bricolage in Arts Entrepreneurship: Building a Jazz Society from Scratch. In: *Artivate: A Journal of Entrepreneurship in the Arts,* 3(1), 165-184.

Rae, D. (2007) Creative industries in the U.K.: cultural diffusion or discontinuity? In: Henry, C. (Ed.) *Entrepreneurship in the Creative Industries: An international perspective.* Cheltenham: Edward Elgar.

A Journal of Entrepreneurship and the Arts. Before joining the OSU faculty, Professor Wyszomirski taught at other universities including Rutgers, Georgetown and Case Western Reserve.

—

Wyszomirski.1@osu.edu

THEORY

Dr Shoshanah Goldberg-Miller is Assistant Professor in the Department of Arts Administration, Education and Policy at The Ohio State University, with a courtesy appointment in the City and Regional Planning Section of OSU's Knowlton School of Architecture. Dr. Goldberg-Miller's research focuses on arts and cultural entrepreneurship, creative economic development, global cultural policy, and management and fund development in nonprofits.

An experienced fundraiser, Goldberg-Miller was on the executive team at The Paley Center for Media, American Cancer Society, Greenwich House Pottery, March of Dimes, American Museum of Natural History, and Museum of Holography. Prior to joining OSU's faculty, she taught at The New School, Hunter College, and Columbia University. As a management consultant, Dr. Goldberg-Miller has served clients such as Parsons School of Design, Aspen Institute, National Geographic and Sesame Workshop, as well as numerous individuals and community-based organizations.

—

Goldberg-Miller.1@osu.edu

Reid, N., Smith, B. & Carroll, M. (2008). Cluster Regions: A social network perspective. In: *Economic Development Quarterly,* 22(4), 345-352.

Rentschler, R. (2002). *The Entrepreneurial Arts Leader.* St. Lucia: University of Queensland Press.

Roberts, Joseph S. (2013). Infusing Entrepreneurship Within Non-Business Disciplines: Preparing Artists and Others for Self-Employment and Entrepreneurship. In: *Artivate: A Journal of Entrepreneurship in the Arts*, 1(2), 53-63.

Schoales, J. (2006). Alpha Clusters: Creative innovation in local economies. In: *Economic Development Quarterly*, 20(2), 162-177.

Schumpeter, Joseph. (1983). *Theory of Economic Development (with Translation by John E. Elliott)* New Brunswick: Transaction Press (original Copyright by President and Fellows of Harvard College, 1934).

Scott, A. J. (2004). Cultural-products industries and urban economic development. In: *Urban Affairs Review, 9,* 461-490.

Thrift, N. (2001). It's the romance, not the finance, that makes the business worth pursuing: disclosing a new market culture. In: *Economy and Society*, 30(4): 412-432.

Throsby, David (2001). *Economics and Culture.* Cambridge: Cambridge University Press.

W. K. Kellogg Foundation. (2010). *Cultural Entrepreneurship: At the Crossroads of People, Place and Prosperity*. Battle Creek.

Wyszomirski, M. (2014). Shaping a triple-bottom line for cultural organizations: Micro-, macro-, and meta-policy influences. In: *Cultural Trends*, 22(3-4), 156-166.

Wyszomirski, M. & Chang, W. (2014). *Arts Entrepreneurship: A Literature Review*. Paper presented at the 40th Annual Conference on Social Theory, Politics and the Arts held in Ottawa, Ontario, Canada. October 9-11.

THEORY

Manuel Montoya

POETICS AS A DYNAMIC CONCEPT IN CREATIVE AND CULTURAL ENTERPRISE

THEORY

Abstract

This paper will critique the current state of debate regarding the creative and cultural enterprise (CCE). Furthermore, it will place the concept of poetics as an essential component of CCE. Poetics can be broadly defined as qualities or features that emphasize beauty, imagination, or elevated thoughts. Milton once referred to poetics as the state of *'words when words are insufficient.'* During the last decade, forces within the global cultural economy have mobilized the need for social innovation while also attending to the artistic and cultural forces endemic to economic identity. Why does CCE distinguish itself from social entrepreneurship? How will educators preserve higher order concepts that can apply broadly to the practitioners, students, and policy makers as these terms become subject to disciplinary boundaries?

Hence, this paper will achieve the following:

1. Define poetics as a fundamental concept to management practices in a changing world, particularly the economic identity of a business and its production of a value chain.
2. Trace the theoretical roots of poetics, derived from philosophy and cultural theory in the context of contemporary international management strategies.
3. Describe and characterize trends in the global economy to discuss the reasons poetics is a relevant and urgent part of global economic development.
4. Prescribe a set of basic learning outcomes that can be utilized in both traditional academic teaching and community outreach, using poetics as a core concept in the study and practice of cultural and creative enterprise.

Introduction

Social entrepreneurship is a term that has gained mobility in the last few years. Business schools have experienced an unprecedented growth of students interested in social entrepreneurship, social innovation, or other related topics of study (Dees and Anderson, 2003; Montgomery and Ramus, 2008; Bloom and Chatterji, 2009). It has become the largest growth sector in business school education, and has caused universities to emphasize entrepreneurship as part of its overall strategic planning (Anderson and Dees, 2006; Saul, 2012). As the business world absorbs, interprets, and capitalizes on the idea that one can go into business while addressing social problems, teaching and learning institutions (including business schools) are challenged to adapt their thinking in order to train this new generation of professionals. Social activists, public servants, artists, and community organizers are among the many people transforming their credentials to include terms like *'business leader'* and *'entrepreneur'.*

Concurrently, many have refined their interests to focus on *'creative entrepreneurship'* and *'cultural entrepreneurship'* (hereafter referred to as *'CCE'*). These terms have been used to distinguish work that is not only socially-minded, but attentive to the forces that sustain artists, preserve cultural institutions, and emphasize the intangibility involved in certain modes of production (Steaveart and Hjort, 2003). Furthermore, as CCE shapes the imagination of the business world, it will confront challenges that, until recently, rarely captured the attention of the business professional in a deep and meaningful context.

What is CCE?

Simply put, CCE is the process whereby creativity and culture serve as the principal forces that start a business or organization. A creative entrepreneur is one who sees creativity, or rather, the intangible work of the mind as the main part of their productivity and sells their work accordingly. The cultural entrepreneur is one who sees culture, perhaps the institution of culture as something that should be preserved. Moreover, this entrepreneur is one who may believe deeply in the value of cultural self-determination and by extension is in the business of supporting cultural rights as part of their work. But one could argue that anything that is produced requires some level of creativity, and one could also argue that culture is endemic to everything. So why have these terms? Why separate a carpenters' work from the work of a poet, or an engineer from a painter? To what extent are these categories helpful, if they are productive at all? These concepts can doom themselves to subjective relativity and remain there to be admonished by hard-line empiricists. But still these concepts remain, and they remain because often, production is defined, refined, and mobilized by these ambiguous forces. The answer lies less in whether the categories themselves are valuable, but to what extent entrepreneurs' view their work as participants in the problems associated with creativity and culture (Raffo, et al., 2000). To emphasize creativity implies that perhaps the conventional way of doing things has turned into a larger social or political problem. To emphasize culture also implies that certain traditions or bodies of knowledge are vulnerable, exploited, or threatened. The carpenter who makes modular homes may be less interested in characterizing her work as having creative value, perhaps because her work may entail a lot of replication. This does not mean she is not creative, but this is different from the carpenter who makes one-of-a-kind homes, someone who partakes in the design of a home and puts time and effort into rendering her work exclusive or unique in some way. The carpenter as creative entrepreneur may see herself as an artist and differentiate herself through the monetization of her unique work. The carpenter as cultural entrepreneur may see herself as a social problem-solver. For example, she may see gentrification as a problem that institutionalizes housing for the poor and may use her talents to address issues of displacement and structural poverty. In either case, the creative and cultural entrepreneur is stimulated by different thinking – thinking that comes from intellectual traditions not normally associated with the training of a business student.

Like all things that become popular very quickly, it is easy to forget its deep historical precedent. Creative and Cultural Entrepreneurship is not a new concept (Dacin, et al., 2010). In ancient economies, matters that dealt with art, culture, or the intangible were primarily the domain of monarchs. In more complex social hierarchies, these issues were within the purview of the priestly classes and scribes (i.e., Sumerian or Akkadian civilization). Merchants, whose work was mobilized by the presence of a medium of exchange (i.e. gold or barter) created and maintained the marketplaces. These hier-archies existed mostly because the highly subjective nature of art and language was associated with the divine. The maintenance of cultural institutions and community identity were the intellectual property of a privileged few. Moreover, the interpretation of complex ideas were limited by the literacy of the people and the centralized power of

THEORY

ancient autocrats (Berlin, 2013). People had always been able to tell stories, to incorporate ritual into craft, and to express themselves creatively. However, as democracy became more popular, the socio-political gap closed between scribes and merchants. These new professionals created new public spaces. Artists and writers became self-employed businesspeople who could influence society in new ways. At the heart of this were thinkers like Aristotle who viewed poetry, literature, and art as an essential feature of democracy.

What is Poetics?

Poetics, a Greek word that means *'making'* is traditionally thought of as the study of poetry, but more directly, it focuses intensively on the process where an idea is mastered and transformed into something material, or at least representational. By studying the form and content of a thing (the methods and modes of artistic creation), the idea that it represents (imitation), and the commonality it shares with other ideas (genre), one had a specific and shared vocabulary to describe what was once intangible. Big ideas could be associated with objects (aesthetics), and those objects could then be explored in relation to the ethics and politics contained by those ideas. But even more fundamentally, the value of a thing was given nuance and a new set of reasoning to explain worth and value in comparison to one another. Marxist thinkers of the 20th century would study how these forces of capital participated in the making of the modern world system. One could argue that the combined discourse of democracy and poetics produced the first discussions of intellectual property, and as society has become increasingly focused on individual rights and freedoms, poetics itself became an essential ingredient in the foundations of economic theory. Martin Heidegger argued in his writings that the world was heading into a state of disconnect between what is produced and what is consumed (2008). In his treatise *'On the Origin of the Work of Art'* he attempted to trace how one focused on *Art* as a finished product, but systematically lost the *Work* associated with the production of that art. Later, writers from the Frankfurt School would combine this thinking with the atrocities of the Holocaust. Walter Benjamin would note in his seminal article *'The Work of Art in the Age of Mechanical Reproduction,'* that as mechanical reproduction slowly replicated objects that were once unique, the thing that made unique works special, the *'aura'* of a thing became more vulnerable, and with it came a detrimental loss to humanity (1968). He famously criticized the death camps not merely for their barbarism and dehumanization of its victims, but also for dehumanizing the killers and propagators of the death camps through the methods of mass production. These writings highlighted the deep political and ethical dimensions of all forms of production, and as a result searched for life-affirming forces that responded directly to these atrocities. At each point, poetics served as a point of reference to illuminate how meaning, authenticity, beauty, and craft contributed to processes and systems that defended vulnerable cultures, rituals subject to erasure, and rights that preserved the dignity of consumers and producers.

Global Distance and the Demand for Storytelling

The systematic removal of work from art corresponded with the systematic detachment of consumers from what they consumed, and poetics was seen as a problem that could be introduced to repair those connections. As the interaction of people and commercial institutions increase on a planetary scale, the landscape that mediates these interactions has fundamentally changed. While most of this activity creates a significant amount of closeness, it also produces an unprecedented level of *'difference and disjuncture,'*

THEORY

(Appadurai, 1990). Far from creating the digital utopia that thinkers of the 1990s forecasted, local identities have been marginalized and in some instances threatened with extinction. Moreover, the industrialization of many parts of the world has created a rise in discretionary income amongst most of the world's population. Those at the '*base of the income pyramid*,' have encountered sharp growth in discretionary income, fundamentally changing the social and cultural welfare of the world's population. We must not only revisit the way that structural poverty is understood, but we must also prepare for the deep and thick descriptions that will construct the 21st century economic narrative. As the poor encounter more income opportunities, what will this do to foundational cultural practices? Furthermore, industrialization has directly created social, cultural, and environmental challenges that has manifested in frustrating economic obstacles that bear massive human cost. Beyond the more obvious issues revolving around exploited labour and human rights are questions of agricultural and environmental sustainability, the production of conflict resources, and the production of parallel economies. What were once considered externalities are now understood as an integral part of today's production costs. Currently, more students are entering business schools with the intention of engaging in socially-conscious practices.

As stated earlier, social entrepreneurship is cited as being the most popular trend in business management coursework within the past four years[1]. This has been prompted by increased collaboration between the academy, NGOs, governments, and businesses (small and large). In a changing world, business schools will have to rely on bodies of knowledge that have long investigated the meaning-making processes endemic to cultures, particularly cultures in crises. CCE remains a distinct component of social entrepreneurship precisely because in order to do a good job confronting challenges to creativity and culture, one can be encouraged to explore the intellectual traditions that help one take tools such as interpretation and critique seriously. How can one be effective at preserving culture if one's understanding of culture is superficial? How can one lead discussions on creative production when creativity is seen as touchy-feely, or worse yet, never receives serious, critical reflection despite its centrality to the entrepreneurial causes in question?

Today it has become popular to incorporate storytelling as a part of CCE. Consequently, learning institutions have emerged to emphasize the value of storytelling, mostly as a component of marketing, sales, and operations management (Rae, 2005; Montoya, et al. 2012). The International Folk Art Alliance (IFAA), for example, annually trains artists approximately 150 artists each year, representing over 75 countries to participate in the world's largest folk art market[2]. By emphasizing the value of telling the story behind one's product, the artists create a unique marketplace founded on quality and cultural authenticity that creates economic opportunities for the many communities throughout the world represented in the market. The IFAA serves as a market channel (managing dozens of entrepreneurs that capitalize on folk traditions), an educational institution (sharing ideas about how to let authentic folk art reach the consumer through narrative), and as a thought-leader (promoting the value of folk art as a response to mass production

THEORY

---

[1] *Retrieved from: http://chronicle.com/blogs/wiredcampus/universities-foster-entrepreneurship-and-innovation-federal-report-says/48059*

[2] *Retrieved from: http://www.folkartalliance.org/*

on a global scale). The mere presence of the market and its success[3] highlights the presence of social, cultural, and political issues that are as powerful today as they were in ancient times – some even more urgent. The world has become so complex that it doesn't merely demand narratives that close distances between one another, it is starving for those narratives. Those stories must navigate the protection of ancestral traditions while simultaneously encouraging the development of new vocabularies to name the 21st century world economy. As CCE evolves into a way of dealing with these specific problems, poetics can serve as a useful organizing concept to address the vast differences and disjuncture produced in the world economy of the 21st century.

Avoiding the forced Choice between Artist and Businessperson

Poetics as a teaching tool can help address an important challenge in CCE: the separation perceived between artists and businesspeople. How does one teach business in such a way that it doesn't compromise artistic integrity while simultaneously training that person to be a businessperson that is practical and reliable? In order to appreciate this challenge-writ-stereotype, one must first understand how teaching and learning institutions are encountering this challenge. The distance between the vocabularies used to train these two professionals is vast (Haussman, 2010). In 2012, the Skoll World forum proposed several takeaway points regarding social entrepreneurship, including:

1. it's ok to make a return solving social problems
2. measurement is no longer an option
3. *'solving problems'* should replace *'doing good'*

In each of these points, social entrepreneurship has been mobilized by a need for better metrics, and terms such as *'ROI'* (return on investment) and *'social impact'* are prominent, quantifiable components of an entrepreneurs' toolkit (Dees, 2008). These trends have created highly refined ways of accounting for one's work and has made management of social issues more commensurate and clearly identifiable across institutions. But like any quantifiable outcome, numbers are only as good as the concepts that inform them. Part of the unspoken tension within CCE is located in the disciplinary biases that mediate higher education. Artists and the humanities are seen as too *'touchy feely'* while the social and physical sciences are perceived as inflexible and lacking an authentic connection to creative thinking. These biases are perpetuated by professional politics and they are augmented by the politics of university funding. Fine arts and humanities students find great difficulty moving across campus to take courses in a business school, and business schools rarely consider coursework in the humanities an outcome of their professional training. Taken to their logical conclusion, these stereotypes serve as a powerful obstacle in the development of a new generation of entrepreneurs.

But there is hope. Interdisciplinary programs are utilizing the strategic frameworks and metric based outcomes of business schools and offering them in conjunction with special topics that one would more likely see in schools of liberal arts.

THEORY

---

[3]*In 2014, the folk art market generated over $3 million in one weekend, 90% of which went back to the artists' home community.*
http://www.folkartalliance.org/market-facts/

In the United States, degree granting programs at the University of Minnesota Duluth have connected to European programs such as the University of London and HKU University of the Arts. These programs draw upon trends in the economic development of particular regions and place them in the context of fields within the Liberal Arts. Programs such as the United Nations Institute for Training and Research division for Knowledge Systems Innovation (UNITAR KSI) and the US Global Centre for Cultural Entrepreneurship (GCCE) represent the way that large governing bodies and small NGOs respectively have organized resources to support the dynamic connections people are making within broadly conceived fields of study to their practical application in support of the robust economic engagement possible through creative and cultural enterprise.

On both ends, these few institutions are rising to the challenge of their students and the needs proposed by the world around them. While empirical forms of analysis have dominated with the social sciences, and the social sciences have largely dominated within business and management schools, globalization has opened up new spaces for methods grounded in the humanities (Bloom and Chatterji, 2009). In the field of international management, for example, it is becoming increasingly popular to view the world as a system with relatively little structure (Henry, 2007; Cunningham, 2009). The resulting institutional dissimilarity produced by the lack of structure has produced the desire to become more culturally adaptive to connect business practices across vast cultural, administrative, geographic, and economic distances (Ghemawat, 2011). This includes exploring culturally intelligent components of strategic management, where the audience for business research is largely directed to practitioners (Peng, 2001). As cultural-based strategies become more popular, for example, telling one's story as part of their supply and value chain, there is renewed space to integrate and connect new and old humanities-based research toward practitioners and traditional academics alike.

THEORY

Poetics-based Curriculum Design

Poetics can serve as a powerful teaching tool, especially when one considers:

1. That creative and cultural entrepreneurship remain distinctive with the larger discourse on social entrepreneurship because creative freedom and the value of creativity is still misunderstood (Rae, 2004). Furthermore, issues of cultural self-determination remain urgent problems in the global political economy.
2. The rapid growth of the world economy, combined with the forces of mass production has made ancestral cultures vulnerable, especially where historically structural poverty has encountered unprecedented growth (Tepper, 2010). Concurrently, the world struggles for a common cultural vocabulary, which demands new forms of creative production that is culturally adaptive but is globally significant (Wry, 2011).
3. A balanced approach where evidence-based methods for measuring social impact incorporates meaning-making practices where critical thinking is needed. Otherwise, future professionals will repeat the tension that alienates creative production from economic gain, and will allow progress of any kind to create distinctions that prevent economic initiatives from sustaining themselves in the long run.

Here are a few central concepts that one can incorporate in the design of a CCE curriculum based on these considerations:

Theories of Language and Capital

The post-structuralist philosophers as well as Marxist critics spent a great deal of time connecting capital to language. Students of culture and creativity should have a basic understanding of how value is as much a problem of language and interpretation as it is quantitative. Teaching a student the methods of critique and cultural criticism trains the mind to understand the connection between culture, creativity, and economy. Furthermore, if storytelling is becoming an essential feature of CCE, then one should employ the long and established traditions whereby storytelling is critically evaluated.

Sacred vs. the Profane: Theories of Space

While many CCE understand that profit-based enterprise can be a good thing, learning how people have resisted naming the things they value could help one understand the logic that resists commodification. By engaging in philosophical inquiry that explores the nature of sacred things and how they resist language, one can gain a greater appreciation for those cultural values that view capitalism as threatening and or exploitative (Mulcahey, 2003). Culture and creativity have both been associated with the fundamental questions of human vulnerability and survival. Many of the great social problems of the 21st century will not be solved with oversimplified solutions. Understanding the vast nature of cultural trauma and the logic behind community are heavily undervalued modes of thought. Despite this, the discourse on poetics is also a discourse on memory and forgetting and the way that consumption patterns are determined by violence and trauma. Arjun Appadurai (1990) and the recent trends in cultural geography have demonstrated that globalization has transformed spaces with such power, that we are displaced from spaces that were once immediately familiar to us. Our displacement from our own time and place is a function of theories of identity that need to be continually evaluated. As creative entrepreneurs appropriate and popularize words such as 'design', educators must equip these practitioners with a way to critically evaluate the tremendous body of knowledge that has been established on, space, time, and place (Pratt, 2004).

Authenticity, Identity, and the Politics of Representation

Both cultural self-determination and creativity rely heavily on a concept of authenticity. Several scholars of the Frankfurt school argue that power is derived from the sense of awe and wonder derived from authentic relationships (Adorno, 1967). Poetics serves as a way to understand the architecture of meaningful social relations and how images, signs and objects mediate the relationship between people and truth (Banks, 2006). Learning how people construct meaning around images and how one deconstructs the meaning behind ritual, signs, and objects leads one to questions of beauty and the life affirming properties that make societies resilient (Lounsbury and Glynn, 2001).

Creative and Cultural Enterprise is a powerful subset of the recent discourse on social entrepreneurship. Its distinctiveness must continue to be appreciated and teaching and learning institutions will have to reach ambitiously across its bodies of knowledge to create professionals who do not merely study content or delineate a set of problems. Instead, our educational institutions should be encouraged to draw upon the deep resources of humanistic inquiry to consolidate the ever-increasing toolkit of the business professional.

About the Author

*Prof Dr Manuel (MJR)
Montoya is a professor of
global structures at
the University of
New Mexico, Anderson
School of Management. He is
an interdisciplinary scholar of
globalization and the factors
that produce
a global political
economy and is a member
of the Council on Foreign
Relations. A Rhodes and
Truman Scholar, he runs his
own global consulting firm,
In Medias Res Consulting,
which has provided
support to global NGOs and
INGOs. His research focuses
on global culture and
its impact on economic and
management issues;
including work on human
security, global culture as
an intangible firm resource,
epistemologies of capital,
international trade, emerging
economies, and global
economic sustainability.
He was recently appointed
as UNM Endowed Professor
of Creative Enterprise and is
on the Board of Directors for
the International Folk
Art Alliance. He was born
and raised in Mora,
New Mexico, educated at
UNM (BA),
Oxford University (M.Litt),
New York University (M.A.),
and Emory University (PhD).*

—

mrmonto@unm.edu

References

Adorno, T. (2001). *The Culture Industry: Selected Essays on Mass Culture*, J.M. Bernstein (ed.). Routledge Press.

Anderson & G. Dees (2006). Rhetoric, Reality, and Research: Building a Solid Foundation for the Practice of Social Entrepreneurship, forthcoming in: *Social Entrepreneurship: New Paradigms of Sustainable Social Change*, Nicholls (ed.), Oxford University Press, 2006.

Appadurai, A. (1990). Difference and Disjuncture in the Global Cultural Economy. In: *Public Culture* 2(2):1-24.

Banks, M. (2006). Moral economy and cultural work. In: *Sociology*, 40(3), 455-472.

Benjamin, Walter (1968). Hannah Arendt, ed. *The Work of Art in the Age of Mechanical Reproduction*, Illuminations. London: Fontana: 214–218.

Berlin, Isaiah (2013). *The Crooked Timber of Humanity*, 2nd ed. Henry Hardy ed. Princeton University Press.

Bloom P. & Chatterji (2009). Scaling Social Entrepreneurial Impact, In: *California Management Review*, Spring 2009.

Cunningham, S. (2009). Trojan horse or Rorschach blot? Creative industries discourse around the world. In: *International Journal of cultural policy*, 15(4), 375-386.

Dacin, P. A., Dacin, M. T., & Matear, M. (2010). Social entrepreneurship: why we dont need a new theory and how we move forward from here. In: *The academy of management perspectives*, 24(3), 37-57.

Dees, G. (2008). Philanthropy and Enterprise: Harnessing the Power of Business and Social Entrepreneurship for Development, In: *Global Development 2.0*: Can Philanthropists, the Public, and the Poor Make Poverty History?, edited by Lael Brainard and Derek Chollet, Brookings Institution Press, 2008 Reprinted in Innovations, vol. 3, no. 3, Summer 2008: 119-132.

Dees, G. & Anderson (2003). For-Profit Social Ventures, In: *International Journal of Entrepreneurship Education*, vol. 2, 2003, special issue on Social Entrepreneurship.

Ghemawat, P. (2011). *World 3.0: Global Prosperity and How to Achieve It.* Cambridge: Harvard Business Review Press.

Hausmann, A. (2010). German Artists Between Bohemian Idealism and Entrepreneurial Dynamics: Reflections on Cultural Entrepreneurship and the Need for Start-Up Management. In: *International Journal of Arts Management*, 17-29.

Heidegger, Martin (2008). *Basic Writings, On the Origin of the Work of Art.* 1st Harper Perennial Modern Thought Edition., ed. David Farrell Krell. New York: HarperCollins: 143-212.

Henry, C. (Ed.). (2007). *Entrepreneurship in the creative industries: An international perspective*. Edward Elgar Publishing.

Lounsbury, M., & Glynn, M. A. (2001). Cultural entrepreneurship: Stories, legitimacy, and the acquisition of resources. In: *Strategic management journal*, 22(6-7), 545-564.

THEORY

Montgomery, D. and C. Ramus (2003). *Corporate Social Responsibility Reputation Effects on MBA Job Choice*. Stanford GSB Working Paper No. 1805.

Montoya, M. and S. Saba, J. Gilroy, E. Reed, J. Evans, T. Borror (2012). *An institutional analysis of the Santa Fe International Folk Art Market*. Anderson School of Management, University of New Mexico.

Mulcahy, K. V. (2003). Entrepreneurship or cultural Darwinism? Privatization and American cultural patronage. In: *The Journal of Arts Management, Law, and Society*, 33(3), 165-184.

Peng, M.W. (2001). The Resource-based view and International Business. In: *Journal of Management* 27(6): 803-829.

Pratt, A. C. (2004). The Cultural Economy A Call for Spatialized Production of CulturePerspectives. In: *International journal of cultural studies*, 7(1), 117-128.

Rae, D. (2005). Entrepreneurial learning: a narrative-based conceptual model. In: *Journal of small business and enterprise development,* 12(3), 323-335.

Rae, D. (2004). Entrepreneurial learning: a practical model from the creative industries. In: *Education+ training,* 46(8/9), 492-500.

Raffo, C., Lovatt, A., Banks, M., & OConnor, J. (2000). Teaching and learning entrepreneurship for micro and small businesses in the cultural industries sector. In: *Education+ Training*, 42(6), 356-365.

Saul, J. (2012). Flex to Flux Takeaways from the 2012 Skoll World Forum. In: *Stanford Social Innovation Review*. April 9, 2012. Retrieved from: http://www.ssireview.org/blog/entry/flux_to_flex_takeaways_from_the_2012_skoll_world_forum

Steyaert, C., & Hjorth, D. (2003). Creative movements of entrepreneurship. In: *New Movements in Entrepreneurship*, 3-19.

Tepper, S. J. (2002). Creative assets and the changing economy. In: *The Journal of Arts Management, Law, and Society*, 32(2), 159-168.

Wry, T., Lounsbury, M., & Glynn, M. A. (2011). Legitimating nascent collective identities: Coordinating cultural entrepreneurship. In: *Organization Science*, 22(2), 449-463.

THEORY

Erin Bass
Ivana Milosevic
Dale Eesley

EXAMINING AND RECONCILING IDENTITY ISSUES AMONG ARTIST-ENTREPRENEURS

Abstract

In business schools, research and pedagogy in entrepreneurship focus on new venture creation and management. Developing individuals to think like an entrepreneur and adopt an *'entrepreneurial identity'* enables them to more effectively build and grow businesses and enjoy financial success. However, the assumption that all entrepreneurs desire financial success may not hold across non-business entrepreneurs. For example, for artists, sacrificing for arts' sake - or enjoying artistic success at the hands of financial success - is a constant struggle. This *'artist identity'* stands in stark contrast to the *'entrepreneurial identity'*. Artists create to satisfy an artistic need, rather than a market opportunity. Given the continuing decay of artistic endeavours due to the lack of financial support, we ask: can these identities be reconciled so that the artist can be a successful entrepreneur?

To explore this question, we turn to identity theory for insight into the differences in identities of entrepreneurs and artists. Building on findings from identity theory and entrepreneurship pedagogy research, we develop a framework for an identity reconciliation process that artist-entrepreneurs experience. For researchers, this framework suggests artist-entrepreneurs are a unique form of entrepreneur, and that identity plays a central role in the artist's creative and financial success. For pedagogues, this framework unveils that designing curricula around the theoretical roots and approaches of identity research can help these individuals grapple with identity-issues to more successfully breed entrepreneurship among artists.

THEORY

Examining and Reconciling Identity Issues among Artist-Entrepreneurs

Entrepreneurs do much more for society than simply creating jobs and contributing to economic development. Entrepreneurs play a vital role in communities by creating unique and innovative outputs, developing and funding social programs, and becoming an institution with which employees, consumers, and community members can identify (Audretsch, 2005; Tracy, 2005). Similarly, artists contribute to society by creating artwork that can foster social inclusion, improve education and health, prevent crime, and increase the quality of life for those that live in the communities touched by the artist and their work (Stuckey & Nobel, 2010; Swan, 2013; U.S. Department of Justice, 2000). Thus, both entrepreneurs and artists produce something novel and unique that contributes to the development of society. Yet, they operate in very different social segments with very little interaction. Indeed, artistic endeavours are often only ancillary to entrepreneurs who may choose to support them for social or personal reasons. Further, financial betterment and market opportunities are often seen as detrimental to art (Griff, 1960). Given both entrepreneurs' and artists' importance to the development of communities, it seems that bringing together these two groups of individuals may be critical. Here, we propose that this may occur through an identity reconciliation process through which artists become artist-entrepreneurs. We define artist-entrepreneurs as those individuals that achieve artistic and financial success by creating their own business of selling their artwork.

Burke (2004, p. 5) defines identity as *'the sets of meanings people hold for themselves that define what it means to be who they are as persons, as role occupants, and as group members.'* Individuals learn what these meanings are and the categories with which they are associated through interactions with others as well as through the work they perform, such as being an entrepreneur or being an artist (Burke, 2004). Being an entrepreneur is a core facet of the individual's identity and is directly linked to the enterprise's (and, relatedly, the entrepreneur's) financial success (Fauchart & Gruber, 2011; Navis & Glynn, 2011). Similarly, the artist's identity dictates who they are and what they do, and is the driver of creative success and artistic satisfaction (Stohs, 1991). In the words of influential American painter, Jackson Pollock, *'Painting is self-discovery. Every good artist paints what he is.'*

To this end, both artists and entrepreneurs engage in creative construction—innovating and driving change (Agarwal, Audretsch, & Sarkar, 2007; Duchamp, 1975; Ketchen, Ireland, & Snow, 2007; Mark, 2003). They do so to develop and protect distinctiveness from other artists or other entrepreneurial firms (Mark, 2003; Van de Ven, Sapienza, & Villanueva, 2007). Thus, their work is a visual brand they create, reflecting of who they are and what they do (Fauchart & Gruber, 2011; Schroeder, 2005). Despite these similarities, differences in what drive satisfaction between artist's and entrepreneur's identities create a chasm between them. The entrepreneur identity seeks creation, innovation, and change for financial success to support organizational viability and continued operations. The artist identity also seeks creation, innovation, and change. However, the purpose is creative success, or the assemblage of *'novel combinations or rearrangements of ideas, technologies, and processes'* (Fleming, Mingo, & Chen, 2002, p. 447), which generates intrinsic satisfaction for the artist. In other words, the work itself is the ultimate reason for the artist's efforts—either because of its contribution to the arts community or due to the level of satisfaction the artist experiences while creating it.

As a consequence of these differences, artist-entrepreneurs face a conflict in identity not experienced by other entrepreneurs. On one hand, they ought to create work to satisfy a market demand and thus gain financial success (driven by their entrepreneur identity). On the other, they work to fulfil their artistic drive, thus gaining creative success (driven by their artist identity). The purpose of this article is to explicate the dynamics of the artist-entrepreneur identity—or coexistence of opposing entrepreneur and artist identities—and why these identities might be in conflict.

Theoretical Context
Identity Theory
Identity theory is rooted in the works of Mead (1934) and Cooley (1902), who explained how social structure can influence self, and reciprocally, how self then affects social behaviours. Society, through an identity theory lens, represents *'a mosaic of relatively durable patterned interactions and relationships, differentiated yet organized, embedded in an array of groups, organizations, communities, and institutions and intersected*

by crosscutting boundaries of class, ethnicity, age, gender, religion and other variables' (Stryker & Burke, 2000, p. 285). Accordingly, individuals hold multiple identities to answer these complexities of society.

To understand how identity impacts one's tendencies and behaviours, (1) individuals hold multiple identities based on who they are as an individual (*person identity*) and what they do (*role identity*), and (2) these identities differ in terms of both their *salience* and the individual's *commitment* to them. Identities that are more salient will form a base for action in diverse situations (Stryker, 1987). According to Burke (2004), the most salient identity is a person identity: it distinguishes one as a unique, identifiable individual who possesses certain characteristics and qualities that other individuals use to verify their own identities. Person identity is at least partially enacted regardless of the context expectations (Stryker & Burke, 2000). Whereas person identity is relatively stable and not dependent on context, role identities are context-specific. An individual holds multiple role identities that are triggered through interactions with others and groups. This simultaneous existence of person and role identities provides some independence of behaviour from immediate contextual demands. This accounts, at least partially, for creativity and unpredictability of human behaviour (Stryker & Serpe, 1994).

Identity commitment is a process through which individuals establish and maintain their different identities (Burke & Reitzes, 1981). More specifically, commitment is represented by the extent to which an individual maintains relationships with others by thinking, acting, and reacting in ways that are in line with others' expectations of that individual (Stryker & Statham, 1985). The salience of the identity is a function of the individual's commitment to it—as the identity is reinforced through interaction with significant others, commitment to that identity increases, hence increasing its salience.

THEORY

Thus, *'an identity is like a compass helping [individuals] steer a course of interaction in a sea of social meaning'* (Burke & Reitzes, 1981, p. 91). Identifying as an artist or an entrepreneur not only indicates identity to others, but it also solidifies the identity for the individual by guiding how they live. As indicated by, Niklas Zennstrom, co-founder of Skype, *'If you want to be an entrepreneur, it's not a job, it's a lifestyle. It defines you.'* Similarly, Elbert Hubbard, an artist of the Arts and Crafts Movement, stated, *'Art is not a thing, it is a way.'*

The Entrepreneur Identity vs. the Artist Identity

Within business schools, research and pedagogy in entrepreneurship focus on new venture creation, growth, and survival (Gartner, 1985; Gilbert, McDougall, & Audretsch, 2006; Shepherd, Douglas, & Shanley, 2000; Timmons, 1999). Entrepreneurs are trained to adopt or develop three main attributes: innovativeness, opportunity recognition, and propensity to take risks (Baumol, 1968; Falck, Heblich, & Luedemann, 2012). For example, Falck and colleagues (2012, p. 42) argue that entrepreneurship courses in business schools generally provide students with experiences such as *'[writing] business plans, [meeting] successful entrepreneurs who tell their powerful and attractive success stories, and also often [receiving] individual level technical advice and assistance in starting up a business.'* These experiences are important for developing entrepreneurs because through it they learn *'who they can be'*, construct stories of *'who they want to be'* and work towards enacting their storied identity. In this sense, *'learning is becoming"* (Rae, 2000, p. 151). By developing individuals to think like an entrepreneur and adopt an *'entrepreneur identity'*, they can more effectively build and grow businesses with the goal of financial success.

Similar to entrepreneurs, an artist's work is a reflection of self (Bain, 2005). For artists, identity stems not only from the work they create, but also from their drive to oppose conformity and challenge societal assumptions (Sternberg, 1999; Stohs, 1990). Artistic success implies work that is *'unusually distinctive, satisfying, and/or productive in opening new ground'* (Caves, 2000, p. 202) and is independent of financial success (Delmestri, Montanari, & Usai, 2005). It is possible, then, for artists to achieve artistic success without financial success. Given this, a salient identity that most artists experience at one time during their careers is that of a *'starving artist'* (Filer, 1986). Part of being an artist means sacrificing for art's sake, or enjoying creative success without experiencing financial success (Stohs, 1991). In fact, artists that focus less on financial success may in fact be more artistically satisfied with their career (Stohs, 1990, 1991). For artists, the importance of embracing the identity as an artist—which means being *'creative, varied, and useful'* (Mishler, 1992, p. 22) is paramount and outweighs the financial independence or even societal recognition for their work (Griff, 1960).

The Emergence of Identity Conflict

Identity conflict emerges (1) when there is a mismatch between situational and identity meanings; or (2) when multiple salient identities are invoked at the same time. First, the conflict may emerge due to the inability to verify an identity in a particular context (Burke & Stets, 1999; Stryker & Burke, 2000). Certain contexts will enable salient identity verification, while others will severely limit or disallow verification. This constrains and/or eliminates behaviours associated with the salient identity. In the situation in which verification of the highly salient identity persistently fails, individuals may resist further negotiation efforts, reject identities others are seeking to impose on them, and leave the situation (Cast, 2003). In other words, *'when choice is possible, people choose roles and groups that provide opportunities to verify their person identity'* (Burke, 2006, p. 11).

Second, the conflict may also occur when meanings contained in two identities are opposing but activated together at the same time, leading to an inability for both to be verified (Burke, 2004). The artist identity, focused on artistic success, rivals the entrepreneur identity, which seeks financial success. Can these identities be reconciled so that the artist can be a successful entrepreneur, without sacrificing either identity? Identity theory suggests that in the situation where identities are not highly salient, identity standards will shift toward a compromise so the conflict can be removed (Burke, 2004). However, we have limited insight into how the conflict is reconciled when conflicted identities are high in salience. In the following paragraphs, we provide a theory-driven framework for identity reconciliation in the context of artist-entrepreneurs. In doing so, we seek to provide insight into the dynamics of reconciliation and explicate theoretical and pedagogical implications.

A Framework for Reconciling Identities
in Artist-Entrepreneurs

Identity is a fluid dynamic (Burke, 2006) due to the continuous negotiation of meanings that individuals engage in as they enter different contexts and assume new roles. Burke (2006, p. 93) argues that identities *are always changing (though slowly) in response to the exigencies of the situation. Insofar as an identity cannot change the situation (and the meaning contained therein), it adapts slowly, gaining control where it can, and adapting where it must.'* We build on this insight to argue that artist-entrepreneurs endure a process of identity reconciliation that occurs as they endeavour to make sense of the new context (i.e., assume an entrepreneurial identity). This process provides the opportunity for identity becoming (Rae, 2000) in which their artistic and entrepreneur identities are integrated as exemplified through the work that they do. We suggest that artist-entrepreneurs experience at least three stages in the identity reconciliation process: *detachment*, wherein the artistic and entrepreneur identities are kept separate; *fusion*, where the artistic and entrepreneur identities conjoin; and *integration*, where the artistic and entrepreneur identities merge to shape the person identity of the artist-entrepreneur.

Detachment

In the detachment stage of the process, the artist keeps two identities separate and enacts each one in the context in which it will be verified. In one context, the individual creates art for artistic success (thus enacting and verifying the artistic identity) without generating much if any sales from it. In other words, the artist identity enables the individual to create artistically successful work regardless of its potential to generate financial returns. These artistically valuable pieces of art allow the individual to further develop their common theme or style (Mark, 2003). At the same time, however, the artist also creates pieces solely to sell to others (thus enacting and verifying the entrepreneurial identity). This can be contract work (for individuals, organizations, or institutions) or art that has commercial appeal (Griff, 1960). The financially valuable art generates financial success for this artist. However, the artist does not derive artistic satisfaction from these creations.

This implies that the artist-entrepreneur must be ambidextrous in their ability to detach their activities and maintain two opposing, yet equally salient, identities. However, the artist-entrepreneur that detaches their artist identity from their entrepreneur identity will never be associated with the work they gain artistic success from, but only with the work they sell for financial success. The consequence is that artist-entrepreneurs maintain two salient, yet detached, identities connected to the two separate activities in which they engage, thus reaching limited development as an artist or an entrepreneur (Burke, 2004; Cast, 2003; Stryker & Burke, 2000). In this sense, the artist's work never secures full artistic value (because the artist pursues and sells work that they feel less artistic satisfaction from), nor does it secure full financial value (because the artist still creates work that they gain artistic satisfaction from, but there is no market for).

Fusion

A lack of congruity between the differing identities (i.e., entrepreneur identity and artist identity), forms a state of tension that individuals look to resolve by altering the conflicting meanings and searching for alternate contexts that will allow them to fuse two identities (Burke & Reitzes, 1981). In doing so, the artist searches for market

THEORY

opportunities for which their artistic work fits. The artist can capitalize on these market opportunities (Caves, 2000; Griff, 1960) to concurrently generate artistic and financial success. The artist-entrepreneur begins to recognize how the two identities can coalesce.

Creating art that simultaneously generates artistic and financial success verifies the emergent identity of the artist-entrepreneur. The artist creates artistic success through the work they create, but also gains credibility as an entrepreneur by exploiting a market opportunity specific to their work and subsequently generating financial success as well. However, that market opportunity for the artist's work is restrictive (Griff, 1960)—it may be small or temporary. As a consequence, the tension that the individual experiences is at least partially fuelled by differing meanings, requiring the identities to negotiate when financial success supports (and when it corrupts) artistic success (Burke, 2006). Thus, similar to the identity conflict occurring in detachment, in this instance, the artist-entrepreneur still creates art solely for artistic success, and other art for financial success. The difference lies in the artist-entrepreneur's additional creation of art that fuses both artist and entrepreneur identities, creating artistic and financial success simultaneously. Artist-entrepreneurs that fuse their artist and entrepreneur identities gain market recognition not from the art they create for artistic success, but rather the art they sell for financial success.

Integration

The final stage in the identity reconciliation process entails verification of the artist-entrepreneur identity and full integration of meanings. This verification began in fusion, where individuals occasionally searched for opportunities to create pieces of art that enable them to achieve both financial and artistic success. Over time, these opportunities created a context in which the fused identity is repeatedly verified (Burke & Stets, 1999; Cast, 2003). As their identity is verified and meanings are accepted, the new identity—identity of artist-entrepreneur—is stabilized (Mcfarland & Pals, 2005). The conflict between the two identities is removed as the artist-entrepreneur's identity becomes legitimized by society (Griff, 1960) and the artist engages in work that has potential to be sold to the market but generates artistic value as well.

Discussion

Using existing literature on artist-entrepreneurs and identity theory, we examine how artist-entrepreneurs might reconcile two competing identities of artist and entrepreneur. The framework identifies a process of identity reconciliation in which the artist-entrepreneur moves from detachment of identities, to fusion, to integration. In the first stage of the process—detachment—the artist-entrepreneur keeps their artist and entrepreneur identities separate. This results in the artist separating the work that creates artistic success from that which generates financial success. In the second stage of the process—fusion—the artist-entrepreneur identifies ways to fuse the artist and entrepreneur identities. They still separate the work that generates artistic success from that which creates financial success, but also search for market opportunities to sell some of their artwork. In the final stage of the process—integration—the artist-entrepreneur fully integrates their artistic and entrepreneurial work to sell art that has both financial and artistic value without any separation between the two.

Theoretical Utility of this Research

This framework suggests artist-entrepreneurs are a unique form of entrepreneur because they do not just search for market opportunities—they also search for artistic actualization. We suggest that identity plays a central role in guiding the work that the individual pursues—whether it be of artistic or financial value. To this end, our framework contributes to the existing entrepreneurship literature that suggests that the entrepreneur's identity is a reflection of who they are and what they do (Navis & Glynn, 2011). More specifically, we show that artist-entrepreneurs that detach their artist identities from their entrepreneur identities (who they are) will never be associated with the work they gain artistic success from, but only with the work they sell for financial success (what they do). The artist-entrepreneurs that fuse their artist and entrepreneur identities (who they are) are associated with some of the art they sell for financial support and success (what they do). The artist-entrepreneurs that integrate their artist and entrepreneur identities (who they are) are associated with work that gives them artistic satisfaction, and this work also creates financial success (what they do). As a consequence, our framework illustrates that additional theoretical and empirical research is needed to understand the process of identity reconciliation in this context.

Pedagogical Utility of this Research

This framework suggests that putting artists in traditional business entrepreneurship courses may not be the most effective way to create and develop artist-entrepreneurs. This is because many of these courses focus on exploiting market opportunities to satisfy demand (Timmons, 1999). However, the product that artists create—art— is not made to exploit a market opportunity. Oftentimes, it is made to intrinsically satisfy the artist—translating thoughts, experiences, or emotions into something tangible (Griff, 1960). Thus, the artist struggles with identifying how to create art with market, rather than artistic, value.

Instead, a curriculum specific to artist-entrepreneurs is needed—one that addresses the potential conflicts between the artist and entrepreneur identities and that allows artist-entrepreneurs to reconcile the two identities and achieve sustainable financial and artistic success. Our framework illustrates that going through the identity reconciliation process allows artist-entrepreneurs to achieve a better understanding of how their identity shapes the work they create, and the process of detaching, fusing, and integrating their artist and entrepreneur identities. Students should be exposed to varying contexts in order to discover opportunities for new identity verification.

An Exercise for Discovery and Identity Verification

Identity is discovered through self-reflection and learning about oneself (Stryker & Burke, 2000). As a consequence, in order for students to learn how to reconcile their different identities, they must engage in discovery and self-reflection first. Here, we offer a three stage project encompassing both in- and out-of-class activities that help students learn about their person identity and discover different role identities through interaction with others. The three stages encompass (1) identity discovery; (2) understanding alternative identity claims and how they may exist in tension with identity; and (3) reflection on the tension and integration of the two identities.

THEORY

THEORY

In the first stage, students are required to complete an identity chart. The chart allows them to discover their person and role identities by providing words to describe who they are and how others see them (person identity) and words describing what they do and how they define success (role identity). Based on this description they should identify as either an artist or a business person/entrepreneur.

In the second stage, students are required to interview a person (outside of the class) that identifies with the opposite category that they selected (e.g., if the student identifies more with the business person/entrepreneur category, they must select an artist to interview). The interview provides insight required to complete an identity chart for the interviewee, as well as learn about the opposing identity claims. The student conducts an interview with this person seeking discovery of their person identity (e.g., How would you describe who you are? How would others describe who you are?) and their role identity (e.g., How do you describe what you do? How do you define success?). The student also asks the interviewee a series of questions about the knowledge they've gained in their profession (What do you attribute your success to? What obstacles have you overcome? Tell me about a time or event that you believe had an impact on your career.). After the interview, the student completes an identity chart for the individual they interviewed.

In the third stage of the project, the student is required to integrate the information they collected about themselves and the interviewee, and reflect on the complete experience. The student compares and contrasts their identity chart from the interviewee's noting similarities and differences. The student also reflects on what they learned from the interviewee, and how they might utilize that information to further their own career, despite the fact that the student and the interviewee differ in the categories with which they identified (i.e., artist vs. business person/entrepreneur).

A classroom experience, such as the project described above, helps students to discover more about their own identity but also explore the identity of a person that is seemingly different than themselves. In doing so, students become aware of how identity plays into career choices and how success is defined. Further, it allows students, through comparing and contrasting with a dissimilar other, to learn from the insights of a person with an ostensibly different identity. As a point of departure, students are equipped to understand that a person's own career can be positively influenced by the integration, rather than conflict, of seemingly different identities.

Artist-entrepreneurs are a unique part of today's society—contributing to both economic and social value creation. However, artist-entrepreneurs also deal with a unique problem that other entrepreneurs do not likely experience—that of identity conflict. The suggested framework puts forth a process of identity reconciliation in which individuals reconcile the artist and entrepreneur identities by detaching, fusing, or integrating them. Once fully reconciled, the two identities form a whole identity of an artist-entrepreneur, with the purpose of creating art that generates both artistic and financial success simultaneously.

About the Authors

*Dr A. Erin Bass is
an Assistant Professor of
Management at
the University of Nebraska
Omaha. Her teaching and
research centre on strategy,
entrepreneurship, and ethics,
focusing on firm innovation,
corporate governance,
and social entrepreneurship.
She is particularly interested
in the emergence of entrepreneurship in unlikely contexts
- ranging from emerging markets to arts communities.
She has experience in
the energy and non-profit
sectors.*

—

andreaerinbass@gmail.com

*Dr Ivana Milosevic is
Assistant Professor at
the Department of
Management at the
University of Wisconsin-
Oshkosh. Her research
interests include identity
theory and exploration of
learning processes in
complex organizations.
She is particularly
interested in doing ethnographic research to
understand organizations
as complex adaptive systems,
with a focus on how
practices are enabled or
restricted through formal
and informal structures.*

ivana.a.milosevic@gmail.com

References

Agarwal, R., Audretsch, D., & Sarkar, M. B. (2007). The process of creative construction: knowledge spillovers, entrepreneurship, and economic growth. In: *Strategic Entrepreneurship Journal, 1*(3-4), 263–286.

Audretsch, D. (2005). *The entrepreneurial society*. Oxford, UK: Oxford University Press.

Bain, A. (2005). Constructing an artistic identity. In: *Work, Employment & Society, 19*(1), 25–46.

Baumol, W. J. (1968). Entrepreneurship in economic theory. In: *The American Economic Review, 58*(2), 64–71.

Burke, P. J. (2004). Identities and social structure: The 2003 Cooley-Mead Award address. In: *Social Psychology Quarterly, 67*(1), 5-15.

Burke, P. J. (2006). Identity change. In: *Social Psychology, 69*(1), 81–96.

Burke, P. J., & Reitzes, D. C. (1981). The link between identity and role perfor-mance. In: *Social Psychology Quarterly, 44*(2), 83-92.

Burke, P. J., & Stets, J. E. (1999). Trust and commitment through self-verification. In: *Social Psychology Quarterly, 62*(4) 347-366.

Cast, A. D. (2003). Identities and behaviour. In P. J. Burke, T. J. Owens, R. T. Serpe, & P. A. Thoits (Eds.), In: *Advances in Identity Theory and Research* (pp. 41–53). Boston, MA: Springer.

Caves, R. (2000). *Creative industries: Contracts between art and commerce.* Cambridge, MA: Harvard University Press.

Cooley, C. H. (1902). *Human nature and the social order.* New York: C. Scribner's sons.

Delmestri, G., Montanari, F., & Usai, A. (2005). Reputation and strength of ties in predicting commercial success and artistic merit of independents in the Italian feature film industry. In: *Journal of Management Studies, 25*(5), 975-1002.

Duchamp, M. (1975). The creative act. In M. Sanouillet & E. Peterson (Eds.), *The essential writings of marcel duchamp.* London: Thames and Hudson.

Falck, O., Heblich, S., & Luedemann, E. (2012). Identity and entrepreneur-ship: Do school peers shape entrepreneurial intentions? In: *Small Business Economics, 39*(1), 39–59.

Fauchart, E., & Gruber, M. (2011). Darwinians, communitarians, and mis-sionaries: The role of founder identity in entrepreneurship. In: *Academy of Management Journal, 54*(5), 935–957.

Filer, R. K. (1986). The 'starving artist'--myth or reality? Earnings of artists in the United States. In: *Journal of Political Economy, 94*(1) 56-75.

Fleming, L., Mingo, S., & Chen, D. (2002). Collaborative brokerage, generative creativity, and creative success. In: *Administrative Science Quarterly, 52,* 443–475.

Gartner, W. B. (1985). A conceptual framework for describing the phenomenon of new venture creation. In: *Academy of Management Review, 10*(4), 696–706.

THEORY

Gilbert, B. A., McDougall, P. P., & Audretsch, D. B. (2006). New venture growth: A review and extension. In: *Journal of Management, 34*, 926-950.

Griff, M. (1960). The commercial artist: A study in changing and consistent identities. In M. R. Stein, A. J. Vidich, & D. M. White (Eds.), In: *Identity and anxiety*. Glencoe, IL: Free Press.

Ketchen, D. J., Ireland, R. D., & Snow, C. C. (2007). Strategic entrepreneurship, collaborative innovation, and wealth creation. In: *Strategic Entrepreneurship Journal, 1*(3-4), 371–385.

Mark, N. P. (2003). Culture and competition: Homophily and distancing explanations for cultural niches. In: *American Sociological Review, 68*(3), 319-345.

Mcfarland, D., & Pals, H. (2005). Motives and contexts of identity change: A case for network effects. In: *Social Psychology Quarterly, 68*(4), 289–315.

Mead, G. H. (1934). *Mind, self and society*. Chicago: Chicago University Press.

Mishler, E. G. (1992). Work, identity, and narrative: An artist-craftsman's story. In: G. C. Rosenwald & R. L. Ochberg (Eds.), *Storied lives*. New Haven: Yale University Press.

Navis, C., & Glynn, M. A. (2011). Legitimate distinctiveness and the entrepreneurial identity: Influence on investor judgments of new venture plausibility. In: *Academy of Management Review, 36*(3), 479–499.

Rae, D. (2000). Understanding entrepreneurial learning: a question of how? In: *International Journal of Entrepreneurial Behaviour & Research, 6*(3), 145–159.

Schroeder, J. E. (2005). The artist and the brand. In: *European Journal of Marketing, 39*(11/12), 1291–1305.

Shepherd, D. A., Douglas, E. J., & Shanley, M. (2000). New venture survival. In: *Journal of Business Venturing, 15*(5-6), 393–410.

Sternberg, R. J. (1999). The influence of personality on artistic and scientific creativity. In: *Handbook of creativity*. Cambridge: Cambridge University Press.

Stohs, J. M. (1990). Young adult predictors and midlife outcomes of male fine art careers. In: *Career Development Quarterly, 38*(3), 213-229.

Stohs, J. M. (1991). Young adult predictors and midlife outcomes of 'starving artists' careers: A longitudinal study of male fine artists. In: *The Journal of Creative Behaviour, 25*(2), 92–105.

Stryker, S., & Burke, P. J. (2000). The past, present, and future of an identity theory. In: *Journal of Social Psychology Quarterly, 53*(4), 284–297.

Stryker, S., & Serpe, R. T. (1994). Identity salience and psychological centrality: Equivalent, overlapping, or complementary concepts? In: *Social Psychology Quarterly 51*(1), 16-35.

Stryker, S., & Statham, A. (1985). Symbolic interaction and role theory. In G. Lindszey & E. Aronson (Eds.), In: *Handbook of social psychology*. New York: Random House.

Dr Dale T. Eesley is the Director of the Centre for Innovation, Entrepreneurship, and Franchising (CIEF), the John Morgan Community Chair in Entrepreneurship and an Associate Professor of Entrepreneurship and Strategy at the University of Nebraska Omaha.
He has been teaching entrepreneurship and working with start-ups and small businesses for over 15 years. His courses focus on Entrepreneurship, Innovation, Entrepreneurial Finance, and Corporate Strategy.
—
deesley@unomaha.edu

THEORY

Stuckey, H. L., & Nobel, J. (2010). The connection between art, healing, and public health: a review of current literature. In: *American Journal of Public Health*, *100*(2), 254–63.

Swan, P. (2013). Promoting social inclusion through community arts. In: *Mental Health and Social Inclusion*, *17*(1), 19–26.

Timmons, J. (1999). *New venture creation: Entrepreneurship for the 21st century*, (5th ed.). Boston, MA: Irwin/McGraw-Hill.

Tracy, B. (2005, June). The role of the entrepreneur. *Entrepreneur*. Retrieved from: http://www.entrepreneur.com/article/78478

U.S. Department of Justice. (2000). *Arts and performances for prevention. Youth in Action*. Washington, DC. Retrieved from: https://www.ncjrs.gov/pdffiles1/ojjdp/178927.pdf

Van de Ven, A. H., Sapienza, H. J., & Villanueva, J. (2007). Entrepreneurial pursuits of self- and collective interests. In: *Strategic Entrepreneurship Journal*, *1*(3-4), 353–370.

THEORY

Rene Kooyman
Ruben Jacobs

THE ENTREPRENEURIAL ANT
RE-THINKING ART MANAGEMENT EDUCATION

THEORY

Abstract

For the past decade the sector of Cultural and Creative Industries (CCIs) has gained a growing interest, both within the political arena and amongst policy developers. Within the sector we can identify two different positions. On the one hand find Art Managers, holding managerial responsibilities within cultural and art organizations. In this article we concentrate on a second profile; the Cultural and Creative Entrepreneur. The largest part of the Cultural and Creative Industries consists of very small, independent entrepreneurial initiatives. This Cultural Ant works within a continuous, fast changing environment, characterized by uncertainty. We challenge the educational dilemma's facing the support of these small-scale entrepreneurs.

Introduction

In 2000 the German sociologist Ulrich Beck announced the '*end of the employee society*' in his book *The future of work and democracy*. According to Beck the future of work no longer finds itself in employed labour alone, but is increasingly being formed into new descriptions, constructions and models (Beck, 2000). Now, fifteen years later a (relatively) new character, the '*entrepreneurial individual*', found its way to the top of the modern workforce pyramid. Especially in Cultural and Creative industries this multi-skilled, flexible and psychologically resilient is what the current entrepreneurial creative culture demands (Ellmeier, 2010). The strong trend in the recent years, towards a more entrepreneurial-minded European Welfare-state labour market, has undoubtedly its implications for arts management education and training. The main question rises; how does an art '*management*' school handle this modern entrepreneurial dimension? How do we prepare students for this shift in the creative labour market?

Managers and Cultural Entrepreneurs

For the past decade the sector of Cultural and Creative Industries (CCIs) has gained a growing interest, both within the political arena and amongst policy developers. The UNCTAD Creative Economy Report proved that the cultural and creative sectors are a significant driver of growth and jobs in Europe (Dos Santos Duisenberg, 2010). In addition they offer a key source of creativity and innovation, as well as contributing significantly to social cohesion and well-being. In the follow-up of the economic success, a lot of statistical data supported the growing interest of policy-makers in culture and its role in society, the economy and the cohesiveness of Europe (European Commission, 2010). The Educational Institutions have followed suit. Various universities have initiated professional educational curricula, both at a Bachelors and Masters Level.

Often the CCIs are treated as one homogenous sector. Within the CCIs however, one can identify different types of organizations, with different positions included. On the on hand we find institutionalized art- and cultural organizations like museums, organizations in the performing arts (theatre, dance and music), event organizations and production houses, etc. Within these formal organizational structure one identifies '*arts managers*': people officially appointed at a specific post within a formalized organizational structure. They operate within hierarchical structures, hold explicit responsibilities, comparable to '*regular*' institutions; hiring and firing personnel, steering the different departments, deciding about policy and strategy issues, etc.

At the other end of the spectrum we find the *entrepreneurs*; those that look for new products, new opportunities and markets, initiating things that '*have not been there before*'. Often these – mostly small scale – entrepreneurs operate from a local level, creating multiple networks in order to find a sustainable existence. In this article we will concentrate on these Cultural and Creative Entrepreneurs.

The Entrepreneurial Dimension
When discussing the entrepreneurial dimension of the Cultural and Creative Industries (CCIs), one can identify two general positions. Either one argues that the sector is like any other business, or one can stress the specific characteristics of the Creative sector (Kooyman, 2009). The entrepreneurs in the Creative Industries share a number of common characteristics with their colleagues in other sectors. Seen from an occupational perspective creative entrepreneurs own and manage one's own business enterprise. They can be categorized as '*business owners*'; they create value. In essence, the creative entrepreneur is a creator of economic value (Sternberg & Wennekers, 2005, April, p. 193).

Moreover, they are engaged in innovative practices, and/or assuming entrepreneurial risk - i.e. pursuing new untapped markets, developing product innovations; recognizing and seizing economic opportunity, or the pursuit of change, etc. (Roberts and Woods, 2005). In accordance with Joseph Schumpeter a number of embody entrepreneurial behaviour: developing new and innovative products, proposing new forms of organization, exploring new markets, introducing new production methods, searching for new sources of supplies and materials (Schumpeter, 1975).

Entrepreneurs in general share the willingness to assume risks in the face of uncertainty. For example, risks such as a possible loss of business capital or the personal financial security, risk associated with the uncertain outcome of an entrepreneurial undertaking (Knight, 1921). As other entrepreneurs they share the change perspective. As Peter Drucker states: '*Entrepreneurs see change as the norm and as healthy*'. They do not have to bring about the change themselves. But, and this defines the entrepreneur and entrepreneurship — the entrepreneur always searches for change, responds to it and exploits it as an opportunity (Drucker, 1985, p.28). In general entrepreneurs are involved in networks of multiple and changing clients, competitors, colleagues, etc. In accordance with the perspective of Gartner (1988) entrepreneurship share the activity to create organizations. '*What differentiates entrepreneurs from non-entrepreneurs is that entrepreneurs create organizations, while non-entrepreneurs do not*' (Gartner, 1988, p.11). Entrepreneurs are actively involved in the search for constituents, contracts, projects, location, etc.

THEORY

The specific Characteristics of the Creative Industry

In general the Creative Industries share the common entrepreneurial characteristics mentioned above. Yet, a number of arguments can be found in order to express the specific characteristics of the Creative Industries. Characteristics that underpin the need for specific attention for the creative entrepreneur. What are characteristics of the creative industries that set them apart from standard concepts of an industry?

Differences in the Labour Market

The cultural fabric of the Creative Industries is complex and thrives on numerous small initiatives. In 2001 a first European report was published covering the topic *'Exploitation and development of the job potential in the cultural sector'*. It stresses the importance of the relationship between the creative sector and the digital culture; Telecommunication, Internet, Multimedia, E-commerce, Software and Security (TIMES). The study points both at the growing attention for the cultural sector, and stresses the fact that *'The cultural sector is characterized by a high share of freelancers and very small companies. A new type of employer is emerging in the form of the 'entrepreneurial individual' or 'entrepreneurial cultural worker', who no longer fits into previously typical patterns of full-time professions.'*

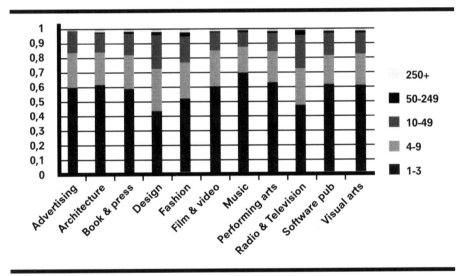

Figure 1 Distribution of Enterprise among Industries per size class (Eurokleis 2009)

The majority of the Creative Industries consists of micro-enterprises, some 70 to 80 % is smaller than 10 persons. Even further, some 58 % operate on a semi-individual basis, or share their activities with no more than one other person. As a consequence most enterprises are classified by one or two entrepreneurs. We might have to position them as a separate category, in order to differentiate them from the micro-enterprises; the very small micros, the *'nano-enterprises'*.

These very small micro-enterprises do not follow the standard entrepreneurial habits. Creators are far more likely to hold non-conventional forms of employment – part-time work, temporary contracts, self-employment – than the workforce in general (e.g. Benhamou 2003). In most of the cases, full-time workers receiving regular pay, are in the minority (Thorsby 2001).The simple dichotomous work/leisure choice of standard theory is complicated in the case of creative entrepreneurs, by the phenomenon of multiple job-holding. Often regular working hours are not relevant. Often multiple job-holding is a very common formula as the cultural workers need a minimum income for survival and some degree of financial security.

In addition, the sectors show specific dynamics of frequent job changes, and working on short term contracts is normal (Ernst & Young, 2014). And numerous overlaps occur within the different sectors: *'at the creation level among authors, composers, visual artists, designers, directors, screenwriters, and writers; at the production level, between TV and films, visual arts and video games; as well as at the distribution level, with the emergence of various platforms for mixed-media distribution'* (Ernst & Young, 2014, p. 16)

It leads to a situation in which the distinction between *'employed'* or *'unemployed'* is obscure, blurred and problematic. The share of independent workers is more than twice as high in the cultural sector as in total employment. The traditional categories of the *'full-time job society'* (here the worker; there the employer) no longer apply. (KEA 2006, pg 91).

In addition the Creative Industries in general contains heterogeneity of human resources categories. Entrepreneurs can enter the market as a result of a higher professional training, from a vernacular background, craft industry or any other category. And there is an abundant supply of established practitioners and new entrants, supplemented by the presence of a sea of semi-professionals and amateurs that blur the existing quality criteria applied when judging the potential entrepreneurs. Commissioners in the arts place little reliance on certification based on formal schooling and often use their own screening devices (art competitions, referees, etc). Certification by means of a degree or diploma also plays an ambiguous role in the creatives' labour markets. Besides formal schooling, there are other screening devices available, such as prizes and competitions, awards from Arts Councils and other forms of informal certification that offer information regarding the quality and reputation.

THEORY

Given the variety within the different sectors it is difficult to analyse the sector as a homogenous group, due to the fact that inside the Creative Industries – and within the individual sectors - there exists a considerable diversity of occupational status.

As a result on average creators accept below average pecuniary earnings (Wassal and Alper 1992, Towse 2001). This is explained either by risk-seeking behaviour (Towse 2001) or a preference for creative work over other types of work (Throsby 1994, Frey 2000, Caves 2000). Often, the non-monetary rewards of being a creative entrepreneur – the spin-off effects - represents an important argument. Also the over-supply of entrepreneurs and ferocious competition might be a factor involved. This is complemented by the motivational aspects of the entrepreneur and the lifestyle of the creatives, the inner drive of the creative spirit, *'creativity-as-a-way-of-life'*, which offers to the creatives non-pecuniary rewards. Creatives often receive their rewards in private satisfaction and other non-monetary income such as social and cultural status, based on authenticity and individualism. Their cultural orientation leads to *'being different'*; creating a cultural distinction between those networks that possess the same kind of cultural capital as they do, and those social strata that hold other values (Bourdieu, 1984).

As a consequence one has to realize that it is unrealistic to assume that within the creative industries all self-employed individuals act in an entrepreneurial manner (Carey & Naudin, 2006). There are several push- and pull factors at stake. In most cases the cultural dimension interferes with the entrepreneurial one. In some cases one can even describe workers in the creative industries as 'accidental entrepreneurs', as many are faced with significant (self) exploitation, and challenges in adopting entrepreneurial practices (Banks & Hesmondhalgh, 2009).

Creative and Cultural Entrepreneurs:
Independent Interdependency

Especially in the start-up phase, the cultural and creative entrepreneur needs to find his specific position, profile and business model (Hagoort, 2009). This requires a certain level of independence in order to develop one's specific position. Yet, at the same time the (starting) entrepreneur depends on sources of external initiatives, drives and inspiration. In this sector the individual entrepreneur is looking for a situation in which he can combine his independent status with a social cooperative networking configuration.

Cooperative networks are created and sustained for a number of reasons. The Creative Entrepreneur wants to create a product that is interesting for himself, yet that will also be appreciated by his peers, and will hold the potential of being bought by a (potential) client. Hence, Creative Entrepreneurs are involved in networks of multiple and changing clients, competitors, colleagues, etc (Gardner, 2007). Consequently, creative initiatives are developed within a cooperative context that has the potential of sustainable value creation.

The Educational Dimension

'Educational training and employment are increasingly diverging, i.e. education serves as the basis of knowledge but is no longer a guarantee of a specific job.'
(Ellmeier 2010)

Within our educational curricula, we often use the 'general' theoretical notions derived from the 'regular' managerial theories. We teach students to develop a business plan, taking into account the regular market analyses, pricing procedures, entrepreneurial planning and alike. Most of these theoretical notions are based on the traditional goal/ means rationality (Weber, (1922) 1973) (Habermas, 1979) ; if we want to reach this goal, we should develop such a product that fits in our market analyses, and will have to be priced in such a way that it can create a sustainable income.

As mentioned, however, the individual micro-entrepreneur is less driven by rational arguments. They often work on multiple pulses, derived from very different sources. Often products are developed on intuitive, non-rational drives and motivations. The entrepreneurs are primary interested in the development of their product. The notion of 'selling the product' often is a secondary one. 'R&D is the main activity, while production is secondary'. Creativity is their core-business; developing those things that have never been here before. Among the factors leading to financial success within the Cultural Industries, 'learning-on- the-job' plays a more significant role than the formal training, and to the role of talent is attached indefinable appreciations.

The Lack of entrepreneurial Skills

The EU funded study on The Entrepreneurial Dimension of the Cultural and Creative Industries has shown that there is a general lack of entrepreneurial skills within all sectors of the CCIs. Limited business skills were cited as the second most important business-related challenge when starting a company (HKU, 2010, p. 139). In the OECD's entrepreneurship framework, the *'culture of entrepreneurship'* is included as a determinant of entrepreneurship, being influential in developing a conductive environment for fostering entrepreneurial activity (OECD, 2009, p. 9). Despite its importance, there is insufficient integration of entrepreneurship education in general curricula and in arts education (DCMS , 2006).

Cultivating the 'entrepreneurial Imagination': Educational Dilemma's

So, if we depart from the point that society in general, and in specific the creative and cultural industries, is becoming more flexible, digital and entrepreneurial, then the question arises: how can we prepare our students for this dynamic, but at the same time uncertain modern work sphere?

From the teacher's point of view a number of dilemmas arise. Can we teach entrepreneurship? Can we train people to operate in uncertain environments? How do we develop self-confidence, individual initiatives, and network-building? We will sketch a number of dilemmas that we are dealing with.

Dilemma 1: How do we teach Risk Taking?

'There can be no question of merely taking a negative attitude towards risk. Risk needs to be disciplined, but active risk-taking is a core element of a dynamic economy and an innovative society.'

According to Kuratko (2005) *'risk taking'* is not common in modern management education curriculum and it's probably hard to find educators who will put *'risk'* at the centre of their own curriculum. Kuratko analyses modern entrepreneurship education as follows:

> *'Too many faculty pursue tenure as their only goal and they leave the challenges of entrepreneurship education 'later in their career.' What message is being conveyed in our classrooms? That students should take risks while faculty pursue security! It is a real dilemma that exists in academia.'*
> *(Kuratko, 2005: 589)*

It's obvious that this old tendency to *'secure the environment'* is nowadays not fully sufficient anymore and should be seen as part of a larger quest for creating an *'entrepreneurial culture'*. As organizational psychologist Geert Hofstede (1980) already concluded in the early eighties *'cultural factors' highly determine the entrepreneurial activity of individuals.'* Or as Klamer (2006) states: *'the cultural factor reminds us that people are not entrepreneurial on their own.'* Historical experiences, beliefs, attitudes and values within a certain educational sphere strongly define the way the students' mind-set is being developed. If a traditional art management education wants to respond to developments on a larger scale, a new entrepreneurial orientation needs to be developed. Taking (calculated) risks should be an important part of art management education and this would inevitably involve a sophisticated demolition of tradition and heritage.

THEORY

Dilemma 2: How can we Develop an Intuitive Mind?

Many studies show that entrepreneurs are rather intuitive than rational thinkers (Kirby, 2004). To cope with dynamic environments it is important to have a well-developed sensitivity for the context in which one is working; something we would like to call *context sensibility*. This acquires a more holistic and syntactical way of looking at the world instead of a sequential reasoned and randomized method of exploration. According to the German philosopher Wilhelm Schmid (2011) the modern human needs to acquire a trained sensitivity (and additional intuition) to deal with the contemporary world. He distinguishes three levels of sensibility:

1. Sensory sensibility: observing volatile, changeable and striking details in order to be able to make choices based on a *'feeling'*;
2. Structural sensibility: theoretical knowledge and understanding of (societal) structures in order to see hidden association, such as power structures whom are hidden under the surface of the sensory perceptible (media structures, policy structures, urban structures etc.)
3. Virtual sensibility: recognizing the possibility of new technologies in order to sharpen the intuition for the movement in the virtual space.

Although the general understanding of concepts like *'sensitivity'* and *'intuition'* leaves no room for nurturing, many psychological research shows that this human attribute is definitely something which can be developed. It is thereby necessary to cultivate a *'critical sensitivity towards hidden assumptions and subtle relationships in social situations which lend themselves to entrepreneurial interventions'*. Techniques like divergent thinking, ethnographic imagination and hermeneutic interpretation could help to enhance this ability.

Dilemma 3: How do we Prepare Students for an uncertain World?

Being a nano-entrepeneur means dealing with a great amount of uncertainties. Students, but also teachers, have to learn how to confront uncertainties because *'we live in a changing epoch where our values are ambivalent and everything is interconnected'*. And because circumstances change rapidly, students need to attain a great amount of flexibility and psychological resilience. The status-quo of today might not be the right point of departure, but rather the status quo of the future. Today's modern students assign great value to *'autonomy'* and *'authenticity'*; both human conditions that are highly valued in modern Western culture. If we want students to be prepared for this uncertain world, one of the most important learning outcomes would have to be *'self-awareness'*. Not in an egocentric way by saying *'what is own to me'* but in a social sense by stressing the proverb *'who am I in the light of the other'*. Becoming an authentic entrepreneur then means to become someone who fully incorporates the art of self-fulfilment and self-actualization, by going into *'dialogue with, sometimes in struggle against, the things our significant others want to see in us'*. This asks for personal leadership, the ability to put one self on the line, being accountable, taking charge and accept failure as inherent to life and work.

Dilemma 4: How do we teach Students to work Together?

An *'individual entrepreneur'* who enters the professional domain will be confronted with the fact that he needs to cooperate with others in small scale, bottom-up networks. It is of the utmost importance to create a solid network in order to survive at all.

THEORY

The Cultural and Creative industries highly depend on cooperation, project-based work, interdisciplinarity, and demand a communal way of thinking. The craft of cooperation is definitely not easy, and according to American sociologist Richard Sennett (2012) it has become weak in the last decades, but by extensive training and reflection it should be promoted in modern education. Project-based education contributes in large part to this need, but is still very much focused on traditional client-assignment situations. Bottom-up community building with external partners, as a more dynamic educational model, might be more in line with this modern entrepreneurial culture.

Dilemma 5: How do we 'Preach' a sustainable Attitude?

Cultural and Creative Entrepreneurs have to create their own income, which forces them to go for 'the fast buck'. They have to generate their individual earnings in a volatile market, with an abundance of cultural products around. Yet at the same time they have to take care of creating a sustainable future. They have to safeguard the opportunities to persist in their endeavours, even in the long run. We have to note that change is one of the main characteristics of the enterprise; change is the only sustainable factor. In addition they have to define a corporate social responsibility, integrating their social concerns in their business, in the interaction with their stakeholders on a voluntary basis. (David Williamson, 2006 Vol 67) This means that we can't ignore moral and ethical questions, which arise in the global community. As being part of a Cultural or Creative industries does not mean that creativity is the preserve of a so- called 'creative class' but 'often resulting from human interaction across boundaries (e.g. across nation states, professions, industries, organizations, disciplines, social and cultural groupings, methods, epistemologies and rationalities)'. Therefor it is important to discuss the social and ecological implications of entrepreneurship. Not by preaching, but by showing students that moral awareness is part of modern entrepreneurship.

Conclusion

We have sketched the characteristics of the Cultural and Creative entrepreneur. Faced with a changing social environment, in which individual networking, coping with permanent change, and handling persisting uncertainty are paramount, we will have to re-think our curricula. More than ever we will have to take the evolving lack of pre-defined career-development and planning into account. We have to prepare the entrepreneurial 'ant' for its lifelong dynamic journey through modern cultural and creative work spheres. A regular income, full-time employment, continuous growth of a micro-enterprise is no longer the standard to long for. Permanent change and innovation has become part of our sustainable surroundings. Our society has more than ever evolved into a dynamic networking environment, asking for basically different entrepreneurial skills.

About the Authors

Drs Rene Kooyman DEA MUAD graduated with a major in Urban and Regional Planning. He received a Diplôme Educations Approfondies (DEA) in Economics and Sociology at the University of Geneva, Switzerland.

References

Abbing Hans (2008). *Why Are Artists Poor? The Exceptional Economy of the Arts*. Dissertation, Amsterdam University Press 2008.

Banks, M. & Hesmondhalgh, D. (2009). Looking for work in creative industries policy. In: *International Journal of Cultural Policy*, Vol. 15, no. 4, 415-30.

Bourdieu, P. (1984). *Distinction. A social critique of the judgement of taste*. New York: Harvard Business Press.

THEORY

THEORY

Carey, C. & Naudin, A. (2006). Enterprise curriculum for creative industries students: An exploration of current attitudes and issues. In: *Education + Training*, vol. 48, no. 7, 518-31.

Chia, R. 2007. Teaching paradigm shifting in management education: university business schools and the entrepreneurial imagination, In: *Journal of Management Studies*, Volume 33, Issue 4, 409–428

DCMS (2006). *Developing Entrepreneurship for the Creative Industries - The Role of Higher and Further Education*. London: Department of Culture, Media and Sport.

Dos Santos Duisenberg, E. (2010). *Creative Economy Report 2010*. Geneva: UNCTAD.

Drucker, P. F. (1985). *Innovation & Entrepreneurship*. New York: Harper and Row.

Ellmeier, A. 2010. Cultural entrepreneurialism: in the changing relationship between the arts, culture and employment, In: *International journal of Cultural Policy*, 9:1, 3-16

Ernst & Young. (2014). *Creating Growth: Measuring Cultural and Creative Markets in the EU*. London: EYGM (Ernst & Young Global Limited).

Eubanks, D, Murphy, S, Dumford. (1996). Intuition as an Influence on Creative Problem-Solving: The Effects of Intuition, Positive Affect, and Training, In: *Creativity Research Journal*, pages 170-184

European Commission. (2010). *Europe 2020; A strategy for smart, sustainable and inclusive growth*. Brussels: European Commission.

Exploitation and development of the job potential in the cultural sector in the age of digitalization. EU DG Employment and Social Affairs. June 2001

Florida, R. & Harris, D. (2002). *The Rise of the Cultural Class*. New York: Harper Collins Publ.

Gartner, W.B. (1988, Spring). 'Who is an entrepreneur?' is the wrong question. In: *American Journal of Small Business*, 12(4), 11-32.

Giddens, Anthony (1999). *Runaway World: How Globalization is Reshaping Our Lives*. London : Profile.

Habermas, J. (1979). Was heißt Universalpragmatik? In: *A.-O. A. (red), Sprachpragmatik und Philosophie* (pp. 174-272). Frankfurt am Main: Suhrkamp.

HKU. (2010). *The Entrepreneurial Dimension of Cultural and Creative Industries*. Utrecht: HKU University of the Arts.

Hofstede, G. (1984). *Culture's Consequences. Comparing Values, Behaviors, Institutions and Organizations Across Nations*, SAGE Publications

Kirby, D. (2004). *Entrepreneurship education: can business schools meet the challenge?*, Emerald Group Publishing Limited, Volume 46, Number 8/9, 2004; pp. 510-519

Klamer, A. (2006). *Cultural entrepreneurship*, Erasmus University and Academia Vitae

Rene Kooyman has been Project Manager for the EU EACEA Research Project on the Entrepreneurial Dimensions of Cultural and Creative Industries. He has been responsible for the EU INTERREG Creative Urban Renewal Project (CURE). At the moment he is an Associated Fellow at the United Nations Institute of Training and Research (UNITAR) in Geneva.

—

www.rkooyman.com

rkooyman@rkooyman.com

*Ruben Jacobs MA MSc
is Lecturer in Cultural
Sociology & Philosophy at
the Utrecht University of
the Arts, and he holds
a Fellowship at The New
Institute in Rotterdam.
Recently he published his
first book Everbody an artist
('Iedereen een kunstenaar'),
in which he explores the
current position of the artist
in the realm of the creative
industries.*

—

www.ruben-jacobs.nl

Knight, F. H. (1921). *Risk, Uncertainty, and Profit. Library of Economics and Liberty*. Retrieved April 9, 2007, from http://www.econlib.org/library/Knight/knRUP1.html

Kooyman, R. (2009). *The Entrepreneurial Dimension of Cultural and Creative Industries.* Preliminary inventory of existing literature. Utrecht: Utrecht University of the Arts HKU.

Kuratko, D. (2005). The Emergence of Entrepreneurship Education: Development, Trends, and Challenges, In: *Entrepreneurship Theory and Practice*, Volume 29, Issue 5, pages 577–598,

OECD, (2009). *Evaluation of Programmes concerning Education for Entrepreneurship*; report OECD Working Party on SMEs. Paris: OECD.

R. Towse (ed)(2003). *A Handbook of Cultural Economics*, Cheltenham, Edward Elgar

Reidl Sybille, Franziska Steyer: *Zwishen unabhängigkeit und Zukunftsangst; quantitatieve Ergebnisse zur Arbeit in der Wiener Creative Industries*. Wien 2006

Schumpeter, J.A. (1975). *Capitalism, Socialism, and Democracy*. New York: Harper.

Sennet, R. (2012). *Together: The Rituals, Pleasures and Politics of Cooperation*, Yale University Press

Sternberg, R. & Wennekers, S. (2005,April). Determinants and effects of new business creation using global entrepreneurship monitor data. In: *Small Business Economics*, 24(3), 193-203. Retrieved April 9, 2007, from EBSCO Online Database Business Source Complete.

Throsby, David (2001). *Economics and culture*. Cambridge, University Press

Towse Ruth: Towards an economy of creativity?. In: *Creative Industries A measure for urban development*? FOKUS, Vienna 2004

Weber, M. (1922/1973). *Ueber einige Kategorien der verstehenden Soziologie*. Tubingen: Mohr.

Williamson, David G. L.-W. (2006 Vol 67). Drivers of Environmental Behaviour; Manufacturing SMEs and the Implications for CSR. In: *Journal of business ethics*, 317 - 334.

THEORY

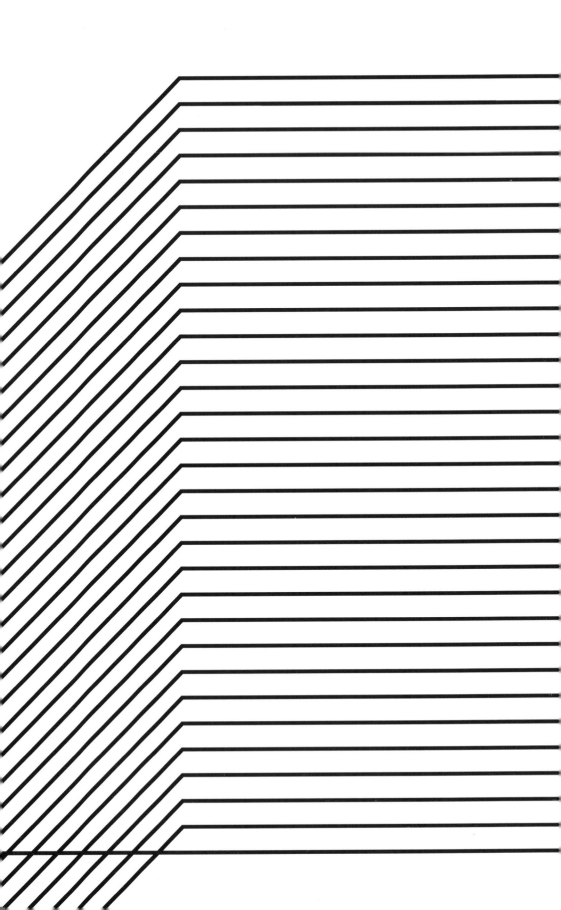

PEDAGOGY

Richard Strasser

GRADUATE MUSIC INDUSTRY EDUCATION A HOLISTIC APPROACH TO PROGRAM CREATION

PEDAGOGY

Abstract

Creating value in music education has become of paramount interest to faculty, students and employers. As questions about the validity of higher education continue, especially in relation to the creative industries, institutions are struggling to meet stakeholders' expectations. This article examines the creation of an innovative graduate music industry program, designed to address the needs of three major stakeholders. The program began with the construction of a structure based on three guiding principles.

First, the program must be student centred (Weimer, 2002), with curricular choices focused on four possible outcomes (Entrepreneurship, professional, practice and research). This principle guaranteed curricula flexibility for students and their divergent career aspirations. Second, the program must make use of experiential learning. This could be in the form of co-ops, internships or job shadowing, imbedded in the curriculum to facilitate reflection on that experience (Rogers, 2001; Schön, 1983). Third, the program must be part of a network of external organizations such as businesses, non-profit organizations and the general community. These networks are expressed via business/college ventures, community advocacies and social entrepreneurship projects.

With these three guiding principles in place issues of appropriate learning strategies, student access, technical capabilities, curriculum design, and assessment were addressed. Through this process the faculty adopted a holistic curriculum that strove to engage students through active and cooperative learning, inquiry and problem-based learning, learning communities, and team projects. This case illustrates the opportunities, challenges, and benefits that music departments face, when developing new degree programs that simultaneously meet academic, student and business needs.

Introduction

The musical landscape has inextricably changed in the past decade. The traditional modes of creating, manufacturing and distributing musical products have been replaced with a fluid model. As the workplace and the drivers of the knowledge based economy (Di-Conti, 2004) continue to evolve, so must music industry education. *'The modern workplace no longer resembles the factory assembly line but rather a design studio, where core values are collaboration and innovation …'* (Mandel, 2007, p.45).
The old rubric of simply transferring knowledge to students has been replaced with the preparation of employees to assume leadership roles in this new malleable environment. (Massimiliano, 2004) Educational administrators and music leaders realize that music organizations face complex challenges well beyond traditional sector boundaries. To address these issues effectively educational programs need to train the next generation of music professionals to adopt knowledge and skill sets that are fluid and reach beyond traditional music industry boundaries. This need requires the creation of educational programs that address the aesthetic, business and legal requirements of music organizations by utilizing a multidisciplinary and interdisciplinary

approach. Furthermore, attributes including problem solving, high readiness for change, self-efficacy and creativity must be adopted in an experiential environment to ensure graduate success in the music industry workplace. (Cantor, 1997; Chapman, et al, 1995; Cross, 1994)

An academic degree is both a cultural artifact and a symbol of postsecondary education. Degrees are linked to the ritual of graduation, signifying the completion of a program of study, and mark a recipient's passage into a higher level of academic endeavour and entry into the workforce. Significant changes occurred when graduate programs were created to assure employment in professional occupations such as accounting, law, journalism, and social work. By the end of the twentieth century professional and graduate programs began to converge into a singularity to meet corporate needs and graduate student career aspirations. (Glazer, 1986)

Music education has traditionally focused on the development of performers, artists, composers, historians and theorists. Professional degrees – music education and music therapy – began as offshoots of European theorists such as Zoltan Kodaly, Carl Orff and Gunlid Keetman. Music industry programs began appearing in the mid-1980s in response to declining enrolment in traditional performance degrees. From this period to the present, the majority of programs have focused exclusively at the undergraduate level. The development of graduate music industry programs emerged in the mid-1990s to offer non-music industry undergraduates an opportunity to obtain a music industry degree and entrance into music organizations. For the most part music industry graduate programs followed an undergraduate curricula model that focuses on a wide range unrelated courses. An opportunity, therefore, existed for the creation of a program that adopted a holistic approach to the preparation of music executives. (Kolb, 1984)

PEDAGOGY

Music Environment and Education

The music business is an example of an industry that faces a future that is increasingly complex and in flux. Managers of music organizations must make decisions based on information from a variety of fields, including law, (intellectual property) marketing, finance, and economics. In an effort to prepare graduates to enter this environment, undergraduate and graduate music industry programs must be inherently interdisciplinary by nature. To anticipate and manage current operational, legal and financing issues facing music organizations, leaders are increasingly applying solutions from non-music viewpoints. The education and practices of these professionals are often radically different, and within higher education institutions they are often found in separate divisions or colleges. The very separation of these fields often creates a 'silo' mentality that inhibits the collaboration between departments and inhibits students developing a deep understanding of a particular discipline.

This places increasing pressure on music industry programs to meet the demands of an industry that requires executives to possess a broad range of skills and knowledge. As such, many music industry programs have struggled to define their academic mission and prepare students to adopt leadership roles within the music industry.

Apart from the academic barriers created by departmental and educational divisions, music industry education requires a new pedagogical approach. Traditional teaching methods, such as lectures and examinations, are often not seen as the most effective means of encouraging music entrepreneurial or managerial skills to develop. (Gibb, 2002; Sogunro, 2004) In such courses traditional teaching methods need to be complemented by activities such as learning by doing, active learning that includes the creation of new enterprises and accompanying documentation (Financial, business and marketing plans and analyses) and the use of experiential opportunities to gain first-hand experience in the operation and function of music organizations. Research (Glaser, 1992; Simon, 1980; Huba, 2000) shows that 'conditionalised' knowledge (i.e., it includes conditions of applicability within music organizations) assist students in applying general knowledge to the operation of firms. To develop meaningful classroom engagement, faculties are encouraged to use techniques such as simulations, problem-based learning activities, collaborative and cooperative learning activities, and other classroom-based practices that provide the kind of practice and application seen in functional music companies (Paul, 1993; Ash et al., 2004, Barkley et al., 2004). These techniques provide opportunities for students to make connections among ideas, knowledge and theories and to synthesize and transfer what they've learned to new and complex situations.

Justification

The desire for the creation of a graduate music industry program was born out of a distinct educational goal set by the university's leadership. With enrolment at the undergraduate level set at approximately two thousand students per academic year, the potential for substantial departmental growth could only come from the graduate realm. The university leadership begun to systematically encourage the creation of professional graduate education through traditional on-campus degrees and the via a unique regional campus hybrid model (part online and on-campus education) that focuses on professional training targeted to specific business sectors within a region (Christensen et al., 1991).

The goal therefore was not only to create a program that matched the university's mission, but develop a program that was distinctive in the market place. One that trained professionals to meet an ever-changing music industry as well has have value within the market. We saw a unique opportunity to create a one-year music management program that would meet the needs of all stakeholders.

To develop an interdisciplinary management program, we first mapped existing courses within the college and university. While several courses existed in the undergraduate music industry program that could have the potential to transfer to the graduate level, a distinctive graduate curriculum would require an innovative curriculum to support the initial mission of an innovative music industry program, especially against well-established graduate programs at competing universities. A needs based assessment model was created to progress to the next level. A list of specific questions was generated that addressed the concerns of creating a new graduate program, including:

1. Is there a need for a graduate music industry program?
2. Should the program have a specific focus (management, intellectual property management, e-commerce, etc.)?

3. What program structure would be most effective (core courses, elective courses, interdisciplinary courses, etc.)?
4. What delivery system (on-campus, online, hybrid) would be of greatest interest to potential students?

The initial answers to these questions came from a variety of sources including experience from the department's undergraduate program, current research in music industry curriculum development and insight from industry leaders and alumni. The results found that adopting an interdisciplinary approach was appealing to all stakeholders and matched the evolving mission of the university. Furthermore, research on curriculum development demonstrated the benefits of an interdisciplinary program. For example, Ducoffe's (2006) research indicated the perceived benefits of interdisciplinary team-taught business courses among students. His research showed better retention rates and job-placement among graduates.

Program Design
Armed with positive results from the analysis and our own research, the university decided to move forward with the creation of a graduate music industry program. It became clear that simply replicating the university's current undergraduate music industry program would not have the required impact for students entering the music industry as mid to high level executives. The goal of the program is to provide a high level training for music professionals to address complex issues facing the music industry and find solutions for music organizations to flourish in this environment. Hence, the review committee began working on creating an entirely new program structure that could meet these requirements.

This discussion resulted in the committee adopting a 32-credit hour Master of Science program consisting of a set of five (3 credit hour) core courses and elective music industry and business courses over a period of 12 months. The core courses provide students with the essential skills to manage a music organization, irrespective of which sector (live music, publishing, recording, etc.) or field (for-profit or non-profit) it is located in. Each course focuses on key managerial skills required to operate a music organization. These include music management, financial management, Intellectual property management, marketing management, artistic creativity, and research. Before creating each core course we defined specific objectives that meet stakeholder needs expressed in the survey, including:

1. define how leadership and management training provides added value to music organizations
2. illustrate the complex nature of music management and the required understanding of multiple variables in the successful operation of organizations
3. demonstrate how insights from interdisciplinary fields improve operations of music organizations, and
4. develop specific competencies associated with managing music organizations such as analytic and reflective thinking skills, communication skills, ethical and legal abilities, and use of information technology.

PEDAGOGY

As such, the core courses require students to identify problems that currently exist in music organizations and articulate best practices for solving them. The desired result is a fluid approach to problem identification and the creation of solutions based on current music industry practices, as well as knowledge and practices from other fields. 'Management of Music Organizations' for example, was designed to be the entry point for students. As an introductory course it provides the critical management skills involved in planning, creation, leading and assessment of music organizations. To align with the goals of the program, this course utilizes a 'systems' view of organizations, which examines organizations as part of a context, including but not limited to the external environment, creativity, strategy, structure, culture, tasks, people and outputs. The course examines how managerial decisions made in any one of these domains affect decisions in each of the others. A similar pedagogical approach was applied to all the core courses. 'Marketing strategies in the music industry' focuses on the application of strategic planning in marketing to achieve competitive advantage in the music industry. It examines the role of strategic planning in developing effective marketing programs that enhance the overall performance of a music organization. In keeping with interdisciplinary approach used throughout the program, this program makes use of business concepts such as consumer behaviour management, market segmentation, targeting, customer equity, brand equity, brand positioning, pricing strategies, and social marketing with specific application to the music industry. The inclusion of research as core course - typically not considered a core function of operational music companies - was added to meet the demands of an ever-increasing data driven industry. Success as a music industry manager often hinges on the ability to find solutions effectively and efficiently. The objectives of the course 'music industry research methodology', include the acquisition of skills to in organizational settings, as well as, to plan, organize, design, and conduct research to help solve identified problems.

By providing students with a solid foundation in their core courses, we sought to equip them with the knowledge and understanding needed to address more complex issues. The second phase of the curriculum development included the creation of electives that address specific skills required in a variety of music organizations. Electives were divided into two groups. The first group included specific music industry courses that focus on specialized skills essential in the operation of specific music firms. These courses focus on emerging areas within the music industry as well as traditional skill sets required to manage a music organization. Courses such as music industry leadership, small business creation, strategic analysis and negotiation offer student specifically target skills required to successfully lead organizations.

We also created a series of courses that provide training in e-commerce. With the music industry moving indescribably towards a digital delivery system, courses such as music and mobile technologies, data-mining in the music industry and online marketing provide students with the necessary skills and knowledge to manage emerging e-commerce companies. The second group of elective courses requires students to select from a range of graduate business courses to broaden the range of skills they can apply to impending problems. Students have an opportunity to enrol in a verity of MBA courses, such as social entrepreneurship, enterprise growth and innovation, early stage venture management, design thinking, etc. By combining business courses with specialized music industry electives students would be able to gain the knowledge to make effective and appropriate management decisions around complex issues that have emerged in the music industry.

After the specific curriculum was established program outcomes were further delineated through four specific concentrations that allow students to focus their education on specific career aspirations. These four areas (professional, research, practice and entrepreneurship) allow students to develop a curricula map that matched specific skills associated with a particular career.

1. The **professional concentration** was created to address the need by practicing professionals who require a graduate degree to validate their position within an increasingly '*professional*' music corporation. Traditionally music executives gain access to leadership roles internally (i.e. climbing the corporate ladder). With non-musical pressures increasing in the decision making process of music organizations, a new generation of leaders must be able to balance artistic acumen with business (especially financial management) and legal know how. The standard educational attainment for such positions has traditionally been a professional masters' degree, either in business (MBA) or law (JD). Students participate in the core requirements, music industry electives and electives at the business school. Any specialization occurs within the course choices, either through the music industry or business electives.

2. The **research concentration** was created for students interested in an academic career. This concentration is centred on the creation of a thesis that replaces the business electives. The thesis attests to the students' mastery of theoretical and methodological literatures in a given specialty, and to connect these literatures to a concrete problem or issue of interest to music industry organizations. Students are expected to produce a work describing original research, with the general expectation that the finished product is of publishable quality, meets professional standards, and is useful to some external audience (e.g. journal readers, practitioners, advocates, other researchers).

3. The **entrepreneurial concentration** was developed to assist students with the creation and commercialization of actual products and/or services. The key feature of this concentration is a capstone that requires students to identify and address issues within the music industry and develop a working business solution. Working with a faculty mentor, students explore alternative strategies to these issues by employing concepts and techniques from business, law, and music industry studies. This '*real world*' project is not only intended to create new businesses, but to develop a students' ability to synthesize specific non-music knowledge and to apply it directly to a music delivery model. Successful completion of the capstone requires an operational prototype of a music business and accompanying documentation (business plan, articles of incorporation, bylaws, etc.). In most cases, students develop a business idea from an issue they identified during one of the introductory core courses.

4. Finally, a **practice concentration** allows students to experience music organization operation first hand. Using the universities extensive network of organizations that provide internship opportunities at the undergraduate level, graduate students have an opportunity to work with music industry leaders at the conclusion of their course work. The goal in this concentration is to allow students to gain invaluable experience working directly with organizations. Furthermore, the experiential

PEDAGOGY

experiences provide students with a unique opportunity to apply their music industry knowledge and skills in a corporate environment. Understanding the subtleties of music industry transactions and decision making allows the students to develop their problem solving skills and find unique solutions not found in traditional textbook cases. In keeping with the programs' focus, students have the opportunity to take a range of experiential experiences, from six-month cooperatives, short-term internships, job shadowing and individualized experiences via a directed study. As with the other concentrations, students complete core requirements along with music industry and business electives prior to commencing their experiential training.

Discussion

Developing an innovative graduate music industry program that has relevance in an ever changing environment was extremely challenging. To achieve the intended goal of creating a unique program required us to integrate experiential expertise in an interdisciplinary fashion to meet the demands of a multi-discipline music industry environment. (Breunig, 2005; Warren, 1995) Moreover, the curricular design, rather than offering a set of unrelated discipline-specific courses, focuses on an integrated model that embrace the very interdisciplinary nature of the music industry. Unlike other programs, that package course offerings from an existent undergraduate curriculum, faculties were challenged to create new courses that embraced interdisciplinary areas beyond the music department. For example, a course such as *Management for Music Organizations* embraces topics from business, law, psychology and sociology. This approach recognizes that a range of disciplinary approaches are important constituents in creating an innovative program that addresses key components of organizational management, operations efficiency, and financial solvency.

To address complex music management problems more effectively, this program also encourages music students to engage in *systems thinking*. Most programs have under-appreciated the magnitude, complexity, and operational challenges facing music organizations. As a result, not enough music professionals view the music commercialization process as a system, rather than an independent practice that integrates program management techniques from unrelated fields. In this program students are encouraged to seek out alternative views and solutions by embracing non-traditional disciplines. Through the programs' electives students solve issues by adopting the skills and knowledge from fields such as computer science, business, and economics and incorporate these results into their own businesses. Improving the overall music industry will require considerable changes in music industry education, especially in regards to adopting techniques from different and at times unrelated disciplines. Yet, the rewards for such training will create organizations that seamlessly function in the knowledge-based economy.

This graduate program offers a variety of benefits to meet the challenges associated with the creation and operation of music organizations.

1. First, it addresses the coordination and functional issues facing many music industry organizations. Music professionals must work with other professionals from other fields to solve very complex problems. Finding solutions to impending short and long-term issues requires music leaders to cooperate and

adopt techniques from fields such as business, economics, computer science, and law. This program embraces this interdisciplinary approach, by building integrative courses and requiring students to move beyond the confines of the music department by gaining knowledge from other fields.

2. Second, given the complexity of music delivery, this program provides graduates with an understanding of the values, beliefs, language, and practices of other professionals. This enhances a music executives' ability to work directly with non-music professionals in the management and growth of music companies.

3. Third, by targeting critical music organization performance measures (innovation, quality, and efficiency) students gain specific skills that will enable them to achieve positive outcomes in key performance organizational performance areas.

This curriculum also has the advantage of encouraging instructors to utilize avoid an '*insular*' model of education. The program aims to impart new insights regarding (1) how to use interdisciplinary methods to create solutions within the music industry and (2) how best to conceptualize crucial aspects of music industry practice as complex inter-related systems while (3) encouraging students to use conceptual tools to re-examine customary workplace practices. Through guided re-examination, students experience professional growth as they come to understand how to apply interdisciplinary knowledge to specific application within the music industry.

Conclusion

Reports from key stakeholders including business, government and students indicate that institutions of higher education must provide graduates with appropriate and practical skills to meet the demands of an ever changing knowledge-based economy. (Heller, 2001; Huisman et al., 2004; Plamer, 2007) This priority has led institutions to develop programs that require students to possess an understanding of function and operation of music organizations, but to do so from multiple perspectives. As music departments begin to explore options to increase student enrolment and retention, they will be looking for innovative models as guides in the development process. Many departments have created music industry programs as an alternative to attract students. Simply merging music courses with business courses does not address the skills required by music organizations.

Students are not the only beneficiaries of an interdisciplinary music industry education. Employers value graduate that have the experience as well as the interdisciplinary skills to handle complex multi-variable issues. Students benefit by designing their own courses based on personal interest and specific career aspirations. This in turn, benefits the institution as it produces satisfied graduates and improves retention rates. As such, this model draws directly from the expertise and needs of a broad range of educators, business people, and lawyers to create a cohesive interdisciplinary program. Courses based upon key performance indicators such as organizational innovation, effectiveness and return on investment produce an environment that requires graduates to think beyond their own respective disciplines and viewpoints, in order to develop music organizations that can operate in a world that requires creative and original solutions. Therefore, the success of this program lies in a model that focuses on problem identification and problem-solving using a broad range of diverse disciplines. While our application focuses specifically on music industry graduate education – an area of exploration and

PEDAGOGY

reform – the approaches used in this program could be used by non-music disciplines in the arts and entertainment fields that are striving to develop a successful inter-disciplinary program.

References

Arum, R., & Roksa, J. (2011). *Academically adrift: limited learning on college campuses.* Chicago, IL: University of Chicago Press.

Ash SL, Clayton PH. (2004). The articulated learning: An approach to reflection and assessment. Innovative. In: *Higher Education,* 29, 137–154.

Barkley, E., Cross, K.P., & Major, C.H. (2004). *Collaborative learning techniques: a practical guide to promoting learning in groups.* San Francisco, CA.: Jossey Bass.

Bloom, B. S. (Ed.). (1956). *Taxonomy of educational objectives, handbook I: Cognitive domain.* New York, NY: David McKay Company.

Breunig, M. (2005). Turning experiential education and critical pedagogy theory into praxis. In: *Journal of Experiential Education, 28*(2), 106–122.

Cantor, J. A. (1997). *Experiential learning in higher education: Linking classroom and community.* (ERIC Digest No. ED404948). Washington, DC: George Washington University, Graduate School of Education and Human Development.

Chapman, S., McPhee, P., & Proudman, B. (1995). What is experiential education? In K. Warren, M. Sakofs, & J. S. Hunt (Eds.), In: *The theory of experiential education* (3rd ed., pp. 235–248). Dubuque, IA: Kendall/Hunt.

Christensen, C.R., Garvin, D.A., & Sweet, A. (1991). *Education for judgment: The artistry of discussion leadership.* Cambridge, MA: Harvard Business School.

Cross, K. (1994). The coming of age of experiential education. In: *NSEE Quarterly,* 19(4), 1–9.

Dall'Alba, G. (2009). *Learning to be professionals: innovation and change in professional development.* New York: Springer.

Donahue–Di Conti, V. (2004). Experiential education in a knowledge-based economy: Is it time to reexamine the liberal arts? In: *Journal of General Education,* 53(3-4), 167–183.

Ducoffe, S. J. S., Tomley, C. L., & Tucker, M. (2006). Interdisciplinary, team-taught, undergraduate business courses: The impact of integration. In: *Journal of Management Education,* 30, 276–294.

Estes, C. A. (2004). Promoting student-centered learning in experiential education. In: *Journal of Experiential Education,* 27(2), 141–160.

Eyler, J. (2009). The power of experiential education. In: *Liberal Education,* 95(4): 24–31.

About the Author

Dr Richard Strasser is an Associate Professor of Music Industry at Northeastern University. Dr. Strasser is a graduate from the Australian National University with a Bachelor of Music (distinction) and a Graduate Diploma in Music. After winning both the Queen Elizabeth II Silver Jubilee Award and the Arts Council of Australia Scholarship, he continued his studies at the Manhattan School of Music, where he received a Master of Music and Doctor of Musical Arts degree. Richard Strasser also has an arts administration degree from New York University.

Dr. Strasser has served as a faculty member of numerous universities including John Cabot University in Rome, Clarion University of Pennsylvania, and as Coordinator of the Music Business program at the University of Massachusetts Lowell. Dr. Strasser served on the Board of Director's for the Music and Entertainment Industry Educators Association, the Cultural Organization of Lowell and the working group for the development for national music industry education standards for the National Association of Schools of Music.

—

r.strasser@neu.edu

PEDAGOGY

Gibb, A.A. (2002). In pursuit of a new enterprise and entrepreneurship paradigm for learning: creative destruction, new values, new ways of doing things and new combinations of knowledge. In: *International journal of management review*, 4(3): 233-269.

Glaser R. (1992). Expert knowledge and processes of thinking. In D.F. Halpern (Ed.), *Enhancing thinking skills in the sciences and mathematics.* (pp. 63–75). Hillsdale NJ: Erlbaum.

Glazer, J. S. (1986). *The master's degree: Tradition, diversity, innovation*. ASHE-ERIC Report No. 6 Washington, DC: George Washington University.

Heller, D. E. (2001). Introduction: The changing dynamics of affordability, access, and accountability in public higher education. In: D. E. Heller (Ed.), *The states and public higher education policy: Affordability, access and accountability.* (pp. 1–11). Baltimore, MD: John Hopkins Press.

Huba, M. E., & Freed, J. E. (2000). *Learner-centered assessment on college campuses: Shifting the focus from teaching to learning*. Needham Heights, MA: Allyn & Bacon.

Huisman, J., & Currie, J. (2004). Accountability in higher education: Bridge over troubled water? In: *Higher Education*, 48, 529–551.

Kolb, D. (1984) *Experiential learning*. Englewood Cliffs, NJ: Prentice Hall.

Kuh, G. (2008). *High impact educational practices: What they are, who has access to them, and why they matter*. Washington: American Association of Colleges and Universities.

Mandel, M. (2007). Which way to the future? Globalization and technology are drastically changing how we do our jobs – and that's both a promise and a problem, In: *Business Week*, 45

Massimiliano, V. (2004). Globalization and higher education organizational change: A framework for analysis. In: *Higher Education*, 48, 483–510.

McArthur, J. W., & Sachs, J. (2009). Needed: A new generation of problem solvers. In: *Chronicle of Higher Education*, 55(40), 1–4.

Palmer, P. J. (2007). A new professional: The aims of education revisited. In: *Change: The Magazine of Higher Learning*, 39(6), 6–12.

Paul, R. (1993). *Critical thinking: What every person needs to survive in a rapidly changing world*. Santa Rosa, CA: Foundation for Critical Thinking.

Rogers, R. (2001). Reflection in higher education: A concept analysis. In: *Innovative Higher Education*, 26, 37–57.

Schön, D. (1983). *The reflective practitioner: How professionals think in action*. New York, NY: Basic Books.

Simon, H.A. (1980). Problem solving and education. In Tuma, D.T., & Reif, R., (Eds.), *Problem solving and education: Issues in teaching and research*. (pp. 81–96). Hillsdale, NJ: Lawrence Erlbaum Associates.

PEDAGOGY

Sogunro, O.A. (2004). Efficacy of role-playing pedagogy in training leaders: some reflections. In: *Journal of Management Development*, 23(4), 355-371.

Tyler, K. (2004), 'Getting value from executive MBA programs', In: *HR Magazine*, 49(7), 105- 109.

Uchiyama, K. P., & Radin, J. E. (2009). Curriculum mapping in higher education: A vehicle for collaboration. In: *Innovative Higher Education*, 33(4), 271–280.

Warren, K. (1995). The student-centered classroom: A model for teaching experiential education theory. In: K. Warren, M. Sakofs, & J. S. Hunt (Eds.), *The theory of experiential education* (3rd ed., pp. 297–307). Dubuque, IA: Kendall/Hunt.

Weimer, M. (2002). *Learner-centered teaching: Five key changes to practice*. San Francisco, CA: Jossey Bass.

PEDAGOGY

Irene Popoli

FROM ART MANAGER TO SOCIAL ENTREPRENEUR REDESIGNING ACADEMIC PROGRAMS IN A TIME OF CHALLENGES AND OPPORTUNITIES

Abstract

During the last decades, public and private universities in Europe have started to design and offer undergraduate and master's degrees, as well as specialized courses, workshops and seminars, focusing on cultural management and entrepreneurship, with the explicit purpose of forming a class of knowledgeable, skilled professionals to operate specifically within the cultural industry. Among other European countries, Italy has witnessed a flourishing of countless initiatives from public and private universities aimed at fitting up a new generation of cultural professionals. Much has been done regarding the integration of knowledge from humanities and business administration, and this has been proven successful in equipping new administrators with the right skills to tackle challenges of organizational and cultural fitness.

However, what appears to be still missing from the existing academic training is the preparation cultural managers with specific social skills necessary in the digital age: Digital technologies and social media, in fact, are still kept on the side-lines of most academic curricula when instead they are pivotal in building up an integrated set of skills. The professional ability to guarantee administrative efficiency, cultural excellence and social impact equally is crucial for the fulfilment of political expectations; and this cannot be achieved today without a full set of digital and social media skills.

This article makes a few propositions as to why and how existing academic curricula for arts managers should be integrated with complementary digital and social skills, to the advantage of financial sustainability and social innovation.

Introduction

Arts and cultural management is, in itself, a young subject that has progressively found some space on the shelves of the academic literature on business administration (Evrard & Colbert 2000): in this sense, full acceptance within the general academic field is still an ongoing process. Among other aspects, the design of ad-hoc university curricula having arts management as the main subject can be considered one of the most important phenomena concurring to promote the integration of this new discipline among other academic streams.

During the last decades, the progressive extension of new public management theories (Dunleavy & Hood 1994; Hood 1991; 1995) to the cultural sector (Griffin 1991; Tobelem 2010) has created a radical shift in the managerial and governance approach to arts organizations. A progressive necessity to professionalize the field has led to a mandatory update of existing professional figures and, most significantly, to the definition of new ones which specifically include managerial knowledge in their curricula (McLean 1995). In general, then, a sector characterized by relative professional closeness, organizational rigidity and almost non-existent turn-over has been progressively forced to redefine the boundaries of many of its professional roles and to give more space to new figures with hybrid sets of skills (DiMaggio 1988).

PEDAGOGY

The traditional academic background of most museum and arts professionals – largely based on study of the humanities– has proved insufficient to keep up with the demand for managerially-trained practitioners: to compensate these inadequacies the higher education system has started to propose academic courses specifically designed to bring up both managerially and artistically educated practitioners explicitly trained for the changed cultural sector. The mentioned concurrent emergence of arts management as a sub-topic of the general management literature – and the avocation for its full inclusion by preeminent academic scholars – has supported the implementation of undergraduate and graduate courses dedicated to this discipline.

Overall, then, the combined forces – at both the professional and the academic levels –, pushing for the definition of new academic curricula destined to form ad-hoc cultural practitioners, together have determined the proliferation of courses and the concurrent institutionalization of the professional figure of the *arts manager* (and of all its specialized versions).

The Development of Cultural Management Curricula in Academic Programs: The Italian Case

The necessity to educate highly trained specialists with both artistic and managerial skills has emerged similarly in most European countries (López 1993): despite inherent national differences, the preeminent public nature of the sector in all Europe has led to the relatively simultaneous transformation of the professional framework in the cultural field (Kotler & Kotler 2000). At the same time, however, the social, economic, and political peculiarities of some countries have contributed to accelerate – or to intensify – the process, making it more visible, established, diffused, and, ultimately, researchable. The Italian academic system, in particular, has witnessed a boom in the offering of programs specifically dedicated to cultural and arts management: the significant dimension and capillary territorial diffusion of the national heritage, the scope of the cultural industry within the Italian economy, and the increasing entrance in the market of new organizations specialized in providing services to the cultural sector, together have pushed the agenda of a new class of cultural professionals to be educated through ad-hoc designed academic courses (Zan 2000).

From a preliminary analysis of archival data, it is possible to identify a progressive diffusion of undergraduate/master courses in arts management, cultural economics and similar subjects from the late 1990s, in correspondence with the progressive reduction of public funding designated for the cultural sector, with the opening of the market to private players (Van Aalst & Boogaarts 2002), with the increase in the competition at an international level, and with the emergence of a new institutional and governance paradigm regulating public organizations (Anderson 2004).

The quick introduction of new courses by universities was the result of the presence of faculty previously interested in the topic – thus making it easier to design an appropriate curriculum – and it is reflective of the opportunities offered by the local environment (Venice, Rome, Florence, Milan). Both private and public universities have engaged in offering courses in arts management, which administrative governance has often been split between two different departments (usually the Humanities and the Business Administration ones).

By analysing curricula of the longest-standing courses (at least five graduated classes), in fact, it is possible to verify the hybrid nature of the designed study plans, where half of the courses results as teaching management-related topics and the other half clearly involving cultural and artistic subjects (figure 1).

Moreover, it must be reported that, beside traditional undergraduate/master's degrees, an increasing plethora of specialized courses, executive and professional masters, and other educational programs have "invaded" the market, with many of these dedicated to experienced practitioners in need of a professional update.

Overall, then, during the last decade, the educational offer on arts and cultural management has flourished all around Italy, with the inevitable increase in competition over prospective students: in this sense, then, the necessity to be more attractive has led many universities to update and to redesign their curricula at a relatively fast pace compared to other traditional courses: new additions have been made – including the definition of sub curricula separating performing arts from visual ones, for example – and the original study plans have been refined – increasing the number of courses and reducing their respective credits weight.

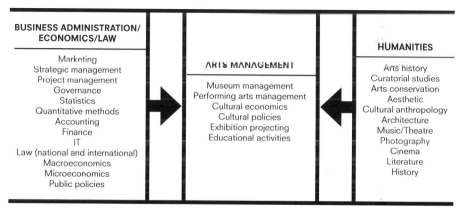

Figure 1 Academic Curricula in Cultural Management – Subject Structure

However, as it will be discussed later, more recently, the necessity to keep at pace with the job market's requests for new professional figures has not been promptly satisfied for what concerns the most recent professional opportunities emerged in the cultural sector, in Italy and elsewhere.

The Diffusion of Digital and Social Media Tools in Cultural Organizations

The boom of the digital and social media market (Hanna et al. 2011) that occurred in the last decade has opened up new possibilities in all sectors (Qualman 2010): from big corporations (Gallaugher & Ransbotham 2010; Culnan et al. 2010) to small start-ups, the diffusion of a faster and more direct way to communicate and to exchange information (Baird & Parasnis 2011; Vernuccio 2014) has determined the emergence of countless business opportunities (Mount & Martinez 2014; Kaplan & Haenlein 2010), not yet fully exploited to this day. In this sense, then, for-profit organizations have more or less understood the potentialities of engaging resources to develop these technologies (Kane 2015).

On the other hand, in the not-for-profit sector, many firms have easily acknowledged the possibilities that digital media could have in terms of cost reduction and social impact (Briones et al. 2011), putting their full exploitation as a top priority in their organizational strategies (Curtis et al. 2010).

The opportunities offered to cultural forms by the strategic use of social media (and correlated technologies) have progressively emerged and they are still far from being fully understood by the top management teams of many cultural and artistic organizations (Giaccardi 2012). The fragmentation of the diffusion of digital media and technologies among them, in fact, represents a point of departure to build up a more cohesive application that could involve, in particular, public cultural organizations – often resistant to change and innovation (Liew 2014).

From the definition of an integrated social media strategy (using multiple channels) to the promotion of the in-site use of digital technologies (apps with maps, audio-guides, etc.), from the engagement of local and virtual communities in project design (crowd-sourced exhibitions) to the efficient communication of results and annual reports to institutional and private stakeholders, digital and social media are particularly effective in supporting cultural organizations in a time of radical change of their social and economic environment (Brock, 2010; Liu 2011).

At the same time, the application of these new tools in the cultural sector has caught the attention not only of public organizations but also of actual and potential private entrepreneurs, interested in exploiting business opportunities and in taking advantage of the progressive expansion of a relatively unexplored market. Funding opportunities from private angel investors and public agencies have promoted the founding of new cultural start ups (For example the MakeACube platform, the IC-Innovazione Culturale fund, and the CheFare initiative, all of which are engaged in promoting new cultural start ups via financial and strategic support, from the initial idea to its implementation). Furthermore, we have seen the emergence of organizations specialized in digital services for the arts sector, spurring the expansion of a new market within the cultural field. *Musement*, for example, is a digital platform where perspective visitors to museums can buy tickets and tours online, thus planning their cultural visit beforehand.

Still, despite the occasional acknowledgement of the importance of social media and digital technologies in the cultural sector and their evident necessity for cultural professionals to get a minimum level of social and digital skills, very few specialized academic courses on this topic have been created, in Italy and elsewhere in Europe.

From the Arts Manager to the Social Entrepreneur: Designing new Academic Curricula for the Future

As discussed before, academic degrees in arts management have been designed and offered out of the explicit necessity to create professional training that was requested after the progressive change in the institutional paradigm in Italy. However, this ability to respond to external necessities on the part of universities seems to have been relatively lost, if we look at the lack of academic courses in cultural management with study plans somehow comprising topics involving entrepreneurship, innovation management, social media and digital technologies. As already mentioned, in fact, the most recent developments in communication and technology have increased the range of job opportunities within existing organizations as well as offered a variety of potential business ventures to be explored by cultural entrepreneurs.

To take full advantage of these potentialities and, at the same time, to keep up with a fast changing market such as the cultural one, current and new professionals are then pushed to update (or to form *ex novo*) their set of skills to include a minimum '*package*' of digital and social media abilities. In Italy, when looking at the current offers of professional and specialized courses in social media marketing, digital strategies and so on, it is possible to understand the progressive flourishing of extensive educational programs targeting present and future practitioners: As a minimum knowledge of IT is requested in almost all industries and sectors, and further specialized training in digital and social media is more and more perceived as an added value to compete in a crowded job market.

However, what seems more difficult to find is the needed redesign of existing undergraduate and graduate study plans in the arts management field: While we see more and more specialized courses are offered to the general professional public (and to graduates interested in enriching their résumés), no concurrent updates of existing programs in arts management can be reported, at least looking at the Italian educational system. Unfortunately, those universities that had recognized the transformations in the cultural market by proposing new specialized academic courses in cultural economics, entrepreneurship and management don't seem at the present state to have responded to external market requests to build expertise for social and digital-savvy cultural managers.

In fact, as cultural organizations – museums, theatres, exhibition centres, concert halls, galleries, cultural sites – are requested to be more engaged and connected with their local communities, while, at the same time, being able to compete at a national and international level to attract visitors, the potentialities of an effective use of social media and digital technologies have hardly been exploited by most organizations. When new challenges from a changed institutional, cultural and economic environment had arisen to force cultural organizations to request practitioners with new professional requisites, universities had felt sufficiently compelled to design a new offer in line with those demands. Now, as most cultural organizations seem still quite unaware of the full potentials of the new digital '*revolution*' (currently, the panorama of digital and social media integrated programs in cultural firms results extremely fragmented, with some best practices detectable in a landscape of non-engaged organizations), the academic system doesn't have sufficient external pressures to induce them towards a further integration of their offer.

For it, despite the foreseeable possibilities – for local growth, cultural enrichment, financial rationalization, social impact – coming from the application of new media and technologies to the management of arts and heritage (Giaccardi & Palen 2008; Paganoni 2012), almost no attempts have been done, by public and private universities in Italy, to complement current curricula with courses specifically dedicated to these matters.

Even worse, in parallel, so far neither traditional universities nor business schools are reported to have proposed new undergraduate and graduate courses destined to form cultural and social entrepreneurs, who could take advantage from the opportunities coming from the present cultural market (with reference to the mentioned application of new digital technologies but not only, as service and consultancies firms specifically dedicated to cultural organizations are still very rare, compared to those operating in other industries).

PEDAGOGY

In this sense, then, even just an unsystematic analysis of the current situation can clearly detect the relative stillness of the higher education system in respect to the new opportunities for further modernization and growth that new digital and social media skilled cultural practitioners could match to great benefit of the cultural and economic enrichment of the communities where they operate: by providing cultural managers with these professional skills, universities would move further into a path started with the discussed implementation of their offer, making themselves even more pivotal in contributing to the successful governance and management of the existing cultural heritage (in all its forms).

Final Considerations

Overall, during the last decades, the European – and Italian – cultural sector has expanded in scope and in variety and, at the same time, it has witnessed a radical transformation at the institutional, social, and economic levels. Cultural organizations have been then forced to rethink their organizational structure and to acknowledge the necessity to update their personnel profiles with new knowledge and competences. A response to these requests coming from the job market has been given by the higher educational system, with the activation of a multiple offer of undergraduate and graduate courses designed to form a new class of cultural professionals, equipped with both artistic and managerial skills.

The progressive emergence of new business and employment opportunities coming from the various application of digital technologies and social media to different industries and services has involved, among others, the cultural sector also: although, at the present state, the process is still on-going, it is nonetheless possible to foresee the countless opportunities that these new developments can have if put into practice in cultural organizations (and in public ones, in particular). The possibility to rationalize costs, the chance to have a closer and more engaged relationship with foreign visitors and local citizens, the opportunity to design and plan a more complete and diversified cultural and educational offer, the occasion to build a long-term relationship with public and private institutional stakeholders, with the concurrent reciprocal economic benefits that it may bring, and so on: a thoughtful and integrated use of digital technologies and social media by cultural organizations could open up a new spectrum of opportunities not to be missed, especially in times of financial and social struggle such as the one that the artistic field is living in the last years (Janes 2009). However, it is only by providing cultural organizations with a skilled class of cultural managers and by increasing the presence of resourceful cultural and social entrepreneurs in the cultural market that an effective growth and implementation of the cultural system can be achieved – to the great benefit of the public.

To ease and promote this progressive evolution, it is then necessary, for the educational system, to provide academic offers to match these necessities, at it has already demonstrated to be able to do with the designing of new courses in arts and cultural Management. It is up to those universities to take on this new challenge by updating their current offers with new programs (or a new version of the existing ones) more in line with the necessities of the professional market, the ultimate ambition, of course, being to contribute successfully to the sustainable and successful development of the cultural sector in all its versions.

About the Author

*Irene Popoli BSc Msc is
a Ph.D. Candidate in Business
Administration and a member of
the Centre for Arts, Business and
Culture at the Stockholm School
of Economics (Department of
Management and Organization).
She has earned her BSc in
Economics and Management of
Arts and Cultural Activities at
Ca' Foscari University of Venice,
and her MSc in Management
of Cultural Organizations at
Catholic University of Milan.
Before starting her Ph.D.,
she has worked at the performing
arts office at the Italian Cultural
Institute in New York and as
a strategic consultant at
the National Museum of Science
and Technology 'Leonardo da
Vinci' in Milan. A strong believer
in the crucial importance of
a strategic approach to the management of cultural organizations,
her research concentrates on
the multi-level effects of institutional and economic changes
on museums' organizational
structures and strategies.*

—

irene.popoli@hhs.se

References

Aalst, I. van & Boogaarts, I., 2002. From Museum to Mass Entertainment: The Evolution of the Role of Museums in Cities. In: *European Urban and Regional Studies*, 9(3), pp.195–209.

Anderson, G., 2004. *Reinventing the Museum: Historical and Contemporary Perspectives on the Paradigm Shift*, Lanham: Rowman Altamira.

Baird, C.H. & Parasnis, G., 2011. From social media to social customer relationship management. In: *Strategy & Leadership*, 39(5), pp.30–37.

Briones, R.L. et al., 2011. Keeping up with the digital age: How the American Red Cross uses social media to build relationships. In: *Public Relations Review*, 37(1), pp.37–43.

Brock, T., 2010. Communicating Cultural Heritage Through Digital Social Media. *Cultural Heritage Informatics Initiative.* Retrieved from: http://chi.anthropology.msu.edu/2010/11/communicating-cultural-heritage-throughdigital- social-media/

Culnan, M.J., McHugh, P.J. & Zubillaga, J.I., 2010. How Large U.S. Companies Can Use Twitter and Other Social Media to Gain Business Value. In: *MIS Quarterly Executive*, 9(4).

Curtis, L. et al., 2010. Adoption of social media for public relations by non-profit organizations. In: *Public Relations Review*, 36(1), pp.90–92.

DiMaggio, P., 1988. *Managers of the arts: careers and opinions of senior administrators of U.S. art museums, symphony orchestras, resident theatres, and local arts agencies*, Santa Ana, California: Seven Locks Press.

Dunleavy, P. & Hood, C., 1994. From old public administration to new public management. In: *Public Money & Management*, 14(3), pp.9–16.

Evrard, Y. & Colbert, F., 2000. Arts Management: A New Discipline Entering the Millennium? In: *International Journal of Arts Management*, 2(2), pp.4–13.

Gallaugher, J. & Ransbotham, S., 2010. Social Media and Customer Dialog Management at Starbucks. In: *MIS Quarterly Executive*, 9(4).

Giaccardi, E., 2012. *Heritage and Social Media: Understanding Heritage in a Participatory Culture*, London; New York: Routledge.

Giaccardi, E. & Palen, L., 2008. The Social Production of Heritage through Cross-media Interaction: Making Place for Place-making. In: *International Journal of Heritage Studies*, 14(3), pp.281–297.

Griffin, D., 1991. Museums - Governance, management and government. Or, why are so many of the apples on the ground so far from the tree? In: *Museum Management and Curatorship*, 10(3), pp.293–304.

Hanna, R., Rohm, A. & Crittenden, V.L., 2011. We're all connected: The power of the social media ecosystem. In: *Business Horizons*, 54(3), pp.265–273.

Hood, C., 1991. A Public Management for all Seasons? In: *Public Administration*, 69(1), pp.3–19.

Hood, C., 1995. The 'new public management' in the 1980s: Variations on a theme. In: *Accounting, Organizations and Society*, 20(2-3), pp.93–109.

PEDAGOGY

Janes, R.R., 2009. *Museums in a troubled world: renewal, irrelevance or collapse?*, London; New York: Routledge.

Kane, G.C., 2015. Enterprise Social Media: Current Capabilities and Future Possibilities. In: *MIS Quarterly Executive*, 14(1).

Kaplan, A.M. & Haenlein, M., 2010. Users of the world, unite! The challenges and opportunities of Social Media. In: *Business Horizons*, 53(1), pp.59–68.

Kotler, N. & Kotler, P., 2000. Can Museums be All Things to All People?: Missions, Goals, and Marketing's Role. In: *Museum Management and Curatorship*, 18(3), pp.271–287.

Liew, C.L., 2014. Participatory Cultural Heritage: A Tale of Two Institutions' Use of Social Media. In: *D-Lib Magazine*, 20(3/4).

Liu, S.B., 2011. *Grassroots Heritage: A Multi-Method Investigation of How Social Media Sustain the Living Heritage of Historic Crises.* ProQuest LLC. Retrieved from: http://www.proquest.com/en-US/products/dissertations/individuals.shtml.

López, S., 1993. The cultural policy of the European community and its influence on museums. In: *Museum Management and Curatorship*, 12(2), pp.143–157.

McLean, F., 1995. A Marketing Revolution in Museums? In: *Journal of Marketing Management*, 11(6), pp.601–616.

Mount, M. & Martinez, M.G., 2014. Social Media. In: *California Management Review*, 56(4), pp.124–143.

Paganoni, M.C., 2012. L'heritage in rete: social media e promozione del territorio. In: *Altre Modernità*, pp.233–247.

Qualman, E., 2010. *Socialnomics: How Social Media Transforms the Way We Live and Do Business*, John Wiley & Sons.

Tobelem, J.-M., 2010. *Le nouvel âge des musées: Les institutions culturelles au défi de la gestion*, Paris: Armand Colin.

Vernuccio, M., 2014. Communicating Corporate Brands Through Social Media: An Exploratory Study. In: *International Journal of Business Communication*, 51(3), pp.211–233.

Zan, L., 2000. Managerialisation processes and performance in arts organisations: the Archaelogical Museum of Bologna. In: *Scandinavian Journal of Management*, 16(4), pp.431–454.

Majda Tafra
Ana Skledar
Ines Jemrić

THE IMPACT OF BLENDED LEARNING ON STUDENTS' SKILLS AND COMPETENCIES
THE UNIVERSITY OF APPLIED SCIENCES BALTAZAR, CROATIA

Abstract

Blended learning is broad by definition, but always includes a combination of face-to-face and online activities. The digital transformation usually takes time because the innovation lies not only in the technology to be used, but also in the methods of instruction. Teachers need to be learning alongside their students and students, though digital natives; they need additional training as well.

UAS Baltazar Zaprešić, the only institution of higher education in Croatia with an undergraduate programme of cultural entrepreneurship and management, aiming to better meet the needs of the market and increase job opportunities for its graduates, has initiated a pilot blended-learning project. It includes a group of third-year *Cultural Management* undergraduate students and *Communication Management* graduate students. The desired outcome would be a flex model of blended learning which includes face-to-face lectures complemented by online activities. These activities are accompanied by an action research which aims to assess how blended learning affects student skills and competencies in the areas of culture and communication.

Each teacher included in the project has given their course a new design, in order to accommodate the desired course outcomes. Action research will use triangulated qualitative and quantitative methods, targeting not only to assess the impact on competencies and skills through the grading system but also the attitudes and experiences of participants in the process, teachers and students alike.

Background

University of Applied Sciences (UAS) Baltazar was founded in 2001 and today, with almost three thousand students enrolled, it is the biggest private business UAS in Croatia. It is the only higher education institution Croatia that provides higher education for entrepreneurs and managers in the sector of culture.

One of the specific goals is to prepare and train students and graduates for lifelong learning and for this reason UAS Baltazar has initiated a number of long-term strategies involving the application of new technologies and capacity building of teachers, in order to meet the needs of innovative development of higher education for managers, cultural managers included.

Cultural Management, the only such higher education programme in the country, and Communication Management have, in general, been attracting students who are more interested in new teaching methods and communication technology. Baltazar

PEDAGOGY

has decided to pilot blended learning in these two study groups. An action research has been accompanying these activities in order to deepen the understanding of the process and enable planning future improvements.

Blended Learning

There are numerous definitions of blended learning (BL), but all of them include a combination of face-to-face and online activities. According to Staker and Horn (2012) there are two components of the definition:

1. online delivery of at least a part of content and instruction of a formal education programme, with some elements of student control over time, place, path, and/or pace;
2. a supervised physical location away from home where at least a part of the learning must take place.

Bonk and Graham (2006) define BL as the combination of instruction from two historically separate models – face to face and distributed learning systems. According to Zemsky and Massy (2004), e-learning - understood as electronically mediated learning - offers a student-centred approach to learning, which is *customized, self-paced and problem-based* and therefore easily adapted to students' personal learning styles. This corresponds to the online/distributed component of blended learning.

Staker and Horn (2012) mention four models of blended learning:

1. Rotation model – students rotate between learning modalities, at least one of which is online learning;
2. Flex model – content and instruction are delivered primarily online and students move among learning modalities on their individual schedule. Some implementations have substantial face-to-face support, while others have minimal support;
3. Self-Blend model – students take one or more courses entirely online in addition to their on-site courses;
4. Enriched-Virtual model – students divide their time between attending a campus and using online delivery of content and instruction.

Whatever model is chosen, the focus should be on providing student and teacher support. Based on the findings of the research of over thirty universities and colleges in the USA, Bates (2000) recommends that higher education institutions focus on innovation in the design and delivery of content and instruction and on providing support.

False Assumptions about E-learning

This, however, is a time-consuming process and the S-curve of diffusion of innovations (Rogers, 2003) has to be taken into account. Also, there are some other issues to be considered. As reported by Zemsky and Massy (2004), there are three false assumptions about e-learning:

1. students will engage simply because online activities are offered;
2. students will engage because they are digital natives (Prensky, 2001);
3. e-learning will force a change in the way of teaching.

These assumptions are false because they imply that the e-learning process will start and evolve spontaneously. According to Jeffrey, Milne, Suddaby and Higgins (2012) the focus should be on student engagement, i.e. capturing engagement, maintaining engagement, and re-engaging those who have either never engaged or have become disengaged. Student support is of utter importance here.

Two related concepts, the concept of cultural entrepreneurship and the concept of (economic) entrepreneurship are treated here in the sense of compliance and fusion, beyond the perception of the cultural entrepreneur as an artist with a sense for business or the other way around. The assumption implied aims therefore at redefining the seemingly often accepted idea of cultural entrepreneur as someone who would be a miscast as a cultural entrepreneur if he/she sees cultural trade as a way of adding profit. (Klamer, 2011). The issue is therefore not whether a cultural entrepreneur is an artist with a business goal and high moral standards in regarding culture or a profit searching economist.

The debate about the raison d`être of entrepreneurship and cultural entrepreneurship alike is the debate focusing on two concepts: profit and purpose. Entrepreneurship, cultural entrepreneurship included, should not be primarily about profit; it is about purpose and the profit follows.

When the stakeholder theory and its implications for education of future entrepreneurs and managers are brought to the cultural entrepreneurship equation it becomes clear that cultural entrepreneurship education, as well as communication management education, should be considered, debated and improved in line with the broad understanding of culture as a way of life (Bennett, Slatter, 2008). This approach stresses the significance of shared meanings in relation to both cultural practices and cultural products; meanings naturally shared by communication.

The strategic direction of UAS Baltazar aims at embedding these approaches in our education of entrepreneurs and managers, cultural and communication managers included. Students receiving their B.A. at our university, in most cases, continue their studies at Communication Management and Project Management graduate programs, which is also an illustration of a certain consistency on the part of the teachers in pursuing an integrated approach to entrepreneurship education.

Consequently, the tasks of educators in both programmes need to include, among others: (adapted list by QAA, 212):

- Creating a learning environment that encourages (cultural) entrepreneurial behaviour in students
- Curricula with learning outcomes that encourage entrepreneurship behaviour
- Empowerment of students by means of relating learning outcomes to the cultural context
- Innovation in teaching approaches and willingness to experiment
- Engagement of external communities and appropriate practical contexts

These elements define some of the tasks included in the conceptual elaboration of the pilot introduction of blended learning in UAS Baltazar. We try to test this

PEDAGOGY

conceptual framework by studying the BL practice in UAS Baltazar introduced in education of cultural and communication managers. We scrutinise models of BL used by teachers, the expectations and perceptions of students and teachers about its efficiency and the challenges for both teachers and students, the issue of engagement included.

Research Methodology

Primarily concerned with understanding of the teaching practice and improving it, we have chosen an action research approach. As practitioners, we have experienced the validity of understanding education as a practice, whose problems can only be considered and resolved through action, which includes teachers' history, values and personal commitment to profession. The analysis within the action research concerns possibilities, not certainties, that it is dynamic and ever evolving (Hannan, 2008). We have, consequently, tried to continue analysing the material and our practice in a dialectical analysis of elements of both ideas and action in a holistic manner and as a learning process.

Our action research is covering the beginning of the pilot project of introducing blended learning in a number of courses of the undergraduate programme of Cultural management and graduate programme of Communication management (see Figure 1).

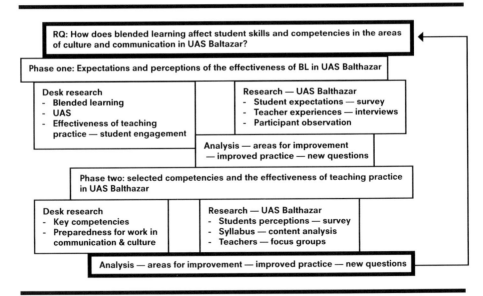

Figure 1 Action Research of Blended Learning in UAS Baltazar

In the first phase of the research, a methodological triangulation is implemented and both quantitative (survey) and qualitative (interviews) methods are used. The questionnaire was used to determine the preferred type of teaching, to assess the level of IT literacy, the access to a desktop computer/laptop/tablet and the Internet and to measure the expectations regarding blended learning. The research included the entire population of third year students of the undergraduate study of Cultural Management and the first and second year students of specialist graduate study of Communication Management, who embarked on BL in the academic year 2014/2015. The survey was carried out at the beginning of the academic year in order to avoid getting experience-contaminated data. The survey was carried out in a group-setting, and took place during classes in the winter semester. Each respondent answered the questions individually upon receiving instructions.

In total, the survey included 75 students, 44% Cultural Management, and 56% Communications Management. In the qualitative part of the research, open in-depth semi-structured 40-60 minute interviews with six teachers – participants in the pilot programme were held. The teachers, aged 32 to 64, all had previous experience the method which has been used in UAS Baltazar since 2006. Content analysis was used for the interpretation of data. The interviews were transcribed; key words and phrases identified in transcription, and later categorized according to themes and cor-related with the survey data.

Results and Analysis

The questionnaire opens with a question about the preferred type of teaching. Almost 70% of the respondents mention that the combination of face-to-face and online teaching is what they prefer. 28% of the respondents consider that face-to-face teaching carried out exclusively on-campus is the most acceptable form of teaching, while only 2.7% choose exclusively online teaching.

Since least an elementary level of IT literacy is required, the respondents were asked to assess the level of their own IT literacy. The aim was to determine whether the level of accepting BL is affected by the level of IT literacy on the one hand, and by the access to a computer or any other device the students can use. The results show that this fear is not grounded as 97% of students own a device with Internet access which can be used and 65% of students rate their IT literacy as very good or excellent.

With the aim of determining the attitudes about blended learning and the expected advantages and difficulties, an instrument[1] with 29 statements was constructed. The respondents were asked to indicate the extent to which they agree with each of the statements. A five degree Likert scale was offered, in which 1 stands for strong dis-agreement and 5 stands for strong agreement.

The highest ranking statements reveal anxiety regarding the new approach to teaching. Almost 91% students expect clear instructions from the teachers regarding online activities, as well as teacher feedback regarding the completed activities, and a slightly lower but nevertheless significant 86% expect the teachers' support in online activities while 89% expect technical support from the institution. 81% of the respondents see the flexibility of online as an advantage of bended learning. This is followed by a high percentage of agreement that emphasize the possibilities blended learning offers students in terms of easier exam procedure an overall studying, better time-management, continuous studying and flexibility. Respondents' expressed the lowest level of agree-ment with statements that emphasise the shortcomings of blended learning or potential difficulties with online assignments.

PEDAGOGY

---

[1] Al – Ani (2013); Al Zumor et al. (2013); Dela Torre (2013);
Owston and York (2012); Barnard et al. (2009)

Just above a third of the respondents believe that online activities will take up a lot of their time. A third of the respondents think the teaching process will be more difficult and that their interaction with other students will be hindered. A quarter of students indicate that the flexibility negatively influence their motivation for meeting the online assignments' deadlines, and under a quarter fear technical difficulties in online assignments.

The three lowest ranking statements refer to completely rejecting the blended learning concept. However, around 60% of respondents disagree with these statements. An even higher number, 83% of respondents, disagree with the statement *I do not have a sufficient level of IT literacy for this kind of teaching*, which partly corresponds to the findings of the assessment of students' own IT literacy level.

In order to process this dimension in more detail, the statements were scrutinized by factor analysis.

The results of the interpretation of the varimax solution matrix confirm the existence of five different models of perceived advantages, disadvantages and needs of the student population regarding blended learning; *Positive aspects of blended learning, Teacher and institutional support, Personal motivation, Negative aspects of blended learning*, and *Additional support*.

An additional analysis shows that there is no significant difference in scores on any of the factors between male and female respondents. Neither any significant difference can be found regarding the student status (part-time or full-time) and programme module – Cultural management or Communications management; nor between part-time and full-time students. A statistically significant difference was determined only on factor 5 *Additional support*. Part-time students expect additional support in completing online activities to a greater extent than full-time students. As for the programme module, a statistically significant difference was determined on the factor *Positive aspects of blended learning*. Communication Management students recognize positive aspects of blended learning significantly more than Cultural Management students.

In the semi-structured in-depth interviews six variables were investigated; Acceptability *of blended learning*, Perception *of student satisfaction with blended learning*, Institutional support *for blended learning*, Teacher burden *in blended learning*, Advantages and disadvantages *of blended learning*, Presence or absence *of engagement strategies in blended learning*.

Our analyses learned that there were only a few opposing attitudes regarding main aspects of blended learning. Regarding acceptability of BL at UAS Baltazar, all teachers expressed their positive view that BL is acceptable as a teaching method. Some were quite enthusiastic about the future prospects of BL as '*giving the students the best of both worlds, classic and on-line teaching*'. Some were rather reserved, admitting the potential but pointing out that neither the teachers nor the students were ready.

Prior to the introduction of the BL pilot project in the academic year 2014/2015, the teachers were using LMS Moodle[2] mainly for posting materials in electronic form and giving students the option to submit papers. However, online testing, although possible, was not widely used and the final evaluation was mainly summative. The introduction of BL has given the teachers the opportunity to expand in methods used. The students have been given the opportunity to better use their time in what was mainly the implementation of the Enriched-Virtual model. The students of Cultural Management had, in a way, been groomed in the previous two years by various project-based tasks and stimulated to welcome innovation, particularly because there is a certain collective culture implying their innovative spirit as future cultural entrepreneurs.

The teacher of Cultural Management took a lead in using BL techniques and the statistics he had gathered after the end of the winter semester led him to the conclusion that BL for future cultural entrepreneurs is at the good start and needs to be developed further. Thus, 55% of 65 students enrolled in the course completed all the online assignments. A total of 66.2 % passed both their mid-term exams in the form of two online tests (which has never happened before) and thus fulfilled the requirements for the final oral exam.

Regarding their perception of student satisfaction with blended learning, two teachers claimed that students were fully satisfied, while four teachers claimed that there were big differences between full-time and part-time students. Teachers claimed full-time students expressed some dissatisfaction with the new method, while part-time students valued the flexibility in time for studying. Teachers insisted that students should be better prepared for BL.

The overall response regarding institutional support was rather critical towards the institution. While all admitted that support undoubtedly existed on a declarative level, some teachers said they felt completely abandoned and isolated, while other teachers looked for support among themselves. All complained that some type of support is needed, not only technical but also pedagogical and methodological. They claimed that the opportunities were not promising without a support system in place, person, centre, or a network.

Teacher Preparation

All interviewed teachers claimed that teacher preparation for BL was a huge, extremely time-consuming task and that online activities reduced the opportunities for inter-active contact. One teacher admitted to not having prepared extensively as the materials were already prepared in previous years, but others described a lot of time and energy included in the preparation and in monitoring students' progress online, correcting assignments etc. This correlates with the survey findings that clear instructions and support are expected from teachers. Again the issue of methodological preparation and the need for support and additional capacity building in course design were stressed. This corresponds to survey findings that the teaching process would be more difficult and interaction with other students hindered.

PEDAGOGY

---

[2]*Moodle: a free, open-source PHP web application for producing modular internet-based courses*

All teachers but one claimed that advantages of BL (better student results, better online interaction, saving time and studying costs, compliance with modern online mobility of student population) outnumbered the disadvantages (lack of preparation, somewhat sceptical attitude of students and teacher workload). Even reserved teachers claimed that the advantages would be great if all the conditions were met (support, preparation of both teachers and students).

A last group of questions was about the presence of five engagement strategies as identified in literature research: primer, social presence, challenge, authentic tasks and re-engaging. All teachers claimed to be implementing at least three of the five strategies. The one not followed was re-engaging which included monitoring and early identifications as well as personal contact and negotiated conditions for re-engagement. Teachers claimed to be so focused on the content, form and online interactive exchange with students and monitoring their success, that in this stage they could not deal with individuals who disengaged. Furthermore, it was clearly stated that no particular *one size fits all* model would be found acceptable. Teachers have adopted and adapted three of the four models (Staker and Horn, 2012).

Based on the survey data and interviews with teachers, a SWOT analysis drafted below suggests that this phase of the project has pointed to a number of strengths and opportunities.

PEDAGOGY

STRENGTHS	WEAKNESSES
- BL programme is more cost-effective - Accessibility of learning for all categories of students (part-time students) - Innovative potential of further development of BL methods - Students own the technology needed students reduced - Better time management for students - Easier exam procedure and overall studying for students - Preferred type of teaching for majority of students	- No preparation of students - No preparation of teachers – left on their own - Institution support only on declaratory level - Interactivity with teachers and other - No focal point for teacher support - No expert in course design at hand
OPPORTUNITIES	THREATS
- Compliance with increasing on-line mobility of student population - Adapting to communication style closer to students - Part–time students need additional support which opens new areas of engagement - Flexibility of studying	- Increasing teacher burden - Monitoring by teachers time consuming - Pressure by competition - Some students drop out of on-line activities and disengage, posing a problem to course community

Figure 2 SWOT analysis of blended learning in UAS Baltazar

In addition, areas for improvement were found on the level of all three key stakeholders: management, students and teachers. Regarding management, it is clear from the results that policy introduction and declarative support will not suffice for sustainable introduction of BL but additional operational measures are needed. These refer to financial and human resources. Additional elaboration of teachers' performance management might also be required in the future.

On the level of students the attitude is generally positive towards the new method but they need to be prepared and their growing expectations need to be met. This means that teaching process planning needs to be considered in-depth in the new circumstances. If the management and teachers fail at this, the opportunity to increase the quality of learning will be lost.

Finally, the main burden of these new methods is obviously on the teachers. They need institutional support and help in awareness raising and capacity building. As participants in the process they should be able to plan future elaborations of BL introduction in the teaching process.

Conclusion and Recommendations

The action research has shown that the introduction of blended learning in UAS Baltazar has proved to have a number of advantages that range from cost-effectiveness and time management to easier exams and overall studying for students, to being a preferred type of teaching for the majority of students.

These are encouraging results for this phase of the pilot project that has only been introduced in the academic year 2014/2015. It also reveals numerous challenges and opportunities that need to be dealt with as a part of the process of introducing blended learning and developing new programmes and new teaching techniques.

At this stage the main recommendations concern an urgent need for teacher support and the preparation of students. It is recommended that these two strategic interventions be developed in a participatory manner. In addition, both students and teachers should be included in the process of planning corrections and alterations of blended learning in UAS Baltazar.

PEDAGOGY

About the Authors

Prof Dr Majda Tafra is a life-time tenure professor at the University of Applied Sciences Baltazar Zapresic, Croatia. She also teaches courses in communication and business ethics and sustainable business at the University of Dubrovnik and Rochester Institute of Technology, Croatia. She holds a doctors degree in communication sciences from the University of Zadar, Croatia and postgraduate certificates in sustainable business and cross-sector partnership and sustainable development from the University of Cambridge, UK.

References

Al-Ani, Wajeha Thabit (2013). *Blended Learning Approach Using Moodle and Student's Achievement at Sultan Qaboos University in Oman*. Retrieved from: http://www.ccsenet.org/journal/index.php/jel/article/viewFile/28509/17543

Al Zumor, Abdul Wahed Q.; Al Refaai, Ismail K.; Bader Eddin, Eyhab A.; Aziz Al-Rahman, Farouq H. (2013). *EFL Students' Perceptions of a Blended Learning Environment: Advantages, Limitations and Suggestions for Improvement*. Retrieved from: http://www.ccsenet.org/journal/index.php/elt/article/view/30165/17872

Barnard, Lucy; Lan, William Y; To, Yen M.; Oslan Paton, Valerie; Lai, Shu-Ling (2009). *Measuring self-regulation in on-line and blended learning environments*. Retrieved from: http://www.sciencedirect.com/science/article/pii/S1096751608000675

Bates, A. (2000). *Managing Technological Change: Strategies for College and University Leaders*. San Francisco: Jossey-Bass

Bennett, P., Slater, J. (2008). *Communication and Culture*. New York: Routledge

Bonk, C. J, Graham, C. R. (2006). *The Handbook of Blended Learning: Global Perspectives, Local Design*. San Francisco: Pfeiffer Publishing

Dela Torre, Jennifer M. (2013). *Variances on Students' Blended Learning Perception According to Learning Style Preferences*. Retrieved from: http://www.iiste.org/Journals/index.php/JEP/article/view/7914/7990

Hannan, A. (2008). *Writing Up Research, Faculty of Education, University of Plymouth*. Retrieved from: http://www.edu.plymouth.ac.uk/resined/writingup/WRITING%20UP%20RESEARCH.htm

Jeffrey, L.M., Milne, J., Suddabay, G (2012). *Help or Hindrance. Blended Approaches and Student Engagement*. Retrieved from: https://akoaotearoa.ac.nz/download/ng/file/group-3089/help-or-hindrance-final-report.pdf

Klamer, A. (2011). Cultural entrepreneurship. In: *Rev Austrian Econ*. Retrieved from: http://download.springer.com/static/pdf/449/art%253A10.1007%252Fs11138-011-0144-6.pdf?auth66=1425750820_4dba6b96e37efe923ba4b-755de114bfa&ext=.pdf

Owston, Ron; York, Dennis (2012). *Evaluation of Blended Learning Courses in the Faculty of Fine Arts – Fall/Winter Session 2011 – 2012*. Retrieved from: http://irdl.info.yorku.ca/files/2014/01/TechReport2012-4.pdf

Prensky, M. (2001). *Digital Natives, Digital Immigrants*. MCB University Press, 9(5).

QAA, (2012). *Enterprise and entrepreneurship education, The Quality Agency for Higher Education*. Retrieved from: www.qaa.ac.uk

Rogers, E. M. (2003). *Diffusion of Innovations*. New York: Free Press

Staker and Horn (2012). *Classifying K-12 Blended Learning. San Francisco: Innosight Institute*. Retrieved from http://www.christenseninstitute.org/wp-content/uploads/2013/04/Classifying-K-12-blended-learning.pdf

Zemsky, R. and Massy, W. F. (2004). *Thwarted innovation: What Happened to e-learning and Why?* Retrieved from: http://www.thelearningalliance.info/Docs/Jun2004/ThwartedInnovation.pdf

She published five books and numerous articles on communication management and corporate responsibility. Before joining the academia Majda worked as a journalist and as a public affairs manager in UNICEF and in Coca-Cola.

—

majda.tafra@gmail.com

Prof Dr Ana Skledar is a college professor at t he University of Applied Sciences Baltazar Zapresic, Croatia. She is Assistant Dean for Academic Affairs and also teaches English for Specific Purposes (ESP). She earned her PhD in literature from the Faculty of Philosophy, University of Ljubljana, Slovenia. She is an ESP textbook author and publishes papers in the area of ELT and ESP, language and literature. Ana's areas of interest are interdisciplinary and experimental approaches to teaching ESP and new technologies in education.

—

a.skledar-matijevic@bak.hr

Ines Jemrić BA MA is a senior lecturer at the University of Applied Sciences Baltazar Zapresic, Croatia, where she teaches sociology. She is the head of the Department for Sociology, Psychology and Related Disciplines. She holds a BA in Sociology from the Faculty of Philosophy, University of Zagreb, Croatia and an MA in Sociology of Culture from the Faculty of Philosophy, University of Ljubljana, Slovenia. Her areas of interest are sociology of culture, sociology of gender and cultural/creative industries.

—

ines.jemric@bak.hr

PEDAGOGY

Bruno Verbergt
Laila De Bruyne

COMPANIONS, NOT GENERAL MANAGERS WHAT MAKES ARTS MANAGEMENT GRADUATE STUDIES SUCCESSFUL?

Abstract

Starting from a philosophical investigation of the specificities of arts management and cultural entrepreneurship and their consequences for management education in the fields of arts and culture, this paper addresses the labour market response to curriculum design in the Cultural Management master program at the University of Antwerp, Belgium. A survey amongst alumni was held in 2009 and repeated in 2014. This study gives an insight into the distinctive qualities of an arts management master program compared to a general management program, and how such a degree can meet the labor market needs of the arts and culture industries. It supports the Janus syndrome conclusion of Brkić (2009), who stated that a simultaneous look at general management and the arts is essential to the success of an arts management education program. Arts managers and cultural entrepreneurs need to be acquainted with both banks of the river, as well as with the techniques needed to build solid, beautiful and *'challenging'* bridges. Besides being general managers and producers, arts managers and cultural entrepreneurs also act as mediators and as companions of artists, associated with them in the same way that a pianist accompanies a singer.

Introduction

The establishment of arts administration and arts and cultural management master programs at universities in North America and Europe reveals a need to separate these education programs from other management, business and arts degrees. This contribution examines the distinctive qualities of an arts management program in comparison to a general management program and how such a degree can meet the labour market needs of the arts and culture industries.

First, we analyse the debate surrounding the specific characteristics of arts and cultural management and subsequently the ideal education model for this field, as an extension of the debate on what general management is, and how it should be taught. Second, we describe our case study: the Cultural Management master program at the University of Antwerp and two surveys investigating the arts and culture labour market response to this program.

Terminology

The 1965 Rockefeller Panel paper was the first policy paper to call for a more professional managerial framework for the arts. The keyword was arts *administration*, and universities subsequently began offering graduate and postgraduate studies in arts administration. This term was far less popular in Europe, when new arts and cultural *management* master programs were established towards the end of the 20th century. Şuteu (2006) notes that the term *'management'* is more strategy and enterprise oriented. When it comes to management, there is a stronger focus on the market as opposed to the hierarchical approach of organizations. Alternatively, as Bridgstock (2013) puts it,

PEDAGOGY

PEDAGOGY

arts *entrepreneurship* concerns skills that are associated with '*the application, sharing and distribution*' of art and creative work as opposed to '*its creation or making*'. More programs, especially in the U.K. and the Netherlands, are now adding cultural entrepreneurship to their diploma titles, and universities are developing research and competence centres under that name[1]. The qualitative survey made by Beckman (2007) of U.S.-based '*adventuring*' arts entrepreneurship programs reveals that the entrepreneurship approach is not limited to Europe. While there are some differences between the three terms with respect to the dynamics of the subject matter (administration and management now have a more static flavour, focused on '*running the business*', while entrepreneurship is far more dynamic, focusing on '*creating the business*'), we have opted to use the word '*management*' to refer to the entire field.

The Specificities of Arts and Cultural Management
The academic evolution of management as a science, following its launch by scholars such as Henri Fayol, Frederic Taylor, Max Weber, Mary Parker Follett and Elton Mayo, has been challenged since the early seventies by Henry Mintzberg's research on what managers really do. '*The trouble with 'management' education is that it is business education, and leaves a distorted impression of management. Management is a practice that has to blend a good deal of craft (experience) with a certain amount of art (insight) and some science (analysis)*', writes Henry Mintzberg in his introduction to *Managers Not MBAs* (2004). Thus, management is neither a science nor a profession. Mintzberg (2009) elaborates on this view using his own doctoral research (1973) and supports other authors such as Whitley (1989; 1995). Barker (2010) also defends his view. Baily and Ford (1996) criticize the practice of American business education established since the 1950s, claiming too little distinction has been made between scholarship (the act of generating knowledge) and education (the act of training practitioners): '*The practice of management is best taught as a craft; rich in lessons derived from experience and oriented toward taking and responding to action.*' Baily and Ford call for an alternative model that views management as a craft involving creativity, experimentation and judgment. Laermans (2012) reminds us that the very skilfulness of a craft rests on the paradoxical ability of the practitioner to transform the not-knowing that the activity necessarily involves into a workable delusion of knowledge or expertise.

When it is defined as a practice, we might argue that management can be taught by transferring knowledge, practicing the craft and enhancing students' insight and '*artistic*' (hidden) talents. A similarity emerges with the educational challenges of arts academies and with the history of the concept of the academy and academism (Boime 1986; Gielen & De Bruyne 2012): art is also a practice, fuelled by knowledge, craftsmanship

---

[1] *Of the 152 graduate and postgraduate study programs listed on www.artsmanagementnetwork.net, 96 (63%) have the word 'management' in their title and 27 (18%) the word 'administration'. Of this latter group, 17 are taught in the USA. Two educational institutions offer a degree in 'arts administration and management'. The website lists three institutions that offer master programs in arts entrepreneurship, all based in the U.K. or the Netherlands. A Google search ('master cultural entrepreneurship', 'maîtrise entrepreneuriat culturel' and 'maestria empresario culturales' performed on 21 December 2014) yielded nine results: five courses in the U.K., two in the Netherlands and one each in Ireland, Bulgaria and Indonesia. Beckman (2007) lists 42 programs (all levels) in the U.S. that focus on 'adventuring' arts entrepreneurship.*

and talent or artistic creativity. Thus, being an artist or manager is not a profession; it is a vocation. This definition suggests that the distinctive qualities of arts management postgraduate programs should be investigated within three domains: management, arts and arts management knowledge; management, arts and arts management craft; and management, arts and arts management creative capacities, competences and insights.

It is clear that there is a significant difference between the knowledge and craft of management and the knowledge and craft of the arts. However, both managers and artists are expected to use their '*creative*' talents and insights in their jobs. Alongside the economization of the concept of culture, we are seeing a growing interest from the management side in creativity (Lampel, Lant & Shansie 2000; Sutton 2001; Bilton & Leary 2002; Florida & Goodnight 2005; Amabile & Khaire 2008) and even in the arts (Nissley 2002). Creativity is seen as essential to success in any discipline or industry, and is one of the most sought-after traits in leaders today. Creative thinking has enabled the rise and continued success of countless companies (Kelley & Kelley, 2012). Besides this common interest in creativity and its management, Hagoort (2007) mentions the commonly held belief that management and the arts are incompatible, echoing Horkheimer, Adorno and Benjamin. The rational mind-set of managers might lead to massification and profit-making activities, which are opposed to artistic integrity, and thus undermine the quality of cultural products (see also Chiapello 1998). Management is supposed to be free of the values that are so inherent to arts and culture. Kuesters (2010) acknowledges the functional differences between arts managers and artists, but also proposes the use of theoretical frameworks that see arts managers as liaisons between finance and arts. Hence the image of building a bridge between the worlds of management and the arts and culture. Hence, also, the relevance of investigating structural differences between general management and cultural or arts management.

A separate Knowledge Base for Cultural Management?

Within the knowledge domain we can distinguish a number of very different theories and models specific to cultural management. The first group of these concern the value appreciation of culture, which is variously seen as different from, broader than or even reducible to economic value equations (see e.g. Klamer 1996, Hutter & Throsby 2008, Snowball 2008). Gielen *et al.* (2014) give an overview of all empirical evidence of the value of culture. Evrard & Colbert (2000) and Noordman (2010) stress that value in arts and culture is experiential, thus immaterial and specific in the sense that it does not diminish after use. The second theory of note is Baumol and Bowen's law on cost disease, the productivity lag that is inherent to the live performing arts. A third group consists of leadership theories that are specific to artistic leadership (Hagoort 2005). Taken as a whole, the scientific knowledge base that is specific to cultural management is rather limited compared to that of general management and there is no convincing argument for treating it as a separate discipline.

The Art and Craft of Cultural Management

Many authors who advocate a clear distinction between management and arts management do so on the basis of a distinctive or '*deviant*' application of management models and theories. Still, as Noordman (1993) points out, we need to be aware that there were no theoretical motives for starting new arts management education programs. It was a number of rather practical concerns that drove universities to offer cultural management programs, such as the growth of cultural organizations and the expanding

PEDAGOGY

complexity of their environment. It seemed obvious to offer separate programs, distinct from general management, because of the interdisciplinary approach required by arts administrators and managers.

If we consider management to be a practice, combining knowledge, craft and insight, it is clear that while the craft concerns working in the artistic, cultural and creative sectors, it is their insights that distinguish cultural managers from general managers. Cultural managers should be aware of the tacit weakness of general management, which implicitly focuses on large-scale, industrial and profit-driven organizations (Hagoort 2005). However, they should also be aware of the dangers of viewing general management as a set of generally applicable theories and models that need no further craftsmanship or insight. In what follows, we outline a number of relevant discussion points and conclusions, derived from the literature.

1. Specific talents and insight with respect to strategic management. Cultural managers need specific talents and insight with respect to *strategic management*. Hagoort (2005) stresses external orientation and innovation, cultural mission, societal responsibility, passion and affection as crucial elements of cultural entrepreneurship. De Corte (2011) notes, however, that the basic principles of entrepreneurship, as summarized by Shumpeter, are still relevant to arts and culture. Șuteu (2006) observes that the cultural manager's relation to society and especially to cultural policy is typical of European contexts.

    Arts organizations need a supply-side marketing approach (Evrard & Colbert 2000, Bendixen 2000). Fillis (2006) describes how the arts industries demonstrate the implications of ignoring market demand and customer wishes. Noordman (2010) describes programming as a meeting of production and taste, while De Roeper (2008) views it as a cultural gatekeeping activity linking audience and artist. Of course, the degree of supply orientation varies: cultural organizations (such as public libraries) are less supply driven than arts organizations. In addition, cultural and creative profit industries are often primarily demand driven: Chong (2002) uses this tendency towards market orientation as an indicator of cultural entrepreneurship. Hagoort (2007), meanwhile, puts far more emphasis on the organization-specific elements of cultural entrepreneurship.

Evrard and Colbert (2000) state that *project and innovation management* are important for the arts and for the cultural manager. Also, cultural managers should be adept at managing discontinuity, and artistic activities are prototypical. Their experiences in working with intermittent workers, dealing with dual management and specializing in what Evrard and Colbert refer to as '*immateriality and patrimoniality*' in finance and accounting may make cultural managers excellent role models for general managers. We might also refer to the peculiarities of authorship and the very special contracts related to buying in top artists (Noordman 2010). Evrard and Colbert (2000) conclude that the differences between general management and arts management may not be that big in many ways, but that just as neurology and cardiology are subdisciplines of medicine, cultural management should be considered a sub discipline of management. For example, Bendixen (2000) notes that artists acquire value not only through sales, but also through reputation. Even given the description of arts management as a creative activity in itself, attracting public attention and launching images based on reputation,

PEDAGOGY

it cannot replace classical management and its marketing, financing, labor relations and accounting functions. Again, the peculiarities of arts management seem to demand a different kind of insight. '*First*', Bendixen (2000) writes, '*serious arts production follows the criteria of the arts and artists; in contrast to commodity industries, its primary purpose is not to satisfy the ordinary needs of consumers, but to challenge their interest in the art, which is more or less independently produced*'. Second, arts and culture embrace a broader range of target groups than does the consumer market. However, when it comes to shaping a stable and far-reaching public sphere in which to secure a reputation, arts management and business management are in many ways rather similar.

2. Besides marketing strategy, Evrard & Colbert (2000) and Noordman (2006; 2010) also identify specific approaches to *promotion* (the dominance of word of mouth; the larger amounts of time spent on public relations), branding (a particular means of image building which uses a combination of brands) and market research (which is primarily qualitative). Sometimes, word of mouth marketing and branding work so well, that the arts manager neglects other essential marketing techniques (Noordman 2006). Durrer and Miles (2009) focus more on the social dimension of relationship building, which they found in arts marketing practices in the U.K.

3. Leadership, too, requires special attention in the context of arts and cultural organizations. Besides the dominance of dual leadership in arts organizations (Chiapello 1998, Evrard & Colbert 2000, Cliché *et al.* 2002, Cray, Inglis & Freeman 2007, Noordman 2010), a special kind of charismatic, highly dedicated and perfectionist artistic leadership has been identified in the literature (Hagoort 2005, Noordman 2010). Leaders in arts and culture face specific challenges: managing and leading creative personnel and processes (DeFilippi *et al.* 2007) means dealing with leadership paradoxes, such as finding a balance between personal initiatives and common goals and benefits, and between stimulating collaborators' autonomy and setting up functional teams (Andriopoulos 2003). Hagoort (2005) and Şuteu (2006) list an entire set of specific values of relevance for cultural leaders, including human rights-related, ethical, social, democratic, and idiosyncratic artistic values. Such leaders must be able to understand and critically react to the culture of stereotypes as well as to label diversities (Şuteu 2006).

4. In the area of *human resources (HR) management*, cultural managers need to have specific insight into working in small teams, where work relations are informal and the environment is dynamic. The adhocratic organization culture is prominent: decentralization, creativity, change and experimental drive are key values (Hagoort 2005). Intrinsic motivation can be so high in cultural organizations that managers need to temper it, to prevent physical, mental and relational damage. In such cases, managers may also neglect other basic HR issues (Noordman 2010).

The '*art*' of cultural management, namely the vision or insights surrounding the subject matter, is a far broader domain than the scientific base of general management. A more intense and field-specific type of education is required to prepare managers to cope with the huge number of potential constellations and organizations that are present in the artistic and cultural realm.

PEDAGOGY

The Roles of the Cultural Manager

Some authors describe the differences between cultural management and general management on the basis of the specific roles cultural managers need to play. As the performing arts show us, roles are embodied through rehearsal and repetition. *Oefening baart kunst*, goes the Dutch proverb: practice makes perfect, literally '*practice gives birth to art*'. Which roles exactly should aspiring cultural managers be practicing?

Radbourne and Fraser (1996) attribute to the cultural manager the role of facilitating the exchange of artistic experience between the artist and the consumer through innovative cultural leadership. As this transfer is often related to government cultural policy, the cultural manager thus acts as a mediator for legislation, artists and the cultural industry itself. Bendixen (2000) also focuses on this facilitating role: the exchange, or mediation, should occur through images based on reputation and distinction, in a supply-driven manner. This is especially the case with arts products which aim beyond easily reachable audiences. Many other authors mention this bridging role as essential and distinctive to arts and cultural managers. It can be grounded historically in the role of the *impresario* and producer (Noordman 2010) or the cultural gatekeeper (De Roeper 2008). It can also be conceived as developmental (UNESCO's aim, as described in Boylan 2003), entrepreneurial (Hagoort 2005, 2010), or as dealing with or shifting between two different logics (Cray, Inglis & Freeman 2007, Brkić 2009, Eikhof & Haunschild 2007, Kolsteeg 2014) or languages (Rooijakkers 1990, Bendixen 2000). Chiapello (1998) focuses on the role of the cultural manager as a companion of artists, where the logic of love, with its elements of trust and belief in non-exploitation, runs parallel with the logic of art.

Implications for Cultural Management
Graduate Education

At the end of introductions to cultural management textbooks, we often find statements such as: '*These characteristics [of cultural organizations] have implications for the way art managers apply general management theory to their own situation*' (Hagoort 2005). Devereaux (2009) remarks in her '*state of the field*' that many authors pay lip service to arts and cultural management as a separate discipline, but eventually conceive of art and culture as the next thing to be managed. Textbooks on cultural management such as Byrnes (1999), however, remain faithful to the classical management approach. Ebewo & Sirayi (2009) also see cultural management education as an education in traditional management, followed by specialization in the management of one or more arts disciplines. Eventually there might be a future, Ebewo & Sirayi conclude, in which '*cultural management will not be a tenant in another department but an autonomous department that will cater effectively to the teaching of the relevant and related subjects; it could even become an independent school within a university*'. Using Mintzberg's definition of management as a practice combining knowledge, craft and insight, we are far better equipped to understand the differences between general management and cultural management. The latter can then be seen as a sub discipline of the first, adding only a few findings and laws of its own to the knowledge base, enriching the craft by defining clearly the bridging or mediating and companion roles of the cultural manager, and unveiling peculiarities in the application of general management and leadership theories as well as in the dynamics of the arts and cultural industries. This implies that all academic discourse on general management education should be part of a reflection on cultural management education – something that has not been done to date in studies or reflections such as those by Şuteu (2006), Ebewo & Sirayi (2009) and Brkić (2009). Discourses that originate from arts education, such as Beckman (2007) and especially Brigdstock (2013), exclude the challenges encountered in business school education, by claiming that its entrepreneurial philosophy is too narrow to apply to arts and culture. Even though it has been acknowledged that corporate social responsibility in fact offers opportunities to broaden the classical concept of management. Statements like that of Howkins (2001) that successful creative entrepreneurs must '*realize their success will be measured in financial terms; the rest is in shadows*' have not only had a devastating impact on the open mind-set: it is a statement that even many general business managers would not endorse.

The Janus head

Brkić (2009) uses the metaphor of the Janus head (introduced by Şuteu 2006): cultural management education should include both artistic or cultural education *and* managerial education, and its basis should be cultural. The ability to shift between two logics, one artistic-cultural and one business (market oriented and/or institutional/policy oriented), is a skill cultural managers need to master, both as mediators and as companions. Bendixen (2000) distinguishes the cultural manager's mediating role from the bridging role of a general manager, who also mediates but as an agent, trader or broker. The cultural manager does not value both sides equally, '*but firmly plants reputation and distinction in the minds of the customers, audiences and consumers, as well as in the media, in the relevant political scene, and among the experts, critics and whomever else may be of importance.*' The same goes for the companion role of the arts manager as producer. Here, being a companion is comparable to the pianist accompanying the singer. It is a subtle game of leading and following, and of following and leading.

Trust is tremendously important: it is given, understood and built. In the end, however, it is the singer who is the star. What the '*academy*' of cultural management needs to achieve, by providing examples, cases, tools for application, internships and so on, is the delivery of insight to students: insight into how management works, how art and culture work and how the bridge between the two worlds works. Subsequently, students will develop insight into what roles to play and what crafts to practice.

The University of Antwerp Case

Brkić (2009) distinguishes four types of curriculum: those that copy directly from business management; those that focus on the technological process of producing artwork; those that link cultural management and cultural policy; and those that take an entrepreneurial approach to arts management, connecting it to issues of creativity and innovation. The University of Antwerp (Belgium) has offered a graduate program in cultural management in the Faculty of Applied Economics since 1999. While the program mainly falls into the first category mentioned above, it also has elements characteristic of the third type, and of the fourth type, primarily because of the involvement of a competence centre devoted to the creative industries at the Antwerp Management School. Undergraduate students in any discipline (often with a supplementary preparatory or conversion year) learn to master the art of combining arts, culture and the creative industries with management in one year.

PEDAGOGY

During this year, the students acquire knowledge, experience and insight by thoroughly auditing an arts organization or cultural institution: what do these organizations actually do in the areas of general and strategic management, marketing management, financial management and HR management? Finally, their master thesis tackles a real management problem within one or more arts organizations.

Methodology and Data Collection

We used data from two electronic surveys taken in 2009 and 2014. Both surveys consisted of quantitative and qualitative study about the employment of graduates of the master in Cultural Management and their opinion of the direct usefulness of the master in their first and/or current job. Since the master program is still running, and given the distribution of survey participants over the graduation years, we consider the data collection to be representative, albeit with a slight overweight for the more recent years.

Respondents' current Work Situation

Of all respondents in the two surveys, 87% (2009) and 91.4% (2014) had a paid job. The majority (almost 90%) were employees; the others were self-employed. Taking both surveys together, 57.6% of respondents worked in the cultural sector or creative industries. A decline was observed in the more recent years, which might be attributed to the effects of the economic crisis. Furthermore, 39% of all respondents (2009 & 2014) were found to work in management-related functions. In 2014, 90% of respondents said that they were working at university level.

A clear relationship can be observed between graduates' major choice and their current profession. However, care must be taken when drawing conclusions about causal relationships: students that are motivated to choose a particular major, will also be motivated to look for and find a job within the same sector. The qualitative section of the survey should provide more evidence. The high score for 'other' sectors in which alumni of the creative industries major are employed can be explained by 77% employment in the private, more commercial sectors such as banking, transport, retail, consulting and pharmaceuticals.

DESCRIBE YOUR JOB? I HAVE A JOB IN...	2009 (in %) n = 145	2014 (in %) n = 105	BREAKDOWN OF THE 2014 SURVEY		
			2009-2014 (in %) n = 28	MAJOR CCI (2010-2013) (in %) n = 36	MAJOR A&C (2010-2013) (in %) n = 41
The cultural sector (government inclusive)	53,8	36,2	39,3	16,7	51,2
The creative industries (publishers, film productions houses, concerts, design, etc.)	7	14,3	10,7	27,8	4,9
The social sector	4,8	3,8	7,1	0	4,9
Education (incl. teaching cultural courses, excl. educational services in cultural organizations)	11	9,5	14,3	5,6	9,8
Government (other than above)	5,5	11,4	14,3	5,6	14,6
Other	17,9	24,8	14,3	44,3	14,6

Table 1 Masters' current work situation

PEDAGOGY

Evaluation of the Program

Results on the value of the program in relation to the respondents' current/most recent recruitment, first recruitment and its usefulness in the implementation of the job are displayed in Table 2. Here, we consider only one subset of the respondents, namely those that found work in the cultural sector and/or creative industries.

VALUE OF THE PROGRAM FOR RECRUITMENT AND IMPLEMENTATION OF	NOT SIGNIFICANT		NEUTRAL		SIGNIFICANT	
	2009 (in %)	2014 (in %)	2009 (in %)	2014 (in %)	2009 (in %)	2014 (in %)
Last or current recruitment (2009: n=86; 2014: n=51)	15	13	15	4	70	83
First recruitment (2009: n=57; 2014: n=27)	35	22	12	11	53	67
Useful in the implementation of the job (2009: n=85; 2014: n=52)	22	13	22	28	58	59

Table 2 Evaluation of the program

The descriptions given by respondents of the usefulness of the management education in their current job are effectively related to the way this master study program is organized. Three main topics stand out: teamwork is needed in order to finish tasks (as in professional life); an overview of different management processes and management domains is provided; and it offers deep insight into the specific structure of the sector (policy, legislation, subsidies). The qualitative data from the 2014 survey on the curriculum elements - being perceived as important for employment - support the principle of including practical experience in education. The practical internship, combined with the research for the master dissertation, was mentioned as the second most important course after Cultural Management Forum, a course in which managers are invited as guest speakers.

The final goal of our research was to investigate whether or not certain competences were developed during the cultural management program. In educational science, four types of competence are defined: knowledge, skills, insight and attitudes (Bloom 1956, De Block & Saveyn 1985, De Block & Heene 1992, Hauenstein 1998). The results from the 2014 survey show that the top six (of eleven) competences evaluated positively by alumni are: learning to work effectively in a team; being able to work in an entrepreneurial manner; using your skills in a network; reflecting on your work and yourself easily; translating reflections into constructive activities; having insight into/understanding/implementing scientific knowledge of cultural management and make critical reflections; and processing and synthesizing scientific management literature.

Discussion and Conclusion

Although several attempts have been made to define arts and cultural management in relation to general management, the results of the debate on general management education have not yet been applied to any discussion of the ideal graduate study program for the sub discipline of cultural management. The understanding that management is a practice reveals several important issues. First, although scientific management

PEDAGOGY

knowledge is clearly one of the foundations of the practice, it is not the only one. A too-narrow scholarly focus on this scientific aspect and on scientific research in graduate programs will not contribute to preparing graduate students for the cultural manager's job. Second, management as a practice means it is a craft, whose main learning mode is experience. Graduate study programs in cultural management that focus on experience, for example through internships, produce students that are better prepared for the labor market. Third, almost all of the qualities that distinguish arts and cultural management from general management are related to the '*art*', '*vision*' or '*insight*' managers deploy in their specific working environments.

Our studies, carried out at the University of Antwerp among cultural management graduates from 14 academic years, support the view that cultural management education needs to fosters the acquisition of experience and insight into the '*bridging*' relationship between management and arts and culture practices.

- The authors would like to thank master students Sonja Deschrijver, Evelien Dockx, Margot Teblick and Nele Verreyken for their contribution with a wikipaper on this topic.

PEDAGOGY

References

AMABILE, Th. & KHAIRE, M. (2008), 'Creativity and the Role of the Leader'. In: *Harvard Business Review*, 86(10), 100-109.

ANDRIOPOULOS, C. (2003). 'Six Paradoxes in Managing Creativity: An Embracing Act'. In: *Long Range Planning* 36/4: p. 375–388.

BAILEY, J. & FORD, C. (1996). 'Management as science versus management as practice in postgraduate business education'. In: *Business Strategy Review*, 7(4), 7-12.

BAUMOL, W. & BOWEN, W. (1966). *Performing arts: the economic dilemma*. New York: Twentieth Century Fund.

BARKER, R. (2010). 'No, Management is NOT a Profession'. In: *Harvard Business Review*, 88(7-8), 52-60.

BECKMAN, G. (2007). "Adventuring' Arts Entrepreneurship Curricula in Higher Education: An Examination of Present Efforts, Obstacles and Best Practices'. In: *Journal of Arts Management, Law, and Society*, 37(2), 87-112.

BENDIXEN, P. (2000). 'Skills and Roles: Concepts of Modern Arts Management'. In: *International Journal of Arts Management*, 2(3), 4-13.

BILTON, Ch. & LEARY, R. (2002). 'What Can Managers Do For Creativity? Brokering Creativity in the Creative Industries'. In: *International Journal of Cultural Policy*, 8(1), 49–64

BLOOM, B. S. (ed) (1956). *Taxonomy of Educational Objectives: The Classification of Educational Goals; Handbook I, Cognitive Domain*. New York: David McKay.

BOIME, A. (1986). *The Academy and French Painting in the Nineteenth Century*. New Haven: Yale University Press, 344 p.

About the Authors

Bruno Verbergt MA MBA is associate professor in general and strategic cultural management at the University of Antwerp. After his studies in Philosophy and in Business Administration, he pursued a career in the arts and government sectors, as artistic director, producer and CEO of the culture, sports and youth department of the city of Antwerp. He recently started TouchTime.coop, a studio for cultural entrepreneurship. His academic interest is in competitive advantage within the arts industries and in cultural industries as experience economies.

bruno.verbergt @uantwerpen.be

Laila De Bruyne MA is education assistant of the master program in cultural management at the University of Antwerp (2011-2015). In addition to having a master in history and cultural management, she is a certified teacher. From the summer of 2015 onwards, she will be working for Herita vzw, *a Flemish organization that manages and exhibits heritage sites.*
—
*laila.debruyne
@uantwerpen.be*

BOYLAN, P. J. (2003). 'Survey of institutions and organisations providing training for cultural development personnel in Western Europe'. In: UNESCO/ ENCACT. *Training in Cultural Policy and Management. International Directory of Training Centres. Europe, Russian Federation, Caucasus, Central Asia*, Paris: Unesco, 15-24.

BRIDGSTOCK, R. (2013). 'Not a dirty word: Arts entrepreneurship and higher education'. In: *Arts & Humanities in Higher Education*, 12(2-3), 122-137. doi: 10.1177/1474022212465725

BRKIĆ, A. (2009). 'Teaching Arts Management: Where did we lose the core ideas?' In: *The Journal of Arts Management, Law and Society*, 38(4), 270-280. doi: 10.3200/JAML.38.4.270-280

CHIAPELLO, E. (1998). *Artistes vs Managers. Le management culturel face à la critique artiste*. Paris: Métailié.

CLICHÉ, D., MITCHELL, R., WIESAND, A., HEISKANEN, I. & DAL POZZOLO, L. (2002). *Creative Europe. On governance and management of Artistic Creativity in Europe. An ERICarts report to the NEF*. Bonn: ARCult Media.

CRAY, D., INGLIS, L. & FREEMAN, S. (2007). 'Managing the Arts: Leadership and Decision Making under Dual Rationalities'. In: *The Journal of Arts Management, Law and Society*, 36(4), 295-313. doi: 10.3200/ JAML.36.4.295-314

DEBLOCK, A., SAVEYN, J. (1985). *Didactische werkvormen en leerstrategieën*. Deurne: Planteyn.

DEBLOCK, A., HEENE, J. (1992). *Inleiding tot de algemene didactiek*. Antwerpen: Standaard Educatieve Uitgeverij.

DE CORTE, D. (2011). 'Schumpeter voor Kunstenaars'. In: [Studiebureau van Professionele Vereniging voor creatieve beroepen – Smart (Red.)]. *De Kunstenaar. Een ondernemer?*, Brussel/Leuven: Smart-Lannoo Campus, 117-123

DeFILLIPPI, R., GRABHER, G. & JONES, C. (2007). 'Introduction to para-doxes of creativity: managerial and organizational challenges in the cultural economy'. In *Journal of Organizational Behavior* 28(5), 511–521.

DE ROEPER, J. (2008). 'Serving Three Masters: The Cultural Gatekeeper's Dilemma'. In: The *Journal of Arts Management, Law, and Society* 38(1), 51-69.

DEVEREAUX, C. (2009), 'Arts and Cultural Management: The State of the Field. Introduction'. In: *The Journal of Arts Management, Law, and Society*, 38(4), 235-238.

DURRER, V. & MILES, S. (2009). 'New perspectives on the role of cultural intermediaries in social inclusion in the UK'. In: *Consumption, Markets and Culture* 12(3): 225-241.

EBEWO, P. & SIRAYI, M. (2009). 'The Concept of Arts/Cultural Management: A Critical Reflection'. In: *The Journal of Arts Management, Law and Society*, 38(4), 281-295. doi: 10.3200/JAML.38.4.281-295

EIKHOF, D. R. & HAUNSCHILD, A. (2007). 'For Art's Sake! Artistic and Economic Logics in Creative Production'. In: *Journal of Organizational Behavior*, 28(5), 523-538.

PEDAGOGY

EVRARD, Y. & COLBERT, F. (2000). 'Arts Management: A New Discipline Entering the Millennium'. In: *International Journal of Arts Management*, 2(2), 4-13.

FILLIS, I. (2006). 'Art for Art's Sake or Art for Business Sake: An exploration of artistic product orientation'. In: *The Marketing Review*, 6, 29-40.

FLORIDA, R. & GOODNIGHT, J. (2005), 'Managing for Creativity'. In: *Harvard Business Review*, 83(7-8), 124-131.

GIELEN, P., ELKHUIZEN, S., VAN DEN HOOGEN, Q., LIJSTER, Th. & OTTE, H. (2014). *De waarde van cultuur*. Onderzoeksopdracht (onderzoekscentrum Arts in Society. Rijksuniversiteit Groningen), Brussel: Socius, 187 p.

GIELEN, P. & P. DE BRUYNE (eds.) (2012). *Teaching Art in the Neoliberal Realm: Realism versus Cynicism*. Amsterdam: Valiz, 304 p.

HAGOORT, G. (2005). *Art management: Entrepreneurial Style (3rd edition)*. Delft: Eburon Publishers, 296 p.

HAGOORT, G. (2007). *Cultureel ondernemerschap. Over het onderzoek naar de vrijheid van kunst maken en de vrijheid van ondernemen. Oratie 6 juni 2007*. Utrecht: Faculteit der Kunsten - vakgebied Kunst en economie, Universiteit Utrecht/Faculteit Kunst en Economie-Lectoraat Kunst en Economie, Hogeschool voor de Kunsten Utrecht, 69 p.

HAUENSTEIN, A. D. (1998). *A Conceptual Framework for Educational Objectives: A Holistic Approach to Traditional Taxonomies*. Lanham, MD: University Press of America.

HOWKINS, J. (2001). *The Creative Economy: How People Make Money from Ideas*. London: Penguin, 288 p.

HUTTER, M. & D. THROSBY (eds.). (2008). *Beyond Price. Value in Culture, Economics and the Arts*, Cambridge: Cambridge University Press, 315 p.

KELLEY, T. & KELLEY, D. (2012), 'Managing yourself. Reclaim your Creative Confidence'. In: *Harvard Business Review*, 90(12), 115-118.

KLAMER, A. (1996). *The Value of Culture. On the Relationship between Economics and Arts*. Amsterdam: Amsterdam University Press, 243 p.

KOLSTEEG, J. (2014). *Shifting Gear. The daily deliberation between arts and economics in cultural and creative organisations in Utrecht, 2010-2012*. Delft: Eburon Publishers, 209 p.

KUESTERS, I. (2010). 'Arts Managers as Liaisons between Finance and Arts: A Qualitative Study Inspired by the Theory of Functional Differentiation'. In: *The Journal of Arts Management, Law, and Society*, 40, 43–57. doi: 10.1080/ 10632921003603976

NISSLEY, N. (2002). 'Arts-based learning in management education'. In: WANKEL, Ch. & R. DEFILLIPPI (eds.). *Rethinking Management Education for the 21st Century. A Volume in: Research in Management Education and Development*, Greenwich, CT: Information Age Publishing, 27-61.

NOORDMAN, Th. B. J. (1993). 'Op zoek naar de fundamenten van een Kunstmanagementtheorie'. In: BEVERS, T., A. VAN DEN BRAEMBUSSCHE & B. J. LANGENBERG (red.). *De Kunstwereld. Produktie, distributie, en receptie in de wereld van kunst en cultuur*, Rotterdam: Erasmus Universiteit, 385 p.

PEDAGOGY

NOORDMAN, Th. B. J. (2006). *Kunstmanagement: een introductie (4ᵉ herziene druk)*. Den Haag: Elsevier, 259 p.

NOORDMAN, Th. B. J. (2010). *10e Carl Birnielezing. Afscheidscollege Dirk Noordman op 21 januari 2010*. Rotterdam: Erasmus Universiteit, 16 p.

LAERMANS, R. (2012). 'Teaching Theory and the Art of Not-knowing: Notes on Pedagogical Commonalism'. In: *Krisis. Journal for contemporary Philosophy*, 1, 63-73.

LAMPEL, J., LANT, Th. & SHAMSIE, J. (2000). 'Balancing act: Learning from organizing practices in cultural industries'. In: *Organization Science* 11(3), 263 – 269.

MINTZBERG, H. (1973). *The Nature of Managerial Work*. New York, NY: Harper & Row, 298 p.

MINTZBERG, H. (2004). *Managers not MBAs. A Hard Look at the Soft Practice of Managing and the Development of Management*. San Francisco: Berrett Koehler.

MINTZBERG, H. (2009). *Managing*. San Francisco: Berret-Koehler.

RADBOURNE, J. & FRASER, M. (1996). *Arts management a practical guide*. Sydney, Docupro, 285 p.

ROCKEFELLER BROTHERS' FUND, INC (1965) *The Performing Arts: Problems and Prospects. Rockefeller Brothers' Panel Report on the Future of Theatre, Dance, Music in America*. New York: McGraw-Hill Book Company.

ROOIJAKKERS, G. (1990). 'Opereren op het snijpunt van culturen: middelaars en media in Zuid-Nederland'. In: TE BOEKHORST, P., P. BURKE & W. FRIJHOFF (reds.), *Cultuur en maatschappij in Nederland, 1500-1850*, Amsterdam: Meppel, 245-283.

SNOWBALL, J.D. (2008). *Measuring the Value of Culture. Methods and Examples in Cultural Economics*. Berlin: Springer Verlag, 230 p.

ŞUTEU, C. (2006), *Another Brick in the Wall: A Critical Review of Cultural Management Education in Europe*. Amsterdam: Boekmanstudies.

SUTTON, R. I. (2001). 'The Weird Rules of Creativity'. In: *Harvard Business Review*, 79(8), 94-103.

WHITLEY, R. (1989). 'On the Nature of Managerial Tasks: Their Distinguishing Characteristics and Organisation'. In: *Journal of Management Studies*, 26(3), 209-225.

WHITLEY, R. (1995). 'Academic Knowledge and Work Jurisdiction in Management'. In: *Organization Science*, 16(1), 81-105.

PEDAGOGY

Valérie Ballereau
Christine Sinapi
Olivier Toutain
Edwin Juno-Delgado

DEVELOPING A BUSINESS MODEL
THE PERCEPTION OF ENTREPRENEURIAL SELF-EFFICACY AMONG STUDENTS IN THE CULTURAL AND CREATIVE INDUSTRY

PEDAGOGY

Abstract

The need for entrepreneurial skills development has become a significant issue for both cultural policy makers (Hearn and Saby, 2014) and the educational community (HKU, 2010). Yet, while artists and entrepreneurs have long been compared, the distance between them often seems abysmal. In this article, we defend entrepreneurial educational experiences built on the hybridization of the artistic and entrepreneurial worlds. Entrepreneurial learning is recognized as a tool for people to acquire attitudes, behaviours and entrepreneurial culture. Designing entrepreneurial learning among diverse populations helps to build these skills, as recently suggested by (Regele and Neck, 2012): entrepreneurship education to be a *'nested sub-ecosystem within the broader entrepreneurship ecosystem'* (2012:25).

Our research presents an innovative pedagogic experiment consisting of collaborative workshops on new business model generation (Osterwalder and Pigneur, 2010), bringing together students and academics of three higher education institutions in music, the visual arts, and management, as well as professionals from these sectors. We describe and assess the perceived self-efficacy regarding entrepreneurial competencies of this experiment. The research is qualitative. We compare the results between art and management students. We question these results regarding the entrepreneurship educational models.

Introduction

Entrepreneurship is a heterogeneous and multi-faceted phenomenon (Fayolle and Gailly, 2008), observable in its natural environment: society. Entrepreneurship is a rapidly growing field in the academic community. Its growth is mirrored by the increasing number of programs in higher education (EuropeanCommission, 2008), in primary and secondary schools (EuropeanCommission, 2013), and in a multitude of initiatives with governmental support to build entrepreneurial skills through new and creative ways of teaching and learning.

This development is accompanied by a wide diversity in the development of programs, teaching their content, and defining their learning objectives. In addition, many studies show that education has an impact on the perception and desirability to start a business, the related intentions, knowledge, entrepreneurial skills, self-efficacy (Bandura, 1977, McGee et al., 2009) or results in terms of the number of created businesses (Martin et al., 2013).

The need for entrepreneurial skills development in the arts and creative industries has similarly become a growing issue among both cultural policy makers (Hearn and Saby, 2014) and the educational community (HKU, 2010). Yet, while artists and entrepreneurs have long been compared regarding their ability to create or to take risks, the distance between them often seems abysmal.

The purpose of this article is to determine students' perceptions of this entrepreneurship training in terms of self-efficacy. The research is exploratory and qualitative, based on 31 questionnaires. We compare the results of art students with those of management students, as well as between visual arts and musical arts students.

Entrepreneurship Education through Culture and Creative Industry State of art of Entrepreneurship Education (EE)

Entrepreneurship is an academic field whose roots lay outside of academia, in the process of human activities that create economic, social and/or cultural value. These actions and processes are guided by the willingness to develop a project.

The significant expansion of entrepreneurship in the academic community (EuropeanCommission, 2008, Rizza and Varum, 2011) is accompanied by a wide diversity in the creation of programs, as well as teaching and defining learning objectives (Béchard and Grégoire, 2005). In general, these initiatives aim at teaching how to create and grow businesses, and they also explore how to acquire an entrepreneurial mind-set (Blenker et al., 2011). That is to say; learning a general attitude towards personal or professional life (Blenker et al., 2011, Verzat and Toutain, 2014). Each of these approaches targets the acquisition of different skills. In the first approach, the expected competencies are connected to the skills needed to develop entrepreneurial know-how and behaviour. In the second approach, the targeted skills are more focused on the value and meaning of being an entrepreneur.

Thus these targeted competencies differ according to three different dimensions:

1. **learning object** (the creation of a business or the transformation of the individual through the acquisition of an entrepreneurial mind-set and entrepreneurial behaviour);
2. consideration of **the environment** (nature of the learning ecosystem by opening outward with extramural partnerships and experience);
3. **the trainers' role** (transmitter of knowledge, facilitator, coach)

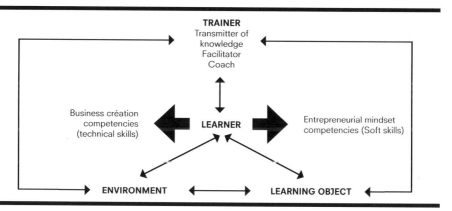

Figure 1 The process of acquiring entrepreneurial competencies

1. Learning Object

The learning object covers two aspects:

a. *Competencies related to business creation.* In this first category, curricula are more focused on the exploration and development of partner networks and knowledge connected to methods and tools that help to create and develop a business. In this way, knowledge related to technical skills and expertise is privileged to allow learners to create businesses and consequently become entrepreneurs. In this learning process, the '*teaching paradigm*' leads the learner to provide rational explanations and produce a logical and argued thought (Barr and Tagg, 1995) about the business creation and development process.

b. *Skills related to the entrepreneurial mind-set.* In the second category, teaching is mainly based on acquiring s*oft skills*' that is to say, capabilities and attitudes such as motivation, self-confidence, adaptation to the environment and uncertainty, exploration of resources in the environment, risk assessment, creativity, projection, empowerment, leadership, teamwork or calling into question (EuropeanCommission, 2013, Verzat and Fayolle, 2013). The teachers' mission is focused on supporting students in their own process of transformation (Mezirow, 1997): people learn from questions raised about their daily experience (Dewey, 1938). He or she helps learners to change their thoughts, to discover new ways of seeing the world around them and to experience themselves (Harrison and Leitch, 2005). In this model, the concept of entrepreneurship education takes on its full sense.

2. Environment

Two perspectives on the environment can be identified:

a. *The entrepreneurship education ecosystem.* In open learning environments, entrepreneurship program managers and trainers create the benefit of an entrepreneurial ecosystem by building strong collaborative networks (Tuunainen, 2005), and ultimately transform their school or university into an entrepreneurial academy (Clark, 2001). The entrepreneurship education ecosystem which influences the nature of the target competencies (closed / open, centred around the acquisition of knowledge / know how-to-be / know-how) is defined by five dimensions (Toutain and Mueller, 2015): the type of curriculum (centred around creativity and knowledge diversity or focused on the acquisition of technical knowledge), the nature of networks (external / internal), the learning space (open and collaborative or individual enclosed space), the entrepreneurial culture targeted (managing a new business or developing an extended entrepreneurial mind-set), and pedagogical choices (transmissive learning or experiential learning).

b. *Learning stakeholders.* Actors in the environment can be considered as stakeholders in the learning process. If the objective of entrepreneurship education is to acquire technical skills to start a business, solicitation of internal and external stakeholders of the school tends to be lower, and the teacher is at the heart of the learning process. Most pedagogical solutions relate to the model of transmissive learning. In contrast, if the training aims to support the learner in acquiring an entrepreneurial mind-set, the learning process is more open. In this case, the learner tends to increase interaction with the actors of its environment in order to obtain the required

PEDAGOGY

knowledge (Toutain and Mueller, 2015). The skills building process is then often collective: the learner and actors within the schools' local environment co-build '*actionable knowledge*' (Jones and Spicer, 2009, Löbler, 2006, Lewin, 1951).

3. The trainer

According to Fayolle (2013) '*there is commitment, intellectual and emotional investment and passion among the educators, instructors and all the people engaged in the EE*' (p. 693).

Recent research (Ruskovaara, 2014, Surlemont and Kearney, 2009) has defined an approach to teach entrepreneurship. Typically, the teacher is considered as a person who 1) has entrepreneurial experience and several years of teaching experience; 2) has leadership and team management competences; 3) develops internal and external networks in schools; 4) plays the role of guide, coach and facilitator in the learning process. In addition to the characteristics set out above, leaders of entrepreneurship programs may also appear as dissidents, straying from standardized education systems (Toutain and Mueller, 2015).

Culture and Creative Industries' Entrepreneurship Education: main debated Questions

The need for entrepreneurial skills development within cultural and creative industries has also become a critical issue, related both by cultural policy makers and the educational community. In the last decade, a growing number of initiatives have aimed at developing entrepreneurship programs. Although relatively low compared to other disciplines, the involvement of universities in arts entrepreneurship is growing (Katz et al., 2014), more than 400 arts entrepreneurship courses are currently offered.

These initiatives take different forms: dedicated curriculum, incubators and peer-to-peer networks, as well as emerging initiatives involving different populations, such as transdisciplinary approaches and cross campus initiatives, coaching between matching CCI entrepreneurs and individual business, and cross disciplinary support networks (Roberts et al., 2014, White, 2013, Essig, 2014).

Entrepreneurship education in culture and the arts is also a growing field of research (Scherdin and Zander, 2011). It was initiated to answer three main concerns: the unemployment level of art students and the relative lack of skills of self-employed artists to monitor their careers (White, 2013) and, more generally, the lack of entrepreneurship skills of CCI entrepreneurs (HKU, 2010).

Contrary to long lasting prejudices, which predict that artists and CCI students would be unwilling or even unable to acquire entrepreneurship skill (Eikhof and Haunschild, 2006, Brown, 2005), recent works have shown that CCI students not only recognize their need for entrepreneurship skills but would also be willing to enrol in entrepreneurship training programs (Shinnar et al., 2009).

A consensus exists on the need to develop entrepreneurship education for CCIs. Because CCIs are based on specific values, driven by critical creativity and cultural achievements and not primarily by profit, narrow models of entrepreneurship training focusing mainly on commercial success are not adapted to CCIs: entrepreneurship education has to be contextualized (HKU, 2010, White, 2013, HEAADMSC and NESTA, 2007).

PEDAGOGY

Related to the state of entrepreneurship education (section 1), two approaches to arts entrepreneurship education co-exist (Pollard and Wilson, 2013). The first and most common, focuses on business models and business start-up skills. The second focuses on behavioural aspects of entrepreneurship, innovation abilities and the development of an 'entrepreneurial mind-set' (Beckman, 2007, Essig, 2014). A combined approach should certainly prevail. However, no clear consensus, in terms of knowledge, skills and abilities, has so far emerged.

Roberst (2013))defends 'infusing' entrepreneurship skills in arts courses. White emphasizes the need for transdisciplinary programs (White, 2013). For art-institutions (HKU, 2010), entrepreneurship education should combine sector specific training and essential general entrepreneurial skills such as finance, marketing or law related topics and core competencies to develop alongside the entrepreneurial lifecycle (a vision, market positioning, business modelling based on cultural values applicable to CCIs, etc.).

In addition, the efficiency of ongoing initiatives needs to be assessed, in terms of learning outcome and enhancement of students' self-efficacy (Roberts et al., 2014, Essig, 2014). This requires valid and reliable methods that are currently lacking.

CCI entrepreneurial education is thus emerging but detailed contents and approaches remain debated. Contextualization of entrepreneurship programs and creation of a common core of accepted approaches are needed, as well as formal and reliable assessment of the ongoing buoying experiments.

Considering all these elements, this article presents an exploratory study measuring the impact of awareness training about entrepreneurial projects on student perception of self-efficacy. Perceived self-efficacy is concerned with peoples' beliefs in their ability to influence events that affect their lives (Bandura, 1994). Previous findings in psychology support the hypothesized relationship between perceived self-efficacy and behavioural changes (Bandura, 1977). In entrepreneurship in particular, self-efficacy is a significant feature of entrepreneurial behaviour.

Factors influencing the process of self-efficacy arise from four principal sources (Bandura, 2001):

1. performance accomplishments (empowerment)
2. vicarious experience (vicarious or observational learning, influence of role models)
3. verbal persuasion (influence of the coach)
4. physiological states (expression of a positive -or negative- emotional feedback, emotional stimulation). Our analytical grid is derived from these four sources of self-efficacy.

Methodology
Pedagogical experiment
Our research presents an innovative pedagogic experiment conducted within the Culture and Creative Industries Master Program (Burgundy School of Business). This experiment consists of collaborative workshops about new business model generation (Osterwalder and Pigneur, 2010), bringing together students and academics of three higher education institutions in music, the visual arts, and management, as well as professionals from these sectors. Herewith we sketch the basic characteristics of the program.

Learners. Our participants were graduate students in CCIs' management program, in music and in visual arts, in their last year of study before professionalization. They did not know each other.

Learning goals. This training aimed at introducing business modelling and contributing to the development of an entrepreneurial mind-set among students, in order to develop students' perceived self-efficacy to conduct a project. In this study, we assess this last objective.

Design. This experiment consisted of collaborative workshops on the generation of a new business model. Professionals and experts from the arts industry were also involved.

Each workshop lasted one full day and was identically structured: the mornings were spent on business modelling with interdisciplinary teams in order to produce a Business Model Canvas[1] for one entrepreneurial project in the arts; in the afternoons, each team presented its BM Canvas to a jury (composed of professionals, mainly from extramural structures).

Pedagogical method. The pedagogy was based on active learning and was project-oriented. It implicated collaborative teamwork allowing students to share their views, and requiring them to come up with common and new business ideas in the arts.

Trainer. The trainers fulfilled the above discussed key characteristics of trainers in entrepreneurial education: 1) they have several years of entrepreneurial and teaching experience, 2) they are competent in leadership and team management and 3) they develop networks inside and outside the university. They took a facilitating role to guide students in their learning.

Research Method

Given the exploratory nature of our research, we used a qualitative method including participant observation and interview analysis. The theoretical concepts derive from the literature on entrepreneurship in arts and cultural education.

Sampling and data collection. Data collection consisted of an online questionnaire completed one week after the training by each student. The sample included 31 students and displays a diversity of 1) profiles from the arts and management; 2) gender; 3) nationality (cf. table 1 below).

STATISTICS		
Number of respondants		**31**
of which:	Arts students	45%
	Management students	55%
	Female	67%
	Male	33%
	French	85%
	International	15%

Table 1 Student samples

---

[1] *For more information on the Business Model Canvas©,*
see http://www.businessmodelgeneration.com/

PEDAGOGY

Data analysis. Collected data cover appraisals, feedback and emotions expressed by students. The set of questions was developed based on the work of Kirkpatrick (1975), with complementary questions focusing on perceived self-efficacy as defined by Bandura (1994).

Data analysis consisted of three stages:

1. The first was a textual analysis of the global perception of students regarding the educational process.
2. The second stage consisted of a qualitative analysis of the same data, guided by the objective of assessing perceived self-efficacy. Data analysis was based on axial coding, as defined by (Maguire and Phillips, 2008, Corley and Gioia, 2004). The data collected were computerized and processed using a qualitative data analysis software (QSR N'Vivo 10). Verbatim transcripts were coded and grouped into first order concepts.
3. The third stage consisted of complementary quantitative data analysis.

Findings and Discussion
Global perception of the training

The first part of the analysis dealt with the general perception of the training on the 4 components of the Entrepreneurial Education System (cf. table).

GLOBAL PERCEPTION OF THE TRAINING	NUMBER OF SOURCES	NUMBER OF VERBATIM QUOTES
Total number of coded data	31	190
1-1 Learning object	29	64
1-1-1 Business creation tools	24	49
a. Discover business modelling	17	23
b. Develop project management competencies (esp. analytical methods and oral presentation competencies)	9	13
c. Practice team management basic competencies	5	6
d. Apply business model in the arts	4	4
e. Some contents shoud be added, especially financial aspects	2	3
1-1-2 Entrepreneurial mindset	11	15
a. Emergence of entrepreneurial intents during the day	7	7
b. Obstacle to entrepreneurshp mindset development among art students (prejudice against business)	3	7
c. Obstacle to EM development-reluctance to self-determination	1	1
1-2 Environnement	25	87
1-2-1 Type of curriculum (Design of the program)	16	29
a. Insufficient time dedicated to the experiment (1 day)	14	22
b. Reluctance toward the uncertainty inherent in the pedagogy	6	7
1-2-2 Diversity in the ecosystem	22	36
Declared interest for intercultural differences (diversity in study background arts or management and in nationality)	22	36
1-2-3 Learning stakeholders	17	22
a. Interest from professionnal network feedback	13	17
b. Interest from extra-muros experts	5	5
1-3 Trainer	4	4
Trainers were perceived as motivatiing, stimulatin, supporting	4	4
1-4 Learner		
a. The learner expressed some personnal satisfaction	17	28
b. The learner felt motivated	5	5
c. The learner felt some frustration	2	2

Table 2 Global perception of the training

PEDAGOGY

Generally, the pedagogical objective of the training was reached. Students felt they had developed the competencies in the targeted business creation tools, in particular regarding general business modelling as applied for the arts. They also mentioned project management and team management related competencies (cf. 1-1.1, table 2). We find indications that the training contributed to developing their entrepreneurial mind-set (cf. 1-1.2, table 2). The '*one day*' format is however perceived as too short.

Regarding the Entrepreneurial Education System, three major positive outcomes are identified:

- Learners point out a general satisfaction and motivation regarding the training (1-4, table 2), confirmed by quantitative data (cf. table 3): 100% of students are globally satisfied.
- Exchanges with professionals from the arts and learning stakeholders from outside schools is repeatedly highlighted (1-2-3, table 2). It is praised by 97% of students and perceived as very satisfying (4.5/5).

The diverse study background among students is perceived as a major contribution to the training and a key factor in the development of personal competencies (1-2-2, table 2). Less significantly, some criticism to the design of the course was mentioned, but it did not appear as essential. Overall, it was remarked that 1) insufficient time was dedicated to the learning process, and that 2) students wished to focus more on their personal entrepreneurial projects. We interpret their remarks as evidence of a need for more entrepreneurship courses in their curriculum, even if time limitations make it challenging to implement such active pedagogy (Vygotsky, 2012, Holt, 1966, Nunan, 1996).

PEDAGOGY

	GLOBAL SATISFACTION	INTEREST FUTURE PROFESSIONAL LIFE	EXPRESSED LEARNER IMPLICATION	PERCEIVED TRAINER'S IMPLICATION	PERCEIVED INTEREST FOR A PROFESSIONAL JURY
All students					
Number of answers	**31**	**31**	**31**	**31**	**31**
Globally satisfied	100%	90%	100%	87%	97%
Average satisfaction*	4,0	3,9	4,2	4,1	4,4
CIC Management students					
Globally satisfied	100%	100%	100%	92%	100%
Average satisfaction	4,5%	4,1%	4,3%	4,2%	4,5%
Visual Arts students					
Globally satisfied	100%	90%	100%	90%	90%
Average satisfaction	3,9%	3,9%	4,2%	4,2%	4,0%
Music students					
Globally satisfied	100%	90%	100%	90%	90%
Average satisfaction	3,9%	3,9%	4,2%	4,2%	4,0%

Table 3 General satisfaction amongst the learners

Overall, the qualitative data confirm the relevance of the training regarding the pedagogical objectives and underline the entrepreneurial ecosystem as a key success factor. Interestingly however, differences among students' backgrounds are observed. Art students, and particularly music students, were less satisfied, less interested and less involved in the training than were the management students.

This may relate to the differences in the learning context and culture of each school. In our sample, management and, to a lesser extent, visual arts students were familiar with entrepreneurship courses and entrepreneurship ecosystems. In contrast, the music students had little exposure to both the topic and the pedagogy. This suggests that entrepreneurial education courses and their inclusion in an entrepreneurial education eco-system are relevant but should not be a one-shot (or one day) experiment.

Perceived Self-efficacy

Findings regarding perceived self-efficacy are synthetized in tables 4 (axial coding) and 5 (quantitative data).

PEDAGOGY

THEORITICAL CONCEPT CATEGORY (SECOND ORDER CONCEPT FIRST ORDER CONCEPT	NUMBER OF SOURCES	NUMBER OF VERBATIM QUOTES
2 Self efficacy	31	124
2-1 Performance accomplishement	18	39
a. Enriching experience; acquisition of competences useful for future entrepreneurial projects	14	22
b. Increasedself-confidence, feeling that now I my entrepreneurial project will be succesful; emergence of entrepreneurial intents		
c. Obstacle to performance accomplishment-prejudice of arts students against any non artistic element, perceived as anti-artistic	2	5
2-2 Vicarious experience	24	32
a. Influence of students - stimulation, learning by interaction with other students	19	23
b. Learning by interaction with the jury	7	7
c. Influence of role model	1	2
2-3 Verbal persuasion	13	29
a. The coaches were perceived as supportive	11	16
b. The jury was perceived as supportive	7	9
c. The coaches supplied technical support	2	4
2-4 Emotive sources of self efficacy	15	24
a. Expression of positive regarding the experience (happiness, enthusiasm)	14	17
b. Expression of negative emotional feedback (frustration, apprehension, perplexity)	6	7

Table 4 Perceived self-efficacy – data structure

Axial coding confirms the literatures' theoretical concepts. Generally, students' perceived self-efficacy was enhanced after the training.

The results tend to confirm that the training reinforced participants' perceived self-efficacy, in particular performance accomplishment and vicarious experience, which was itself enhanced by multicultural teams mixing art and management students. They also suggest that such an experiment should be repeated in order to overcome initial apprehensions and to arouse positive emotional factors.

Additional Findings

Some additional findings also emerged. In a minority of cases, art students expressed reluctance towards business and entrepreneurship, which they perceived as incompatible or detrimental to the arts. This limited their feeling of self-confidence regarding entre-preneurial projects. This corresponds to a long-lasting debate in the literature on arts entrepreneurship which relates a series of obstacles to entrepreneurial education to such supposed prejudice. Business model approaches would disengage art students who are more interested in creative practices than running businesses (Brown, 2005). Antagonism between the arts and business (Eikhof and Haunschild, 2006), the idea that money harms rather than enabling art (Beckman, 2007), and the identification of creative students as *distinguished from the rest of society, especially the bourgeoisie and business*' (Eikhof and Haunschild, 2006), p234), would disengage students from entrepreneurship courses. Eventually, faculty and program design officials would be reluctant to recognize arts entrepreneurship as essential.

In contradiction to this however, we observe that the training also tends to reduce art students' *'anti-business'* prejudice. *'We consider it as easier now to talk about 'taboo' topics such as budget, finance, wages'* (PE13). This result constitutes one of the important promising outcomes of the experiment. It should be discussed in future research and related to the mechanism of defensive routines in the learning process (Argyris and Schön, 1987).

Interestingly, students spontaneously related their acquisition of competencies to an increased confidence in their employability, although the training was only dedicated to entrepreneurial projects. *'I have learned to consider my artistic work differently. This will enable me to face my future professional life 'head-high'* (PE13). This side-result, although unexpected, is in line with previous works in arts entrepreneurship, which have attributed to arts entrepreneurial education the goal of improving artists' employability (Roberts, 2013, White, 2013). It may also relate to the increasingly positive perception of entrepreneurship by society, which has become fashionable for *stagnating or declining economic activity in both developed and developing countries*' (Matlay and Carey, 2007).

Conclusion

This article describes the outcome of an innovative entrepreneurial learning experiment that was project-oriented, based on active learning, and deployed campus wide and multicultural teams by mixing art students and management students. The objective of the training was to familiarize students with entrepreneurial project development by introducing business modelling and enhancing an entrepreneurial mind-set.

This research aimed to determine the students' perceptions of self-efficacy. Qualitative analysis findings support an enhancement of perceived self-efficacy after the training, in particular, performance accomplishment and vicarious learning. Diversity of back-ground in the teamwork appears as contributing to this result. Verbal persuasion is observed, but to a lesser extent. Findings regarding emotional sources of self-efficacy are mitigated, and suggest that such campus-wide entrepreneurial education systems should be repeated to overcome prevailing prejudices and apprehensions. Eventually, the entrepreneurial and educational ecosystem appears as a key feature of the training experiment. These results lead us to defend the interest of entrepreneurial educational experiences built on the hybridization of both artistic and entrepreneurial worlds.

Limits to these results lay in potential declarative biases linked to the qualitative method and more especially the use of on line questionnaires. Moreover, the progression of self-efficacy perception has not been measured in this research. Reluctance to express emotions may have also limited our findings.

To conclude, learning stakeholders and teachers play a fundamental role in activating the entrepreneurial ecosystem. Dynamic interplays guarantee open learning, based on the diversity of views and on a more complex approach of entrepreneurial processes. Thus, an interdisciplinary approach to entrepreneurship education in CCIs implies not only a focus on students, active learning methods and tools, but also on teachers' roles as guides and facilitators throughout the training (Ruskovaara, 2014).
Moreover, we believe that the links we explore between learning processes and multidisciplinary and entrepreneurial self-efficacy perceptions provide both a better understanding of key learning processes to develop entrepreneurial attitudes and behaviours, and relevant measurement instruments in an entrepreneurial context. This supports the idea that learning context, teachers' role, and active learning pedagogy have an impact on self-directed learning.

- The authors would like to thank the Institut Supérieur des Beaux Arts Besançon in Besançon, Franche-Comté and the Pôle d'Enseignement Supérieur de la Musique in Dijon, Burgundy with whom this pedagogic experiment was developed.

References

ARGYRIS, C. & SCHÖN, D. 1987. Reasoning, action strategies, and defensive routines: The case of OD practitioners. Research in organizational change and development, 1, 89-128.

BANDURA, A. 1977. Self-efficacy: toward a unifying theory of behavioural change. *Psychological review,* 84, 191.

BANDURA, A. 1994. *Self-efficacy,* Wiley Online Library.

BANDURA, A. 2001. Social cognitive theory: An agentic perspective. *Annual review of psychology,* 52, 1-26.

BARR, R. B. & TAGG, J. 1995. From teaching to learning - A new paradigm for undergraduate education. *Change: The magazine of higher learning,* 27, 12-26.

BÉCHARD, J.-P. & GRÉGOIRE, D. 2005. Entrepreneurship education research revisited: The case of higher education. *Academy of Management Learning & Education,* 4, 22-43.

BECKMAN, G. 2007. Adventuring arts entrepreneurship curricula in higher education: An examination of present efforts, obstacles, and best practices. *The Journal of Arts Management, Law, and Society,* 37, 87-112.

BLENKER, P., KORSGAARD, S., NEERGAARD, H. & THRANE, C. 2011. The questions we care about: paradigms and progression in entrepreneurship education. *Industry and Higher Education,* 25, 417-427.

BROWN, R. 2005. Performing arts creative enterprise: Approaches to promoting entrepreneurship in arts higher education. *International Journal of Entrepreneurship and Innovations,* 6, 159-167.

About the Authors

Dr Valérie Ballereau is associate professor of entrepreneurship at the Burgundy School of Business (Dijon, France), affiliated to MECIC (Management of Culture and Arts Research Cluster) and to ICE (Innovation, Cluster, Entrepreneurship). She holds a PhD in Management Science. After several years in consulting and as an entrepreneur in Ireland, she has joined an academic career in 2001. She launched the incubator of the Burgundy School of Business, Incub'ESC©, which she co-manages today. Her research topics are dedicated to SME's management and entrepreneurship, particularly applied to cultural industries and tourism.

—

Valerie.Ballereau@escdijon.eu

Dr Christine Sinapi is associate professor of finance at the Burgundy School of Business (Dijon, France), where she is also scientific Coordinator of the Management of Culture and Arts Research Cluster (CEREN/MECIC), and Head of the Finance - Law - Control Department. She graduated from ESSEC and holds a PhD in Economics. Her research interests include financial market instability, monetary economics, and cultural economics. She has recently conducted a research project on performing arts or ganizations shared practices in Europe.

—

Christine.Sinapi@escdijon.eu

Dr Olivier Toutain is associate professor of entrepreneurship and managing director of the incubator in the Burgundy School of Business. He was the manager of a business training agency and business owner (consulting firm) for 12 years. He is co-founder of ALICE-Lab research centre (Action Learning for Education, Creativity and Entrepreneurship) and member of CEREN (Business Research Centre of Burgundy School of Business) and the Research Centre for Entrepreneurship (EM Lyon Business School). He also works as independent expert in Entrepreneurship Education for the OECD. His current research is focused on innovative learning methods in entrepreneurship education, a topic on which he accumulated more than fifty publications.

—

olivier.toutain@escdijon.eu

CLARK, B. 2001. The entrepreneurial university: New foundations for collegiality, autonomy, and achievement. *Higher Education Management,* 13.

CORLEY, K. G. & GIOIA, D. A. 2004. Identity Ambiguity and Change in the Wake of a Corporate Spin-off. *Administrative Science Quarterly,* 49, 173-208.

DEWEY, J. 1938. Education and experience. New York: Simon and Schuster.

EIKHOF, D. & HAUNSCHILD, A. 2006. Lifestyle meets market: Bohemian entrepreneurs in creative industries. *Creativity and Innovation Management,* 15, 234-241.

ESSIG, L. 2014. Ownership, Failure, and Experience: Goals and Evaluation Metrics of University-Based Arts Venture Incubators. *Entrepreneurship Research Journal,* 4, 117-135.

EUROPEANCOMMISSION 2008. Entrepreneurship in higher education, especially within non-business studies. Final Report of the Expert Group. *Brussels.* European Commission.

EUROPEANCOMMISSION 2013. Entrepreneurship education. a guide for educators. Brussels: European Commission.

FAYOLLE, A. 2013. Personal views on the future of entrepreneurship education. *Entrepreneurship & Regional Development,* 25, 692-701.

FAYOLLE, A. & GAILLY, B. 2008. From craft to science: Teaching models and learning processes in entrepreneurship education. *Journal of European Industrial Training,* 32, 569-593.

HARRISON, R. T. & LEITCH, C. M. 2005. Entrepreneurial learning: Researching the interface between learning and the entrepreneurial context. *Entrepreneurship Theory and Practice,* 29, 351-371.

HEAADMSC & NESTA 2007. Creating Entrepreneurship: higher education and creative industries. London: Higher Education Academy Art Design Media Subject Centre and NESTA.

HEARN, S. & SABY, O. 2014. Rapport sur le développement de l'entrepreneuriat dans le secteur culturel en France. Paris: Ministère de la culture et de la communication, Ministère de l'Économie, du redressement productif et du numérique.

HKU 2010. The Entrepreneurial Dimension of the Cultural and Creative Industries. Utrecht, Netherlands: Hogeschool vor de Kunsten Utrecht (HKU).

HOLT, J. 1966. How children fail. *Literacy Research and Instruction,* 6, 4-7.

JONES, C. & SPICER, A. 2009. *Unmasking the entrepreneur,* Edward Elgar.

KATZ, J. A., ROBERTS, J., STROM, R. & FREILICH, A. 2014. Perspectives on the Development of Cross Campus Entrepreneurship Education. *Entrepreneurship Research Journal,* 4, 13-44.

KIRKPATRICK, D. L. 1975. *Evaluating training programs,* Tata McGraw-Hill Education.

LEWIN, K. 1951. *Field theory in social science,* New York, Harper and Row.

LÖBLER, H. 2006. Learning entrepreneurship from a constructivist perspective. *Technology Analysis & Strategic Management,* 18, 19-38.

PEDAGOGY

MAGUIRE, S. & PHILLIPS, N. 2008. 'Citibankers' at Citigroup: A Study of the Loss of Institutional Trust after a Merger. *Journal of Management Studies,* 45, 372-401.

MARTIN, B. C., MCNALLY, J. J. & KAY, M. J. 2013. Examining the formation of human capital in entrepreneurship: A meta-analysis of entrepreneurship education outcomes. *Journal of Business Venturing,* 28, 211-224.

MATLAY, H. & CAREY, C. 2007. Entrepreneurship education in the UK: a longitudinal perspective. *Journal of Small Business and Enterprise Development,* 14, 252-263.

MCGEE, J. E., PETERSON, M., MUELLER, S. L. & SEQUEIRA, J. M. 2009. Entrepreneurial self-efficacy: refining the measure. *Entrepreneurship theory and Practice,* 33, 965-988.

MEZIROW, J. 1997. Transformative learning: Theory to practice. *New directions for adult and continuing education,* 1997, 5-12.

NUNAN, D. 1996. The self-directed teacher: Managing the learning process, Cambridge University Press.

OSTERWALDER, A. & PIGNEUR, Y. 2010. Business Model Generation: A Handbook For Visionaries, Game Changers, and Challengers, Wiley.

POLLARD, V. & WILSON, E. 2013. THE 'ENTREPRENEURIAL MINDSET' IN CREATIVE AND PERFORMING ARTS HIGHER EDUCATION IN AUSTRALIA. *Artivate: A Journal of Entrepreneurship in the Arts,* 3, 3-22.

REGELE, M. D. & NECK, H. M. 2012. The Entrepreneurship Education Subecosystem in the United States: Opportunities to Increase Entrepreneurial Activity. *Journal of Business and Entrepreneurship,* 23, 25.

RIZZA, C. & VARUM, C. A. 2011. Directions in entrepreneurship education in Europe.

ROBERTS, J. 2013. INFUSING ENTREPRENEURSHIP WITHIN NON-BUSINESS DISCIPLINES: PREPARING ARTISTS AND OTHERS FOR SELF-EMPLOYMENT AND ENTREPRENEURSHIP. *Artivate: A Journal of Entrepreneurship in the Arts,* 1, 53-63.

ROBERTS, J., HOY, F., KATZ, J. A. & NECK, H. 2014. The Challenges of Infusing Entrepreneurship within Non-Business Disciplines and Measuring Outcomes. *Entrepreneurship Research Journal,* 4, 1-12.

RUSKOVAARA, E. 2014. Entrepreneurship Education in Basic and Upper Secondary Education–Measurement and Empirical Evidence. *Acta Universitatis Lappeenrantaensis.*

SCHERDIN, M. & ZANDER, I. 2011. *Art entrepreneurship,* Edward Elgar Publishing.

SHINNAR, R., PRUETT, M. & TONEY, B. 2009. Entrepreneurship education: attitudes across campus. *Journal of Education for Business,* 84, 151-159.

SURLEMONT, B. & KEARNEY, P. 2009. *Pédagogie et esprit d'entreprendre,* De Boeck Supérieur.

Dr Edwin Juno-Delgado is associate professor of law at the Burgundy School of Business (Dijon, France), where he is head of the Culture and Creative Industries Concentration (Master degree). He is affiliated to MECIC (Management of Culture and Arts Research Cluster). He is a Peruvian and French jurist, specialist in cultural law and regulations. He holds a PhD in International Public Law. His research interests are dedicated to cultural organizations legal framework, international comparative law in culture, mass cultural topics, and copyright and cultural consumption.

—

Edwin.Juno-Delgado @escdijon.eu

PEDAGOGY

TOUTAIN, O. & MUELLER, S. 2015. The Outward Looking School and its Ecosystem. Entrepreneurship 360, OECD (Forthcoming).

TUUNAINEN, J. 2005. Contesting a hybrid firm at a traditional university. *Social studies of science,* 35, 173-210.

VERZAT, C. & FAYOLLE, A. 2013. Comment faire éclore des talents d'entrepreneur. *L'Expansion Management Review*, 100-108.

VERZAT, C. & TOUTAIN, O. 2014. Entrainer l'esprit d'entreprendre à l'école, une opportunité pour apprendre à apprendre? *Cahiers de l'action*.

VYGOTSKY, L. S. 2012. *Thought and language*, MIT press.

WHITE, J. C. 2013. Barriers to recognizing arts entrepreneurship education as essential to professional arts training. *Artivate: A Journal of Entrepreneurship in the Arts,* 2, 28-39.

PEDAGOGY

Melanie Levick-Parkin

WHAT WE TALK ABOUT WHEN WE TALK ABOUT ENTREPRENEURSHIP

Insights into students' and lecturers' thoughts on learning and teaching creative/cultural entrepreneurship

Abstract

This article explores the attitudes to creative entrepreneurship of students and staff engaged in creative education on a graphic design programme at a university in the UK. It will include first hand voices of the participants interviewed, whilst conceptually building on existing literature.

In line with the UK governments' drive of the employability agenda, many creative and design programmes now include elements or modules explicitly focusing on entrepreneurship or enterprise. How effective are these specific modules in encouraging entrepreneurial attitudes and behaviour in creative students? What do these modules add to the traditional art and design curriculum in relation to entrepreneurial attitudes? What are the underlying values that drive entrepreneurial behaviour in creative students?

Art and Design has well established and successful pedagogic methods and strategies for encouraging creative behaviour. Creative disciplines also have their own specific value systems that motivate them to engage in entrepreneurship. This article will show some links between art and design pedagogy and general advice on teaching of entrepreneurial behaviour, whilst trying to reveal some the values underpinning motivation for entrepreneurship in a creative subject area. We provide insights into these aspects discussed, but more importantly we stress that there is scope to deepen and widen this research in the context of creative education; its values and motivations in relation to cultural entrepreneurship.

Introduction

This article is linked to a *'Teaching enhancement project'* at the University where the research took place. The aim of the project is to gain a better understanding of how students and staff conceptualise enterprise and entrepreneurship teaching and learning in the context of a visual communication programme, as well as finding out how they thought these things linked to (creative) employability. The programme is host to approximately 350 students, who are spread across level 4-7 and are all engaged in creative disciplines in relation to Graphic Design. In the UK level 4 students would typically be in their first year of an undergraduate programme, having completed their A-levels or achieved equivalent educational attainment. On this particular programme students are also interviewed and submit a portfolio of creative work in order to gain their place. Level 5 students are in the second year of the Degree and level 6 students are either in their final year of a Ba (Hons) or are students who have elected and qualified to study on the MDes Course, which enables them to leave with a post-graduate qualification at level 7.

PEDAGOGY

The research was conducted by a practitioner researcher, with students and staff from the BA and MDes programmes, levels 6 and 7. Data was collected with a small student group and six members of staff, but because the data collected was very rich, this article will primarily concentrate on findings in relation to student data. It is envisaged that this article will form part of a larger body of work at some point in the future.

The Research Project and its Questions

The overall questions directing the research were concerned with the uncovering of underlying, un-expressed, and potentially un-reflected on, attitudes of students and staff to enterprise and entrepreneurship education within a creative context.

The questions asked centred around:

1. What does '*Enterprise and Entrepreneurship*' mean to students and staff in the context of the creative subject they are studying or teaching?
2. What do they think a module that is explicitly about *enterprise and entrepreneurship* adds/should add to the design curriculum?

Underlying themes involved are what values drive the application or adoption of entrepreneurial or enterprising behaviour in the creative field, as well as the question whether creative entrepreneurship was perceived to be different from '*other*', business oriented entrepreneurship.

Research Approach and Methods

Overall the project was governed by a mixed methods research approach and could be considered to have grown from within a pragmatist paradigm (Cohen et al. 2011). It has been developed out of several parallel strands of educational research in relation to creative entrepreneurship and art & design pedagogy. In order to gain an understanding of the kind of environment that creative entrepreneurship education in the UK stems from and resides in, a small-scale policy overview was conducted from within a critical paradigm.

Data gathering for this project has been at a micro scale and was conducted with staff and students from a visual communication subject group within an Art and Design department. This research is qualitative with interpretive research methods, centred on semi-structured interviews with a small number of staff and students.

Enterprise and Entrepreneurship Education

Entrepreneurship, including creative and cultural entrepreneurship is increasingly being discussed as an answer to all manner of economic and societal ills (Mazzucato, 2013, Viladas, 2011; Cox & Sperry, 2005). The call for more entrepreneurial behaviour and an enterprising mind can be found in policy documents, speeches, articles, interviews and many more places if one cares to look closely enough (Ball, 2008; DBI&S 2013; Crainer & Dearlove 2000). For the creative community some of the proclamations of '*new found*' insights by business of the benefits of lateral thinking, experiential learning, multi-modal communications, learning from failure and sacrificial labour (Cox & Sperry 2005, Crainer & Dearlove 2000) resembles an indigenous community, hearing some conquistadors declaring that they just landed in a previously undiscovered country.

PEDAGOGY

There is some recognition that a creative or liberal arts education seems to be particularly effective in instigating entrepreneurial behaviour and success (P.J.C., 2010, QAA 2012). Yet little evidence is given that there is a real widespread understanding why that might be (Oakley et al. 2008; ADM-HEA, 2007). In the UK Organisations and bodies such as 'Creative England' and NESTA (ADM-HEA, 2007) have been making the case that entrepreneurial education is intimately linked to creative and cultural education.

The current government has followed previous governments in their call for more enterprise and entrepreneurship education (MIoIR, 2013), whilst at the same time implementing a return to a narrower, more traditional curriculum, that side-lines creative subjects and advocating didactic teaching methods such a rote learning; known to be counter-productive when wanting to develop entrepreneurial behaviour (Gibb, 1993).

Cultural and Creative Entrepreneurship in the UK and its European Context

It is difficult to pinpoint the first origin of the desire to explicitly connect education to enterprise and entrepreneurship (Taylor, 2014) in the UK through educational policy. This desire is so intimately intertwined with economic policy (Fairclough, 2010; Ball, 2008), that when looking at enterprise and entrepreneurship educational policy, it is difficult not to think that one is merely looking at an economic policy lever.

Policy is often validated and driven by a narrative of necessity and or even fear. Warrants are constructed around 'truths' that are usually stated as if pre-established facts (Hyatt 2013, Fairclough, 2010). Connected to the 'necessity' of entrepreneurship education is the narrative of an urgent need for building a workforce that can adapt to rapidly changing markets. The idea, that education needs to play its part in protecting the country from imminent economic ruin, is not a new one (Danvers, 2003; William & Haukka 2008; Ashton, 2010; Design Commission, 2011). In their 1962 book 'Educating the Intelligent', Hutchinson and Young state that '... we must have people who are prepared for very rapid change in the conditions of their work. The job which a child will start on today may have ceased to exist when he retires for work ...' (1962:27). The 2012 QAA document titled 'Enterprise and entrepreneurship education: Guidance for UK higher education providers' states that 'driven by a need for flexibility and adaptability, the labour market requires graduates with enhanced skills who can think on their feet and be innovative in a global economic environment.' (2012:2). One might be forgiven for thinking that things hadn't really moved on much despite the underlying tone of immediate urgency in both sources.

Klamer (2011) argues that the peculiarities and particularities of the arts world need to be taking into account, in order to make sense of the cultural/creative entrepreneur and warrant his/her inclusion as a separate character. Several reasons why the pursuit of entrepreneurial behaviour in art and design may be fundamentally different from a more business-oriented pursuit of enterprise and entrepreneurship can be mentioned (Design Council 2011). The most fundamental one of those is connected to held values that drive individuals in the creative community (Levick-Parkin 2014). Their motivation for engaging in enterprising and entrepreneurial behaviour is different from a more main-stream, financial reward one, because in their economy financial reward is not usually the top priority (Klamer 2011, ADM-HEA 2007). Despite of this apparent discrepancy, the actual outcome is one of overall financial economic gain

PEDAGOGY

(Cox and Sperry 2005). In '*A Manifesto for the Creative Economy*', published through NESTA in the UK, the authors highlight that the UK's creative economy provided more jobs than the financial, advanced manufacturing or construction sector (Bakshee et al. 2013) and that the country is finally starting to take this seriously.

The UK is not the only place that is now recognises that cultural entrepreneurship in particular as an important factor in the generation of social and economic capital. A study prepared by KEA (2006) notes that the role of the cultural and creative sector in boosting innovation and contributing to the '*knowledge economy*' (European Commission 2006). Eight years on in the European Unions' Research programme Horizon 2020, there are a broad variety of calls, whose aim it is to encourage enterprise and entrepreneurship in the cultural sector (Horizon 2020, 2015). At the same time reports such as the '*Effects and impact of entrepreneurship programmes in higher education*' report (2012), brought a wide range of empirical research data together that discussed the importance of entrepreneurship provision within the Higher Education (HE) sector.

The UK 2012 QAA document finds itself within this broader context of entrepreneurship discourse and explicitly draws on several European reports, whilst focusing on its immediate remit of UK HE provision. The QAA guidance document introduces itself as reflecting current thinking in enterprise and entrepreneurship education (2012). It goes on to say that '*it is intended to illuminate contemporary best practice in order to inform, enhance and promote the development of enterprise and entrepreneurship education in the UK.*' (QAA, 2012:2).

The QAA defines the content and quality of Higher Education (HE) degrees in the UK with a list of '*benchmark*' requirements for each subject. It is an independent body that monitors and advises on standards in UK HE and one of its aims is to '*be at the forefront of policy debates on the quality of higher education, to support providers, students and decision-makers in meeting future challenges*' (QAA, 2014). The creative provision discussed here is part of a larger re-approval early in 2012.

How Art & Design Pedagogy links to Entrepreneurship

The *raison d'être* for art and design pedagogy is the establishment of successful methods and strategies that encourage creative behaviour. Central to this is a '*learning to be*' rather than a '*learning about*' approach, which is intimately linked to experiential learning (Shreeve et al. 2010; Danvers, 2003; Orr & Bloxham, 2012). The art and design curriculum is centred on project work, much of which is set in the context of particular themes or external partners. Problem based learning and studio based pedagogies are central to creating pedagogic spaces in which students are able to take creative risks and learn to tolerate the ambiguity that comes with an aesthetics-based value system (Danvers, 2003).[1]

---

[1] *Here we note that aesthetic values are inherently subjective, experiential, and dialogic in nature (Clews, 2009; Danvers, 2003).*

PEDAGOGY

Gibb (1993) found that when looking at effective learning modes for enterprise teaching, that the didactic mode, traditionally very common in HE, was entirely unsuitable. The learning modes outlined by Gibb as being conducive to enterprise learning in this figure are almost indistinguishable from traditional art and design modes of learning (Orr & Bloxham, 2012; Shreeve et al. 2010; Book & Phillips, 2013; Henry, 2007). Indeed, experiential learning, which is widely associated with the creative subjects, also features in the QAA guidance for enterprise teaching in HE (2012). The document highlights that courses that are focusing on creating enterprising mind-sets through experiential learning, normally involve the setting of learning opportunities within meaningful and relevant contexts (QAA 2012).

Our study covers two courses that offer specialisation in a variety of creative disciplines such as graphic design, illustration, motion design, advertising and packaging (to name a few): a BA(Hons) Graphic Design Degree level 4-6 spanning 3 years, and a Graphic Design MDes course, which spans level 4-7 over a 4-year study duration.

When the BA students enter their third and final year they go straight into the graduation projects module, which may or not be linked explicitly to outside clients or entirely self-generated depending on their choice of study. When entering level 7 on the Mdes the student will have previously been on semester-long industry placements and are starting on a module called Mdes Enterprise.

During this module they are asked to develop a product/concept or service that can be taken to market or contribute to a business start-up. The outcome has to be proto-typed, tested and then pitched in the style of a business funding pitch. Additional to this the students have to submit a 6000-word enterprise plan that includes current enterprise research and business theory.

Most of the learning outcomes directly relate to the kind of learning the QAA (2012) recommends in order to foster entrepreneurial behaviour in students:

> 'The learning mode is active, exploring problems and opportunities as vehicles for active learning and creative problem solving to enable students to develop generic skills in enterprise. Business simulations can also be valuable. Activities are often group based, especially when team-working skills are desired outcomes. Learning through action and reflection features prominently'
> (QAA, 2012:4).

Students' conceptions of creative/ cultural entrepreneurship

> 'It's weird, … I mean it's weird …with design, it's like, in our area; you kind of ehm, have to be entrepreneurial anyway.'
> (Mdes Student Level 7).[2]

---

[2] As this was just a very small study, the sample of the students who were interviewed or invited to complete the questionnaire was very modest. Data collected consisted of contributions from 4 Ba level 6 students, 5 Mdes Level 6 students and 3 Mdes Level 7 Students.

The QAA (2012) defines enterprise as *'the application of creative ideas and innovations to practical situations'* and entrepreneurship as *'the application of enterprise skills specifically to creating and growing organisations in order to identify and build opportunity'* (p8). As a consequence the first question students were asked was: *'What does enterprise and entrepreneurship mean to you in the context of the creative subject you are studying?'*

In their answers the students identified a range or markers of entrepreneurship and enterprise in the context of their creative subject, which are also identified in the QAA document. These were:

1. The link to **Innovation and Creativity**: *'Creativity and Innovation - Ideas led by enterprise and entrepreneurship are founded on the ability to think and act creatively.'* (QAA, 2012:18).

The students' answers included the following phrases: *'new venture or idea'*, *'unique and different'*, *'designing something new'*, *'think of an idea and make it into something'*, *'coming up with new ideas to make money'*. This suggest that the students identify the need to engage with what the QAA (2012) lists under essential requirements, such as thinking speculatively, generating ideas & concepts, innovation and understanding the values of intellectual property, to name a few.

Two other themes that emerged from their answers were related to the idea of how self-employment and starting a new business was linked to enterprise and entrepreneurship. The QAA talks about the importance of these as part of the *'warrant'* (Hyatt 2013) for the document as a policy driver:

2. **Entrepreneurial effectiveness**: *'the ability to function effectively as an entrepreneur or in an entrepreneurial capacity, for example within small businesses or part of portfolio careers, where multiple job opportunities, part time work and personal ventures combine.'* (QAA, 2012:2)

In their answers the student differentiated between being self-employed and starting a new design business: *'I think I'd understand it more in terms of going freelance or setting up your own studio after graduation, trying to make it on your own.'* (Level 6 Ba Student)

On the whole, students differentiated between the two, but obviously felt that both variations were important to be listed separately. In relation to self-employment they mentioned: *'going freelance'*, *' making money in self-employment'*, *'to sell your designs'*, *'making money from what you do'*, *'self-employment and private commission'*, *'marketing yourself'*, *'trying to make it on your own'*, *'Graphic design: selling it, getting paid for it or freelancing.'* In general, they considered the relevance of self-employment and new venture creation in the same breath, mostly it was expressed within one sentence. The terms they used to describe venture creation were: *'setting up your own studio'*, *'successful design business'*, *'to sell your designs'*, *'creating your own business'*, *'create a successful business'*, *'go to market'*. These ventures were generally described in the context of having ideas or practicing design.

PEDAGOGY

Although the majority of the answers were no longer than two sentences, a few students also managed to start alluding to what attributes were needed in order to achieve '*entrepreneurial effectiveness*' (QAA 2012). They mentioned the need to '*have multiple skill sets*', '*skills to sell*', '*to combine technical and taught skills*', '*do things, make things, have a plan*', '*marketing yourself*', '*being proactive*'.

3. **Entrepreneurial capabilities**, which according to the QAA guidance, encompass a range of behaviours, attributes and skills (QAA 2012).

The students also start touching upon issues of motivation for becoming entrepreneurial when they mention things such as *greater creative freedom, trying to make it on your own*', '*getting paid for it*', '*making money from what you do*', '*coming up with new ideas to make money*'. Although four out these six include an economic incentive, we feel that these warrant closer inspection in terms of the way the student envisage the motivation for entrepreneurial and enterprising behaviour. Creative students are known to show high levels of what is known as '*sacrificial labour*' (Oakley et al., 2008), where labour invested far outweighs any immediate financial gain. This may relate to the idea that the creative economy is built on a different value system (Levick-Parkin, 2014), in which financial reward and sustainability is an important aspect, but no-where near as important as self-realisation and recognition from (creative) peers (Oakley et al., 2008). And indeed one student mentions '*greater creative freedom*' as a reason for becoming entrepreneurial and another one '*trying to make it on your own*', which is very closely aligned with goals of self-realisation.

Even some of the reasons mentioned, which are seemingly about financial motivation are not necessarily that straight forward. When students talk about '*getting paid for it*' and '*making money from what you do*', they are actually referring to the idea of pursuing their creating practice with the added benefit of gaining a financial reward from their pursuit. The students clearly identify the need to make money, but overall their response would suggest that these may not the overriding factors of motivation.

What is interesting about their responses is the fact that students from all three previously outlined modules responded in a very similar way to the question, which warrants further investigation, but might suggest that taking modules with Enterprise or Entrepreneurship in its title does not substantially add to their understanding of it in the context of their discipline.

The students were also asked if they thought that creative/cultural entrepreneurship was the same as '*other*'/ more business focused entrepreneurship.

Here all the students on the BA and the Mdes level 6 answered that they thought along the lines of '*It's certainly similar, but not the same*'. The main way they seemed to differentiate between the two was that creative entrepreneurship started with a tangible product, i.e. the a-fore mentioned creative labour one pursued anyway. Business entrepreneurship in that context was seen as primarily the '*midwife*' that would deliver the creative output into the world. Some students commented that they felt that creative entrepreneurs did more than '*business entrepreneurs*', because they had to '*parent*' the idea, the production, the service, the finances, etc. This sentiment is also echoed in some of the literature aimed at creative entrepreneurs (Heller, 2008).

With the Mdes Level 7 students, who had just taken the enterprise module, the answers were leaning more towards creative entrepreneurship being the same as *'business'* entrepreneurship and that the name creative/cultural merely situated it in their specific subject area.

Staff Conceptions of Creative/Cultural Entrepreneurship

Semi-structured interviews were conducted with 6 members of staff, who were involved in the delivery of the previously outlined provision one way or another.

The questions used to structure the interviews mirrored the questions we had asked the students. When we asked staff about what enterprise and entrepreneurship meant in the context of the creative discipline they were teaching, the majority of them mentioned how so called entrepreneurial behaviour was part and parcel of the education of a creative student. But quite few of them were also quite adamant that creative entrepreneurship was not the same as *'other'* entrepreneurship. The following response is quite representative in term of what staff thought:

> *'I think it means an ability to spot opportunities and often that's not about financial gain, I suppose that's the difference between what we do and what more business orientated course might consider it to be. It's about getting involved with people and opportunities in the outside world, which often has no financial drive to it at all. Especially not if you are trying to get into that position, it often means that you are volunteering or being part of something.'*
> *(Graphic design tutor, level 6 Ba).*

this seems clearly to support the idea of a creative economy not necessarily being built on the same value system as a financial economy (Levick-Parkin, 2014), and it is therefore likely to be more appropriate for creative entrepreneurship to build on social enterprise theory than on business enterprise theory, because of the complimentary value systems (Ridley-Duff & Bull, 2011).

Conclusion

Our study gives some insights into what creative/cultural entrepreneurship means to a small group of creative students. The research conducted highlights that the creative students interviewed seem to have a good understanding of what enterprise and entrepreneurship means to them, although there are some issues of semantic discord when describing specific entrepreneurial attributes in the creative context. As previously discussed, those students who had taken modules specifically dealing with enterprise, were more inclined to see creative entrepreneurship as being directly linked to business based activities, than students who had taken primarily creatively focused modules.

Both groups of students showed a high level of enterprise awareness and evidence of an entrepreneurial mind-set, as well an appreciation of what it meant to be entrepreneurially capable. Yet, the interviews and questionnaires highlighted that they didn't always make links between their creative capabilities and overlapping entrepreneurial ones.

Both groups showed consistent levels of confidence in their creative practice, but low confidence in possessing enough of the business specific expertise necessary to be entrepreneurially sustainable. The research also indicated that their level of confidence

PEDAGOGY

in their ability to deal with business requirements did not appear to be markedly improved by having taken an explicitly named 'enterprise' module, though it is difficult to generalise this as the sample was so small. However, questions of confidence are notoriously difficult to evaluate, especially without looking at the enterprise modules impact on their subsequent employment patterns.

In order to show the operational impact of enterprise teaching within creative provision, whether integrated into modules or explicitly delivered through entrepreneurship modules, systematic research with our alumni would be needed, similar to the research exemplified in the previously mentioned 'Effects and impact' report by the European Commission (2012).

Whilst it is encouraging that cultural entrepreneurship is taking a more centre stage in the broader educational discourse, we can't help but feel that the creative and cultural community needs to beware of entering into these discussions solely based on an economic value system defined by others. Creative enterprise and entrepreneurship is more akin to social enterprise in its values (Heller and Talarico 2008, Ridley and Bull 2011). In this study most of the answers given, by both students and lecturers, in relation to motivating factors for entrepreneurial behaviour, chime with other findings (ADM-HEA 2007) that suggests that creatives primarily behave entrepreneurially because they are motivated by goals of creative self-realisation, or to fulfil a desire to contribute to 'the greater good' in their immediate surroundings.

Although financial viability is important to them it is not the sole, or primary driver for their activities. Kooyman and Jacobs also (2015) note that 'creatives often receive their rewards in private satisfaction and other non-monetary income such as social and cultural status, based on authenticity and individualism' (2015:6). Rather than trying to incentivise creative and cultural entrepreneurial behaviour with overtly financially focused promises and goals, we need to harness these attitudes and values as being central to socially *and* economically sustainable cultural enterprise models.

References

ADM-HEA, (2007). Creating Entrepreneurship: entrepreneurship education for the creative industries, ADM-HEA, UK, pp. 57, 58, 59, 126, and 126. In: *Towards an entrepreneurial University* (Gibb 2005).

Ashton, D. (2010). Productive passions and everyday pedagogies: Exploring the industry-ready agenda in higher education. In: *Art, Design & Communication in Higher Education*, 9(1), pp.41--56.

Bakhshi, H., Hargreaves, I. and Mateos-Garcia, J. (2013). *A Manifesto for the Creative Economy*. London: NESTA.

Ball, S. (2008). *The education debate*. Bristol: Policy Press.

Book, L. and Phillips, D. (2013). *Creativity and entrepreneurship*. Cheltenham: Edward Elgar.

Cohen, L., Manion, L. and Morrison, K. (2011). *Research methods in education*. 7th ed. London: RoutledgeFalmer.

PEDAGOGY

About the Author

*Melanie Levick-Parkin
BA studied visual
communication &
graphic design and
then re-incarnated as
an advertising creative for
a number of years.
After abandoning a
teenage crush on
photography, Melanie moved
into an academic career.
Being involved in Art
& Design education for over
a decade, she has become
passionate about
the relevance of creative
education beyond
the 'Art School' setting.*

*Her current research
interests revolve around
Design Anthropology,
Co-design and other
participatory approaches,
which she is exploring in
relation to projects focussing
on heritage, archaeology and
cultural tourism.
She is currently studying
for a doctorate at
the University of Sheffield,
and is involved in a variety
of research projects ranging
from small explorative visual
communication projects,
to teaching enhancement
project and the EU funded
meSch Project. Personal
interests include archaeology,
Cretan history and culture.*

m.levick-parkin@shu.ac.uk

Cox G., Sperry B., (2005). *Cox Review of Creativity in Business: building on the UK's strength*. UK, pp. 2,3,

Clews, D. (2009). *Dialogues in art and design*. 1st ed. [S.l.]: GLAD.

Crainer, S. and Dearlove, D. (2000). *Generation entrepreneur*. 1st ed. London: FT.com.

Danvers J., (2003). Towards a Radical Pedagogy: Provisional Notes on Learning and Teaching in Art & Design, JADE 22.1 NSEAD, UK, pp.51, 53,

Department for Business Innovation & Skills, (2013). *Enterprise education impact in higher education and further education*. London: Crown

Design Commission, (2011). *Restarting Britain: Design Education and Growth, UK*, pp.15,

European Commission, (2006). *The Economy of Culture in Europe*. Brussels: Director General for Education and Culture

European Commission, (2012). *Effects and impact of entrepreneurship programmes in higher education*. Brussels: Entrepreneurship Unit: Directorate-General for Enterprise and Industry

Fairclough, N. (2010). *Critical discourse analysis*. 2nd ed. London: Longman

Heller, S. and Talarico, L. (2008). *The design entrepreneur – Turning Graphic Design into Goods That Sell*. Beverly, Mass.: Rockport Publishers

Henry, C. (2007). *Entrepreneurship in the creative industries*. 1st ed. Cheltenham, UK: Edward Elgar

Hyatt, D. (2013). The critical policy discourse analysis frame: helping doctoral students engage with the educational policy analysis. In: *Teaching in Higher Education*, 18(8), pp.833-845

Horizon 2020, (2015). *Horizon 2020 - European Commission*. Retrieved from: http://ec.europa.eu/programmes/horizon2020/h2020-sections [Accessed 3 Feb. 2015]

Hutchinson, M. and Young, C. (1962). *Educating the intelligent*. Baltimore: Penguin Books

Klamer, A. (2011). Cultural entrepreneurship. In: *Rev Austrian Econ*, 24(2), pp.141-156

Kooyman, R. and Jacobs, R. (2015). *The entrepreneurial ant: re-thinking art management education.* Academia.edu. Retrieved from: ttps://www.academia.edu/5453559/The_entrepreneurial_ant_re-thinking_art_management_education [Accessed 2 Feb. 2015]

Levick-Parkin, M. (2014). Creativity, the muse of innovation: How art and design pedagogy can further entrepreneurship. In: *Industry and Higher Education*, 28(3), pp.163-169

Manchester Institute of Innovation Research (MIoIR), (2013). *The Impact and Effectiveness of Entrepreneurship Policy*. NESTA, Manchester

PEDAGOGY

Mazzucato, M. (2013). *Entrepreneurial State: Debunking the Public vs. Private Myth in Risk and Innovation.* Anthem Press

Oakley K., Sperry B., Pratt A., (2008). *The art of innovation: How fine arts graduates contribute to innovation.* NESTA, London, UK

Orr, S., Bloxham, S., (2012). *Making judgements about students making work: lecturers' assessment practices in art and design*, Arts and Humanities in Higher Education. ISSN 1474-0222 (In Press)

Point Judith Capital, The Liberal Arts Entrepreneur, Online, (2010). Retrieved from: http://pointjudithcapital.com/blog/blog-post-3/ (Accessed 20th of April 2014)

QAA. (2012). *Enterprise and Entrepreneurship Education: Guidelines for UK Higher Education Providers.* The Quality Assurance Agency (QAA) for Higher Education 2012

Ridley-Duff, R. and Bull, M. (2011). *Understanding social enterprise.* 1st ed. London: SAGE

Shreeve A., Sims E. and Trowler P., (2010). 'A kind of exchange': learning from art and design teaching, In: *Higher Education Research & Development*, 29:2, 125-138, pp.132

Viladas, X. (2011). *Design at your service.* 1st ed. Barcelona: Index Books.

William Mc E. and Haukka S., (2008). Educating the creative workforce: new directions for twenty-first century schooling, In: *British Educational Research Journal*, 43:5, 651-666, pp.652

Oluwayemisi Abisuga

DEVELOPING CREATIVE EDUCATION IN SOUTH AFRICA
A CASE OF WESTERN CAPE PROVINCE

Abstract

This article explores entrepreneurial education in the creative industries. Traditional entrepreneurship training is concerned with providing knowledge, but there is a lack of understanding and research about the processes of creative entrepreneurship (Kellet, 2006). This article attempts to gain a clearer understanding of creative entrepreneurship as a whole, and skill developments needed to successfully overcome the over-supply of university graduates in a very difficult employment market. The substantial conceptual confusion as to what constitutes enterprise education worsens the dilemmas being faced when attempting to identify effective educational strategies and examples of good practice (Penaluna and Penanula, 2006a).

This article questions the relevance and effectiveness of entrepreneurship education, and inadequacy with the development in entrepreneurial activities that are accessible within higher education in the Western Cape of South Africa. The primary question this research attempt to answer is how higher education inspires a creative, entrepreneurial student in business schools, in the context of the institutional programme of developing the Creative Industries. Also, the researcher proposes a six phase conceptual framework of entrepreneurial training to help creative discipline students develop a vision for a business.

PEDAGOGY

Introduction

In South Africa the Arts, Culture, Heritage and Creative Industries were affected by apartheid as all other aspects of human, social, political and economic life of the people. The educational scheme of blacks did not offer arts education, and there were little or no job opportunities in the Creative Industries for black people. The South African White Paper on Arts, Culture and Heritage (2013) blames this unfair skill development practice of the apartheid era, to a narrow understanding of the role of Creative Industries since 1994. Considering the new national Creative Arts curriculum (CAPS, 2011) and the past deficits experienced at schools in arts education, the current school reality showed a picture far from ready to meet the welcome changes and new challenges.

Isaacs, Visser, Friedrich and Brijlal (2007) assessed the levels of entrepreneurship education and training at the Further Education and Training (FET) level in the South African context, and stress the opinion that entrepreneurship education and training is a necessity, which must fulfil a primary role in preparing the nation for its future. But, the traditional academic entrepreneurship theory sometimes lacks the Creative Industries context to attract and motivate the talented students who stand out with a determination to become business owners in the future. Isaacs, Visser, Friedrich and Brijlal indicate that the entrepreneurship education at school level does not receive a high priority in the South African context. Entrepreneurship in the creative industries and the related development of entrepreneurial skills are not well understood, and traditional approaches cannot be assumed to be effective. Hence, the development of a training model is potentially valuable (Rae, 2004).

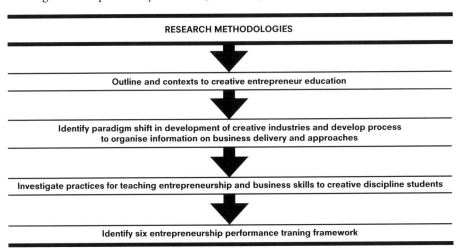

Figure 1 Research methods

The Western Cape Province

A core factor in the development of creative entrepreneurship in South Africa is education. All the stakeholders involved, including state, educators, and learners themselves have to be included.

Within the Western Cape Province the utmost limitations of economic development can be attributed to its lack of entrepreneurs. The ratio of entrepreneurs to workers in South Africa is approximately 1 to 52, whereas the ratio in most developed countries is approximately 1 to 10 (Friedrich & Visser, 2005; Gouws, 2002). However, there is a sound ambition in the area. WESGRO (2013) indicates that: *'The Western Cape is poised to become a world-class destination for creative industries with Cape Town being awarded the World Design Capital 2014 designation'.*

At present Western Cape Province has many excellent arts service providers, recognized nationally for making outstanding creative learning opportunities and events available to students outside and within the schools. The after-school creative arts learning providers have influenced quality arts experiences for youths and are on the edge to make a larger contribution and commitment. There is a requirement for the district to provide an opportunity to rebuild the creative learning curriculum and reach outside school walls to establish a province's rich arts community.

However, creative education and training opportunities are declining in schools and community life. In many schools within the Western Cape Province, creative learning is mostly forced to compete against other district priorities for time and funding. To worsen this issue, various educators in this province themselves are part of a generation that did not encounter arts education when they were students. Due to the artistic shortage of skill in schools, the creative education is not accessible to all learners in South Africa.

PEDAGOGY

This article will question the principles, frameworks, and on current concepts found in the literature, followed by practitioner-based reflection to provide an understanding into the process of developing entrepreneurship education in higher education institutions (HEIs). Our study indicates a paradigm shifts in the development of the Creative Industries concept in South Africa, and reflects on the role of Higher Education. It indicates the change which might contrast with the more traditional entrepreneurial business school approach for students specifically wishing to enter the Creative Industries field. A literature review discloses a dominance of texts that have been made by authors within the business environment and creative industries as educators or practitioners. Six phases conceptual framework of entrepreneurial training to help creative discipline students develop a vision for a business was identified.

Creative Entrepreneurship Education

The Confederation of British Industry (CBI, 2014) verifies that, in order for the creative industries to continue to be the world's leading creative hub, one must have access to a broad talent base, particularly to young people from different backgrounds. This must be supported by an education framework that embraces a commitment to creativity, and that inspires the youth to desire a career in the creative industries. Thus, there is a strong message from the Creative and Cultural Industries that the education which young people receive in school in Creative and Cultural subjects has a direct bearing on feeding into the talent pool for those who take up employment in this sector (DCMS, 2012).

The plea for creative entrepreneurial education in South Africa is not grounded on what has been taught in the traditional business education in the past. To a greater extent, the key issues revolve around what is presently not available in South Africa, and what should be provided for in future curriculae.

Many times, creative students have problem in changing their ideas into entrepreneur planning, due to a lack of experience and understanding of the business world. Kellet (2006) gives requirements for that as comprising research, training, business planning, networking, expert advice and mentoring, incubation facilities, prototype and piloting of products or services, supply chain investigation, finance and fundraising, investment, customer profiling, sales and marketing.

Educating creative discipline students in business related training such as presentation skills, self-promotion, sales and marketing, intellectual property rights, client handling, financing and managing businesses is often not available as part of their course. Kellet (2006) suggests that, creative education subjects should be acknowledged as an intellectual rigour and practical skills should be taught to entrepreneurial creatives. DCMS (2012) also, believes there should be a clear signal from the government that these subjects are both valuable and valued as part of the full package of education offered to students.

The Creative entrepreneurs extend support and advice to creative individuals across the Western Cape region through a range of high-quality development programmes. The developments are of two main categories; those which are focused on students and graduates at the Universities and Colleges, and those creative individuals who live and

PEDAGOGY

work in the Western Cape region. Hence, professional based creative entrepreneurship workshops and business support should be developed and implemented, in order to encourage and support those students who are keen to develop their own business.

Cox' *Review of Creativity in Business* (2005) provides that the HEIs are assigned to render the education and skills that produce business people who understand creativity. Business leaders should know when and how to use the creative specialist, and be able to manage innovation.

At the same token, creative specialists are needed, who understand the environment in which their talents will be used, and can talk the same language as their clients and business colleagues; often engineers and technologists who can speak the language of business. Therefore, educators are charged with incorporating business expertise into all programmes outside business schools and developing the essential skills for creativity and idea protection within them, with a key challenge is to make available a curriculum that motivates students in art and design subjects (Penaluna and Penaluna, 2005 cited in Penaluna and Penaluna, 2009).

PEDAGOGY

EDUCATIONAL ENTREPRENEURIAL FRAMEWORK CONDITION	MEAN SCORE 2010	MEAN SCORE 2013
Primary and secondary education encourages creativity, selfsufficiency and personal initiative	1,75	1,96
Primary and secondary education provides adequate instruction in market economic principles	1,67	1,63
Primary and secondary education provides adewuate attention to entrepreneurship and new firm creation	1,87	1,75
Colleges and universities provide good and adequate preparation for starting up and growing new firms	2,33	2,33
Business and magagement education provides adequate preparation for starting up and growing new firms	2,60	2,50
Vocational, professional and continuing education provides good and adequate preparation for starting and grow new firms	2,32	2,13

Table 1 Average expert ratings education and training for entrepreneurship in South Africa, (2010 & 2013) Source: Herrington and Kew, 2013

The table 1 above shows that rating for different aspects of education and training are well below average. This seems to indicate that the current schooling continues to provide almost no foundation in the preparation for starting up and growing a new business.

SKILL SHORTAGE	PROBLEMS	WAY OUT SCORE
Business idea formation	Lack of creativity and business planning practice	Ideas development training and workshops. Practical business research
Recognising opportunities	Identifying the current business openings	Understanding of crative industries business operations.
Communication skills	Problems with oral, reading and written communication	Exposure to practical experience
Self-awareness	Inability of self-branding to be able to sell their product or services	This can be built upon by the mentoring or practical development materials
Presentation skills	Inexperience, anxiety and lack of self-confidence	Practical experience through group assessment and role-play
Marketing skills	Inability to identify the target market and opportunities	Self-development through research and business start-up guidelines
Team work	Lack of practice and cooperative work with others	By role-playing, business teams groups and projects works.
Business development	Growth and sustainability of business is important	Mentoring and use of case studies in training
Risk taking	Inexperience on risk taking and business environment security	Making up a fake business situation for student to manage, with allocation of budget
Decision making	Students needs fast decision making ability to survive as business owners	Making an assumed situation for student to work with
Project management	Student's inability to complete project to industry standard within time and budget	Mentored through live project, or a fake project scenario
Financial planning	Understanding the pricing, costing and profit constraints	Marketing research on competitor's product, and costing strategies. Knowledge through experience

Table 2 Skill Shortage in Creative Students

The Business School Perspective

The subject of business and entrepreneurship has traditionally come under the responsibility of the business school and historically been part of a hidden curriculum within art and design schools. Its presence has been totally absent, and it has not been part of the key remit of the everyday curriculum, which has focused more on creative subjects (Kellet, 2006). Rae (1997) argue that: *'the skills traditionally taught in business schools are essential, but not sufficient to make a successful entrepreneur.'* In addition, Collins, Hannon, Smith (2004) stipulate that business schools provide one-size-fits-all education outputs that are not applicable to all students across different disciplines. Having identified that a successful entrepreneur has personal skills, attributes and behaviours that covers outside the purely commercial (Gibb, 1998), the challenge to Higher Education's is to develop students with entrepreneurial abilities that meet the entrepreneurial challenges of the 21st century knowledge economy.

Cox Review provides indications, supported by other studies (Pelaluna and Penaluna, 2006a), that curriculum development in higher education should integrate business school and should develop the fundamental skills for developing creative ideas security for those within the school (Penaluna and Penaluna, 2006b). The implication of

PEDAGOGY

this for educators and cross-faculty mentors is to introduce the suitable curricular developments that will be needed to overcome the unwillingness of the many academics who will not welcome entrepreneurship education (Penaluna and Penaluna, 2006b).

Self-employment and Entrepreneurship

Traditionally, higher education institutions (HEIs) perform the role of educating, training and preparing individuals to turn out to be employees. Hartshorn and Hannon (2005) observe self-employment and entrepreneurship has not been traditionally viewed as the career choice for graduates. However, HEIs play an essential role in the development of the required behaviours and skills that would allow graduates both to create their own job (business start-up) or become an effective job seeker (Lewis, 2005).

Entrepreneurship Education and Training

The business schools are faced with the responsibility for providing a great part of the future professional creative industry workforce. It is required to develop and teach students to be more enterprising through pedagogical practises. Gibb (2010) states that this type of education has been criticised for its use of traditional pedagogical approaches. These traditional approaches over-emphasise theory and handle functional knowledge as an *'end'* rather than a *'means'*. Such an approach limits the development of entrepreneurial skills, capabilities and attributes. Kellet (2006) states that these approaches give a student a 'feeling' of entrepreneurship, which subsequently raises their understanding of living day-to-day with the uncertainty and risk. By repeating the educational exercises they will learn to transfer the experiences into the reality of life. In order to safeguard this transfer of knowledge, learning and teaching should be well structured around solving problems.

There has been a failure to make relevant provision, for creative businesses, with traditional business courses in South Africa. Creative students have natural entrepreneurial qualities, and are rich in ideas. Yet, without an understanding of their industry and the ways to penetrate it for profit, supplemented with the soft skills for organising and delivering a business, graduates cannot take their ideas for business forward (Kellet, 2006). Isaacs, Visser, Friedrich and Brijlal (2007) defines entrepreneurship education as the meaningful involvement of an educator in the life of the learner to impart entrepreneurial qualities and skills to enable the learner to survive in the world of business. Alberti, Sciascia and Poli (2004) also defines entrepreneurship education as: *the structured, formal transfer of entrepreneurial competencies*. It refers to the concepts, skills and mental awareness used by individuals during the process of starting and developing their growth oriented business ventures.

The fundamental reason for the creative entrepreneur training is to provide students with vital knowledge, skills and attitudes to empower them transform knowledge into entrepreneurship and / or new business practices. By doing this, students will require the capacity to reflect over what skills they have gained amid their course, and what prospects will be open to start their own businesses based on these skills.

Teachers' Skills

The Howard Davies Review (2002) highlighted that many teachers are believed to need substantial support in terms of their knowledge, skills and experience of business and enterprise, likewise, business requires to be more closely involved with education.

PEDAGOGY

A similar problem has been identified by introducing entrepreneurship education at school level, specifically experienced at tertiary level. For instance, Davies (2001) provides that introducing entrepreneurship as a discipline, particularly in tertiary institutions, is elusive due to different mind-sets, funding mechanisms and a mix-up between entrepreneurship training and creation of small business managers.

As stated, business education in South African creative industries has less attention than entrepreneurship education and training. The creative entrepreneurship training is a lifelong learning process which comprises of the following six phases; fundamentals, skill awareness, creative diligence, start, progression and growth as shown in the figure 2, below:

PHASES OF ENTREPRENEURIAL TRAINING

WORK TRAINING AND EDUCATION

PHASE 1 Fundamentals	PHASE 2 Skills awareness	PHASE 3 Creative diligence
- Forming an idea - acquire required fundamental skills - recognise career opportunities - knowledge of business system	- identify entrepreneurial skills - understand problem of the industry	learn entrepreneurship skills - acquire work-related training - learn new business ideas

WORK RELATED EXPERIENCE

PHASE 4 Start business	PHASE 5 Progression	PHASE 6 Growth
- become an entrepreneur - develop business strategies	- formulate business policies and procedures - prepare future business plan	- improving existing business - resolve challenges effectively

Figure 2: Phases of entrepreneurship performance training framework

The training framework devised for this study, help creative student's pioneers develop a vision for a business through a process of forming an idea, understanding how the business will operate and critical activities in the business. Students formulate their thoughts and visions through a sequence of illustrations based on a process of 6 phases of modelling.

The importance of Creative Entrepreneur Training in the Western Cape

The population of the Western Cape in 2013 is estimated at 6 million people and represents approximately 11.4% of the total national population with relatively 60.27% of the regional population being younger than 35 years of age (WESGRO, 2014).

Van Graan (2005) states that: *'The province is well-served with high quality tertiary institutions providing world-class training across all sub-sectors, however, here is an urgent need for high-quality training of managers and entrepreneurs to provide leadership within this field and to unlock its significant economic and social potential.'* The Western Cape, in its working document ONECAPE2040, has identified various key areas centred to enable the province achieve its vision of *'a highly-skilled, innovation driven, resource-efficient, connected, high opportunity and collaborative society'* by 2040 (Herrington and Kew, 2013):

Educational institutions providing education and training in creative industries in Cape Town:

- Government Tertiary Education Institutions: 4
- Government Further Education and Training Colleges: 3
- Government High School Education: 1
- Independent Schools: 43 (WESGRO, 2013)

PEDAGOGY

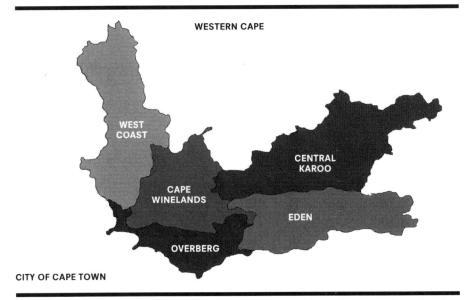

Figure 2 Western Cape Province

REGION	ART	MUSIC	SPEECH AND DRAMA	DESIGN	DANCE
OVERBERG	7	7	3	7	4
METROPOLE	67	45	30	51	14
CENTRAL KAROO/ SOUTH CAPE	7	4	0	4	0
WEST COAST/ BOLAND	11	12	5	10	2
TOTAL	92	68	38	72	20

Table 3 Number of schools offering arts-related courses.
Source Van Graan (2005)

PROFESSIONAL ASSOCIATIONS IN THE CREATIVE INDUSTRY IN CAPE TOWN

- Africa Fashion International
- Animation SA
- Arterial Network — African Arts Institute
- Associaton for Commercials and Advertising (ACA)
- Engineering Council of South Africa
- Institue of Interior Design Practice
- Jewellery Council of SA
- Cape Town Design Network
- Cape Town Fashion Council
- Cape Film Commission
- Cape Institute for Architecture
- Cape IT Initiative
- Ceramics South Africa
- Commercial Producers Association

- Documentary Filmmakers Associaton
- Engineering Council of South Africa
- Institute of Interior Design Practice
- National Arts Council of SA
- Business and Arts South Africa
- Cape Craft and Design Institue
- Professional Photographers of SA
- publishers of SA
- Silicon Cape
- South African Graphic Design Council
- SA Guild of Interior Design
- Western Cape Furniture Initiative
- Visual Arts Network of SA
- Cape Music Industry Commission
- Western Cape Clothing and Textiles Service Centre
- Western Cape Tooling Initiative
- Design Education Forum of South Africa

Table 4 Creative Industries Association in Cape Town Source: WESGRO, 2013

	CAPE METROPOLE	OVERBERG	BOLAND	CENTRAL KAROO	EDEN	WEST COAST
Architecture	2	-	I	-	-	-
Arts management	-	-	-	-	-	-
Craft	2	-	1	-	-	
Dance	1	-	-	-	-	-
Film	3	-	-	-	-	-
Literature	1	-	1	-	-	-
Museum/heritage studies	-	-	-	-	-	-
Music	1	-	1	-	-	-
Opera	1	-	-	-	-	-
Theatre	3	-	1	-	-	-
TOTAL	17	0	6	0	0	0

Table 5 Number of tertiary Institutions providing professional training (degrees/diplomas) in the creative industries (excluding private institutions) Source: Van Graan (2005)

PEDAGOGY

Van Graan (2005) opined that, if education provides the premise for the creative industries, then it would appear that the Western Cape is well-served by institutions that provide training in the various fields. However, there are skills shortages in the area of management, leadership and entrepreneurship. Van Graan (2005) contributes: '*This represents an opportunity for the Western Cape to develop world-class training in these areas at least one of its tertiary institutions, and so form the basis to attract students from around the country and indeed, from around the developing world.*' Van Gran further puts forward that, no institutions track their graduates to determine whether they find employment in the sector or not, how soon they find such employment, what kinds of jobs they are likely to take up within the sector or in other sectors, how long they remain within the sector, whether they remain in the province or migrate to other provinces or abroad.

SUB- SECTOR	TOTAL
Architecture	1880
Community arts	890
Craft	4750
Dance	500
Design and advertising	6300
Fashion (including designers,	2000
Fashion photography, models,etc. Festivals and events	500
Films	600
Heritage and museums	3000
Language schools	175
Publishing, literature, printing and packaging	20000
Music	2000
Musicals and opera theatre	150
Theatre	800
Visual arts	4000
TOTAL	47545

Table 6 Summary of the employment in the creative industries sector in the Western Cape Source: Van Graan, 2005

An estimate of the number of people directly employed and those who earn their primary income in the creative industries sub-sectors would be close to 50 000, at least 50% more than the 30 000 teachers working in the province or four times more than the total number of workers in the mining and quarrying and electricity, gas and water supply sectors in the Western Cape (Van Graan, 2005). Herrington and Kew (2013) put forward that, the Western Cape has the highest rate of high business growth, i.e. businesses that intend generating 20 plus jobs over the next five years. Obviously, there are needs for more research into the number of people employed in the creative industries in the province, even the estimates above, shows that the impact of the creative industries on employment is important.

FDI PROJECTS INTO THE WESTERN CAPE, 2013							
DATE	COMPANY NAME	SOURCE COUNTRY	DESTINATION CITY	SECTOR	BUSINESS ACTIVITY	VALUE (ZARM)	JOBS
Nov 2013	MCI Group	Switzerland	Cape Town	Business Services	Creative Industries	47,83	12
Nov 2013	The Jupiter Drawing Room	Zambia Province	Lusaka Services	Business Industries	Creative	47,83	19
Jul 2013	Snapplify	United States	New York	Software & IT Services	Creative Industries	69,70	40
Feb 2013	Celebrity Services Africa (CSA)	United States	California	Business Services	Creative Industries	39,63	18
Aug 2012	Movile	United States	California	Software & IT Services	Creative Industries	69,70	40

Table 7 Foreign creative projects in Western Cape Source: WESGRO, 2014

The table 7 above, provides an outline of foreign companies who have invested in creative industries in the Western Cape in 2013.

FINDINGS OF THE STUDY

In regards to the study, the researcher identified ten findings as explained below.

1. A gap is identified in relations to inadequate geographic coverage of current programmes offered in the Western Cape Province. These unfulfilled training needs were based on the findings from the literature review, as well as information gathered from previous researchers. The Western Cape has the lowest percentage of businesses with low-growth perceptions (40%, compared to three quarters of the businesses in the rest of South Africa) (Herrington and Kew, 2013).

2. The significance of skills for the creative discipline students such as marketing, sales presentation, communication skills and the shortage of this training within the core curriculum in Higher Education Art and Design Institutions noticeably requires to be addressed.

3. Creative Enterprise Education has traditionally been part of a hidden curriculum within Higher Education as generic business courses fell under the remit of Business School Faculties.

4. There is an increasing need to clearly define new and emergent pedagogical processes used in Creative Enterprise Education, as a means of teaching the creative discipline students the business skills and successful market strategy (Kellet, 2006).

5. Entrepreneurs in the Western Cape are 6.7 times more likely to be opportunity-driven than necessity-driven (Herrington and Kew, 2013). However, if there are opportunities, true entrepreneurs will, through innovative and creative means, find profitable opportunities.

6. There is a lack of case studies to use as teaching resources to support creative entrepreneur educators, and there is a great demand and need from students to have role models to source and learn from (Kellet, 200).

7. It was found that, what is hindering the desires of creative students to develop new businesses is business entrepreneur education failure.

8. Three critical areas were identified as prerequisites for implementing training programmes, namely, development of infrastructure, provision of suitable and appropriate training material, and the need for funding.

9. Developing a business scheme to assist the learner to participate actively in exploring suitable creative models and develop a network of contact to support future goals.

10. Cases of young entrepreneurs and role models are essential in providing a greater visibility of business development.

PEDAGOGY

Recommendations

From the study, therefore, we derived the following recommendations.

- The government should constantly examine the structures of all schools and inclusive education providers to prove their commitment to a changed national curriculum. Also, providing opportunities for young people to study a mixed subjects including creative arts and entrepreneurship.
- The educational courses need to combine business development and business management practice, improved with sector specific material, set as in a contextual framework of the Creative Industries (Kellet, 2006).
- Providing mentorship programmes for new entrepreneurs where the mentors have practical personal experience of running a business and focusing on entrepreneurial education at both secondary and at university level (Herrington and Kew, 2013).
- Cross-departmental government co-operation: the Department of Education and the Department of Art and Culture should establish a new board to work with, sponsored bodies to help them deliver effective creative education across the country (DCMS, 2012).
- Implementing 'Training-the-trainer programmes' for educators in South Africa seven provinces. The reason for this recommendation is built on our findings and observations that: schools teachers are ill-equipped for the role of mentor, advisor and lead promoter of entrepreneurship programmes at schools (Isaacs, Visser, Friedrich and Brijlal (2007).
- Students need to work in groups to provide them with experience of teamwork and offer them a more complete real life approach to learning.
- Training in developing pedagogies of creative entrepreneur education teaching is required for educators who obviously understand the sector works and yet need to modify their skills in teaching business development (Kellet, 2006).
- The educational courses must combine business development and business management practice, set as in a contextual framework of the Creative Industries.
- Developing the skills of the next creative generation: disregarding the creative subjects in educational curriculum, inadequate expertise training for educators and the absence of reliable vocation guidance can make numerous young people be discouraged from chosen a creative career.

Conclusion

This article argues in reaction to the present economic recession and unemployment problems that, graduate creative entrepreneurship is an important intervention. HEIs play a significant role in helping students make the change to be successful entrepreneurs who can create their own job and possible jobs for others (Lourenco, Taylor and Taylor, 2013). Future investigations should also allow other external groups such as enterprise clubs and investors, to increasingly become more applicable to the student experience and actual start-up activity and associated issues of sustainability (Penanula, Penanula and Jones, 2012).

Successively, the study encourages the growth of graduate entrepreneurship in the Western Cape Province of South Africa to overcome the problem of excess supply of university graduates in a very challenging employment market. Rae (2004) contributes that, it may be helpful for emerging entrepreneurs to use the framework, perhaps in dialogue with a mentor, as a structure to think through questions of their personal and social identity and role, the development of their skills in managing the enterprise, and how they use contextual learning in recognising opportunities and in working from natural experience to develop their own repertoire of *'practical theory'*. The findings of this study demonstrate that traditional business school methods have not been efficient when working with creative mind-sets, and calls for the creative entrepreneur subject up-grade to a management position within our business school's curriculum. We suggest that the most effective entrepreneurship educators follow the leaders they recommend and think *'outside the box'* to provide an entrepreneurship education that both fulfils the demands of assessment criteria, and provides a meaningful curriculum. Furthermore, it is recognised that traditional approaches for the development of entrepreneurial skills are not essentially the most effective in the creative sector.

About the Author

*Oluwayemisi Abisuga
is involved in
the Business School of
the Tshwane University of
Technology in Pretoria,
South Africa. She has
published in several
academic gremia, e.a:
the OIDA International
Journal of Sustainable
Development. She participates at several International
Conferences, e.a.: The 2014
International Conference on
Arts, Culture, Heritage and
the National Development
Plan: Vision for 2030.
Tshwane University of
Technology, Pretoria,
October 2014.*

—

yemisuga@yahoo.com

References

Alberti, F., Sciascia, S. and Poli, A. (2004). *Entrepreneurship Education: Notes on an Ongoing Debate*. In: Proceedings of the 14th Annual IntEnt Conference, University of Napoli Federico II, Italy.

CBI. (2014). *The Creative Nation a Growth Strategy for the UK's Creative Industries. The Voice of Business*. Retrieved from: http://www.cbi.org.uk/media/2535682/cbi_creative_industries_strategy__final_.pdf

Collins, L., Hannon, P. and Smith, A. (2004). Enacting Entrepreneurial Intent: The Gaps between Student Needs and Higher Education Capability. In: *Education and Training*, Vol. 46 No, 8&9, pp. 454-463.

Cox, G. (2005). *Cox Review of Creativity in Business: Building on the UK's Strengths*. London: HM Treasury, Executive Summary.

Davies, T. (2001). *Entrepreneurship development in South Africa: Redefining the Role of Tertiary Institutions in a Reconfigured Higher Education System*. Natal Technikon, KwazuluNatal.

Friedrich, C. and Visser, K. (2005). *South African Entrepreneurship Education and Training*. De Doorns: Leap Publisher.

Gibb, A. (1998) Educating Tomorrow's Entrepreneurs. In: *Economic Reform Today*, No 4, pp. 32-38

Gibb, A. (2010). *Towards the Entrepreneurial University: Entrepreneurship Education as a Lever for Change*. The National Council for Graduate Entrepreneurship, Birmingham, UK.

Gouws, E. (2002). Entrepreneurship Education: Implications for Teacher Training. In: South African Journal of Higher Education, Vol.16 No, 2 pp. 41-48.

Hartshorn, C. and Hannon, P. (2005). Paradoxes in Entrepreneurship Education: Chalk and Talk or Chalk and Cheese? A Case Approach. In: *Education and Training*, Vol. 47 No, 8&9, pp. 616-627.

Herrington, M. and Kew, J. (2013). *South African Report, Twenty Years of Democracy*. Global Entrepreneurship Monitor (GEM).

PEDAGOGY

Howard Davies Review. (2002). *A Review of, Enterprise and the Economy in Education*. London: HM Treasury. Retrieved from: http://www.mebp.org/Downloads/Davis%20Review%20main%20report.pdf

Isaacs, E., Visser, K., Friedrich, C. and Brijlal, P. (2007). Entrepreneurship education and training at the Further Education and Training (FET) level in South Africa. In: *South African Journal of Education*, Vol. 27, pp. 613–629.

Kellet, I. (2006). *Emergent Practices in Entrepreneurship Education for Creatives, Research report for the Art Design Media Subject Centre*. Retrieved from: http://www.adm.heacademy.ac.uk/library/files/adm-hea-projects/emergent-practices.pdf

Lewis, K. (2005). The Best of Intentions: Future Plans of Young Enterprise Scheme participants, In: Education Training, Vol. 47 No. 7, pp. 470-483.

Lourenco, F. (2013). Integrating 'education for entrepreneurship' in multiple faculties in 'half-the-time' to enhance graduate entrepreneurship. In: Journal of Small Business and Enterprise Development. Emerald Group Publishing Limited, Vol. 20 No. 3, pp. 503-525.

Penaluna, A. and Penaluna, K. (2006a). *Business Paradigms in Einstellung: Entrepreneurship Education, a Creative Industries Perspective*. Paper presented at the Internationalizing Entrepreneurship Education and Training Conference, Sao Paulo, 9-12 July, 2006.

Penaluna, A. anf Penaluna, K. (2006b). *Stepping Back to Go Forward: Alumni in Reflexive Design-Curriculum Development*. Paper presented at the Internationalising Entrepreneurship Education and Training Conference IntEnt, Brazil.

Penaluna, A. and Penaluna, K. (2009). Creativity in business/business in creativity: transdisciplinary curricula as an enabling strategy in enterprise education. In: *Industry and Higher Education*, Vol. 23, No 3, pp. 209–219.

Penaluna, A., Penaluna, K. and Jones, C. (2012). The context of enterprise education: insights into current practices. In: *Industry and Higher Education*, Vol. 26, No 3, pp. 163–175.

Rae, D. (1997). Teaching Entrepreneurship in Asia; Impact of a Pedagogical Innovation, Entrepreneurship, Innovation and Change. In: *Emerald: Publisher*, Vol. 6 No, 3, pp. 193-227

Rae, D. (2004). *Entrepreneurial learning: a practical model from the creative industries, Education and Training*. Vol. 46 No, 8/9, pp. 492-500.

South Africa. (2013). *Creative Industries Sector Fact Sheet*. The Western Cape Destination Marketing Investment and Trade Promotion Agency (WESGRO).

South Africa, (WESGRO). (2014). *Overview of the Western Cape, Cape Town and Western Cape Research*. District Executive Summary.

South Africa. (2013). Revised White Paper on Arts, Culture and Heritage. Version 2 (4 June 2013). In: *OECD Economic Surveys: South Africa 2013*. OECD: Publishing, March 2013, overview.

United Kingdom. Department for Culture, Media and Sport (DCMS), (2012). *Cultural Education in England, An independent review by Darren Henley*. Published by Department of Education, UK.

Van Graan, M. (2005). *Towards an understanding of the current nature and scope of the Creative Industries in the Western Cape*. Retrieved from: http://www.westerncape.gov.za/other/2005/11/final_first_paper_cultural_industries_printing.pdf

Van Graan, M. (2014). African Creative Industries the Sleeping Giant. In: *African Business: African Creative Industries*. Retrieved from: http://www.racines.ma/sites/default/files/AB_CoverStoryCreativityAll0214.pdf

PEDAGOGY

Brea M. Heidelberg

TRANSITION COURSES IN THE ARTS MANAGEMENT CURRICULUM –
DEVELOPMENT OF A PROFESSIONAL DEVELOPMENT SERIES

PEDAGOGY

Abstract

The job market can be difficult to navigate as a recent graduate. While the global economy, and the United States economy in particular, is on the rebound the competition is stiff. Job seekers who complete an undergraduate degree spend a considerable amount of time and money building their skill sets and resumes. But are academic programs truly preparing students for a successful job search upon graduation? Are we equipping students with a strong foundation upon which they can build their careers?

Research suggests there is room for improvement. There is some concern that students lack the professional writing and technical skills required to successfully enter a competitive job market (Alssid, 2014). There is also concern about the growing disconnect between universities and employers (Rodgers, 2014; Zimmer, 2014) as well as the different perceptions of preparedness between students and employees (Grasgreen, 2013). This issue has been noted across universities, but especially in applied programs such as business, communications, and arts administration.

This article focuses on the development and management of a Professional Development Series - a set of three courses within an undergraduate arts management curriculum at a liberal arts institution in the United States.

Introduction

Arts administration as an academic discipline has long suffered negative perception from administrators in the field that question the rigor or even the point of academic programs designed to teach future arts administrators. In the past many have favoured long-term on the job training (DiMaggio, 1987). Although more recent research into the, perhaps changing, perception of arts administration programs among working arts administrators has not been conducted, past trends suggest that the same issue that impacts other professional programs also impacts arts administration. Core coursework in arts management programs address students' need for field-specific skill sets, but what about the skills required to become a valued member of an organization? Deal with the inevitable interpersonal issues that arise? Take ownership of their professional development?

Here I focus on the development and management of a **Professional Development Series** - a set of three courses within an undergraduate arts management curriculum at a liberal arts institution in the United States. The process of creating these courses combines consideration of curriculum design with developments in the labour market – particularly concern for job preparedness for undergraduate arts management students. This chapter explores areas where knowledge bases from cultural management and other fields converge, pulling some of the focus away from arts management specific skills in order to touch upon more universally acknowledged skills for engaging in the workforce.

Goals of the Professional Development Series

The transition from the classroom to the workplace workplace can be rife with issues. The Professional Development Series (PDS) was created in order to apply the concept of a transition course in a new setting – the undergraduate arts management curriculum. Other academic disciplines have set an example. Transition courses have been discussed primarily in the medical profession (Poncelet & O'Brien, 2008), where they were designed to ease the transition from the classroom to the working context for medical students. The most important aspect of a transition course is that it goes beyond an internship and incorporates aspects of socialization in addition to professionalization.

While each course in the series has its own objectives, as a unit the series is designed to ease the transition from the classroom to the workplace. The collective goal of these courses is to provide opportunities for students to develop hard skills and soft skills simultaneously, while diminishing the work expectation-reality gap (Barnett, 2012; Lent & Brown, 1996). These courses address the need for well trained graduates by focusing on the development of technical skills such as professional writing, production management, patron services, and practical aspects unique to the field of arts management. The aforementioned aspects are arguably part of most internship courses. The PDS is significant because it also empowers students to successfully navigate the workplace by fostering soft skills such as emotional intelligence and conflict resolution.

The overall goal of the PDS is to provide students with holistic preparation to enter the field. The methods of achieving that goal is to first focus on the individual student, then on how the student might engage and interact with the field in their immediate environment, and finally focuses on how the student understands their place within the broad field of arts administration as a discipline of inquiry and practice. Research shows that it is the match between an individual's characteristics and their work environment that leads to career success (Feldman, 2002; Greenhaus *et al.*, 2000). What follows is an exploration of each course within the series and the ways in which they attempt to achieve the aforementioned goal.

Practicum I

Arts Practicum I (hereafter referred to as '*Practicum I*') is the first course in the professional development series. Students typically enrol in this course during the fall or spring semester of their sophomore year. At this point in their academic career they have had, on average, two to five of the thirteen core courses in the arts management curriculum in addition to various courses to fulfil the university's general education requirements.

Practicum I includes both classroom and practical components. Students meet as a class one hour once a week and are required to work eighteen hours in the campus box office. The box office aspect of the course is managed in collaboration with the campus Box Office Manager. During the semester each student learns how to use Seat Advisor Box Office (SABO) Ticketing Software and gain experience with Front of House Management. Students meet these working requirements on evenings and weekends of their choosing, based on the show schedule for the theatre spaces on campus.

PEDAGOGY

PEDAGOGY

Students' personal awareness

Course topics in Practicum I focus on increasing students' personal awareness of their strengths and interests, both in general and as they pertain to the field of arts management. Given that most students will have limited experience in arts management/art entrepreneurship as well as limited exposure to arts management as an academic discipline, course topics and classroom assignments are designed to further acclimate students with the various subfields of arts management and entrepreneurship.

Despite declaring arts administration as their major and taking multiple courses within the core curriculum, many students are unaware of the various career paths available to them. There is some awareness of general job functions. For example, most students enter the course with a basic understanding of careers in marketing and fundraising. However, students are still largely unaware of the many roles arts management plays within non-profit arts organizations, for profit organizations, cultural institutions that may operate outside of the arts (e.g. zoos, aquariums, and historical museums), funding institutions, and various levels of government. Assignments in the course are designed to better acquaint students with other career options that may be a good fit for them. They also provide students with the skills to continue researching those options after the course ends. Career profiles and informational interviews are assigned so that students learn how to conduct these types of investigations.

Evaluation of Students' Work

Early in the semester professional writing topics such as cover letter writing and resume construction are discussed. This information is applied later in the course, as students apply for positions with arts organizations in anticipation of the requirements for the next course in the series, Practicum II – Service to the Field. The process of searching for positions is discussed in depth. Students learn how and where to search for internships including how to craft letters of inquiry. It is assumed that students will not master these skills the first time they are introduced. Instead, these skills are introduced in a way that allows for scaffolding in the next course.

There are two aspects of evaluation for Practicum I: evaluation of students' work in the classroom and evaluation of students' work in the box office. Classroom assignments are assessed based on the associated rubrics. Work in the box office is assessed based on an agreement made between students and the Box Office Manager. At the beginning of the semester students are required to sign a Box Office Code of Conduct. This document outlines all of the responsibilities for working in the box office including: dress code, how to interact with patrons, and expectations for shift starting and ending times. The elements of the code of conduct cover the practical aspects of working in the box office while also introducing students to the concept of being held accountable for the way they present themselves as professionals. Students are evaluated based on their ability to adhere to the code of conduct.

Practicum II

Practicum II – *Service to the Field* (hereafter referred to as '*Practicum II*') - is the second course in the professional development series. Students are encouraged to take this course directly after Practicum I, but it is not required. At this point in their academic career students are either second-semester sophomores or juniors. They have taken between five and seven of the thirteen core arts management courses (including Practicum I) and have likely finished met the university's general education requirements.

As with Practicum I, Practicum II has both classroom and practical components. Students meet as a class for one hour once a week and are required to complete a minimum of 47 working hours for a cultural institution/organisation – although many students work more hours over the course of the semester. Students are responsible for finding and securing their own positions using the skills they learned in Practicum I. However, if a student has difficulty finding a position the professor provides assistance. Each semester 80% of students enrolled in the course secure a position prior to the start of the semester. By the third week of the semester all students are placed with an organization.

Formalising Contacts

Students are required to fill out a pre-agreement form prior to starting their work with an organization. This form was designed to set clear expectations for both the student and the contact at the organization responsible for evaluating the student, hereafter referred to as *the site supervisor*. The form requires the student and their site supervisor to develop a position description and learning objectives, establish a schedule of working hours for the student. The form also explains the methods of evaluation, informing the site supervisor of their obligation to complete a midterm and final evaluation and letting students know about the expectations for record keeping and their final paper. The pre-agreement form was developed with consideration of best practices for internship management (Ciofalo, 1992). The pre-agreement operates alongside the course syllabus, which focuses on the learning objectives and evaluation methods for the classroom component of the course.

Course topics in Practicum II expand upon the information presented in Practicum I. While the focus in Practicum I was on the preferences and strengths of the student, the classroom component of Practicum II focuses on soft skills that will help students navigate the less technical aspects of working: organizational culture and behaviour.

This course starts by introducing students to different theories on management styles. Students will inevitably work with many different management styles throughout their career. In Practicum II we discuss how to identify different management styles, as well as the strengths and weaknesses of each. Most important for where they currently are in their careers, we discuss how their specific working preferences match up with various management styles. We also discuss what to do when their working style does not immediately mesh with their manager's management style. These conversations lead directly into discussions of how to deal with conflict. Various conflict resolution styles are introduced - students are tasked with identifying their own and identifying ways they can engage with the other styles.

Professional Writing Skills

The second half of the course is dedicated to building upon the professional writing skills introduced in Practicum I. Students further develop their abilities to search for and apply to an internship, learning how to best articulate their interest in a position

PEDAGOGY

and showcasing their growing resumes. One of the best aspects of this course is that students have two relevant working experiences on their resumes, prior to entering an increasingly competitive internship market.

Survey-based Evaluation Methods

Evaluation methods specific to the working component of the course are survey-based. These surveys, developed over the course of three semesters in collaboration with site supervisors, are a combination of Likert scale and open-ended questions. The survey is designed to solicit feedback about each student's progress on a combination of practical and soft skills. There is also space for site supervisors to discuss ways in which the student is a strong asset to the organization as well as areas where they can improve.

The midterm evaluation survey is completed by the student's site supervisor and submitted to the professor at the midpoint of the semester. After receiving the written evaluation the professor follows up with a meeting to obtain additional qualitative information regarding the student's work and professional progress. The information gathered from this process is shared with the student in a midterm meeting. The same process is conducted at the end of the semester. Course assignments are comprised of in-class activities and reflective writings.

The final paper asks students to discuss their working experience through the lens of the coursework they have taken to date, including the in-class discussions that have occurred throughout the semester. This paper also asks students to reflect upon whether or not they achieved their learning objectives and to consider the next steps in their professional development as they begin searching for an internship and planning for their first position post-graduation.

Internship

The Arts Management Internship (hereafter referred to as 'Internship') is the final requirement in the professional development series. Students are required to take six credits total and may meet this requirement by taking two separate three-credit internships in different semesters, or by taking on a full six-credit internship. When students enrol for internship credits they are juniors or seniors and have completed a significant portion of the arts management core curriculum.

There is no class component for Internship. Students meet individually with the professor throughout the semester. There are required meetings at the midpoint in the semester and during the last week of classes. Other meetings are coordinated as needed, depending on the needs of the student. Their main responsibility is to work for a cultural organization. Students are responsible for securing their own internships by utilizing the skills they learned in Practicum I and honed in Practicum II. The professor provides assistance to students throughout the application process by reviewing cover letters and resumes. Each semester 90% of students have arrangements made prior to the start of the semester. When a student struggles to find a position the professor provides additional assistance by reaching out to local organizations. All students are placed with an organization by week four of the semester. As in Practicum II students are required to complete a pre-agreement form.

PEDAGOGY

Final Paper and Portfolio

When this course was first developed, students were responsible for completing their working hours and submitting a final paper and portfolio at the end of their experience. This course takes the place of a senior capstone and so it was determined that more academic rigor was necessary. The course needed additional elements if students were to learn how to connect their work to the broader field of arts management and entrepreneurship. Incorporation of this goal began with more clearly articulated requirements for the final paper. The final paper shifted from being merely an accounting of events to a critically reflective assignment that requires students to actively integrate their classroom learning with their internship experience. Students are required to connect their personal experiences to larger trends within the field of arts management and must include at least seven scholarly sources into their final paper. To facilitate this kind of higher-order thinking smaller assignments were added to the course. These assignments are a series of reflective papers based on a reading list that is customized based on the students' internship. The writing assignments increase in difficulty throughout the course of the semester: students are first asked to summarize and reflect on one article and work their way up to discussing and reflecting on three different articles prior to beginning work on their final paper.

Evaluation methods for the working component of Internship mirror those of Practicum II. Site Supervisors complete midterm and final written evaluations that are accompanied by follow-up meetings where the professor gathers additional information. Students are made aware of the results of both evaluations in individual meetings with the professor. Use of the same evaluation tool for both Practicum II and Internship allows both the student and the professor to track the student's professional development in a manner that is easily understandable and translatable into actions items for improvement.

Impact

Each course addresses professional development concerns that match where students are in the core curriculum as well as their working experience. Practicum I introduces students to career options and helps them to begin matching their preferences and strengths to career plans and goals. Practicum II furthers those conversations by asking students to think about themselves within a larger organizational context. Finally, Internship helps to hone students' focus, requiring students to think in more complex ways about themselves and their connection to the field. While each course could stand alone, only having one course would prevent students from growing into their identity as future arts administrators. Callanan and Benzing (2004) found that internships alone are linked to finding employment upon graduation, but they are not linked to higher confidence levels with regard to workplace-personality fit. Information linking workplace-personality fit with higher levels of work performance (Tziner *et al.*, 2002) as well as less burnout (Meir *et al.*, 1995) indicate that the PDS is better equipped as a unit to prepare students for a successful career as an arts manager.

PEDAGOGY

The purpose of these courses is synthesis. These courses are designed to synthesize information students are learning in the classroom with practical working experiences. Students are encouraged to explore potential career paths in Practicum I, seek positions somewhere along that career path in Practicum II, and then determine if they'd like to stay on that path or explore a different one for their Internship.

As a result of these classes, students have lower-stakes opportunities to explore the field in ways they might not otherwise. This results in students who explore working as an arts administrator for various artistic disciplines, organizations of varying size, and work in two or more different capacities before graduation. This provides students with the necessary information to make informed decisions about their career goals upon graduation.

Conclusion

While transition courses are commonly used in medical and business curricula, this chapter demonstrates how this type of course can be applied to an undergraduate arts management context. Each course' objectives, structure, and evaluation methods were discussed to demonstrate how workplace preparedness goals are tied into each facet of the Professional Development Series. Next steps for the Professional Development Series are the development of an evaluation tool that will provide detailed information about the short- and long-term impact of the program on both students and area arts organizations. Now that the program has run for three years it is time to conduct a thorough investigation of the series and its various elements.

Although this particular case of transition courses focused on an undergraduate curriculum, there is evidence that transition courses would find success in a graduate curriculum as well. Graduate arts management programs should explore the possibility of adding one of these courses into their curriculum immediately prior to or in tandem with their internship requirements. Transition courses are designed to equip students with both the practical and soft skills necessary to be competitive on the job market upon graduation and should have a place somewhere in the curriculum of all practical disciplines, particularly a discipline as varied and nuanced as arts management.

References

Alssid, J. (February 27, 2014). *A New Gallup Survey Says Colleges and Employers Disagree About How Workforce-Ready Graduates Are – Whos Right?* Retrieved from: http://www.huffingtonpost.com/julian-l-alssid/a-new-gallup-survey-says-_b_4862669.html

Barnett, K. (2012). *Student Interns Socially Constructed Work Realities: Narrowing the Work Expectation-Reality Gap. Business Communication Quarterly,* 75(3), p. 271-290

Callanan, G., Benzing, C. (2004). Assessing the Role of Internships in the Career-Oriented Employment of Graduating College Students. In: *Education + Training,* 46(2) p. 82-98.

DiMaggio, P. (1987). *Managers of the Arts: Careers and Opinions of Senior Administrators of U.S. Art Museums, Symphony Orchestras, Resident Theaters, and Local Arts Agencies.* National Endowment for the Arts.

About the author

Dr Brea M. Heidelberg is an Assistant Professor & Internship Coordinator in the Arts Administration program at Rider University. Dr. Heidelberg serves as a board member of Artworks Trenton, on Americans for the Arts' Emerging Leaders Council, and on the board of the Association of Arts Administration Educators. She earned a PhD in Arts Administration, Education & Policy from The Ohio State University, where her research focused on arts

PEDAGOGY

*advocacy arguments and
policy entrepreneurship at
the federal level.
Her other research interests
include diversity in arts
organizations, evaluation,
human resources develop-
ment in non-profit arts
organizations, and
professionalization of
the field of arts management.*

—

brea.heidelberg@gmail.com

Grasgreen, A. (October 29, 2013). *Qualified in Their Own Minds*. Retrieved from: https://www.insidehighered.com/news/2013/10/29/more-data-show-students-unprepared-work-what-do-about-it

Lent, R., Brown, S. (1996). Social cognitive approach to career development: An overview. In: *The Career Development Quarterly*, 44(4), p. 310-321.

Poncelet, A., OBrien, B. (2008). Preparing Medical Students for Clerkships: A Descriptive Analysis for Transition Courses. In: *Academic Medicine*, 83(5), p. 444-451

Rodgers, K. (May 20, 2014). *Is College Adequately Preparing Students for the Workforce?* Retrieved from: http://www.foxbusiness.com/personal-finance/2014/05/20/is-college-adequately-preparing-students-for-workforce/

Zimmer, T. (August 6, 2014). *Are Recent Grads Prepared for the Workplace?* Retrieved from: http://www.forbes.com/sites/ccap/2014/08/06/are-recent-grads-prepared-for-the-workplace/

PEDAGOGY

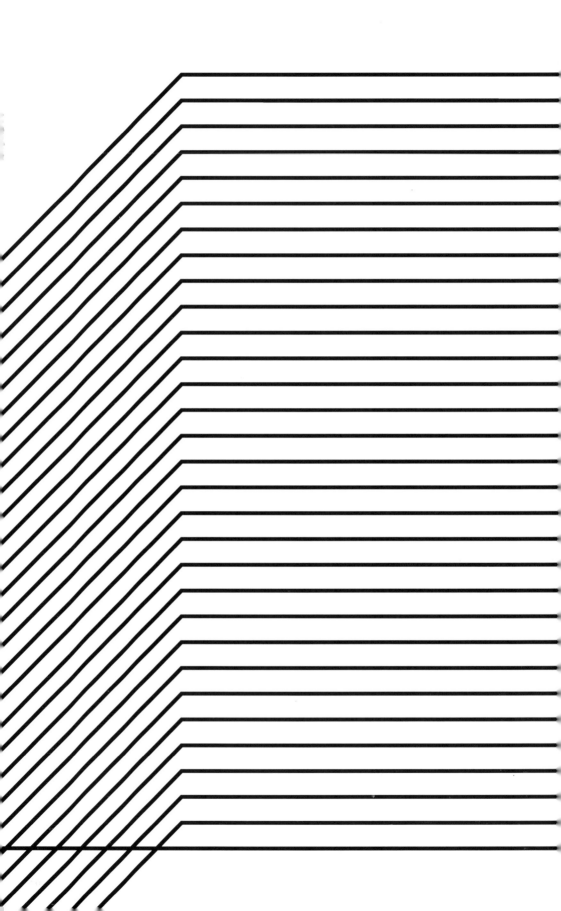

CASES

Ira Levine
Jeremy Shtern

CULTURAL AND CREATIVE ENTREPRENEURSHIP EDUCATION BY DESIGN A CASE STUDY OF THE DEVELOPMENT AND LAUNCH OF CANADA'S FIRST BA PROGRAM IN CREATIVE INDUSTRIES

Abstract

This article will discuss the curriculum design, theoretical roots and pedagogical approaches of the recently launched School of Creative Industries at Ryerson University in Toronto. Ryerson's mix of academic programs traverses the gamut of the Creative Industries. From publishing and digital journalism to TV production, fashion and interior design, dance and film, the University's diverse media, design and artistic units are represented in the BA in Creative Industries and contribute their courses and faculty expertise to the delivery of the Creative Industries curriculum. The School of Creative Industries utilizes these academic resources in combination with the course offerings provided by the Ted Rogers School of Management. Its founding represents an innovative curricular design that, unique among Canadian undergraduate programs, studies the creative disciplines from the perspective of enterprise development and entrepreneurship and blends artistic, media and communication, cultural and business studies to prepare students for employment opportunities in today's creative economy.

This chapter will present a reflexive case study that discusses the theory and methodology behind the intellectual and pedagogical structure of the Ryerson School of Creative Industries. Challenges, both theoretical and practical, implicated in the development of an innovative academic program that aims to provide students with a multi-disciplinary entrepreneurial education are discussed.

Introduction

In Fall 2013, The Faculty of Communication & Design at Ryerson University in Toronto, Canada, launched a new undergraduate program in Creative Industries. This interdisciplinary B.A. program is aimed at the creative, knowledge-based and service-oriented economy that is assuming an increasing proportion of contemporary economies in Canada and globally. In focusing on the Creative Industries, this new program views the cultural products and services that they create, produce and distribute as one of the key cornerstones of this economy. It recognizes that this industrial sector has grown increasingly complex, due primarily to the impact of information and communication technologies, and that the rapid changes it is experiencing requires new skills, new business models and new global perspectives.

Over the course of its first two admission cycles, the BA program in Creative Industries received more than 12 applicants per available space. The admission cut-offs are amongst the highest of any B.A. program in Canada and industry leaders have enthusiastically agreed to join its advisory board.

CASES

Background and Context

The increasing importance of the Creative Industries to national economies has been recognized across the developed and developing world for a number of years. A 2008 Report from the United Nations concluded the following:

> The Creative Industries are among the most dynamic emerging sectors in world trade. Over the period 2000-2005, trade in creative goods and services increased at an unprecedented average annual rate of 8.7 per cent. World exports of creative products were valued at $424.4 billion in 2005 as compared to $227.5 billion in 1996, according to preliminary UN figures (Santos Duisenberg, 2008). Creative services in particular enjoyed rapid growth –8.8 per cent annually between 1996 and 2005. This positive trend occurred in all regions and groups of countries and is expected to continue into the next decade
>
> (Santos Duisenberg, 2008, p. 5)

Originating in the United Kingdom and Australia in the latter 1990s, the term 'Creative Industries' refers to a distinctive group of creative fields pertaining to media, design, entertainment and the visual and performing arts (Flew 2012). While these fields have long been recognized for their cultural value and their role in enhancing social cohesion and quality of life, they are with increasing frequency being appreciated as an important engine of economic prosperity and urban renewal as well.

The city of Toronto plays a central role in this sector, the growing scope of the Creative Industries within Canada and their steadily expanding share of the country's GDP. Based on data provided by Statistics Canada, the Conference Board of Canada has estimated that the output of this sector totalled $46 billion in 2007, or 3.8% of GDP, and that its full economic impact – including its effect on other economic sectors – was approximately $84 billion or 7.4% of GDP. In 2007 these industries contributed more than 1 million jobs to the Canadian economy (Conference Board of Canada, 2008, p. 1). Within the Greater Toronto Area (GTA), more than 130,000 workers are employed in over 9,500 enterprises in this sector and, through 2007, creative occupations grew at a rate more than double that of the labour force as a whole (Creative Capital Gains, An Action Plan for Toronto, May 2011, p. 5) and faster than financial services, the medical and biotechnology industries and the food and beverage industry (Vindorai, 2010).

Within this industrial sector the growth of global markets and the increasing trends toward collaborative and cross-sector creative work are amongst the factors driving a new educational approach to creative disciplines, one in which financial and operational aspects on the one hand and creative processes on the other are studied simultaneously and viewed as a synergistic and inseparable combination. The societal importance of such educational programming is corroborated by recent research, for example the report prepared by the Conference Board of Canada (2008b).

CASES

Goals and Curriculum of the BA Program

The goals and curriculum of the B.A. program in Creative Industries are designed to address key long-term trends impacting the Creative Industries. A number of government and university-based studies have identified challenges that Canadian creative enterprises, both commercial and non-profit, are at present ill equipped to meet. These include the constant introduction of ever-newer digital and mobile technologies and web-based applications that can radically alter marketing, and distribution and consumption patterns and thus transform (if not undermine) the business models upon which these enterprises are based. As well, technological change has generated new complexities around intellectual property and copyright that threaten traditional revenue streams and pose a significant challenge to government policy, legislation and regulation. The internet and other communication technologies have greatly expanded the marketplace for media and cultural products while increasing competition within Canada. In order to prosper in this context and to remain competitive in a global marketplace, Canadian enterprises will increasingly require employees with a working knowledge of international marketing, free trade agreements, import/export regulations and copyright issues.

The creative workforce, employed predominantly in small-scale enterprises, is progressively more in need of legal and governmental expertise if it is to navigate successfully through an increasingly complex and interconnected environment. Canadian content requirements, status of the artist legislation, regulatory mechanisms, cross-border reciprocal agreements, and apprenticeship and training programs are just a few of the factors creating a demand for well-informed cultural and media managers, who can exploit their understanding of governmental structures and processes and the legal environment to advocate effectively for their organizations and take advantage of the opportunities afforded by subsidy programs, tax incentives, and other government initiatives.

Unless these trends are addressed through a reconceived and modernized skill-set such as envisioned in the proposed program, they will exacerbate chronic deficiencies that have handicapped creative enterprises for years. These include well-documented weaknesses in business communication, human resource systems, strategic planning, entrepreneurship and fiscal management.

In a letter endorsing the societal need of the Creative Industries B.A. program Diane Davy, Executive Director of Cultural Careers Council Ontario, describes the current situation in the sector:

Again and again, we hear that, to prosper and grow in a rapidly changing global marketplace, the cultural sector, including the cultural industries, needs a workforce that has stronger business and technical skills. New entrants to the sector need to understand both traditional and evolving business models and to understand the myriad processes that contribute value to a creative product including production, marketing, distribution, financial management, government policy, copyright, etc.

Innovative pedagogy; unlearning embedded assumptions

Hence, post-secondary education programs explicitly have to be focused on the Creative Industries in Canada, in particular in Toronto. Yet, putting that process in motion required a certain degree of both innovative pedagogy as well as the unlearning of some pretty powerfully embedded assumptions about how university programs relevant to this area operate. Typically higher education programs that aim to study and/or feed these industries are distinguished by the polarization between '*suits*' and '*creatives*'; between creative practitioners and those who manage and commercialize the creative process. Business students are taught in one faculty, typically with little focus on the unique professional contexts associated with managing creativity and the would-be-creators or creative professionals are taught separately in professional, humanities or fine arts programs, often with little to no business training.

This approach is fundamentally at odds with what we know from a variety of academic literatures concerned with the contemporary nature of work in arts and cultural industries problematize this pedagogical approach in at least three significant respects.

In the first place, we are aware that most of the enterprises in this sector tend to be small-scale,[1] though the distribution companies (e.g. film companies, broadcasters, cable operators, retailers, global multimedia firms) associated with them may be very large. Many rely on customer perception as a basis of economic value; for such enterprises, copyright is fundamental to their business models, and the right to use their product is often of greater value than the product itself. Businesses in this sector tend to operate with a very high degree of risk and unpredictability. They have distinctive patterns of work and organization, and display a very strong sensitivity to public regulatory, revenue and cultural policies. In other words, analysis suggests that in order to succeed in the contemporary creative economy, most artists must develop and make use of a whole series of entrepreneurial, regulatory, branding and management skills.

Suits and Creatives

On the flip side, literature on managing creativity as well as various ethnographic studies of sites of professional production (c.f. Deuze 2011) underline the value to executives charged with managing creativity of being able to deploy what Collins and Evans (2007) would describe as the '*interactional expertise*' of creativity; a basic, familiarity with not only the knowledge and skills required of the creative talent, but an understanding of the world view, jargon and discourse of their community of practice.[2]

In other words, literature on how work gets done in the Creative Industries are increasingly clear: the distinction between '*suits*' and '*creatives*' does not hold up anymore, if it ever did. In order for organizations to succeed in the knowledge economy, creatives must posses and make use of business skills, and mind-sets and suits have to get their hands dirty, make an effort to understand creative people, communicate effectively with them and be treated credibly within the subcultures of artistic and creative practice. Furthermore, various studies point out the extent to which the defining features of work in the creative economy are precarity and self-directed portfolio careers (c.f. Campbell 2013). It no longer make sense to educate '*suits*' and '*creatives*' in separate silos, doing so creates skill deficits that will lead many graduates to struggle to be competitive and successful in the creative economy.

CASES

---

[1] *Creative enterprises typically range from micro-businesses (privately owned and operated with under 10 employees) to SMBs (small businesses with under 50 employees or medium-sized businesses with under 250 employees)*

[2] *This Collins and Evans (2002; 2007) distinguish from the higher order form of expertise: 'contributory expertise' the capacity to contribute to the work of the community of practice.*

Program Approach

The foundational goals of the Ryerson School of Creative Industries include: contributing to bridging this divide through an academic program that provides opportunities for studies in these creative fields; delivering courses in creativity theory and the management of creativity; incorporating core and elective business and entrepreneurship courses and; providing a curriculum through which students are able to learn how these industries function as creative enterprises and acquire the requisite skills and knowledge to obtain employment in this expanding economic sector.

The program attracts students seeking careers in diverse aspects of the Creative Industries. Some of our students have experience working as talent in the Creative Industries who already recognize that they need more education and training in order to manage their careers effectively and eventually take on leadership roles. Others are young people who know they want to make a career doing something creative, but are not yet ready to commit to making a deep dive into training for one specific field (as would be required, for example of a theatre school student). Generally, these are students who wish to cultivate a broad understanding of possible career paths and who want to acquire a solid foundation of communication and business concepts and practices applicable to creative production. Our hope is that they will study to become leaders who, as they gain experience in the creative economy, will have the capacity to transform creative ideas into commercial products and services.

The BA in Creative Industries program consists of a 42 course curriculum. Core competencies are viewed to be oral and written communication; collaboration and cross-functional teamwork; Information Communication Technology (ICT) literacy; critical thinking and research design and methodology. All students undertake studies in the following core knowledge areas: communication and digital media; innovation and entrepreneurship specific to the Creative Industries; intellectual property and copyright law; creativity theory and business. Optional courses focus on governance (media regulation, cultural policy, tax incentives and subsidies, etc.), emerging technologies, advertising and public relations, gaming and other applicable subjects.

1st Semester:	CRI 100 PLX 111	Creative Industries Overview Imagining the Creative City
2nd Semester:	CRI 200 CMN 210	IP Issues in the Digital Age Text, Image & Sound
3rd Semester:	CRI 300	Digital Design Studio
4th Semester:	CRI 400	Entrepreneurship in Creative Industries
5th Semester:	CMN 323	Introduction to Professional Practice
6th Semester:	CRI 600	The Creative Process
7th Semester:	CRI 700 CRI 710	Human Resources Management in Creative Industries Creative Industries Research Methodologies
8th Semester:	CRI 800 CRI 810	Managing Creative Enterprises and Capstone Project Studies in Creative Collaboration

Figure 1 Required Core Courses in the BA in Creative Industries

The BA in Creative Industries program is industry-based rather than focused on a specific discipline or professional field. This distinctive feature invites and necessitates an interdisciplinary approach that is facilitated by the modular structure of the program. For the purposes of the program, a module is defined as a sequence of six courses consisting of varying combinations of required and elective courses in a discrete subject area. There are, as of press in 2015, fourteen modules to choose from (Figure 2).

School of Fashion	The Fashion Industry: Markets, Aesthetics & Creativity
School of Professional Communication	Communication Studies
School of Image Arts	The Art & Business of Film Visual Culture Curatorial Practices
School of Journalism	The Business and Practice of News
School of Graphic Communications Management	Concept to Reality: Publishing and Printing
RTA School of Media	The Music Industry Storytelling in Media Media Business
Theatre School	Acting/Dance Studies
Theatre School and Department of English	Performance Studies
School of Interior Design	Interior Design: Human scale for Creative Thinkers

Figure 2 Partner Schools and Available Creative Industry Modules

CASES

Students each select any two modules to complete as part of their BA in Creative Industries. These modules are taught by faculty and instructors in the various professional schools of Ryerson's Faculty of Communication and Design, as well as departments in Ryerson's Faculty of Arts. Each of these are professional schools that rank amongst the best university programs feeding their respective professional domains in Canada.

Implementing this approach requires an innovative approach to service teaching and partnerships across campus. Creative Industries students will normally undertake 65% to 74% of their coursework (27 to 31 courses) outside their home program, and anywhere from 31% (13 courses) to 55% (23 courses) outside their home Faculty.

By design, Creative Industry students take these module classes alongside students enrolled in the programs offered by the professional programs.

The intention of these modules is to give Creative Industries students enough exposure to the basic, foundational knowledge of these disciplines as well as the cultures, jargon and worldview of their communities of practice. To go back to the Collins and Evans distinction between 'contributory' and 'interactional' expertise mentioned earlier, the pedagogy of these modules is that one does not necessarily need to be able to design a dress, for example, to be an effective public relations manager at a fashion label. But one's ability to function in that role would surely be enhanced by having had enough exposure to and experience with designers to be able to talk to them, work alongside them and be treated as somebody who can credibly claim to understand their role and perspective.

Within the multi-disciplinary approach of the program, the students' choice of two modules is augmented by an additional series of six business courses that are taught by Ryerson's Ted Rogers School of Management (Figure 3).

REQUIRED COURSES (4):

BSM100:	The New Business: From Idea to Reality
BSM200:	The Growing Business: Breaking Even
FIN 305:	Financial Management
BSM600:	The Mature Business: Market Dominance or Failure (capstone)

ELECTIVES COURSES (2):

GMS410:	Management in the Large Corporation
ENT500:	New Venture Start Up
ENT505:	Small-business Management
GMS455:	Project Planning and Delivery
ITM350:	Online Business
MKT310:	Marketing Plans
ENT520:	New Venture Creation
GMS520:	Fundamentals of International Business

Figure 3 Business Course Progression in the BA in Creative Industries

This business education, as well as a work placement that all students must complete for credit during their third year in the program, is intended to contribute to bridging the management and entrepreneurial training gap that is seen as a holding back many Creative Industry careers. This innovative program design has been implement in the interest of students achieving the following learning objectives by their completion of the four-year B.A. in Creative Industries:

1. Contribute productively to the operation of Canadian Creative Industries by applying a synthesized knowledge of the economic, legal, political, and technological environments in which they function together with an understanding of how these enterprises communicate and how they are managed.
2. Demonstrate an entrepreneurial capacity to engage in independent learning and to transform creative ideas into commercial products and services through the application of business and management concepts and practices applicable to media and cultural production.
3. Facilitate the work of artists, writers, designers and media makers by applying an integrated knowledge of creative and production processes (both individual and system-based) and of funding and investment structures, and by recognizing and responding to future challenges and opportunities in their sector.
4. Communicate effectively in oral and written formats, using a range of media that are widely used in creative enterprises.
5. Conduct research relevant to cultural and industry issues, formulating appropriate research questions and conceptual frameworks; employing data collection techniques and appropriate quantitative and qualitative tools and methodologies
6. Implement and manage projects requiring problem solving, team building, negotiating and collaborative work practices.

7. Put to use a range of ICT skills and an understanding of the ways in which emerging technologies and applications are reshaping creative and business processes so as to assist creative enterprises with recognizing and responding to technological change.
8. Integrate aesthetic sensibility with business acumen by applying a critical knowledge of the aesthetic, theoretical and historical development of one or more creative subsectors to practical realities of production, promotion, distribution and consumption.

Reflections on the Implementation of the Program

As of publishing (spring 2015), the School of Creative Industries has admitted two cohorts and is in the process of doing admissions for its third class. Demand for the program was greater than anyone had imaged. With very little brand recognition, outreach or publicity, the School of Creative Industries received almost 16 applications for every one of its planned 100 places during its first admission cycle in 2013. Even after dramatically increasing the size of the first ever cohort, the admission cut off average was still very high. The number of applicants have held relatively steady over the initial three admission cycles. We have had considerable interest not just from students applying out of secondary school systems, but also from students seeking to transfer into our program from other programs and institutions. This in spite of the fact that in most cases, making that move requires four additional complete years of undergraduate education, despite whatever transfer credits can be granted. Overall, cut off averages for admission are high and have only increased with each successive admission cycle.

We continue to roll out and evaluate the program. Yet, with only two cohorts admitted and none graduated, we are conscious of the need to view a larger sample size before judging the program's ultimate impact and delivery. Thus, even in our minds, though the early returns are largely positive, the jury is still very much out on the significance of our efforts at innovative pedagogy for the creative economy.

Reflections

We would however offer a couple of reflections on some elements of program design that have already presented themselves to us as requiring further research and consideration.

In the first place, it has become clear that many students- even the high achieving, highly motivated students such as the ones we are attracting- struggle to conceive of the soft skills that are associated with developing talent for the creative economy (entrepreneurial thinking, innovation, strategic management of portfolio careers, etc.) as 'hands on' skills. We have learned from experience that education for the creative economy needs to not only address these new competencies, but provide a form of pedagogical scaffolding that reinforces not only their value, but their very status as portable, in demand talents. We need to not only teach the creative economy, we need to teach learning in the creative economy in parallel.

Secondly, we continue to reflect on the question of how to set the admission requirements for our BA in Creative Industries. At present we only consider marks. Yet, we regularly hear from and meet exceptional young people who have performing or design careers, or who have been involved in start-up Creative Industry ventures, who clearly have a great deal to contribute to our program and potential to assume leadership of the Creative Industries in Toronto and beyond, but who don't meet our ratified marks cut off levels.

At the same time, we also recognize that the marks only criteria lets in other students who, in spite of their high marks, might not—for various reasons- be candidates to succeed long term in the highly competitive, emotionally taxing and entirely self-driven careers that define working in many Creative Industries. As we have discussed, we try to effectively straddle the lines between the creative side of our professional program partners and the critical thinking, communication and analytical skills developed in more traditionally academic B.A. programs in every respect.

Where admissions are concerned, we have thus far come down squarely on the side of the practice of traditional academic programs that look only at marks, consciously avoiding the portfolio evaluation that many professional schools in Creative Industries subjects undertake as part of their admissions. This preference is born in part of convenience, of course. With only a skeleton faculty contingent to work with during our start-up phase, 'marks only' represents a path of least resistance. But 'marks only' also represents an epistemological stance at the base of our pedagogical approach, one that suggests that post-secondary education for the creative economy requires thinkers as well as creators. Admission to this program has, as a result, asked for marks to stand in as (an admittedly limited metric for) evidence of thinking at the expense of evidence of creating.

As our program roles out, we are pushing these and other questions about best practice for post-secondary education for the creative economy as suggestions for further research and discussion, in part to reflect further on our own experiences, but also in the hope of contributing to the development of a global network of institutions and instructors committed to the on going innovation of post-secondary education for the creative economy. The aim of this chapter has been to offer a reflexive account of the design and roll out of Ryerson's School of Creative Industries. We hope that its publication diminishes, even slightly, the extent to which other institutions considering planning new academic programs or revising existing programs feel as though they must invent the effort from scratch. After all, as we preach, so should we practice: innovation is an iterative process that is best incubated within a network or community and creativity works best as a collaborative process.

CASES

- The authors wish to thank Ariella Klein for her research and editing assistance

References

Bilton, Chris (2007). *Management and Creativity: From Creative Industries to Creative Management.* Malden: Blackwell Publishing Ltd.

Campbell, Miranda. (2013). *Out of the Basement: Youth Cultural Production in Practice and Policy.* Montréal: McGill-Queen's University Press.

City of Toronto; Economic Development Committee and Toronto City Council (2011). *Creative Capital Gains, An Action Plan for Toronto.* http://www.live-withculture.ca/wp-content/uploads/2011/05/CCI-Final.pdf

About the authors

Prof Dr Ira Levine has been a professor and academic administrator at Ryerson for the past 27 years, during which he has developed numerous undergraduate and graduate programs for the University. While continuing to teach performance history for the Theatre School, he is currently seconded as Chair of the School of Creative Industries. Dr. Levine came to Ryerson with a background in theatre directing and arts administration that encompassed the management of both theatre and dance companies. He has served on the boards of the Toronto Arts Council, the Desrosiers Dance Theatre and the Ontario Cultural Sector Human Resources Council. Dr. Levine has a B.A. Magna Cum Laude in European Intellectual History from the University of Rochester and received his M.A. and Ph.D. in Dramatic Theory and Criticism from the University of Toronto. His publications include Left-Wing Dramatic Theory in the American Theatre.

---

ilevine@ryerson.ca

Dr Jeremy Shtern is assistant professor and a founding faculty member of the School of Creative Industries at Ryerson University in Toronto. He received his PhD at the Université de Montréal and a MSc at the London School of Economics and Political Science. Jeremy Shtern's research focuses on transformations in the structure and governance of communication industries and creative work as they reorganize around globalization and digital technologies. He is co-author of two books: Media Divides: Communication Rights and the Right to Communicate in Canada (UBC Press, 2010, with Marc Raboy) and Digital Solidarities: Communication Policy and Multi-stakeholder Global Governance The Legacy of the World Summit on the Information Society (Peter Lang, 2010, with Marc Raboy and Normand Landry).

---

jshtern@ryerson.ca

Collins, H. M. and Richard Evans (2007). *Rethinking expertise.* Chicago: The University of Chicago Press.

Conference Board of Canada. (2008a). *The International Forum on the Creative Economy.* Retrieved from http://www.conferenceboard.ca/topics/education/symposia/creative_economy.aspx.

Conference Board of Canada (2008b). *Valuing Culture: Measuring and Understanding Canada's Creative Economy.* Retrieved from http://www.conferenceboard.ca/e-library/abstract.aspx?did=2671.

Deuze, Mark ed. (2011). *Managing Media Work.* London: Sage.

Flew, Terry (2012). *The Creative Industries: Culture and Policy.* London: Sage.

Gertler, Meric et al (2006). *Imagine a Toronto ...Strategies for a Creative City.* Creative Cities Leadership Team. Retrieved from http://web.net/~imagineatoronto/fullReport.pdf

Ryerson University (2008). *Shaping Our Future: Academic Plan for 2008-2013.* Retrieved from http://www.ryerson.ca/senate/academicplan.pdf

Santos Duisenberg, E. dos. (2008). *Creative Economy Report 2008.* Geneva: UNCTAD.

Vindorai, T (2010). *Update to Imagine a Toronto: Strategies for a Creative City (2006), based on data from Statistics Canada, Labour Force Survey.* Retrieved from: http://www23.statcan.gc.ca/imdb/pIX.pl?Function=getThemeSub&PItem_Id=97413&PCE_Id=355&PCE_Start=01010001&cc=1

CASES

Paola Dubini

TEACHING AND LEARNING CULTURAL ENTREPRENEURSHIP
HUMANITIES IN BUSINESS

Abstract

This chapter describes how cultural entrepreneurship is taught at Bocconi University, as the result of the development of educational and research activities in the field of arts management and cultural policy. In the following paragraphs, the evolution of the school positioning in these domains is first described, by highlighting the history, philosophy and unique characteristics of the first program launched, CLEACC and the process of legitimization of the leading business school in Italy among practitioners in the arts. We will treat two principles; Liberal Arts for managers (a), and the creation of Managers for the arts (b) . The issue of how to teach and learn cultural entrepreneurship is then addressed, by discussing the parallel evolution of the term amongst practitioners.

Teaching and Researching Arts Management

Università Bocconi launched a four year degree in Management for the Arts, Culture and Communication (CLEACC) in 1999. The school, founded in 1902, is a leading university in Italy in management and economic studies. Within the Italian landscape, Università Bocconi is characterised by an international vocation and a strong link with practitioners; the school started offering career and placement services to its students and developed a series of programs with companies well before the other universities in Italy, and many students choose to attend Bocconi for its placement prospects. According to university statistics, around 95% of graduates are employed six months after graduation. Internally, program directors are measured on the performances of their students, on their evaluation of the quality of teaching and on students' employability.

The decision to offer a degree in arts management came after a long internal debate. At that time, cultural institutions were mostly financed exclusively with public funds and managed by the Government; in 1992 the first law was approved allowing the Ministry of culture to outsource to private enterprises the management of the so called '*ancillary services*' (bookshops, cafeterias, audio guides and so on). In 1999, the 14 opera houses, which were part of the State administration, were transformed into foundations. No museum or theatre director in Italy had an economic background at the time and often even people in administrative positions did not hold a degree in management. The overall perception among practitioners in cultural organisations was that art is a sort of '*zona franca*' in which market logic does not apply; the community of art scholars and practitioners resisted to the presence of managers in the arts and in cultural institutions.

Part of the faculty acknowledged that a need existed for graduates in arts management, but feared the very limited size of the job market. The job market in cultural institutions is very peculiar, particularly in Italy: entry is limited, stability of employment is

CASES

hard to reach, and a graduate in business administration is typically not a choice in job postings of theatres or museums. The salary is low, compared with consulting or investment banking.

Profession and Vocation

Part of the faculty felt that Bocconi, as a leading university specialised in economics and management should contribute to the managerialisation of cultural institutions in Italy, by adapting tools and theories developed for manufacturing and service firms to cultural settings. The curriculum should focus on management and economics and courses should involve testimonials and discuss cases from cultural industries and institutions; in order to overcome the limited size of job market, different industries should be taken into consideration, from visual arts, to performing arts, media, tourism, fashion and design. Thus the appropriate name would be management of the arts, culture and communication.

Another part of the faculty considered arts as a form of knowledge and looked for a program addressing contemporary economic and cultural challenges to '*restore the cultural dimension of societies that are too often represented simply as economies and to restore the calculative dimension to societies that are too often simply portrayed as solidarities*' (Appadurai 1986: 12). A program in management and economics for the arts should thus take arts as a reference to build an economy supportive to arts, instead of transforming arts into products or services and artists into brands. The program should include liberal arts into the curriculum and explicitly address the often problematic relationship between markets and society. Although the curriculum would be particularly suitable for managers willing to work in specific industries and business contexts, the program should not be designed as a vocational course. The experience of art should give a possibility to modify our view on the economy and to open up opportunities for research, innovation, and experimentation.

Eventually, CLEACC was launched in the academic year of 1999 -2000: its name was management and economics FOR the arts, culture and communication. Although the name of the program stated the decision of a more challenging positioning for Bocconi, the tension between these two views has not been fully resolved, has been made explicit and is a constant element of discussion within the faculty, between faculty and students and among students. It is precisely this not fully resolved tension that makes the program highly innovative and unique.

Since its start up, the curriculum has been designed around the two following and complementary principles:

- **Liberal arts and humanities or managers.** Any manager should have liberal arts as part of her curriculum in management, no matter which professional choice she will undertake in the future. Notwithstanding the generic assumption that a varied background is important in any profession, humanities are a fundamental component of a managerial education, as it is accounting, statistics, marketing or law. Managers are no longer asked to be just technocrats, and the capability to play the multiple tasks theorized by Mintzberg (1973) seems inadequate to face the increased diversity and instability of the environment in which managers and enterprises operate. Ability to discern, to assume different perspectives, to critically reconcile often conflicting points of view are crucial competences that require ability to listen, to master different scientific languages and methods. Liberal arts and humanities in a management curriculum remind us that enterprises, public organizations, not-for-profit companies are run by people and offer product and services targeted to satisfy people's needs. Humanities complement a traditional curriculum in management by pushing critical thinking; liberal arts open up to different theories and research methods to prepare managers able to accept ambiguities and complexities intrinsic to the current social cultural and economic world, while at the same time technically well prepared from a quantitative standpoint and able to master the *'typical toolbox'* of business schools graduates.

- **Managers for the arts.** Students interested in the arts and in cultural organisations as a potential career opportunity as managers or entrepreneurs should be aware of the specificities of these domains , so as to get ready early on to develop necessary and complementary skills. Unlike disciplines like medicine, hard sciences or some vocational topics, management and economics are typically not a degree students and their families choose as they have a specific intellectual curiosity or passion. Cultural institutions, not for profit organizations and the so called *'CREATIVE INDUSTRIES'* (which are often put in the same category as cultural organizations in spite of significant differences) seem to be an exception, for their glamorous aura and because arts are often part of interests, hobbies or passions at a young age. This is particularly true in countries – like Italy – where arts and heritage are often mentioned as a distinctive feature of the economy and their institutions are surrounded by a Bourdieu-like aura of charm and elitism (Bourdieu, 1984). In fact, they are complex organizations whose sustainability requires solid management skills, as the *'degrees of freedom'* for managerial action are limited; as an undergraduate degree in management, CLEACC should be instrumental to self-select students for graduate studies in arts management and encourage those interested in investing in the field.

A number of implications follow from this positioning. First of all, CLEACC is in its structure an undergraduate program in management, compliant with the Italian legislation for a curriculum in management studies at undergraduate level, with limited differences in the traditional curriculum. Secondly, liberal arts are given equal role to economics, management, law and quantitative methods in characterizing the program. The true difference in the curriculum from a typical management program at the undergraduate level consists of five courses, three of which are compulsory: aesthetics, theories and methods in artistic research, and cultural anthropology. The remaining two are chosen by the students among ten options ranging from Italian renaissance art, to theatre, to design, to public opinion formation, so as to accommodate a wide variety of interests. Limited size of classes allows for very interactive sections.

Over the years, the program has changed, as a consequence of both the reform of the Italian academia and to accommodate the evolving needs of the job market. The program currently consists of two classes at the undergraduate level (CLEACC – a 3 year program), each of approximately 120 students, in Italian, and one class of a MSc in Management and Economics in Arts, Culture, Media and Entertainment (ACME) in English, attended by nearly 90 students per year. Of particular interest is the modification of the program to take into consideration the emerging issue of *cultural entrepreneurship*. A research centre, ASK (Arts, Science, Knowledge) has been launched in 2004 Projects address the transformation of cultural industries and the relationship between social technological and market pressures on the sustainability of cultural institutions, the interplay between emerging business models and intellectual property regimes. The centre is also in charge of developing new materials to be used in class and new forms of reporting research exploring multimedia narratives.

CLEACC Students and Graduates

The launch of CLEACC was a tremendous success; students and their families fully appreciated the innovative approach of the program. Compared with other Bocconi students, students that chose humanities as a mayor in high school were overrepresented, as those playing an instrument or dancing at professional level and those who are consumers of cultural goods (visit exhibitions, read, assist to performances go to the movie…). Even today, typically students attending CLEACC would not have chosen Economics as a degree if it wasn't for CLEACC and their participation to campus and community life is very strong. We owe to CLEACC students the setup of the university radio and students web TV.

The broad scope of CLEACC is mirrored in the choices after graduation. Every year the program graduates approximately 240 students. As of today there are almost 3.300 graduates. 25% of graduates choose arts management for their graduate studies, 18% management, 18% marketing, 14% international management. 5% stops studying and gets a job, 15% splits between master courses in content production, tourism, service or fashion management and communication studies. 5% chooses arts; among CLEACC graduate there are professional music and jazz players, a composer, several art scholars at PhD level. 25% of graduates work abroad. Graduates work in all types of cultural and art institutions, private and not for profit entities, big enterprises, financial institutions and so. Not surprisingly, while a CLEACC graduate would be considered as a Bocconi graduate by any employer in the business community, it would be difficult to be hired in a cultural institution with a degree in management and economics other than ACME/CLEACC.

An important aspect of the students' education, often underestimated by the students before they come to Bocconi, is the building of a strong peer-community, which is particularly relevant for students pursuing an entrepreneurial career in the arts, in arts management, in the media or other CLEACC related industries. As a matter of fact, although the majority of students is employed in corporations and enterprises, nearly 15 % are either self-employed or work in corporations in entrepreneurial contexts. We feel that this is a quite remarkable percentage, given the young age of the program and its graduates.

CLEACC Legitimization Process

The world of scholars and practitioners in the arts and within cultural organizations is culturally and ideologically very far from a business school; the accreditation of the school and of CLEACC among the professional communities in the arts has been a long process. In the business and academic communities in Europe and increasingly worldwide, Bocconi has a solid reputation as a research university in which quantitative methods are often preferred to ethnographies or case studies. On the contrary,

CASES

artistic and cultural organizations were unaware of Bocconi and, generally speaking, quite suspicious. A series of research projects on the transformation of content industries, on heritage and identity, on cultural policies were started, which eventually led to the formation of the research centre. Each project involved very prestigious scholars from academic institutions specialized in the arts and led to intense and at times confrontational conversations. The guiding principle was *'to put art and the artistic processes at the centre'*. Particular attention was put in choosing the appropriate faculty for the liberal arts classes; whenever possible top scholars in their discipline were chosen, eager at the same time to develop an ad hoc pedagogical approach. It has been a long process of mutual listening and progressive inclusion via joint multidisciplinary research and teaching projects. Out of the ten faculty members in the liberal arts faculty, only two are permanent Bocconi faculty; three out of ten are ex CLEACC students who are respectively a byzantine art historian, a TV author and a jazz musician.

As in any start-up, the legitimization process was crucial for the sustainability of the program (Zimmermann Zelt 2002), and it bounced between the need to conform to the expectations of the university on the one hand and to create a common language and a mutual level of trust with the community of practitioners and academics in the arts.

Of particular difficulty was the breadth of the industries and the variety of related policies included in the program. Building an adequate understanding of how organization works and who are the key-players in a variety of industries in a limited time was and is a big challenge. The world of cultural and artistic institutions consists of very different industries: museums and opera houses are worlds apart and contemporary art museums face different challenges from the big institutions hosting collections from the past. Even in the world of cultural industries, schoolbooks are a different business than children books, and the two segments have different heroes, players, issues. The choice to address several industries was dictated by the need to keep adequate opportunities for placement and long term sustainability to the program.

The faculty started from heritage management and their related policies, and from a selected number of content industries and gradually developed relations and understanding in different domains, in order to strengthen the quality of the program and to broaden placement options for our students. The discipline imposed by the placement requirements and the objectively limited absorption capacity by each industry have driven a constant attention to the job market dynamics.

From Arts Management to Cultural Entrepreneurship

As a degree in management and economics, the program started with a focus on management and policy making. In recent years, though, the need to expose students to the challenges and opportunities of entrepreneurial activities and to increase the international scope of the program has become apparent. The term *'cultural entrepreneurship'*, suddenly so popular in public debates after a rather long but limited incubation in scholarly works, started circulating among faculty and has been encompassed in the last revision of the program, that started with the academic year 2013-14.

The first scholar to explicitly use the term has been di Maggio (1982), to describe the interplay between artistic production and financing of the music scene in Boston in 1800. The focus in this definition is the pioneering, the entrepreneurial spirit associated with artistic practices, and the need to develop an ecosystem around it, in which production, distribution and financial industries converge in sustaining the creation and visibility of cultural and artistic outcomes. In the following years, the term has been used by scholars of cultural studies and sociologists, as a wide encompassing concept, quite ambiguous in its definition (Hirsch & Levin, 1999), at the intersection between social, political, artistic and economic spheres. As the term has become popular, it has been utilised in a variety of settings, ranging from the utilisation of digital technologies to develop start-ups and corporate venturing programs in content industries, events management, artistic productions, tourism, to projects targeted to *'urban cool'* audiences, to the development of markets around heritage valorisation. The term is also used to describe the transformative capacity of territories and communities by cultural and social organizations starting from the valorisation of local identities and unique resources.

The term therefore encompasses initiatives and projects with very diverse governance structures and juridical forms: start-ups, not for profit organisations, associations, committees, consortia, cultural institutions, B corporations, cooperatives, public private partnerships.

In line with its identity CLEACC addresses this field with the ambitious goal to educate students *'for'* entrepreneurship rather than *'about'* entrepreneurship. As Kirby (2005) suggests, entrepreneurship programmes in universities can be categorized as follows:

- Entrepreneurship orientation and awareness programmes which focus on general information about entrepreneurship and encourage participants to think in terms of entrepreneurship as a career.
- New enterprise creation programmes designed to develop competences which lead to self-employment, economic self-sufficiency or employment generation.
- Programmes which focus on small business survival and growth.

We are convinced that the development of an orientation towards entrepreneurship is increasingly an important aspect of a curriculum in management. In order to absorb the risks associated with the liability of newness, students are encouraged to participate in curricular and extracurricular projects, working with and for a selected number of cultural institutions, incubators, start-ups. The effort is oriented towards two directions:

- as far as the students are concerned, to give them opportunities to experiment the difficulties associated with entrepreneurial ventures in cultural settings, while they are still in the protected environment of the university
- as far as the stakeholder associated with cultural projects are concerned, to offer them the opportunity to utilize some specialised resources and to get in touch systematically with important audiences.

Class activities explore some of the common challenges that research carried in ASK has identified across the variety of situations analysed through case studies and the intervention of guest speakers.

CASES

- How to create and nurture networks of physical and virtual relations, leveraging on the diffusion of digital platforms. The analysis and the discussions of the conditions for sustainability of platform based business models on the web is a very important area on which we are training our students. Of particular interest is the evolution of platforms associated with storytelling and audience building.
- How to simultaneously mobilize of a variety of stakeholders by cultural projects: collaborators, clients, audiences, residents, providers of funds. The need for cultural institutions to simultaneously operate in educational, scientific and cultural fields (Baia Curioni 2006) forces them to have an articulated value proposition, no matter how big they are. The effort of consensus and reputation building is time consuming and relatively resilient.
- The conditions for sustainability: cultural projects are structurally in disequilibrium form an economic and often financial point of view. Competition for public and private funds is increasing and the tension on resources forces inevitably the development of collaborative relationships at industry and territorial level.

We are just at the beginning of the process: we have to take into consideration several elements at the same time:

- The need to respect the identity of each institution we deal with; this requires a mutual investment between the institutions and the university. If the program has to act as a mediator and a facilitator between students and the institutions, it has to then educate students to the appreciation of the uniqueness of their counterparts;
- The need to be parsimonious. The involvement of students in activities associated with cultural entrepreneurship is time consuming for them, for faculty and for the institutions involved. The identification of the 'rules of the game' to make the cooperation rewarding for all the parties involved is a process that is crucial for the success of the operation
- The scalability of the project. We are currently in the position to offer to a very small number of students only the possibility to experiment, due to organizational constraints.

Cultural Entrepreneurship

Evidence from companies in the field suggests that curricula should focus on how digital technologies transform value creation and value appropriation processes, opening up opportunities for start-ups, as well as for corporate venturing programs.

In recent years, however, the term has suddenly become fashionable and is released from the sphere of purely academic debates. Inevitably, in the momentum of popularity, cultural entrepreneurship has been enriched with new and different rhetorical meanings. Some recent definitions have attributed cultural entrepreneurship to build markets around cultural institutions, attracting large flows of visitors through cultural initiatives, to diversify income sources through diversification of activities (as in the case of the organisation of concerts and screenings in a Museum), business development, involvement of private sponsors. Currently, the development of studies on innovative start-ups and, in particular, on the one hand, digital, the emergence of hybrid forms of social entrepreneurship often linked to initiatives of corporate philanthropy account or corporate social responsibility.

The massive operation by the European Community of the term Creative Europe to launch invitations Horizon 2020 led to broaden and render even more ambiguous entrepreneurship cultural boundaries to include initiatives that characterize the territories in terms of '*urban coolness*' (kitchen, design, communication, graphics etc.). As these projects for characterizing a high entrepreneurial component and often are highly representative of the identity of a specific territory and culture of a community, this article focuses on the strictly cultural dimension and interaction between different organizational forms that deal with the development of new ways to test, produce and disseminate culture and with an important public dimension.

About the Author

Dr Paola Dubini is Associate Professor in Management and Technology at Università Bocconi – Milano Italy and the Director of CLEACC (Corso di Laurea in Economia per le Arti, la Cultura e la Comunicazione – Undergraduate Management Program in Management for the Arts, Culture and Communication) at Università Bocconi. She is the past Director of ASK Research Centre at Bocconi and the current director of Bocconi Arts Campus.
—

paola.dubini@unibocconi.it

References

Appadurai, A. (1986). Introduction: Commodities and the Politics of Value. In: Appadurai, A. (ed.). *The Social Life of Things: Commodities in Cultural Perspective.* Cambridge: Cambridge University Press, pp. 3-63.

Baia Curioni S. L'intrapresa culturale. Riflessioni sul rapporto fra produzione culturale e logiche d'impresa. In: *Economia & Management* 1,2006 (1-13)

Bourdieu, P. (1984). *Distinction.* London: Routledge.

DiMaggio, P. J. (1982). Cultural entrepreneurship in nineteenth-century Boston. In: *Media, Culture and Society,* 4, 33–50.

Hirsch, P. M., & Levin, D. Z. (1999). Umbrella advocates versus validity police: A lifecycle model. In: *Organization Science*, 10(2), 199–212.

Kirby D.A. (2005). Entrepreneurship Education: Can Business Schools Meet the Challenge? In: *Silicon Valley Review of global entrepreneurship.* Proceedings of the San Francisco-Silicon Valley global entrepreneurship research conference 173-194

Mintzberg, H. (1973). *The Nature of Managerial Work.* New York: Harper and Row.

Zimmermann M.A. Zeitz G.J (2002). Beyond survival: achieving new venture growth by building legitimacy. In: *Academy of Management Review* 27,2, 414-431

CASES

Marilena Vecco

A NEW APPROACH TO TEACH AND LEARN CULTURAL ENTREPRENEURSHIP
THE CEE MASTER AT ERASMUS UNIVERSITY ROTTERDAM

Abstract
Entrepreneurship is by now a well-established educational subject around the globe (Fayolle, 2007; Klein 2006). Entrepreneurship has become a strong field of interest in the educational area. The subject is taught in several education sectors, ranging from business entrepreneurship to social entrepreneurship. Among them also cultural entrepreneurship is increasingly gaining popularity as university degrees all around the world. Why and how can we improve the traditionally taught entrepreneurship? What are the new skills and competencies required by cultural entrepreneurs to cope with a globalised and unstable socio-cultural and economic environment?
This article discusses the Erasmus School of History, Culture and Communication (ESHCC) experience, as a reflection on three years of observation and experiences, focusing on the innovative approach adopted in comparison to more traditional ways of teaching and learning entrepreneurship.

CASES

Introduction
'Tell me and I forget, teach me and I may remember,
involve me and I learn.'
B. Franklin (1706-1790)

Entrepreneurship is by now a well-established educational subject around the globe (Fayolle, 2007; Klein 2006). Whether it is instructed in colleges, workshops and seminars, or it is ascertained in America or Europe, entrepreneurship has become a strong field of interest in the educational area. In several European countries the teaching of entrepreneurship is seen as a *panacea*, to actuate the development and innovation of economy and wealth. The subject is taught in several education sectors, ranging from business entrepreneurship to social entrepreneurship.

Among them, also cultural entrepreneurship is increasingly gaining popularity as university degrees all around the world. Why and how can we improve the traditional teaching of entrepreneurship? What are the new skills and competencies required by cultural entrepreneurs to cope with a globalised and unstable socio-cultural and economic environment? What could be the competitive advantage of this new generation of cultural entrepreneurs?

This article is a reflection, based upon the experience of Erasmus School of History, Culture and Communication (ESHCC) at the Erasmus University in Rotterdam (EUR), in the Netherlands. The EUR has incorporated human sustainability core skills and an innovative approach in teaching and learning in its Cultural Entrepreneurship course (CE) within the master in Cultural Economics and Entrepreneurship (CEE). This article, based on three years observation and experiences, will present the course design and curriculum with its improvements over time and the innovative approach adopted. It will be compared to more traditional ways of teaching and learning entrepreneurship.

Background

The CEE master at ESHCC at Erasmus University is a well appreciated master within the arts and cultural management field.[1] Cultural Entrepreneurship is a compulsory subject within one year master program. The course is related to most of the courses taught in the master and well connected in terms of content and learning objectives with the other management courses.

The overall goal of the master is to impart knowledge, understanding and skills in the domain of arts and culture studies, in order to allow the graduate to fulfil MA level positions at the relevant labour market. They need to develop critical thinking, to apply leading theoretical insights, academic discussions and research on cultural economics and entrepreneurship vis-à-vis the art world; to contribute and develop an academic approach applicable in the cultural sector. The CE course aims to improve students' knowledge on cultural entrepreneurship, the entrepreneurial dimension of the cultural sector and the entrepreneurial skills to start up and to foster their entrepreneurial behaviour within the framework.

The objective is to attract around fifty Master students, attending this course each year. Three years ago the design of the course has been drastically changed to meet the challenges of the economic and social (recently political) context, moving towards an enterprising society. Promoting entrepreneurship among students has become a central issue in universities and governments (Fayolle, Redford 2014). Several studies confirmed the positive role of universities in developing entrepreneurial intentions and the determinants influencing entrepreneurial behaviour of students (Hofer, 2013; Pickernell et al. 2011; CIHE/NCGE/NESTA 2008; GEM, 2007; Fayolle et al. 2006). Within the context of a more entrepreneurial society, there is a widespread need and request for innovation and entrepreneurship within the European economy. Moreover, within cultural entrepreneurship field in the Netherlands, faced with a recent cut in governmental subsidies, different cultural organisations had to develop entrepreneurial activities and behaviours to generate additional income.

Within the CEE master there are two different trajectories: cultural economics and cultural entrepreneurship. Both are structured around three different aspects: theory, applications and skills.

The program should not be confused with a conventional program on cultural management. The program puts a great emphasis on innovative theory and original empirical research, which is an important aspect of market research, strategic management, and many entrepreneurial projects.

CASES

---

[1]*Retrieved from http://www.best-masters.com/ranking-master-arts-and-cultural-management.html.: 2nd ranking in 2015, 1st ranking in 2014 in the category in 'Arts and Cultural Management' (out of 46).*

Moreover, the specific aim of the course is to give to the students the intellectual tools to approach the tasks needed, and to provide them insights into the skills and competences in entrepreneurship in practice through own projects and critical reflections on them (projects and students as future entrepreneurs).

The teaching Philosophy applied

Active learning is the goal of the CEE Master, and the core value of our teaching philosophy. The main objective in teaching is to support the learning process, by helping students to gain and develop the skills to enhance their active participation in their own learning process. This active participation and proactive role can provide sound knowledge that will stay with an individual. The CE Course is offering a co-shared process, whose results are based on the interaction between teaching and learning.

Accordingly, one of the crucial components within our education is answering the question *what might learning be?* Our philosophy starts with the statement that learning is a process instead of an activity. This process can be labelled as a construction. Adopting the constructivist learning theory, knowledge acquisition is compared to a building activity: every person is equipped with more or less basic mental tools and skills to make sense of his or her world, by building mental representations of it, creating knowledge and skills for interacting successfully with and within the society.

a. The first assumption of this approach is that each person is a sort of creative builder of his/her own mental environment. We are not passive receivers but active builders. By using the knowledge structures and meaningful relationships that we construct in the course of our lives, we are able to produce our subjective world-experience representation.

b. Knowledge is a construction, but it needs to be complemented by the ability for practical *use* (cfr. Hymes 1972). The main issue is to create knowledge one can use in everyday life as well in the professional field.

The CE course pays attention to this specific nature of learning and this concept of knowledge, skills and competencies that need to be developed in order to support learning as a process.

Learning – when considered in perspective of life development – is also a process of self–creation and re-creation. According to Colebrook (2002), learning is the process of becoming-other, of moving beyond the given boundaries of a socially stabilised self: '*we are always more than the closed image of the self we take ourselves to be*' (Colebrook, 2002: 142). In line with Foucault's (1986) and Kostera's (2005) perspectives, position learning is a path to self-actualisation. The central point here is again the concept of process, as Hjorth and Johannisson (2007) stated: '*...we share with relational constructivists and poststructuralists (such as Deleuze) the view that processes make people rather than people make processes*' (Hjorth and Johannisson, 2007: 49). The learning itself is seen as an entrepreneurial process, because it breaks the given and prescribed patterns and boundaries, and creates new self-constructs: new self-other and self-world relations.

The CE Course

The cultural entrepreneurship course (CE) is based on three main concepts:

a. The entrepreneurial process,
b. The entrepreneurial behaviour,
c. The student's self-knowledge on his/her own skills and competences in entrepreneurial processes.

The model of the entrepreneurial process (Shane, 2003) represents the blueprint for the course design (Fig. 1). In fact, the main focus is not on start up a business once the student is graduated, but rather on the entrepreneurial behaviour and the understanding of entrepreneurial dynamics and processes. Students will be exposed to this process of understanding entrepreneurship and will develop a disposition to cultural entrepreneurship. The pedagogical dimension of the process is mainly based on the constructivist approach and on Kolb's learning cycle (Fig. 2).

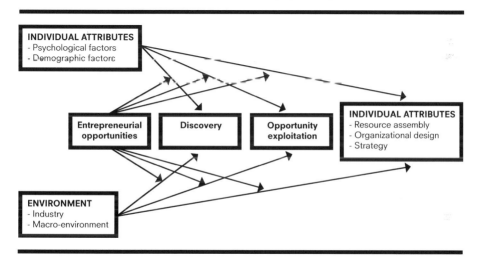

Figure 1 Model of the entrepreneurial process (Source: Shane, 2003: 11)

In Kolb's experiential learning theory (ELT), the learning is not a circular process but is a cycle or spiral where the learner 'touches all the bases'. In other words, it offers a cycle of experiencing, reflecting, thinking, and acting.

Immediate or concrete experiences lead to observations and reflections. These reflections are then assimilated into abstract concepts with implications for action. The person can actively test and experiment with these concepts, which in turn enable the creation of new experiences.

The cycle is structured in four learning stages (which might also be interpreted as a *'training cycle'*:

a. Concrete Experience - (CE)
b. Reflective Observation - (RO)
c. Abstract Conceptualization - (AC) and
d. Active Experimentation - (AE)

Two points have to be stressed. First, often to fully understand the fundamental principles, it is required to go through the four stages several times. Second, it is an iterative cycle, characterized by a progress in depth into the discerning of the analysed problem. Each interaction implies a better and more profound gaining of the concepts. Moreover, this model offers both a way to understand individual people's different learning styles, and also an explanation of a cycle of experiential learning for students and teachers as well.

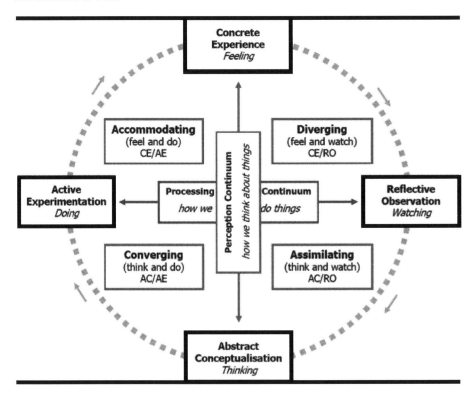

Figure 2 Kolb's learning cycle Source. Kolb 1984, 2005

This model appears to be suitable for future cultural entrepreneurs, because *'learning to learn'* is an important aspect in their activity. Entrepreneurs are dealing with completely new business concepts without any specific external guidelines. Learning by doing, by experimenting and by interacting with their environment is the most relevant tool to develop entrepreneurial knowledge and experience. The central concept of entrepreneurship education is to support students learning experiences through different learning models *('learning by doing'; 'project learning', 'problem based learning', 'action learning',* etc.).

Learning Objectives

It is our perspective that the teaching activity has to support the student learning process of the fundamental content of the courses we offer. Yet, it also has to contribute to long term objectives. Moreover, students have to understand the relevance of being autonomous; they have to play an active role in their own learning process. By this *'active'* engagement, students will be able to develop the lifelong learning skills needed to cope with progress in management and entrepreneurship practice. Our goal is to create the context to support this process. To make clearer the bridge between the theory and the applications, we often use professional experiences taken from the real world. In addition, we refer to current research projects. Students are invited to start the process to be able to master the main concepts and develop connections among the different perspectives. Passive knowledge will not suffice: students have to gain an understanding of the main concepts, and to be able to explain them to their peers.

Since students need to develop their business skills and process understanding, additional attention is given to the development of their entrepreneurial skills and behaviour. This means introducing specific topics and activities promoting a growing awareness and characteristic behaviour of the entrepreneur. In designing the learning objectives of the CE course, a number of sources are used; such as Hisrich and Peters' three categories of entrepreneurial skills (1998) (technical skills; business management skills and personal entrepreneurial skills); Ray's taxonomy of entrepreneurial needs (1997) (table 1).

Communication skills (especially persuasion)
Creativity skills
Critical thinking
assessment skills
leadership skills
negotiation skills
problem-solving skills
social networking skills
time management skills

Table 1 Learning objectives: Ray's taxonomy of entrepreneurial needs (1997)

Course Description

The target group is represented by around fifty CEE master Dutch and international students each year. The use of active teaching methods and the involvement of students in the classroom work (setting to *'learning to learn cultural entrepreneurship'*) is supported by two small working groups (25 students). Each class offers the following components:

- Interactive lectures,
- Principal and small group discussion,
- Game play or computer based simulation Case study discussion or guest lecture (experienced cultural entrepreneurs are invited to speak about their successful and failed experiences, and challenges in starting and running their businesses).

The goal of the lectures is twofold: to raise student's awareness, and provide knowledge on the theoretical side of cultural entrepreneurship, business administration (a), and to consult students on business planning and writing business plans (b).

The students' individual readings of literature, as well as of case studies, offers a preparation to each plenary session, together with a mandatory study of articles during the lectures. After two sessions students groups will be actively involved in the composition of a business plan of a new creative and/or innovative cultural business. They will be expected to apply the notions and concepts of each lecture, and to hand in the part of the business plan relating to the lecture subject a week after.

Since the self-knowledge is a central topic of this course, starting from week 3 until week 6 students have to complete four online tests (one per week). The results of these tests will be part of the student development portfolio and be discussed during lecture 8. Then, students will elaborate on these results themselves and use the first and the last self-assessment tests (week 1 and week 8) to write their development portfolio of skills and competences.

This development portfolio is an essay, reflecting on test results, course material, connecting class theory and concepts with personal experience. Students are expected to state their future entrepreneurial goal, and analyse their knowledge and capability of cultural entrepreneurship competences discussed in this course to achieve it. They are expected to assess their competences and human skills as well as the process they did to acquire and/or develop them, using proper examples from their work completed in their assignments and class discussions.

The Educational Model used

The CE course holds three innovative aspects: the topics taught, the teaching methods and the design entrepreneurial behaviour, process and person-centred process (see above).

The course covers the main entrepreneurial topics in terms of technical, business management and personal entrepreneurial skills, focusing on the concept of human sustainability and core skills recognized as relevant skills for the entrepreneurs in the 21st century (Hovanessian, Vecco, 2014; Dede 2009). In the past entrepreneurial education focused on the students' goals, plans, actions and strategies. , *Deeper personal processes such as emotions, assumptions, cultural paradigms, which makes all those plans and strategies to succeed or fail were not discussed*' (Hovanessian, Vecco, 2014: 81). As affirmed by Carrier (2007), still a lot of entrepreneurship programmes are using traditional strategies and tools for teaching entrepreneurship. However these models of teaching provided mechanics of business to *students ignoring the person who runs the business, the entrepreneur.*' The goal is to develop in students the attributes and behaviour of the entrepreneurial person which are sustainable in the medium and long term' (ivi: 82). As Ray stated (1997): *'The skills traditionally taught in business schools are essential but not sufficient to make successful entrepreneur'*.

Teaching methods utilized in entrepreneurship education vary (see table 3). The CE course doesn't adhere to the traditional classroom teaching. It combines traditional methods (lecture, seminars, case study BP, discussion groups) with some more innovative ones (computer based simulation, games and development portfolio), in order to show the variety of skills that have to be trained and/or developed.

The educational model used is a blended learning, to afford each student a more personalized learning experience, meaning increased student control over the time, place, path, and/or pace of his/her learning (Bonk, Graham, 2006). Within this blended learning we combine:

- Building a Business Plan which is used to establish a connection with the real world;
- Case studies which relate theory and practice, supporting analysis and critical thinking as well handling assumptions and inferences to make decisions, all relevant entrepreneurial skills;
- Computer-based simulation games, which embody the main entrepreneurial skills (seeking opportunity, solving problems creatively, persuading, negotiating a deal successfully, taking decision);
- Dragon's Den, organised to create a more competitive and entrepreneurial environment. Each student group will pitch their business concept in front of (potential) investors. The best group will receive a symbolic award.

Looking Back: Three Years of Experience

In our master education the goal is to create a student-centred environment. Students have to learn cultural economics and entrepreneurship actively rather than passively, which means they have to participate. Skills like critical and creative thinking, entrepreneurial skills are central to our master philosophy.

During these three years we observed that students are sceptical about the development portfolio assignment. As a facilitator, we show the relevance of this assignment and its difficulty, because they have to apply their critical skills and evaluate their learning process in order to be constructive to improve in the future. In this course we try to relativize the concept of success and stress the relevance of a failure, as a moment within the entrepreneur's learning process. In our CE class on entrepreneurial skills our educational motto is: *'Make sure people learn and grow from mistakes and that they share this learning. But don't accept that the same mistake is made twice. Make it clear, the rule is: Only make new mistakes'* (P. Dourando).

Within the CEE master in average 65% of the students are international from other European or extra European countries. This cultural diversity may imply some difficulties in levering students thinking and learning. We always try to show the relevance of this cultural diversity and its positive impact on their learning trajectory. More attention to selection of the students with the right attitudes would seem to be appropriate.

Not only motivation letter has to be mandatory, but also personality test, face-to-face interviews may be adopted to evaluate the applicants. To ensure entrepreneurial attitudes among the students comprehensive interview process might be applicable.

At present, the EUR master is working on expanding and improving the management/entrepreneurship and leadership trajectories at an international level. The main idea is to strengthen the expertise in management of creativity and cultural entrepreneurship, financing, philanthropy, cultural project management, promotion and arts and culture marketing. Moreover, the master is developing some collaborations with other universities in order to develop a new master program. In future, the CEE master may introduce some labs to develop further the skills dimension of the master and new courses focusing on specific segments of the cultural sector.

Within the CE course we are facing different challenges: to have a well-balanced blended learning model, able to motivate and involve students over the whole master, to develop entrepreneurial projects with Fine arts universities and the Conservatory of Music student. At present, the course includes the main topics associated with the early stage of an enterprise. Yet, no room is devoted to the topics covering later phases. The later stages of an enterprise are relevant to assure enterprise and entrepreneur's sustainability as well. The experiences collected lead to additional questions. How can academia be updated, and reflect in its courses what is going on in the cultural entrepreneurial sector. Or, how to understand and strengthen the relationship between cultural entrepreneurship research and practice?

CASES

References

Barbosa, S.D., Kickul, J. and Smith B.R. (2008). The road less intended: integrating entrepreneurial cognition and risk in entrepreneurship education. In: *Journal of Enterprising Culture*, 16(4):411–439.

Bonk, C. J. & Graham, C. R. (Eds.) (2006). *Handbook of blended learning: Global Perspectives, local designs*. San Francisco, CA: Pfeiffer Publishing.

Cassier, C. (2007). Strategies for teaching entrepreneurship: what else beyond lectures, case studies and business plans? In: Fayolle A. (Ed). *Handbook of research in entrepreneurship education*, vol. 1. (pp. 143-159). Cheltenham/Northampton: Edward Elgar.

CIHE/NCGE/NESTA (2008). *Developing Entrepreneurial Graduates: Putting Entrepreneurship at the Centre of Higher Education*. London: The Council for Industry and Higher Education, National Council for Graduate Entrepreneurship and National Endowment for Science Technology and Arts.

Dede, C. (2009). *Comparing Frameworks for '21st Century Skills*. Harvard Graduate School of Education, 19 p.

Fayolle, A. (2007). *Handbook of Research in Entrepreneurship Education: Contextual Perspectives vv. 1 and 2*. Cheltenham: Edward Elgar Publishing Ltd.

Fayolle, A., Dana T. Redford (2014). *Handbook on the Entrepreneurial University*. Cheltenham: Edward Elgar.

Foucault, M. (1986). *The History of Sexuality (Vol. 3) The Care of the Self*. New York: Vintage Books.

About the Author

Dr Marilena Vecco *is Assistant Professor of Cultural Economics at Erasmus University Rotterdam. In the Department for the Study of the Arts and Culture, she lectures in the MA Cultural Economics & Cultural Entrepreneurship. Her research focuses on cultural entrepreneurship, management with a special focus on cultural heritage (tangible and intangible) and contemporary art markets. She holds a PhD in Economic Sciences at University Paris (Fr), a PhD in Economics of Institutions and Creativity at University of Turin (I) and a MBA executive in International Arts Management from the University of Salzburg Business School in collaboration with Columbia College, Chicago.*

Between 1999 and 2010 she was head of research of the International Centre for Arts Economics (ICARE) and Research Fellow and Adjunct Professor of Cultural Economics and Art markets at the University Ca' Foscari of Venice. She has been a consultant for several public and private organisations, including OECD, Centre for Entrepreneurship, SMEs and Local Development, World Bank and The European Commission.

—

vecco@eshcc.eur.nl

GEM (2007). *Graduate Entrepreneurship in the UK: Summary Report*. From GEM UK Data, NCGE Research Report 003/2006, GEM, London, April.

Heinonen,J., Poikkijoki S. A. (2006). An entrepreneurial-directed approach to entrepreneurship education: mission impossible? In: *Journal of Management Development*, 25(1): 80 -94.

Hisrich, R.D., Peters, M.P. (1998). *Entrepreneurship*, 4th ed. Boston, MA: Irwin McGraw-Hill.

Hjorth, D. and Johannisson, B. (2007). Learning as an entrepreneurial process. In: Fayolle, A. (2007, ed. By). *Handbook of Research in Entrepreneurship Education* (46-66). Cheltenham, Northampton, MA, USA: Edward Elgar.

Hofer, A.et al. (2013). *Promoting Successful Graduate Entrepreneurship at the University of Applied Sciences* Schmalkalden, Germany, OECD Local Economic and Employment Development (LEED) Working Articles,2013/02, OECD Publishing.

Hovanessian, S., Vecco, M. (2014). Human Sustainability at the Core of Educating Entrepreneurs. In: Gijón-Puerta, J. & García-Sempere, P. (coords.) (2014). Book of Articles. *Conference on Enabling Teachers for Entrepreneurship Education* (ENTENP2014) (pp. 79-92). Granada: Editorial Universidad de Granada.

Hymes, D. (1972). On communicative competence. In J. B. Pride and J. Holmes (eds.): *Sociolinguistics.* Harmondsworth: Penguin.

Kostera, M. (2005). *The Quest for the Self-Actualizing Organization*, Malmö: Liber.

Mwasalwiba, E. S. (2010). Entrepreneurship education: a review of its objectives, teaching methods, and impact indicators. In: *Education + Training*, 52(1): 20 -47.

Neck, H. M. and Greene, P. G. (2011). Entrepreneurship Education: Known Worlds and New Frontiers. In: *Journal of Small Business Management*, 49: 55-70.

Pickernell, D., Packham, G., Jones, P., Miller, Ch., and Brychan Th. (2011). Graduate entrepreneurs are different: they access more resources? In: *International Journal of Entrepreneurial Behaviour & Research*, 17(2): 183-202.

Ray, D.M. (1997).Teaching entrepreneurship in Asia: impact of a pedagogical innovation. In: *Entrepreneurship, Innovation and Change,* 6(3): 193–227.

Shane, S. (2003). *A General Theory of Entrepreneurship. The Individual-opportunity nexus*. Cheltenham (UK): Edward Elgar.

CASES

Jeannette Guillemin
Wendy Swart Grossman

TEACHING CULTURAL ENTREPRENEURSHIP IN AN ENGAGING, STRATEGIC AND USEFUL WAY
NOTES FROM THE FIELD

abstract

This article describes a Cultural Entrepreneurship course offered within a graduate arts administration program. The course educates students to think in entrepreneurial ways, and to apply newly acquired skills to put ideas into action. The article proposes a working definition of cultural entrepreneurship and introduces two tools designed for this class:

a. The CIIP Personal Inventory tool allows students to assess their professional motivations by defining their Care/Idea/Interest/Passion
b. The 4V Model assesses creative business endeavours by reviewing four attributes: Vision, Venture, Viability, Vitality.

The article outlines four core components: Self-Reflection, Assessment, Spotlight and Action, and provides examples of interactive activities and case studies.

Introduction

When Mara was three years old, her grandmother took her to see The Nutcracker ballet. Mara was transported by the magic that unfolded on stage, and it sparked her life-long interest in the arts. In college, Mara studied theatre performance but discovered her true passion was arts management and decided to enrol in a master's degree program in Arts Administration. In her last year of graduate school, Mara signed up for Cultural Entrepreneurship, a course designed to introduce the creative economy and teach entrepreneurial skills to arts professionals. In the class, she assessed her management and personal skills, identified her passion, interviewed the executive director at a theatre venue and designed a social networking website for theatre artists that addressed an issue raised in her interview.

After graduation, a position became available at the same local theatre and Mara immediately applied. During her interview she shared her website concept designed in the Cultural Entrepreneurship class. From a pool of hundreds of qualified candidates, Mara established herself as an innovative thinker and was hired for her 'dream job'.

Mara applied the skills she learned in her Cultural Entrepreneurship class — developing an entrepreneurial mind-set, building a personal network, and seizing opportunities — to succeed in a competitive job market.

As universities and colleges in the United States evaluate the best ways to educate and prepare students for the 21ˢᵗ century, arts and cultural entrepreneurship courses and programs continue to emerge. Despite increased offerings, there is confusion about how to teach students the tools and techniques used by cultural entrepreneurs to create and sustain cultural projects (Beckman, 2007). Addressing this concern, this article outlines the creation of a Cultural Entrepreneurship course, firmly rooted in real world experiences and taught in Boston University's graduate Arts Administration program. The course explores the dynamism of this emerging field while providing students with practical skills that enable them to translate ideas into action. In the class, entre-preneurial thinking is modelled and students are introduced to tools and methods for identifying innovative initiatives in the for-profit, non-profit, and public sectors.

Limited public financial support and increased competition within the culture sector require non-profit arts organizations to find better ways to secure stable funding and attract audiences. Simultaneously, technological advances have enabled many new ways to experience and participate in arts and culture, expanding the possibilities for artists and arts administrators to engage in the arts beyond the scope of traditional cultural organizations (i.e. museums, concert halls, theatres, and galleries). New tech-nologies have lowered barriers to entry, reduced start-up costs, and created opportu-nities for cultural entrepreneurs to reach a global audience.

By studying cultural entrepreneurship, arts administration students acquire the tools and confidence to market themselves to established arts organizations that seek creative thinkers who can bridge old and new technologies. In addition, it also teaches students how to create their own opportunities, such as working as solo practitioners or found-ers of start-up for-profit and non-profit enterprises. In our course, students are encour-aged to explore all these possibilities and develop projects to further their interests using tools we outline in this chapter.

Cultural Entrepreneurship Definition and Course Research

Cultural entrepreneurship is a term with a wide range of definitions. While many defi-nitions focus on the ability of cultural capital to create financial, social and artistic value (Loy, 2015; Bilton, 2010; Rae, 2005)., there are other definitions that emphasize cultural entrepreneurship as the ability to change belief systems and shift Culture on a grand scale (Martin & Witter, 2011; Mokyr, 2013). After introducing our students to this range of perspectives, and we then established a specific definition for the purposes of our course. While the concept of social responsibility does not necessarily apply to all creative industries, we made the decision to incorporate it into our class definition. By doing so, we attempted to differentiate cultural entrepreneurship from standard business entrepreneurship. Whereas business entrepreneurs are motivated by finan-cial gain, cultural entrepreneurs are more apt to be intrinsically motivated, seeking meaning and purpose in addition the financial gain. (Bilton, 2010; Bridgstock, 2012, Klamer, 1996).

The course thus embraces a definition of Cultural Entrepreneurship as the capacity to leverage cultural products and services at the intersection of arts & culture and business & technology in a socially responsible and financially sustainable way (figure 1).

CASES

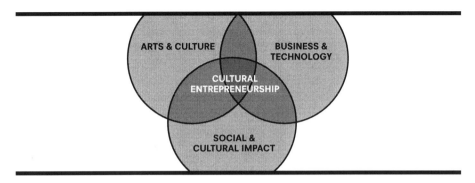

Figure 1 Cultural Entrepreneurship Definition

In our class, when we refer to culture, we emphasize the creative industries; advertising, architecture, art and antiques markets, crafts, design, fashion, film and video, food, music, performing arts, publishing, television and radio (Howkins, 2007). We also model an entrepreneurial mind-set that includes innovative thinking, risk-taking and the ability to generate opportunities.

It was helpful to categorize cultural entrepreneurs into three distinct levels of influence:

1. The individual independent artist who takes on risk and finds entrepreneurial ways to financially support him/herself;
2. Entrepreneurs, sometimes referred to as intrapreneurs, working in the creative industries operating within the creative economy
3. Impact entrepreneurs who are shifting belief systems on a grand scale.

Several authors provide a valuable context for the role of creative professionals in the 21st century. According to Pink (2005)., 'We are moving from an economy and a society built on the logical, linear, computer-like capabilities of the Information Age to an economy and a society built on the inventive, empathetic, big-picture capabilities of what's rising in its place, the Conceptual Age' (p. 1). The research of Gardner (2006) and Zhao (2012) also argue that individual creativity will drive the success of future societies. With this framework in mind, we asserted that Pink described an age where creative or cultural entrepreneurs would thrive.

We found Howkins's (2007) writing on creative industries, Ries's (2011) work on lean start-up business strategies and Bornstein & Davis's (2010) research on social entrepreneurship to provide a diverse yet complementary framework for our course development. Howkins research highlighted the relationship between creativity and economics for value creation and deepened our understanding of the increasing relevance of the creative economy. Ries's outline of the lean start-up model - defined as a 'build-measure-learn feedback loop' to quickly transform ideas into products and services - helped us understand the entrepreneurial mind-set and informed our approach to teaching in an entrepreneurial way. Bornstein and Davis addressed the importance of how entrepreneurial ventures addressed problems in unique ways to promote a social good (arts and culture, in our case) as opposed to having a singular focus on financial gain. We embrace the idea that everyone can be a change maker, and assigned readings on social entrepreneurship to establish a historical context for melding a social mission with business practices (Drayton, 2006).

Finally, we designed our curriculum to serve arts administration students, many who aspire to work in established cultural organizations. Our goal is to help students recognize their potential to bring a vision to life and to think in inventive ways whether working within an institution or independently. By providing a broad understanding of this emerging field, facilitating the process of self-discovery and promoting an entrepreneurial mind-set, we attempted to empower students to chart a unique and self-directed professional path while remaining true to their values and aspirations.

Course Structure

The Cultural Entrepreneurship class [MET AR 789] runs during Boston University's Summer Session and meets for eleven three and a half hour class sessions. The enrolment limit is 25 and most students have some work experience and hold undergraduate degrees in music, theatre and visual arts. We designed each class to include a lecture, a student-led homework review, an interactive activity and student spotlight presentations. In addition to active class participation, students were graded on three articles, the development of a business proposal, a five-minute pitch regarding their entrepreneurial initiative and a final prospectus.

Our course emphasizes four key core components: A. Self-Reflection B. Assessment C. Spotlights and D. Action. Career development theorists emphasize the importance of Self-Reflection as a way to achieve career success (Super, 1983; Bandura, 1978), offering a foundation for the other three components. By developing an entrepreneurial identity, (Rae, 2005) students can begin to see their potential to translate ideas into Action. Assessment and Spotlight components provide students a chance to research and evaluate organizations that are working in their area of interest. Our emphasis on four core components is supported by the research of Ruth Bridgstock (2012) who writes about entrepreneurship and career development in higher education.

In each section below we outline the course objective, introduce tools we designed and give examples of interactive activities and case studies.

A. *SELF-REFLECTION*

   Course Objective. Develop a better understanding of individual strengths to assess the best role for each student in the cultural entrepreneurship field - be it as change agent, entrepreneur, intrapreneur, founder, supporter, thought partner, mobilizer, and administrator.

   Values Assessment. As highlighted in many of our readings, self-awareness is essential to finding a well-suited and meaningful professional path and to sourcing one's strengths, weaknesses and competencies. The course engages students in a process of self-reflection through personal inquiry, value and skills assessment.

   Two weeks before the class begins, students receive a short video introducing the class and an online questionnaire asking about their skills, goals, values and comfort level with risk. The introductory iMovie video self-referentially models new approaches to teaching. Most graduate students have never received a video intro-duction from their professors to any of their classes and thus, we set the stage early that the class will be different - more creative, more interactive, more embracing of new technology and, we hope, more engaging. The questionnaire helps us to establish a connection with students before they enter the classroom.

Introducing the CIIP Personal Inventory. Effective and successful culture entre-preneurs need to be fully invested in their ventures. Likewise, students first must identify what drives them before they can commit and be fully invested in a venture. While some people are issue-driven (world hunger or gun violence)., others might be driven by an idea (a new product or a better system for doing things)., while still others might have a distinct passion (classical music or dance). To facilitate the process of self-exploration, we created a tool to help students define their **CIIP** - Care, Issue, Idea and/or Passion (Figure 2). The term CIIP provides a quick and easy reference that we use in class and connects to a stu-dent's semester-long project. The questionnaire challenges students to identify their CIIP and find the area or topic to which they are deeply invested. Their first article assignment is specific to exploring their CIIP. The process of identifying an ultimate value or interest is challenging; some students have one clear answer while others find identifying or making choices between their passions difficult. Rather than feeling overwhelmed by competing interests or CIIP areas, we chal-lenge students to find unique intersections between seemingly disparate interests that could lead to creative invention. This provides fertile ground for entrepre-neurial and interdisciplinary thinking. In the first article, students are asked how their CIIP connects with their professional goals and whether their CIIP could translate into a viable business venture or initiative.

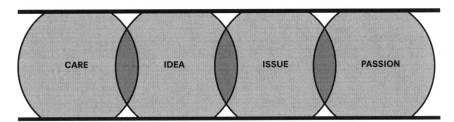

Figure 2 The CIIP Personal Inventory

By delving into students' interests (CIIP) and competencies (skills identified through the questionnaire) with the goal of creating an individualized proposed business venture, we establish a foundation for a more informed and directed professional path.

Interactive Activity: MISSION VS MONEY. The classroom is cleared and bright yellow duct tape lines the floor to create a coordinate grid. The y-axis represents money and the x-axis represents mission. A series of questions are read to the students and they stand and move within the grid based on their values. This activity gives students an opportunity to take a literal stand on where they are on the mission vs. money continuum. It also allows the students a chance to see where their classmates are on the grid and helps to facilitate discussion in order to clarify personal values and priorities around money, work-life balance and career choices. The activity visualizes for the students how these values and priorities shift and change over time, depending on personal circumstances. As part of the activity, we assess comfort level with risk, with money, with taking on debt and then evaluate the level of commitment to their CIIP as an entrepreneurial venture.

Case Study: SHARON - CIIP Combining Politics and Art. By the age of thirteen, Sharon read the news article from cover to cover. She would sit with her parents at the kitchen table discussing and debating politics. Sharon also had a strong passion for dance. In college she studied business and dance and went on to graduate school to study arts administration. When writing about her CIIP, she talked about the critical role both arts and politics play in her life. Through this process, she saw a connection. She realized she could advocate for the arts on a national level. Her final project for the class was the catalyst she needed to create a website that tracks arts-related legislation in the US Congress. She also made a list of US Representatives and Senators voting records specific to the arts. Her project involved a lobbying campaign to educate graduate arts administration students nationwide about arts policy on the national stage and to encourage tracking of elected officials on her website.

B. *ASSESSMENT — THE 4V MODEL*
Course Objective. Identify the challenges and opportunities that creative professionals and creative economies face in the rapidly changing world with an emphasis on identifying, defining and assessing successful cultural entrepreneurship models.

Referencing back to the definition we set for our class, students collectively identify the rising leaders at the intersection of arts & culture, business & technology and social impact arenas. We challenge our students to identify the '*gold standard*' in cultural entrepreneurship and created the 4V Evaluation Model (Vision, Venture, Viability, Vitality) as a lens to use when looking at innovative projects. Each of the 4Vs represents a key aspect that entrepreneurial organizations need to address to be successful. We use the 4V Model to assess both existing cultural entrepreneurial ventures as well as proposed ventures.

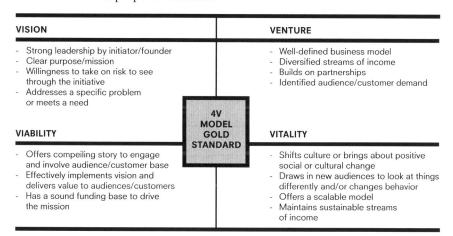

Figure 3 4V Evaluation Model

In the course, we read case studies and meet guest speakers from non-profits, for-profits and public sector organizations and evaluate their business models with our students. We refer to the 4V Model when assessing their programs, rating each of the four areas on a scale of 1-10, fully achieved [7-10], partially achieved [4-6] and not achieved [0-3]. Some ventures may do well in one or two categories while the '*gold standard*' ventures manage to find success in all four quadrants. As students work on their final projects they refer to the 4V Model as an aspirational guideline.

Interactive Activity: STUDENTS AS INVESTORS. During the final presentations, each presenter asks his/her fellow classmates to assume various roles from potential financial investors, to board members, to volunteers, to elected officials. Classmates are given plastic coloured chips to distribute to the project(s) that they feel will best use their time, money and/or talent, based on the role they assume. Students use the 4V Model to assess the strength of project proposals and are expected to distribute their chips accordingly.

Case Study: MELINDA – Music and Business. Melinda requested to take Cultural Entrepreneurship toward her graduate music degree requirements. Her final project was an entrepreneurial initiative to attract future audiences by teaching middle school students to understand and appreciate challenging musical compositions with the measurable goal of improving math scores. For her final presentation, she performed a French horn piece and outlined a partnership with a tutoring organization. Applying the 4V Model, Melinda's classmates rated her initiative high on Vision and Venture and lower on Viability and Vitality because her project was untested.

C. *SPOTLIGHT*

Course Objective: Explore existing entrepreneurial initiatives in the three sectors of our economy (non-profit, for-profit, public) that remain mission-driven and incorporate diverse funding streams.

The purpose of the Spotlight core objective is to inform students of innovative organizations in their CIIP area and to provide tools for evaluation. Throughout the semester, students' research and report on two entrepreneurial initiatives or organizations, spotlighting one in class and adding both to a shared research database accessible to all students. Each class presents student-led Spotlights that include information about the founder, an overview of the organization's mission, an outline of the business model, and an assessment of funding streams. Organizations are assessed in accordance with the 4V Model and discussed and debated in class.

Additionally, in their second article, students investigate what it means to be a leader within the entrepreneurial initiative/organization relating to their CIIP. Students perform a landscape survey to assess existing initiatives and to develop ideas on how they can approach their CIIP in new, innovative ways, working within an existing organization or creating a new initiative.

CASES

Interactive Activity: PIPE CLEANER PROJECT – Building Prototypes. We define creativity by first engaging in the creative process. Small student groups take five minutes and use six pipe cleaners to design and create a functional object that stands independently and has one moving part. The exercise allows students to quickly identify a problem, prototype a product that addresses the problem, and pitch the solution. This activity produces remarkable results. Design solutions include such objects as cameras, birds that lay eggs and swing sets, and the student groups also develop compelling stories about the value and use of the prototype. The activity encourages innovation, creative problem-solving and working in collaboration.

Case Study: JOE – CIIP and Corresponding Spotlight. Joe, a visual artist, used the CIIP process to identify his passions for design and social action. During his Spotlight he focused on a company called Beyt by 2b design (http://www.2bdesign.biz) '*an award-winning home décor social enterprise with 100% of its workers coming from disabled and/or marginalized backgrounds*.' A certified B corporation, Beyt is a social enterprise with a business model that relies on revenues from sales to achieve financial sustainability. This Spotlight ranked high in all quadrants of the 4V Model as well as introducing Joe to a local business working successfully in his CIIP area.

D. **ACTION**

Course Objective: Learn the basic steps necessary to transform an idea into action. After completing the two CIIP and landscape survey articles, students take action. In the final article, they decide whether they will propose an entrepreneurial initiative within a newly discovered organization relating to their CIIP, start an independent initiative or, if they are a working professional, propose an initiative within their current place of employment. The goal is for students to apply an entrepreneurial mind-set to a project that also provides long-term, professional benefits. The final article includes an outline of a program initiative, its deliverables, a draft budget and a timeline for implementation.

The final project must connect to a student's CIIP and include a completed action step toward implementation. Examples include creating a Kickstarter video, creating a product prototype, or conducting in-depth market analysis in a student's CIIP arena. By connecting the final project to a student's CIIP, students leverage the class to build their professional network, gain applied skills and generate their own opportunities. This section of the course includes a teacher-led tour of Boston's Innovation District. Students meet and interact with leaders in the community and see first-hand the exciting intersection between arts, commerce, innovation and ingenuity within our city.

Interactive Activity: CIIP CAFÉS. The CIIP Cafés provide time for students to discuss their interest and get feedback from classmates about a final project proposal. The desks are arranged, face-to-face in one long line in the centre of the room. Like speed dating, students are paired, two at a time for ten minutes, with five minutes for each student to share his/her CIIP. After ten

CASES

minutes, students move to the next desk and begin the process again as a new pair. Student feedback tells us that this is a highly valuable exercise to communicate effectively, to gain new insights and to create new collaborations and partnerships.

Case Study: MOLLY – Eating History. As an undergraduate at Dartmouth, Molly studied Art History and possessed a deep appreciation for local historical sites. Through the CIIP exploration and spotlight research she hit upon her idea: Eating History, a blending of her love of food with architecture and history. H er entrepreneurial business was to bring actors into historic restaurants in Boston and have them perform period skits between courses, attracting new patrons to the restaurant, growing audience appreciation of theatre and illuminating the rich history of historic surroundings. For her final presentation she produced high quality professionally designed marketing materials and her Action step included meeting with a number of local restaurant owners to assess interest, practicality, and costs.

Conclusion

Although we are educators and practitioners, we approached this class as an entrepreneurial venture, determined to have our '*start-up*' succeed. We embraced risk and explored new ways of thinking. We pulled in partners to help fill our knowledge gaps by inviting in entrepreneurial guest speakers and we made the class highly interactive. Using the entrepreneurial model to direct our venture, we consistently updated the course based on student feedback and new literature. Like any entrepreneurial endeavour, some aspects of the course have worked well while others have not. The strengths include the highly interactive nature of the classroom experience, the rich and extensive course content, the guest speakers, and the tour of Boston's Innovation District. The challenges for the course reside in the emerging nature of the topic and in the limitation of time.

We've received positive feedback about the readings for the class, but we want to continue to increase scholarly references specific to the field. With such a broad topic, in order to maintain focus and clarity, it is critical to resist the temptation of trying to cover too much. In one semester, most students cannot realistically take an idea into full implementation. We would like to see a follow-up course, specific to supporting implementation and follow-through of projects so students can have more time to execute their initiatives.

Finally, while we hope the CIIP and 4V Models will add value to other practitioners, they remain untested outside of our course. Because we taught the course with an entrepreneurial mind-set, we saw the failures as opportunities for improvement. If an interactive activity or lecture did not meet our desired results, we would get immediate feedback and change it.

In conclusion, we believe that a course in Cultural Entrepreneurship is an essential component to any arts-based program. While a cultural entrepreneurship course could be approached in many different ways, we found that focusing on four key components, Self-Reflection, Assessment, Spotlight and Action, provided an effective framework for success. The CIIP, used to deepen self-awareness, and the 4V Model,

CASES

used for assessment, were both valuable tools for our students. Class evaluations and alumni feedback confirm that the class is highly effective at teaching students to think with an entrepreneurial mind-set.

Our experience leads us to believe that arts administrators are positioned to combine creativity with entrepreneurial thinking for new ventures and established organizations in the for-profit, non-profit and public sectors. By providing skills and practical experiences as part of a graduate education, arts administrators are well positioned to play an essential role as cultural entrepreneurs and entrepreneurial thinkers in a dynamic 21st century economy.

About the Authors

Jeannette Guillemin BA MS EdM teaches in Boston University's graduate arts administration program and serves as Director ad interim at Boston University's School of Visual Arts. In addition to teaching and advising students, she creates and implements collaborative and experiential programming that expands professional opportunities, ignites entrepreneurial thinking and engages student-artists within the Boston community. Guillemin holds a bachelor's degree in English from the State University of New York at Geneseo and two master's degrees in Arts Administration and Counselling from Boston University.

—

jguillem@bu.edu

References

Adler, Nancy (2006). The Arts & Leadership: Now That We Can Do Anything, What Will We Do? In: *Academy of Management Learning and Education*, *Vol. 5, No. 4* pp. 486-499

Amabile, Teresa and Khaire, Mukti (2010). Creativity and the Role of the Leader, In: *Harvard Business Review, October 2008,* pp 2 - 11

Bandura, Albert (1978). Reflections on Self Efficacy, In: *Advances in Behavior Research and Therapy, Vol 1, Issue 4*, pp. 237 - 269

Beckman, Gary (2010*)*. 'Adventuring' Arts Entrepreneurship Curricula in Higher Education: An Examination of Present Efforts, Obstacles, and Best Practices, In: *The Journal of Arts Management, Law and Society, Vol 37, Issue 2*, pp 87 - 112

Belsky, Scott (2010). *Making Ideas Happen: overcoming the obstacles between vision and reality*, London, Penguin

Bilton, Chris (2010). *Identity, creativity and the cultural entrepreneur*. Article presented at the 23rd EGOS Colloquium, Vienna, Austria 5-7 Jul 2010

Bornstein, David and Davis, Susan. (2010). *Social Entrepreneurship-What Everyone Needs to Know*, Oxford and New York, Oxford University Press

Bridgstock, Ruth (2012). Not a dirty word: arts entrepreneurship and higher education, In: *Arts & Humanities in Higher Education, Vol 12, Issue 2-3*, pp 122-137

dos Santos - Duisenburg, Edna (2009). The Challenge of Assessing the Creative Economy: towards Informed Policy-Making, Article presented in the Creative Economy. In: Report at the United Nations Conference on Trade and Development, Maputo, Mozambique, June 2009

Drayton, Bill (2006). Everyone a Changemaker: Social Entrepreneurships Ultimate Goal, retrieved from: https://www.ashoka.org/files/innovations8.5x11 FINAL_0.pdf

Florida, Richard (2012). *The Rise of the Creative Class — Revisited: 10th Anniversary Edition*, New York, Basic Books/Perseus Books

Gardner, Howard (2006). *Five Minds for the Future*, Boston, MA, Harvard Business School Press

Hagoort, Giep and Kooyman, Rene (2010). *Creative Industries: Colourful Fabric in Multiple Dimensions*, Utrecht, NL, Utrecht School of the Arts

CASES

Howkins, J. (2007). *The Creative Economy–How People Make Money From Ideas*, London, Penguin Books

Klamer, Arjo (1996). *The Value of Culture: On the Relationship between Economics and Art*, Amsterdam, Amsterdam University Press

Loy, Alice (2015). Global Center for Cultural Entrepreneurship, Retrieved from: http://www.culturalentrepreneur.org

Martin, Courtney E. and Witter, Lisa (2011). Social or Cultural Entrepreneurship: An Argument for a New Distinction, Retrieved from: http://www.ssireview.org/blog/entry/social_or_cultural_entrepreneurship_an_argument_for_a_new_distinction

Mokyr, Joel (2013). Cultural Entrepreneurs and the origins of modern economic growth, In: *Scandinavian Economic History Review Volume 61 Issue 1*, pp 1 - 33

Pink, D. (2005). *A Whole New Mind-Why Right-Brainers Will Rule the Future*, New York, Riverhead Books

Rae, David (2005). *Entrepreneurial Learning: A narrative-based conceptual model*, Bingley, UK, Emerald Group Publishing Limited

Reis, Eric (2011). *The Lean Startup: How Today's Entrepreneurs Use Continuous Innovation to Create Radically Successful Businesses*, New York, Crown Business

Super, Donald (1983). Assessment in Career Guidance: toward truly developmental counseling, In: *The Personnel and Guidance Journal, Volume 61, Issue 9*, pp 555-562

Zhao, Yong (2012). *World Class Learners: Education Creative and Entrepreneurial Students*, Thousand Oaks, CA, Corwin Press

CASES

Wendy Swart Grossman BA MSc teaches in Boston University's graduate arts administration program and is a consultant to Non Profits and Family Foundations. With a background in US and South African presidential politics, Wendy is committed to helping her clients and students build effective collaborations, devise strategic plans for their lives and mission, implement board development that makes sense, and use entrepreneurial thinking to maximize their impact and results. She has held positions at Harvard's Museum of Science and Culture, The Science Museum in London and the Social Innovation Forum. Swart Grossman holds a bachelor's degree in Economics and Political Science from St. Olaf College and a Master's in Urban and Environmental Policy from Tufts University.
—
wswart@usa.net

† Dany Jacobs
Tamara Rookus

EXPERIENCES WITH A PRACTICE-ORIENTED MINOR AT ARTEZ INSTITUTE OF THE ARTS

Abstract

Many graduates of art are forced to start a company nowadays. However, it seems that many of the entrepreneurs concerned do not identify themselves as such, and as a consequence only by trial and error develop their entrepreneurial activities on a more professional level. Hence, it is increasingly important to prepare art students for their professional entrepreneurial activities after graduation. Yet it is difficult to develop entrepreneurial education in a proper form, within a context that traditionally focusses completely on *'artistic talent development'*.

Herewith we present hands-on experience within the ArtEZ institute of the arts, with a minor on creative entrepreneurship the last four years. ArtEZ covers a wide spectrum of disciplines in the field of dance, theatre, music, fine arts, design and architecture. In our minor, students learn what entrepreneurship means within the field of the arts (including applied arts such as product and graphic design) by following an artist they admire, and in doing this trying to understand what their business model looks like. The article shortly explains the concepts behind the curriculum development, the structure of the program, and offers a first reflection regarding the results.

The changing Field of Art Alumnus

Many schools of the arts are having a hard time developing a training for their students to become a creative entrepreneur (HBO-raad, 2010). On the one hand there are still many teachers who think that one should focus entirely on the artistic development, on the other hand many students themselves are only concerned about their possible career prospects at the very end of their studies. In this paper we describe our experience with the now four year old minor Creative Entrepreneurship that students of all disciplines can follow at ArtEZ.

Nowadays people who graduate from schools of the arts are often forced to start a company. In the Netherlands graduated artists often work as an entrepreneur (40%), also compared with the average of graduates of other bachelor studies (5%). These percentages vary per art discipline. Especially graduates in *'film and television'* (67%) and *'fine arts'* (62%) work as entrepreneurs (HBO-raad, 2010). One of the major problems for many of these creative entrepreneurs is that they have to learn to become a business professional the hard way. Therefore schools of the arts are expected more and more to prepare their students for the way in which they can practice their profession after graduation (Danielle Arets et al., 2008). Many of these schools, however, find it hard to develop a fitting form of entrepreneurship education and to embed this in training courses that are, traditionally, completely focused on artistic talent.

CASES

Creative Entrepreneurship

We have set up and developed a practical minor in creative entrepreneurship at the Institute of the Arts ArtEZ in the last four years. During this minor the students learn what it specifically means to be an entrepreneur in the arts - including in applied arts such as product and graphic design - and they also learn to write a good paper about it.

ArtEZ houses a broad spectrum of bachelor and master study programmes in the fine arts, fashion, design, architecture, music, dance and drama. With 3000 students it is the biggest art institute in the East of the Netherlands with three locations in Arnhem, Enschede, and Zwolle. Some programmes, especially those in the performing arts, made entrepreneurship a logical part of their training, while other programmes are still searching for the right form. Minors at ArtEZ are elective courses in the first semester of the third year of the bachelor programmes. The minor Creative Entrepreneurship (15 ECTS)[1] is developed for bachelor students of all art disciplines what makes creative entrepreneurship in theory accessible to all students who still miss this in their own training. In reality primarily students from the art and design programmes followed the minor. After four year 9% of the total of 32 students who followed the minor studies Fine Art, 88% Design and 3% Music.

Entrepreneurship; that is not my Concern

Obviously most art students at a school of the arts feel passionate about the profession they choose to be trained in. The fact that they will probably become an entrepreneur after graduation, is something most students are not engaged in during their training; '*it´s a small detail they ignore*' (HBO-raad, 2010). Even if it is mentioned during their training, this information is usually very soon forgotten by most students. Therefore our biggest challenge was to ensure that students truly experienced and learned what their professional life could look like and what they had to do to achieve that goal.

During the years we have observed a change in students at this point. Where the interest among students for the entrepreneurial side of their profession was only moderately present in the beginning, we noted a growing interest for this subject in recent years. We observed this for example at the increasing amount of students following the minor Creative Entrepreneurship (2010/2011: 4 students, 2013/2014: 15 students) and alumni following masterclasses on entrepreneurship and business models (2014: 6 alumni, 2015: 13 alumni). At the Product Design and Graphic Design departments the last 5 to 10 years we see an increasing number of students who put their business cards at the graduation exhibition and have good working websites. We also see changes in the attitude of alumni at '*Arnhemse Nieuwe*'[2]; a yearly evening with live short presentations of the ten best students graduated from ArtEZ Institute of the Arts (location Arnhem). The fresh alumni at '*Arnhemse Nieuwe*' more and more

---

[1]*ECTS stands for European Credit Transfer System and is a system in order to compare study points in Europe. One ECTS-point stands for 28 hours studying. One study year exists of a minimum of 60 ECTS-points. De total course load of a study programme exists thus of 1680 hours per study year.*

[2]'*Arnhemse Nieuwe*' *means 'Arnhems New' and refers to a typical Dutch food delight: raw herring which is called 'Hollandse Nieuwe' (Hollands New). The 'Hollandse Nieuwe' season in The Netherlands starts every year in June.*

show an entrepreneurial attitude in the way they present themselves to the public just a few months after graduation[3]. Some have already started their own business, some tell the public what (commercial) value they have to offer; others are already able to show what position they want to conquer in the creative industries. Untill four or five years ago these presentations focussed mainly on the artistic process.

Creative Entrepreneurship: Master-companion

We have set up and developed a practical minor in creative entrepreneurship at the Institute of the Arts ArtEZ in the last four years. During this minor the students learn what it specifically means to be an entrepreneur in the arts - including in applied arts such as product and graphic design - and they also learn to write a good paper about it. Basically, students of all ArtEZ courses can take the minor in Creative Entrepreneurship (15 ECTS) in their first semester of the third year. It is an elective course, which makes creative entrepreneurship accessible to all students that cannot find these courses within their own curriculum.

Rik Wenting (2008) showed that most fashion designers who have a successful business had usually worked a while for another successful fashion designer. In other words; most successful fashion designers who run their own company first experienced what it means to run a fashion company in the fashion industry by actually working in that industry at another man's business. We translated the idea that a look behind the scenes of a successful master could be an important first step to become a successful designer in the future to the field of entrepreneurship in arts education. That's why we thought it would be a good idea to have students follow the business practice of a colleague as closely as possible, and have them analyse this '*masters*' business and revenue model. So students choose one, sometimes two, professionals they admire, who work in the same discipline as themselves.

Ideally, they do this in a small or larger company, which has acquired a good reputation culturally and is economically successful too. At the Art, Culture and Economy research group of ArtEZ Institute of the Arts we call this the '*double success criterion*' (Jacobs 2012/2014). This criterion explains the tension between cultural and economic success in creative entrepreneurship. The alacrity to ask and receive money for a product or service you deliver as a creative professional is often difficult to manage in relation to attain a culturally successful reputation. An important part of the '*double success criterion*' is that a too big pressure on the extrinsic motivation (*earning money*) can damage the intrinsic motivation (*creating*). Yet, if we talk about *successful* creative entrepreneurship, we need both criteria. In the minor the tension between both criteria is addressed in the research to analyse the company's business model. The students do this research based on interviews and orientation days they spend with the professional. This is how they get a look behind the scenes and get the opportunity to experience what is needed to run a company as creative professional. They also write a report about it. This is done one step at a time, as they write different chapters on every important part of the business model.

CASES

---

[3]'*Arnhemse Nieuwe*' is organized in September since 2006.

To explain the concept of a business model we use the theory of the Business Model Canvas of Alexander Osterwalder and Yves Peigneur (2010). They use the following parts to build a complete business model: value proposition, clients, customer relations, channels, revenue streams, key activities, key sources, key partners and cost structure. These parts form the chapters of the report. In this way the minor is also a good preparation for their end thesis, which is often part of graduation in the fourth year.

Three Learning Tracks

The minor in Creative Entrepreneurship consists of three learning tracks.

1. The first track (Master-Companion) is described above and forms the backbone of the minor.
2. The second consists of supportive lectures in theory and some workshops. They start of by learning to understand and use the Business Model Canvas. This model has become very popular in recent years, because it provides a good overview of a company in a visual way. The very fact that Osterwalder and Pigneur's book is so visual, makes it particularly suitable for art students to study. Our experience is that they can handle it quickly and tell about it as if they invented it themselves. The Canvas model also helps to analyse the professional's business model as an entity of logically connected components. By using the Canvas model students become aware of the mutual influence of the separated parts. Furthermore they take a closer look in class at the forces in the field of art in which the artist works, the double success criterion, at various forms of innovation, at strategy, branding, marketing, and also at legal and administrative matters.
3. The third learning track is focused on the students' development of vision in relation to their own professional practice. Students learn to reflect on the research of their masters' professional practice based on their own personal core strengths and values. By seriously considering the variety of business models that were highlighted during the minor, they learn what they themselves want and what suits them. They realise that there is not just one right way, but a multitude of possible ways to practice art. They also learn to express the vision they have of their own professional practice and to give a short presentation about it, a bit like an elevator pitch, on which they receive feedback.

The purpose of all these is that they become aware of the need to actively take control of their careers. They are supported on this course by guest lecturers who have gained their spurs in the world of art.

In addition to these three learning tracks, excursions are organised to other professionals where the group as a whole then does an interview. Besides this, students visit industrial organisations such as the BNO (Association of Dutch Designers) where they get classes on copyright, cooperative working spaces, incubators and production workshops such as Vechtclub XL and Kapitaal in Utrecht. Who and what gets visited is matched as closely as possible to the art disciplines of the students. This part of the minor is very popular every year:

*'Exploring locations where you meet people who work as entrepreneurs
with lots of passion gives me energy', 'The excursions give a good insight in the possibilities'
(Rookus, 2014).*

The minor is concluded with on the one hand the aforementioned report on the masters' business model and the reflection on their own future, based on this (done individually) and on the other hand with a joint final presentation. This final presentation is put together, designed and organised independently by the students as they see fit. Students are encouraged to organise the final presentation outside the confines of ArtEZ, which forces them to adopt an entrepreneurial attitude and put to practice what they have learned. They start doubtfully with the organisation as a group. Tasks are divided, appointments and deadlines are scheduled, temporary updates take place and all with 0 Euro budget. In the end they experience what it is to really undertake something to show yourself to the world and what the positive effect is if you focus your energy on it. *'The final presentation was nice and satisfying'* (Rookus 2014).

Students' Experiences

After they have completed the minor, students often agree that they have acquired knowledge and experience that every student who graduates a school of the arts should actually have. They indicate that they now have a more concrete idea of what life might look like after college and what to expect after graduation. *'I really knew much less about the professional practice than I thought before. I have learnt more than I could estimate in advance.'*

This does not mean that every student is chomping at the bit to actually start a business after graduation. To some it became clear, for instance, that they still need to follow another master abroad. Others realise that it will be very difficult to make ends meet with just their specialty, and that they have to develop a hybrid professional practice or initiate crossovers with other disciplines. *'A world of potential possibilities opened up for me.'*

But there are also students who found out that they already possessed a natural entrepreneurial attitude and who now have better skills to hone that gift concretely. These students are often the ones who teach, sell products, or do paid projects for clients when they are still studying. Most students realise that if they really want to be able to live off their trade and be successful, they need to develop an enterprising attitude towards their work. *'For me, the threshold for getting started as an entrepreneur has been lowered. I even feel like starting off.'* They understand that passion for the job is a prerequisite, as long as that passion does not blind them. They have to be able to deal with criticism and pick themselves up again after a setback. As an entrepreneur, and ideally as a student as well, they should know in which direction they want to go and focus on that. In addition to that, they need a clear understanding of their businesses' financial side and they have to be able to think commercially. Otherwise they will not be able to carry on in the long run. We observe the latter happening more to artists who approach being both an entrepreneur and an artist with less focus and professionalism.

Enriching Interdisciplinarity

As mentioned before, working in an interdisciplinary group sees to it that the students get to meet other disciplines of art, often for the first time. This is perceived as a very enriching experience. In the evaluation survey students suggest ArtEZ to spend more time on interdisciplinairy projects in the study programmes. *'I have experienced the cooperation with students from Product Design as very positive. They were very enthusiast and hard workers'* (ArtEZ, 2014). Not only are the various other fields of work discussed, but the students really get to know the ins and outs of other disciplines. They for example learn the main differences between regular business and revenue models in the working field of the different disciplines. By comparing the different business models of their colleagues' *'heroes'* in a practical way, they start to understand the possible diversity of these models. On the other hand it is striking how much culture, work attitude and mentality differ between the various departments at ArtEZ. During joint assignments for the minor, but especially during the preparations for the joint final presentation, the students learn to collaborate and communicate with other *'blood types'*. This, of course, can be very frustrating for them, but in the best case scenario this irritation later transforms into mutual understanding.

In conclusion, we think we have developed a nice concept and appropriate working method to teach art students what it really means to become an entrepreneur and experience it first-hand. *'My expectations are proven: the theory and additional knowledge from the master, that's something valuable I can go on with'* (Rookus, 2014). De biggest dispiriting factor for the students was that they had to read some theoretical texts about the working field of the arts. Yet, as long as theory is practiced-based and in good balance with practical workshops it is better appreciated.

We can well imagine that the approach of this minor, especially the master-companion concept, can be used more widely, even outside the school of the arts. We have schools in mind that train students to become professionals who, in order to practice their profession, have a preference to become entrepreneurs. The fact that a minor takes half a year in The Netherlands (albeit at ArtEZ only half that time) makes it possible to establish a practical educational project in which the various aspects of entrepreneurship and supportive research are discussed. We are quite enthusiastic about this working method and even better: so are the students. The material that emerged from the student case studies, is very interesting for the Art, Culture and Economy research group as well, which also accompanied the minor to gain insight into the business and revenue models in various creative sectors.

References

Arets, Danielle e.a.(2008), *Hello Creative World. Entrepreneurship in Arts Education*, Utrecht: Research Group Art and Economics, Faculty of Art and Economics at the Utrecht School of the Arts.

ArtEZ (2014), *Evaluatie minoren 2013-2014. Vragenlijst studenten*, Arnhem: ArtEZ.

Jacobs, Dany (2012) 'Creatief ondernemerschap en het dubbel succescriterium', In: *Holland Management Review*, 146, Nov.-Dec. 2012, p. 37-42.

Jacobs, Dany (2014), *The Cultural Side of Innovation: Adding Values*, New York: Routledge.

About the Authors

Prof Dr Dany Jacobs is Professor of Industrial development and innovation policy at the University of Amsterdam and professor Creative Economy at HKU University of the Arts Utrecht. During the period described, both Dany Jacobs and Tamara Rookus were member of the Art, Culture and Economy Research

CASES

*Group of the ArtEZ and
HAN Universities of Applied
Science in Arnhem,
The Netherlands.*

*Tamara Rookus MA is
an educator, concept devel-
oper and researcher in
the field of creative entrepreneurship. She holds
the Professorship Art,
Culture and Economy at
the Art Business Centre,
of ArtEZ Institute of the Arts
in Arnhem, the Netherlands.*

*At the moment she is
the project leader of the accel-
erator programme
Bridging the gap
(www.bridgingthegap-
holland.nl).
—*

*www.tamararookus.nl
t.rookus@artez.nl*

Osterwalder, Alexander & Yves Peigneur (2010), Business Model Generatie, Deventer: Kluwer.

HBO-raad (2010), **Onderscheiden, Vernieuwen, Verbinden. De toekomst van het kunstonderwijs**, Advies van de commissie-Dijkgraaf voor een sectorplan kunstonderwijs, Den Haag: HBO-Raad.

Rookus, Tamara en Dany Jacobs (juni 2014), 'Ervaringen met een praktijk-gerichte minor in het kunstonderwijs'. In: **OnderwijsInnovatie**, Heerlen: Open Universiteit.

Rookus, Tamara (2014), **Internal evaluation report minor Creative Entrepreneurship 2013-2014**, Arnhem: ArtEZ.

Wenting, Rik (2008), **The Evolution of a Creative Industry. The Industrial Dynamics and Spatial Evolution of the Global Fashion Design Industry**, Utrecht: Utrecht University Press.

CASES

Post-scriptum

*Dany Jacobs, co-author of
this article, deceased recently.
He was the main initiator
of the minor creative
entrepreneurship at ArtEZ
Institute of the Arts, on which
this article is based.
His ideas, inspirational vision
and innovative insights have
largely contributed to
the content and development
of the educational offerings.
This article is a tribute to
this man from whom
the educational community
has been able to benefit
so much. The loss is huge.*

Tamara Rookus. March 2015

Paul Zalewski
Izabella Parowicz

DARE TO TRY! WAKING THE ENTREPRENEUR IN HERITAGE CONSERVATORS

Abstract

Museums, archives and other public institutions, which have their own conservation laboratories, can only to a limited extent absorb the growing number of graduates of conservation studies. As a result, many conservators are forced to launch their own business and to offer their services within the market environment. However, during their studies, conservators are not taught how to apply marketing and management thinking in their future business practice. Which is more, the very nature of conservation services requires training in a complex area of expertise from the services' providers and restricts their undertakings by means of the professional norms and ethical standards that require rigorous adherence. This is, to a large extent, contradictory to the concept of entrepreneurship and the pertinent autonomous, uncontrolled engagement in creative and innovative activities that field necessitates.

The Masters course *Strategies for European Cultural Heritage* is an innovative extra-occupational program of study offered by the European University Viadrina in Frankfurt (Oder), Germany. It is addressed to conservators and other professionals who wish to become more successful on the cultural heritage market. The aim of this paper is to discuss the curriculum design of the above course with special emphasis on how our approach can help turn professional conservators into cultural entrepreneurs.

Theoretical Remarks

The researchers in the field of *cultural entrepreneurship* have so far dedicated little attention to the area of cultural heritage preservation. In addition, a look into the extant, but scarce, literature unveils that the definitions of *heritage entrepreneurship* vary significantly. While Powell, Thomas and Thomas (2011) define this term in reference to *heritage-based tourism*, Paju (2007) draws attention to the usage capacity of cultural (mostly architectural) resources and to its influence on the development of the entrepreneurial attitude amongst the local business people. Pfeilstetter (2014) proposes a totally different, two-sided interpretation of the term *heritage entrepreneurship*: as (1) the construction of cultural heritage (turning cultural elements into cultural heritage) and as (2) promotion of cultural heritage. To the authors' best knowledge, the professional activity of conservators-restorers has so far not been analysed in terms of *heritage entrepreneurship*.

Now, according to the definition drawn up by the European Confederation of Conservator-Restorers' Organisations (E.C.C.O), a conservator-restorer is '*a professional who has the training, knowledge, skills, experience and understanding to act with the aim of preserving cultural heritage for the future*'[1]. The principal role of a conservator-restorer is '*the preservation of cultural heritage for the benefit of present and future*

---

[1] *Source: http://www.ecco-eu.org/about-e.c.c.o./professional-guidelines.html, retrieved on 23rd February 2014.*

CASES

generations.[2] Consequently, in their daily practice, a conservator[3] is in charge of *'strategic planning; diagnostic examination; the drawing up of conservation plans and treatment proposals; preventive conservation; conservation-restoration treatments and documentation of observations and any interventions'*[1].

In economic terms, conservators are providers of what one calls *professional services.* These services are extremely individualised, as they have to be tailored not only to the customers' expectations, but also to the needs identified in the examination of the historical object in question. At the same time, the success of a conservation undertaking is strongly determined by the theoretical know-how and performance of the conservator in charge. It appears moreover that the general public, including owners of historical objects who have never used conservation services, find it difficult to fully appreciate their rationale without being exposed to relevant information from their providers (Parowicz, 2014).

The above remark concerning the fact that heritage conservation belongs to professional services is important in the light of further considerations. It has to be emphasized that most authors who deal with the term *entrepreneurship* consider it in light of the work of Schumpeter (1942) who associated it with *innovation* in any possible economic contexts and promoted a radical approach towards old structures, *creative destruction* as he styled it. Now, such an approach would be inconceivable in the case of heritage conservators whose concern is to save historical objects from damage. As Freidson (2001) emphasises, it is crucial for the work of professional service providers to deal with problems with the utmost care; it is not possible to give up their professional standards and ethical norms and to replace them with a *'creative destruction'* approach. This is why, as Reilhen and Werr (2012) notice, *entrepreneurship* and *professionalism* are two separate phenomena that, to certain extent, exclude each other and therefore they hardly ever interact with each other.

Many authors however emphasise that entrepreneurship is not necessarily defined by *creative destruction* or about creating something completely new. Rather, it is about recognising profitable market opportunities and reacting to the latter accordingly (see e.g. Kirzner, 1979; Shane and Venkatamaran, 2000; Hausmann and Heinze, 2014). For this purpose, it is helpful to find ways to use existing knowledge and skills to innovatively engage customers in the process of value creation (see Drucker, 1993; Alvesson, 2004; Malek and Ibach, 2004, Halinen and Jaakkola, 2012). As Mitchell et al. (2007) suggest, one of the key factors of successfully merging professionalism and entrepreneurship is the motivational disposition of the particular provider of professional services; they should be in a position to recognize opportunities and to benefit from the latter while exploiting their own intellectual know-how and professional potential.

---

[2] *Ibidem.*

[3] *For simplicity's sake, the conservators-restorers will be referred to as conservators throughout the text of the present work.*

[1] *Ibidem.*

Professional Opportunities of Conservators

For heritage conservators — the professional *'doctors'* of damaged historical objects — there are basically two major possibilities of employment. They can either be employed within a larger cultural institution, such as an archive or a museum, or they can offer their services within the free market environment (as freelance conservators or within a multi-person conservation business entity). There are several factors that may determine the selection of a given career path. Quite often, it is the personal predisposition that is the decisive element; there are conservators who value the sense of stability and job security that pertains to being employed at a public institution. Working in a museum is also sometimes considered to be a more prestigious career path, as it enables one to deal with particularly valuable works of art. Younger conservators may also take this opportunity to gain valuable experience when working under the supervision of their more proficient colleagues. Such opportunities are less evident in the cases of freelance conservators. The latter, however, enjoy more freedom in terms of professional independence and flexible working hours. What is more, the reason for which many conservators choose this career path is their expectation to generate financial profit. Obviously, the latter largely depends on the entrepreneurial skills of the conservator in question (Parowicz, 2014).

Yet, practice shows that in most European countries, few conservators can afford to actually choose a type of employment according to their preferences or predispositions. Quite the contrary, the number of conservators has been growing continuously, while – mostly due to the economic crisis - there are fewer and fewer respective positions offered within public, cultural institutions (Kowalski, 2014). As a result, many conservators, especially fresh graduates, have no choice but to go freelance and to face the challenge of market competition. Those whose respective efforts are insufficiently successful or who are still looking for inspiration as to how to reshape their professional career (as well as those who wish to become more attractive on the conservation market), frequently look for additional qualification opportunities. This need becomes even more urgent in view of the aforementioned conceptual discrepancies between *professionalism* and *entrepreneurship*. Conservators are, as a rule, not taught how to be entrepreneurial; since it is of utmost priority that they acquire and consequently apply complex, multidisciplinary know-how and follow ethical principles and professional standards in all their work endeavours (see Abbot, 1988. It is the confrontation with harsh market rules that leads these professionals to the conviction that gaining additional skills is necessary to succeed in terms of their career. Some of them decide to apply for the Master's course *Strategies for European Cultural Heritage* and become our students.

Our Audience

The Master's course, *Strategies for European Cultural Heritage/ Schutz Europäischer Kulturgüter*, (www.denkmalpflege-viadrina.de) was established in 1999 at the European University Viadrina (EUV) in Frankfurt (Oder), within its Faculty of Social and Cultural Studies (Chair of Heritage Sciences). EUV is situated on the Polish-German border, and the offices of our chair are located on the premises of the Collegium Polonicum, on the Polish coast of the Oder river.

CASES

Our study offer is addressed to representatives of various professions. Applicants whose previous career might have been in fields completely different from heritage preservation are very welcome, as we appreciate their enthusiasm and willingness to create multidisciplinary synergies between their original background and heritage preservation. Thus, among our students, there are representatives of numerous fields such as architecture, archaeology, but also economic studies, political science or language studies, as well as arts and media. The extensive variety of professional perspectives that our students have on heritage preservation frequently leads to interesting discussions and exchanges of ideas which, in turn, often result in spectacular projects and sustainable cooperation examples (some of which are described below). Figure 1, which depicts the overview of the original academic and/or professional background of our students within the last six year-groups, reveals that it is predominantly conservators who enrol for our course. Which is more, in the past two years the interest of conservators in our course has increased even more.

STRATEGIES FOR EUROPEAN CULTURAL HERITAGE	YEAR OF ENROLMENT						TOTAL
Original background of students	2009	2010	2011	2012	2013	2014	
Aesthetics/Film history		1					1
Archaeology	1	1		3	1	1	7
Architecture	2	3	3	3	1		12
Archivistics					1		1
Arts (Painting/Sculpture)		1	1				2
Communication Studies		2	1				3
Cultural Science		2			1		3
Economic Studies	1		1	1	1	1	5
European Studies	1					1	2
Heritage Administration			1	1			2
Heritage Conservation/Restoration	2	3	2	4	6	8	25
History	1			2		1	4
History of Arts	1		3	3	2	5	14
Intercultural Management				1			1
International Relations				1			1
Language Studies			1			1	2
Museology		2	1		1		4
Political Science		1	1				2
Soil Science			1				1
Tourism	1						1
Total	10	16	16	19	14	18	93

Figure 1 The original background of students in the last 6 years.
Source: The course's internal statistics

When asked about the reasons for our students choosing this particular course, they always provide various replies, ranging from personal interest in heritage preservation issues to willingness to try something new in life on up to the urgent need to strengthen their attractiveness on the employment market. The conservators, as a rule, bring up the latter reason; they frequently emphasise the struggle and uncertainty that pertain to their profession and the difficulty of making their ends meet. They also express their hope that our course will help them improve their chances of a satisfying career (in terms of both activity and remuneration).

The Course's Curriculum

Our study programme is not necessarily an offer aiming to create a completely new job profile. Rather, our idea is to help our students build on their original qualifications by focusing on entrepreneurial skills and other hands-on competences that are usually not conveyed within such study courses as conservation, archaeology or even architecture. It is not our primary goal to prepare our future graduates for positions in public services, but to help them develop their own initiative, independence and creativity (Zalewski, 2011).

This four-semester course is offered in German with a few lectures delivered in English. It is composed of seven rather intense modules; each of them is two weeks long. There are two modules foreseen in each of the first three semesters. The last module, scheduled at the end of the 3rd semester, includes a field trip to a European city or region, selected by the students. The 4th semester is dedicated to writing the master's thesis (see figure 2).

These modules are intertwined with the independent learning periods during which students are meant to accomplish their required study assignments from home, to prepare for their exams[1] and to work in groups on their study projects. They are also expected to accomplish their internship in a cultural heritage institution of their choice. This system of study may be hard to reconcile with the professional and familial duties of the students, as it requires them to be absent from both work and home for fourteen days, twice a semester. In our experience, however, we find this very necessary, as the students are in a position to get fully immersed in studying, without being too frequently distracted by their usual obligations, as is the case with courses organised on weekend basis.

CASES

---

[1] *The students are supposed to pass two written examinations in Project Management, one written exam in German Heritage Law as well as one written exam in International Heritage Law. They are to write two term papers, one in Art History, the other in the subject of their choice. They are also required to deliver an oral presentation concerning current issues pertinent to heritage preservation and society.*

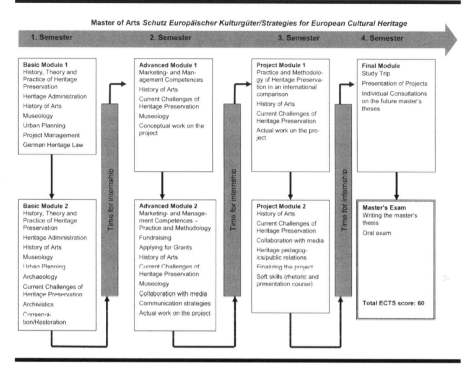

Figure 2 The organisational scheme of the course Strategies
for European Cultural Heritage

CASES

More detailed, our course is structured in the following way:

1. Semester

Basic Module 1: This module focuses on the interdisciplinary introduction into various fields of heritage preservation. The underlying idea is to provide a common knowledge platform for all students whose original backgrounds significantly vary from each other. How cultural heritage is to be dealt with is explained; principles, legal acts, international conventions and their historical development are discussed. The ultimate objective of this module is to convey the significance, the protection requirements and the identity-building role of cultural heritage.

Basic Module 2: In this module, the focus is on conveying methods on academic work with primary and secondary sources concerning material and immaterial heritage. Moreover, the practical applicability of various instruments and procedures pertinent to heritage preservation is presented. The knowledge of how cultural heritage used to be dealt with is developed. The students moreover take part in a simulation game that helps them understand the roles played by institutional and private actors of any heritage conservation endeavour. In this module, the conceptual work on the study projects commences. After a brainstorming session, students present their raw ideas, and the feasibility thereof is analysed.

2. Semester
Advanced Module 1. Based on practical examples from various areas (museums, heritage sites, archaeological excavations), marketing and management strategies and field of actions are presented. This module focuses particularly on methods and strategies of communication with the general public and with the media. The issues of fundraising and applying for grants are discussed with particular attention, and students take part in pertinent workshops that help them conceptualise the strategy for winning funds for study projects

Advanced Module 2. The goal of this module is to analyse the practical applicability of the conveyed aspects of heritage preservation, i.a. the cultural, socio-political, legal and economic aspects of urban planning, town rehabilitation, cultural landscape care, museum and exhibition planning and cultural tourism. The study projects: Analysing the progress of works already carried out.

3. Semester
Project Module 1. The goal of this module is to confront students with the innovative methods of dealing with cultural heritage in manageable administration units (town, rural district, region) and to discuss the applicability of selected administration and management methods. These methods are presented in an international comparison by foreign experts working in cultural institutions in i.a. Amsterdam (NL), London (UK), Montpellier (FR), Poznań (PL), Sibiu (RO) and Zurich (CH). In addition, this module encompasses a seminar on the UNESCO world heritage management.

Project Module 2. This module focuses on the accomplishment of the study projects. Additional time is allocated for working in groups so that these projects can be finalised in the near future. The students receive training in soft skills (e.g. rhetoric and communication) that should further enhance their persuasiveness in their future professional life.

4.Semester
Final Module. The aim of the Final Module is to reflect upon the competences and know-how gained within the whole course. To ensure that this reflection be as practical as possible, a multiple day study trip is organised to the European city or region of the students' choice. Finally, the results of their study projects are presented in front of the whole year-group.

The study Project as a Crucial Tool in Developing Entrepreneurial Attitude

Although the study project has been an integral part of the curriculum since its beginnings in 1999, relatively less attention was paid in the first few years to actually putting the newly acquired marketing or management skills into practice. As a result, a study project was often limited to drawing up a concept and presenting its details at the very end of the course.

The obligation to actually deliver a product or a service as a result of the study project has been introduced with the change of the chair of the course in 2008. Hence, the study project plays a pivotal role throughout the whole curriculum. It has become a key field for implementing theoretical knowledge within the self-generated project ideas. It is not an easy undertaking and can definitely be referred to as the most challenging

CASES

component of the whole course. The students have to conceive an idea that is accomplishable within 3 semesters, taking into account the necessity to strategically plan all the activities that lead to a successful end. They also have to draw up a plan B that can be accomplished should any aspect of the original concept fail to work.

It is important that the students themselves choose the topic of their project, and one that is feasible in view of their place of living and their time capacities. The difficulties that appear within a given project pertain not only to the feasibility of the ideas or the accordance thereof with the needs identified with regard to both heritage and society.

Throughout the whole endeavour, the students are offered assistance from our lecturers in the fields of project management, fundraising, grant application, marketing and any other field that pertains to the given project. Which is more, the university's finance department assist the students on a regular basis in terms of accountancy and any formalities that need to be observed. On the whole, however, the project teams are expected to demonstrate their independence, creativity and – last not least – to be entrepreneurial, especially in all instances in which things fail to work according to the plan.

The entire course design is in line with our understanding of the term *entrepreneurship*, that is, recognizing opportunities and benefitting from them while exploiting one's own intellectual know-how and professional potential (see Mitchell et al., 2007). We offer our students an array of lectures and workshops that aim to make them acquainted with the theoretical and practical aspects of the management of heritage assets. As mentioned above, these skills are, as a rule, completely new to the majority of our students. We understand these skills as tools that can greatly contribute to discovering one's own entrepreneurial potential.

CASES

We believe, however, that the entrepreneurial spirit of cultural heritage professionals is something that can neither be taught in theory nor can it be actualised, unless it is tried in practice. Which is more, the extent and the ways in which this spirit may be released depends largely on one's own professional experience and their knowledge of the circumstances that pertain to their field of expertise.

Nonetheless, the latter factors may also be limiting whenever one does not dare to actually try to go beyond their usual way of handling things. Yet, this limitation can be overcome when the representatives of various fields, who usually do not collaborate with each other in their professional lives, merge their strengths within a project team. For the very purpose of identifying and fostering entrepreneurial potential, the study project phase of the course is supervised by an experienced, successful entrepreneur and practitioner in the field of culture/cultural heritage. The main task of this supervisor is to encourage members of the project teams to go beyond their conventional ways of thinking or acting while applying their newly acquired management and marketing competences. Moreover, it is the responsibility of the supervisor to regularly draw the project teams' attention to the ways in which their own potential can be first identified and then exploited by means of a creative and fruitful collaboration.

Despite this constant support, it is expected that the particular project teams act as independently as possible. Hence, an important aspect of the study projects is that the team members learn from each other. They can, on the one hand, rely on each other's previous competences, but they also gain a deeper insight and understanding for each other's activities and the pertaining difficulties. Thus, they have the chance to discover synergies with representatives of professions with which they have never collaborated before. This in turn may further trigger new, innovative business ideas.

Content Restrictions

There are practically no restrictions in terms of what can be the subject of a project as long as it clearly relates to cultural heritage. From our end, the only indication is that, at the end of the project, a product or a service should be delivered. Among the past projects, the following ideas have been accomplished:

- **Chronos Kids (Students Discover Heritage)** – a campaign addressed to primary school students to stimulate their sensibility towards built monuments in their surroundings;
- **HörMal Frankfurt** – professional audio guides for the selected heritage sites in Frankfurt (Oder), addressed to children (www.hoermal-frankfurt.de);
- **Uncomfortable Heritage of Socialism** – an international conference aiming to compare social acceptance for such heritage in Central and Eastern Europe;
- Designing **Websites** for selected, usually little known heritage sites (e.g. www.kloster-zurehregottes.de, www.musikheim.net, www.schloss-wildenbruch.de);
- **Offene Grenzen - (V)erschlossene Orte** - a bilingual printed guidebook and app on the hidden treasures and peculiarities of Frankfurt (Oder) (DE) and Słubice (PL);
- **Bückeberg - an uncomfortable monument** - a professional documentary dedicated to the contemporary ways of dealing with a site associated with Nazi-regime (bueckebergfilm.wordpress.com);
- **Oranjeroute** – a travelling exhibition depicting 33 German and Dutch towns that were important for the royal House of Orange-Nassau (www.oranjeroute.nl).

While the above examples of projects may be referred to as extremely successful or even spectacular, there have also been projects carried out with but moderate success or, in the worst cases, remained concepts merely written down and never fulfilled. The reasons for this might have been of an objective nature, such as withdrawal of the project's external partners. Or from a subjective nature, for instance, whenever the team members failed to successfully communicate with each other or to allocate their tasks efficiently. Although the results of a study project sometimes appear disappointing, even to the team members, the feedback we usually receive at the end of a whole course is that the study project constitutes the course's greatest educational added value, and our students benefit from it most.

Turning students into cultural entrepreneurs

A successful graduate receive 60 ECTS and a MA diploma which enables them to apply for a PhD course. In fact some of our graduates eventually decide to go for an academic career. Regardless of that, there are the following qualification benefits to be derived by the graduates of our course:

CASES

- Those who continue to work freelance can optimise their activities by means of new methods and competences in the fields of project management, marketing and public relations;
- Thanks to the said competences the graduates can extend their previous activities, or launch completely new business ideas. In the latter respect, the graduates are supported (also financially) by the university's agency for business start-ups (Zalewski, 2011).

Acknowledging the new qualifications gained, many of our graduates have found themselves to be able to find satisfying job positions in various heritage agencies, ministries, museums, NGOs and other cultural institutions. For us, however, the most rewarding instances have been those in which our graduates actually dared to try. They have become more self-confident in terms of their market attractiveness and mustered the courage to launch a business. Among the most successful examples, the following may be mentioned:

- **Art Detox GmbH** – a company run by two graduates – heritage conservators – whose idea was to start offering consulting services with regard to decontamination of historical objects. This idea has proved to be extremely successful and received multiple awards as a most creative business start-up in Berlin-Brandenburg region (www.art-detox.de);
- **Dobro Kultury** – a Polish foundation for the preservation of cultural heritage established by 9 graduates (various backgrounds). It has become an important actor among the heritage preservation institutions at the Polish-German border, specialising mainly in educational and awareness raising activities (www.dobrokultury.org);
- **Kulturerben GbR** – a German agency established by 5 graduates (various backgrounds). Its goals are carrying out projects in the area of heritage preservation (management of events, organising workshops, conferences, study tours, writing publications and analyses etc.) (www.kulturerben.com).

CASES

In their professional life, conservators frequently come across various limitations, difficulties or even burn-out resulting from high competition, awareness deficits in the society, and economic crises that leads to cutting expenses in the field of culture, both by public and private bodies. In the 15 years of its existence, our course has proved to be a reliable offer that helps conservators and other professionals wishing to pursue a career in the field of heritage preservation and to bring out their entrepreneurial potential, thus enhancing their chances for professional success.

About the Authors

*Prof Dr Paul Zalewski
studied art history,
monument preservation and
archaeology in Bamberg,
Heidelberg (Germany) and
Torun (Poland).
In 2000 he received his
doctorate in history of
preindustrial architecture
at the Berlin Technical
University.*

References

Abbot, A. (1988). *The System of Professions.* Chicago, IL: University of Chicago Press.

Alvesson, M. (2004). *Knowledge Work and Knowledge-Intensive Forms*. Oxford: Oxford University Press.

Drucker, P. (1993). *Innovation and Entrepreneurship*, HarperBusiness.

Freidson, E. (2001). *Professionalism: The Third Logic*. Cambridge: Polity.

Halinen, A. and Jaakkola, E. (2012). Marketing in professional service firms: turning expertise into customer perceived value. In: Reilhen, M., Werr, A. (Eds.). *Handbook of Research on Entrepreneurship in Professional Services*, Cheltenham, UK, Northampton, USA: Edward Elgar, 219-237.

Hausmann, A. and Heinze, A. (2014). Cultural Entrepreneurship – Begriffsverwendung, Verortung und Tendenzen innerhalb der Entrepreneurshipforschung, in: *Zeitschrift für KMU und Entrepreneurship*, 62. Jahrgang, Heft, 125-152. Retrieved from: http://www.ecco-eu.org/about-e.c.c.o./professional-guidelines.html

Kirzner, I. M. (1979). *Perception, Opportunity and Profit*. Chicago: Chicago University Press.

Kowalski, Ch. (2014). Mehr Frauen, gut ausgebildet, aber in unsicheren Arbeitsverhältnissen – Schlechte Aussichten für das Berufsfeld der Restaurierung? In: *Restauratoren Handbuch* 2014/2015, München: Callwey Verlag, 106-114.

Malek, M. and Ibach, P.K. (2004). Entrepreneurship. Prinzipien, Ideen und Geschäftsmodelle zur Unternehmergründung im Informationszeitalter, dpunkt.verlag.

Mitchell, R.K., Busenitz, L.W., Bird, B., Gaglio, C.M., McMullen, J.S., Morse, E.A. und Smith, J.B. (2007). The central question in entrepreneurial cognition research.In: *Entrepreneurship Theory and Practice*, 31 (1), 1-27.

Paju, M. (2007) Cultural heritage, entrepreneurship and local development - Remarks on the use of cultural heritage, in: Kobayashi, K. et.al. (Eds.). In: *Social Capital and development trends in rural areas*, vol 3., Umeå University, CERUM, & Kyoto: University, MARG.

Parowicz, I. (2014). *Marketing of Heritage Conservation Services Based on the Example of the Maltese Conservation Market*, an unpublished habilitation thesis submitted at the European University Viadrina in Frankfurt (Oder).

Pfeilstetter, R. (2014). Heritage entrepreneurship. Agency-driven promotion of the Mediterranean diet in Spain. In: *International Journal of Heritage Studies*, DOI:10.1080/13527258.2014.930502.

Powell, L., Thomas, S. and Thomas, B. (2011). Innovation and heritage entrepreneurship development in the South Wales Valleys. In: *Annals of Innovation & Entrepreneurship*, Vol. 2, No. 1.

Reilhen, M. and Werr, A. (2012). Towards a Multi-Level Approach to Studying Entrepreneurship in Professional Services, in: Reilhen, M., Werr, A. (Eds.). *Handbook of Research on Entrepreneurship in Professional Services*, Cheltenham, UK, Northampton, USA: Edward Elgar, 3-20.

Shane, S. and Venkatamaran, S. (2000). The Promise of Entrepreneurship as a Field of Research. In: *The Academy of Management Review*, 25 (1), 217-226.

Zalewski, P. (2011). Bildungsprojekte, PR-Arbeit und Management für die Denkmalpflege. Ein Ausbildungsmodell an der Europa-Universität Viadrina in Frankfurt (Oder). In: *Bildung und Denkmalpflege* (Jahrestagung der Vereinigung der Landesdenkmalpfleger in der Bundesrepublik Deutschland, Brandenburg/ H. 2010). Ed.: Brandenburgisches Landesamt für Denkmalpflege und Archäologisches Landesmuseum 2011, 86-89.

CASES

Afterwards, he became senior assistant at the Bauhaus University in Weimar and coordinated an international program for documentation of Romanesque churches in Burgundy/France.

In 2009 he has been appointed Professor for Heritage Studies and the Head of the Master's Program 'Strategies for European Cultural Heritage' at the European University Viadrina in Frankfurt (Oder).
—
zalewski@europa-uni.de

Dr Izabella Parowicz studied management (international relations/European studies) at the University of Economics in Poznań, Poland and cultural heritage preservation at the European University Viadrina in Frankfurt (Oder), Germany, where she also obtained her PhD degree (with summa cum laude) in 2006. In her PhD thesis she dealt with the issue of the effectiveness of funding architectural conservation.

She was twice awarded a Marie Curie Fellowship by the European Commission. Since 2009 she has been acting as the coordinator of the Master's course 'Strategies for European Cultural Heritage' at the European University Viadrina in Frankfurt (Oder).
—
parowicz@europa-uni.de

Ana Maria de Mattos Guimarães
Cristiane Schnack

CHALLENGES OF TRANSDISCIPLINARY CURRICULA

Abstract

This article presents an ongoing experience at Unisinos, a traditional 30.000-student University in Brazil, with the implementation of its School of Creative Industries. This School is structured around communication, design and languages and conceived of as based on four aspects: centrality of Culture, as a means of producing wealth and of belonging; Creativity; Innovation; Entrepreneurship (GUIMARÃES, 2014). The implementation of the School has brought a call to its 13 undergraduate courses for changing the envisioning of curricula, requiring a professional who is both a specialist and a connector. The proposal transdisciplinarity breaks barriers among long-established courses and allows fluidity of knowledge. This fluidity has been experienced in different scenarios: 1) Students taking educational programs other than the pre-established ones, connecting areas to solve situations they experience (BECK, 2010); 2) Professors proposing integrative academic activities to gather students from different courses who have to bring their specificities to the group working around a given problem; 3) Use of diverse methodologies, specially Design Thinking (BROWN,2009), to find solutions to real social problems in diverse communities, and Action Learning (KOLB,1984), in which students work collaboratively to find solutions for real clients, tutored by Professors coming from diverse areas of expertise. More than only products of the School implementation, these initiatives reveal an entrepreneur professor, who has become a curricula designer, finding other ways of looking at situations, to understand them deeply and thus propose creative, innovative and Culture-sensitive solutions.

CASES

Introduction

Andreia is a Brazilian student who has just finished high school and takes a University entrance examination. She passes it and is called to enrol in the course she chose. On the day of her enrolment, she receives a list of disciplines she will have to take in order to graduate and become a professional in the desired area. All disciplines contribute their share to her professional and human development. The majority of the disciplines, if not all of them, focus on specific aspects of the chosen area. She will soon have nothing than her area of expertise in mind and will focus solely on her career.

Does this sound as a course of your dreams? Perhaps. While this account describes a traditional and common profession-focused undergraduate course in Brazil, what we experience in everyday professional life is more likely to resemble a task-based routine, in which our workmates will be defined according to the task we have to solve, as will the competences required to do so. Our workmates will probably not be the ones who graduated from the same course. This means that experiencing work is constituted of interacting and integrating with other areas of expertise.

In practice, what happens is: students come to us, at University, and ask us if they can take a discipline in another area, because there is something (peripherally) related to their area that they would like to understand better — and from a different perspective.

Take the case of a student of us taking Journalism who asked the coordinator of his course if he could take a discipline related to Fashion in another undergrad course. Even though this is one case of a student asking permission to take disciplines in other courses, this is not the only one — there are several, and the number increases every year. Students are looking for connections, for diverse points of view, for transdisciplinarity. They understood what is clearly out there, in our professional career: one must establish different connections to better understand a problem-solving situation, constituting the so-called 'network society' (CASTELLS; CARDOSO, 2005). This is what enables Creativity to flourish.

Meanwhile, non-governmental institutions, such as UNCTAD, have called artists and other creative-economy professionals to, among others, establish partnerships with NGO's and Universities in order to develop and improve their careers. This called was made based on the understanding that Universities, for instance, are those institutions where there is, by nature and definition, an investment in (human) development and which would, then, be naturally able to respond to these professionals' developmental needs. What brings us here, then, is the sharing of an ongoing experience at Unisinos, a traditional 30.000-student University in Brazil, with the implementation of its School of Creative Industries. This implementation was triggered by the institution itself, which, as a Jesuit University, has long established a communitarian perspective on education. This means Unisinos has opened itself to local and global configurations, which are not only related to Education, but also to Technology, Science and Culture. While discussing new possibilities of acting in the educational scenario, Unisinos proposes that the areas of expertise it offers be organized around what is at the core of each of them. This is when the School of Creative Industries is born, bringing together undergraduate courses, graduate programs and extension courses - and this is the start of the story being told and shared here. What is being shared are less the results of this story than the process itself — and the learnings along the way.

Creative Industries and the way a School of Creative Industries is born

In 2012, forty professors, responding to a University's call for strategic planning, define what would become the School of Creative Industries. Since that time, the University has understood that this School would be structured around communication, design and languages and based on four aspects: centrality of Culture, as a means of producing wealth and of belonging; Creativity; Innovation; and Entrepreneurship (GUIMARÃES, 2014). Organizing academic doings in terms of Schools appeared as a possibility of increasing fluidity of knowledge and experience to take place among the courses the University offers.[1]

What supports the School of Creative Industries and aligns it to the sector of Creative Economy/Industry is the understanding that Creative Industry is based on Culture, seen as possibilities of human development, as well as on Creativity, languages and design. This means that Culture also enhances economic development, fostering the development of (economic) activities which rely on cultural expressions, which does not deny the importance of Culture as an essentially human expression, and does not forget its symbolic importance (BENTZ et al 2013).

CASES

---

[1] *The other Schools Unisinos has: School of Humanities, School of Health, School of Law, School of Management and Business, and Polytechnic School.*

Though the sector is yet not well conceptually defined in terms of having a single definition (UNCTAD, 2010), it has pulled together Creativity, Culture and technology as its recurrent defining concepts, and has, at Unisinos, determined the courses which constitute the School. The School of Creative Industries, at Unisinos, is thus constituted by the courses directly conceived of as courses dealing with '*communication*', '*design*' and '*languages*'. There are 13 undergrad courses, 5 Graduate Programs, 9 Specialization courses, and 1 MBA.

The implementation of the School has brought a call to its 13 undergraduate courses for changing the envisioning of curricula, requiring a professional who is both a specialist and a connector seeker, someone who knows the potential of his/her area of expertise, but also understands that connection and transdisciplinarity enhance this expertise and make it useful to contemporary needs. The proposal transdisciplinarity breaks barriers among long-established courses and allows fluidity of knowledge within them. This fluidity has been experienced in different scenarios:

1. Students taking educational programs other than the pre-established ones, connecting areas to solve situations they experience (Beck, 2010);
2. Professors proposing integrative academic activities to gather students from different courses who have to bring their specificities to the group working around a given problem;
3. Use of diverse methodologies, specially Design Thinking (Brown,2009), to find solutions to real social problems in diverse communities, and Action Learning (Kolb,1984), in which students work in collaboration to find solutions for real clients, tutored by Professors coming from diverse areas of expertise, and
4. Professors and researchers working on a joint venture to propose an MBA which reflects the needs and capabilities of the School. These are the initiatives being reported on in the following sections.

While at an institutional level the creation of the School was achieved on July 2013, its (effective) existence only occurred after other achievements were experienced - which has already happened. According to Bentz et al (2013), this existence entails a three-space existence: a) real existence, b) symbolic existence and c) imaginary existence.

The launch of the School

Creative Economy/Industry requires a multidimensional and collaborative approach, which is seen as opposite to the configurations of traditional market. Taken to our educational level, conceptualizing and conceiving of the School of Creative Industries required a '*joint venture*', one in which professors, researchers, directors and other staff came from different areas of expertise and worked together to construct a common identity, one which would not erase specificities of each area. Throughout several months, two groups met on a regular basis. The first worked on the definition of arenas of action and planned strategically the way the School would act. This group still meets and is formed by the coordinators of the courses which compose the School and other invited professors. They have decided both on strategic actions and plans and routine activities the School takes part in.

CASES

The second group was responsible for thinking the moment the School would become '*visible*' to the greater audience. In 2013, this group decided, then, that there would be an official launch of the School. This launch, firstly proposed by the dean of the School, was thought of and planned by a group of professors of different areas of expertise and office workers who saw this opportunity as a learning opportunity for everyone. Thus, not only did participants learn about the official existence of the School, but also about Creative Industry and its potentialities as a sector. The event was divided in two different moments: a first meeting with two key speakers in the area, internationally and nationally responsible for implementing and configuring the area. After these talks, participants could take part in several workshops, which developed different aspects related to the School. Unisinos professors offered the workshops and had, also, to learn more about the School, and then plan their contribution to this understanding. On the other hand, participants, who were students-to-be, potential students, actual students, Unisinos' staff, partners, media and the general interested public, had the chance to have different experiences, through the workshops and the talks, related to the School. For some of these, the event represented a possibility of knowing more about Unisinos, for others, about Creative Industries and, for most of them, knowing more about Creative Industries at Unisinos.

We can say that, at this institutional level, the wash-back effects we experienced with the launch of the School have shown us that this School is not merely an institutional and administrative act, but a whole new way of experiencing the University. At the same time, however, it has also given us an idea of how many challenges we would face while integrating areas and inviting people to leave their comfort zone.

After this first event, the group decided this event should be transformed into an annual meeting, in which new approaches, new developments in the area could be communicated both to our internal public - students, professionals and partners - and to our external (or potential) public - students-to-be, for instance.

Besides this launch, the University has experienced several other initiatives, which are reported on in the following sections. We organized the presentation of the initiatives as: (a) pedagogically-sensitive initiatives, which will be presented in the following section, (b) taken at an institutional and academic level, which will be presented afterwards, and (c) taken at an institutional and academic level, differing from the previous because it is a result of a group of professors and researchers which create a new arena of action, which is the School's MBA.

Constructing and Implementing the School of Creative Economy in the classroom

In Brazil, after enrolling for a discipline at an undergraduate course, students get to know their professor, the syllabus of the discipline, and what is expected from them. Everything is planned previously, and the product of the semester is a matter of walking through a (known) path, aware that what happens is what people do with the plan (COUGHLAN; DUFF, 1994). What has happened at Unisinos is the increasing number of projects in which the result is co-constructed with the students along the academic term, which means it does not bring the whole semester planned.

CASES

These experiences offer students different views on their subject matter, which enable them to evaluate their own doing from different perspectives. Seen as interdisciplinary projects (FAZENDA, 2002), the possibility of dealing with a same situation with contributions from different areas resembles what happens in real life, in which different areas of expertise will be called into action according to local and situational needs. We will highlight two examples, both of each taking place in Letras/Modern Languages and Advertising and Marketing Undergrad Courses. They were created from the desire professors had to make students establish different relations with their subject matter, with their courses, the University and their colleagues.

The first experience has been developed between the discipline of 'Poetry', which belongs to the BA in Language and Literature (BALL) and 'Visual Programming', which belongs to Advertising and Marketing (A&M). The main objective, in this experience, was to offer students the chance to produce something targeted at a real 'partner', one who would apply concepts which are specific to his/her area of expertise and thus create a 'new' product. Students do not meet, personally, but the results of the work of each group have been, each academic term, shared with the partner group. In practice, this experience has worked the following way: BALL students study about poetry and produce, towards the end of the semester, a poem triggered by some readings and on a common theme to all. These poems are then read and studied by A&M students, who will have the responsibility of translating them to a different format, keeping the original idea printed in other apparently unrelated forms and packaging, a strategy known as 'Blur Marketing'. In a certain academic term, A&M students worked on the poems so that the original idea could be printed onto cups. In another term, ecologic bags carrying the poems printed on them were produced. When these products are ready, BALL students have the chance to experience Literature on a product which can be consumed in other forms[2].

The second experience was born after systematic and routine accounts Letras' students produced in terms of using technology, and specifically video production, as a resource for teaching Foreign Languages. Understanding that teachers need expertise in an area which is not their area by nature, BALL professor sought a partner in order to qualify students' professional role, so that they could respond to social and technological demands. Technology has long been considered an essential tool to be explored in the classroom, and a possibility for students to experience language in a different format when it comes to learning a second language (LEFFA; IRALA, 2012). At the same time, A&M professor was seeking a partner who could help her students in terms of interacting with potential real interlocutors, those who could change the way students conceive of the final product of the discipline she teaches. From these identified needs and known Cultures in the hearing process (BROWN, 2009), professors planned what would become a joint semester, in which students from both courses would have to come to terms with the specificities of their courses mediated by the perspective of the other. Throughout a semester, students discuss educational topics which, in the end, will have to trigger the joint production of a short movie. In this experience, students interact with both areas of expertise, face-to-face, on a weekly basis. In the end of the semester, they have the chance to have learned both the other area of expertise and about their area through the eyes of the other.

CASES

---

[2]Some pictures and more information can be found in
http://www.unicos.cc/alunos-de-comunicacao-produzem-ecobags/

The process, which is enriched by its more flexible approach, has been a challenge for students, who realize and ask for new ways of learning, but who also have to learn how to learn in this new configuration. We have seen that it takes some time for students, and professors, to understanding that this new configurations are also valid learning experiences, because it challenges what is assumed as '*class*'.

Creating a concrete Space for Creative Industry in undergrad Courses

While these two experiences, which are not the only ones at Unisinos, have been motivated by professors who have taken ownership of the process of academic and professional knowledge construction and student development, there are other initiatives which have been triggered by institutional acts and implemented by a careful strategic plan to involve professors and researchers of different areas in a collaborative way.

Even though the Institution has long valued individual and collective initiatives, it understands that enabling students to experience the School of Creative Industries is its institutional responsibility. This means that initiatives which transcend the borders of each area of expertise are as important as creating a concrete space for the School to exist. This has been done through the offering of two new disciplines which will be taken by all School of Creative Industries students. One of them is centred on the relation between Creative and Social Innovation, and is called Creative Industries and Social Innovation, while the other has the development of Entrepreneurship as its core objective, and is called Entrepreneurship and Innovation in Creative Industries.

Following the same reasoning, what is aimed at here is not only related to equipping students with theoretical concepts and practical techniques so that they can innovate and create. Design Thinking (BROWN, 2009) is one of the methodologies chosen in this case. However, at the heart of the decision is the idea that students have to learn about truly connecting areas to actually solve situations they experience (BECK, 2010) in diverse communities, living Action Learning (KOLB, 1984) as a practice, and not as theory. Professors teaching these disciplines come from the School's courses and have come closer and have systematically developed this knowledge. This means that, in Letras courses, for instance, a professor who is commonly associated to theories of second language learning can teach one of these new disciplines. So can also a professor who, in A&M courses, is rapidly related to visual programming. The advantage is that those professors will be able to establish a close connection to real situations professionals-to-be experience in the area of expertise of the course.

What enables a professor to teach these new disciplines is his/her professional trajectory at a first place. Besides this, the University has proposed a series of workshops in which these professors meet, develop and recognize themselves as professors dealing with these areas of expertise. What happens in these workshops is that professors develop both a broad and a specific understanding on Innovation, Entrepreneurship and Creativity, and are invited, then, to rethink the area of expertise of the courses they teach at from these three conceptual perspectives.

In the long term, this initiative will be offered to other professors, who will be able to learn about new areas and to learn about their own area from a different perspective, impacting as well on the group of disciplines they teach.

In this case, we have faced, once more, the challenge of making students recognize these disciplines as important for their professional development and career. So far, not so many students have enrolled for the disciplines. Increasing this number is our aim now.

A further Step: Specializing and Managing in Creative Markets

After the second year of existence, the School of Creative Industries launches its MBA in Creative Markets: Innovation scenarios. This has become possible due to the University's investment in enabling professionals to come together to discuss the format, the purpose and the main concepts which constitute the course[3].

There are two relevant (interrelated) aspects to consider: the process and the product. The process, as said before, entailed efforts from different professionals who act in diverse areas which constitute the School. During staff and informal meetings, professors had the chance to discuss the global format of the course and the contribution their specific areas had to the MBA. From this intense interaction, a proposal was made possible, and additional negotiation was established: the actual design of each of the components of this course. Design, communication, Culture, technology and arts are the main territories covered by the course, all of which sharing a common thread: Innovation and Creativity as resources that organize and constitute them.

The construction of the course showed some challenges as well. Professors negotiating with other professors, who belong to different areas, had to learn about these other areas as well. Once the course qualifies as an MBA, the course also benefits from an approach to management. This means that managerial processes will be studied closely from the perspective of Creativity, Innovation, Culture, design and technology. It differs, thus, from other courses being offered in the sector of Creative Economy/Industry also because of this approach to business management. Another differential is the fact that throughout the course students will experience '*Project laboratory*' as a discipline which will connect groups of disciplines that would otherwise be offered in a one-after-the-other fashion.

The very nature of this MBA, constructed as a joint enterprise, in a co-working space, gives the tone of what has come to be understood as the School's responsibility: take students, professors and researchers to experience their work in collaboration with different areas of expertise, enlarging and reconceptualising each area individually.

Preliminary achievements and Challenges to come

Any structural reorganization takes effort and time. Implementing a new course of actions means and has meant, for the School of Creative Industries, implementing a new and reconfigured way of dealing with knowledge and exercising one's own professional live.

---

[3] *Retrieved from: http://www.unisinos.br/mba/mercados-criativos-cenarios-de-inovacao/presencial/porto-alegre*

The School has been seen as a space defined as a real, a symbolic and an imaginary space (BENTZ et al, 2013), once it requires real and concrete conditions to create and enable the development of actions, it defines social bonds established by different actors who belong to the School, and it creates social representation among institution(s), people, and groups. In this sense, we may say that achievements can be noticed because these three spaces have been established, at different levels and times.

The challenges foreseen are related to monitoring, maintaining and intensifying each space, being able to assess each of them separately and also in relation to the others. The main challenge, and also the main responsibility the School has taken, is related to the way people experience the School, once it should not be taken only as an institutional decision, but as reconfiguring the relation professionals and students establish to knowledge development.

We have, thus, also pointed out the challenges faced in this construction. These challenges are mainly related to the way people perceive their areas and what they expect should happen at a University level. Above all, more than only products of the School implementation, the path taken reveals an entrepreneur professor, who has become a curricula designer, finding other ways of looking at situations, to understand them deeply and thus propose creative, innovative and Culture-sensitive solutions.

CASES

References

BARBOSA, M.C.S. Por que voltamos a falar e a trabalhar com a Pedagogia de Projetos? In: *Projeto - Revista de Educação, Porto Alegre: Projeto*, v.3, n.4

BECK, U. (2010). *Sociedade de Risco. Rumo a uma outra Modernidade*. São Paulo: Editora 34, 2010

BENTZ, I.M.G; GUIMARAES, A.M.M.; LADEIRA, J. (2015). *Projeto Escolas: o desafio da coneitacao escola de Industria Creativa: Comunicação, Design e Linguagens*. Retrieved from: http://www.unisinos.br/images/escolas/apresentacao-escola-industria-criativa.pdf. Last access on: Jan 08, 2015

BROWN, T. (2009). *Change by Design: How design thinking transforms organizations and inspires Innovations*. Harper-Collins e-book

CARVALHO, J. (2012). *A Educação para a Economia Criativa*. Retrieved from: http://www.educacaopublica.rj.gov.br/biblioteca/educacao/0328.html. Last access: Jan 08, 2015

CASTELLS, M. (2003). *O poder da Identidade. A era da informação: Economia, sociedade e cultura*. Lisboa: Fundação Calouste Gulbenkian.

CASTELLS, M; CARDOSO, G. (2005). *The Network Society: from Knowledge to Policy*. Washington, DC: Johns Hopkins Center for Transatlantic Relations

COUGHLAN, P.; DUFF, P. (1994). Same task, different activities: Analysis of a second language acquisition task from an activity theory perspective. In: J. P. Lantolf and G. Appel (Eds.): *Vygotskian approaches to second language research* (pp. 173-193). Norwood, NJ: Ablex

About the Authors

Prof Dr Ana Maria de Mattos Guimarães is full professor at the Applied Linguitics Graduate Program and Dean of School of Creative Industries at Vale do Sinos University (UNISINOS). She has published articles and books in the area of language development, language learning and teaching and literacy development. As the Dean of the School of Creative Industries, she is also interested in cultural aspects related to innovating in teaching, design and leadership.
—
anamguima@terra.com.br

Prof Dr Cristiane Schnack is a professor at the Arts and Humanities Department at Vale do Sinos University (UNISINOS), mainly working with teacher development and language teaching methodologies.
She coordinates a specialization course in Teaching Foreign Languages and an MBA in Creative Markets: Innovation scenarios. She has been working on connecting different areas of expertise and developing interdisciplinary projects at University.
She has published articles and chapters to books in language socialization, literacy and the analysis of talk-in-interaction.

⸻

crischnack@yahoo.com.br

FAZENDA, Ivani Catarina Arantes.(1984). Integração e interdisciplinaridade no ensino brasileiro: efetividade ou. In: Kolb, D.A (1984) *Experiential Learning: Experience as the Source of Learning and Development*, New Jersey: Prentice-Hall

GUIMARAES, A.M.M. (2014). *Lançamento da Escola de Indústria Criativa.* Porto Alegre: Unisinos. Lecture, 2014

HOWKINS, J. (2001). *The Creative Economy*. London: Penguin Books

KOLB, D.A (1984). *Experiential Learning: Experience as the Source of Learning and Development*. New Jersey: Prentice-Hall

LEFFA, V.; IRALA, V. (2012). O Vídeo e a construção da solidariedade na aprendizagem da LE. In: SCHEYERL, D.; SIQUEIRA, S. (Org.) *Materiais Didáticos para o Ensino de Línguas na Contemporaneidade: Contestações e Proposições*. Salvador: Editora da UFBA, 2012, pp. 83-108

CASES

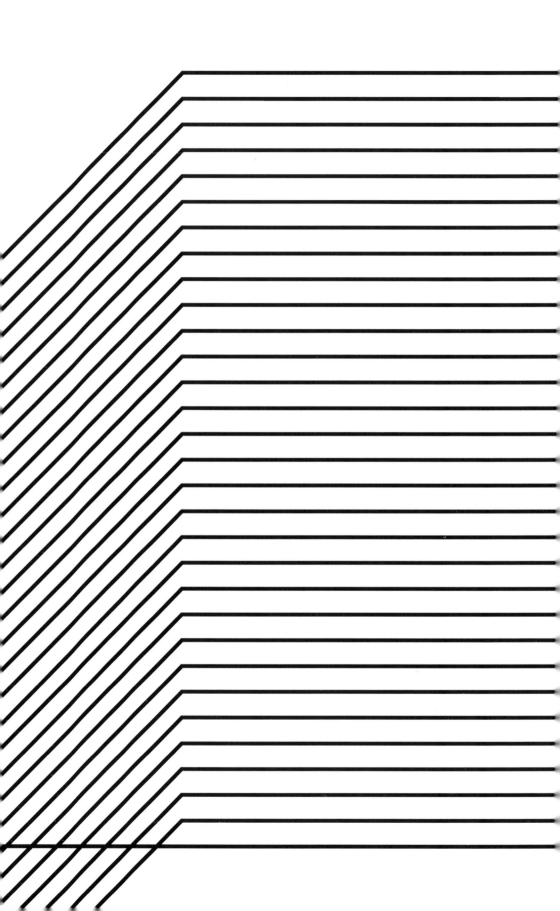

PRACTICE

Robert Davis
Julia Calver
Steven Parker

DISRUPTING DISCIPLINES
MEETING THE CHALLENGE OF THE INDUSTRY-READY AGENDA FOR THE FREELANCE CREATIVE PRACTITIONER

PRACTICE

Abstract

From the late 1990s, successive UK governments have developed a political narrative that presents the cultural industries as a successful and vital component of the economy. Running in parallel with this economic agenda has been an educational imperative, in which the university sector has had to integrate an ability to deliver graduates ready for employment or who have demonstrable entrepreneurial skills. We argue that the notion of an industry-ready workforce in the cultural industries fails to reflect the freelance, self-employed, portfolio or micro-industry models that make up a large proportion of the industry workforce. Drawing on research with industry practitioners, recent graduates and higher education students, our research in the field of music production points to the need to engage with the industry-ready agenda in terms of the freelance practitioner/consultant. Using case studies from the music industry, we explore an initiative for developing entrepreneurial effectiveness to address the implications of the industry-ready agenda.

We argue that for higher education, to actively promote and prepare students to undertake a freelance career, a more innovative approach than the existing rhetoric around employability and entrepreneurship may be required. By placing the freelance practitioner at the centre of the industry-ready agenda, a number of tensions emerge. These tensions challenge existing educational structures, be they physical, pedagogical or ideological. Giving the freelance practitioner, a voice invites us to disrupt disciplines and to allow real entrepreneurial competencies to be developed in the university environment.

Economic and Educational Context in the UK

While the importance of the cultural industries in developing the UK economy can be traced back to the 1980s (Hesmondhalgh & Pratt, 2005), it was not until the late 1990s that the UK government attempted to actively influence the economic potential of the creative economy through a sustained series of policy initiatives and commissioned reports. In 1997 the newly elected Labour Government created the Department of Culture, Media and Sport (DCMS), which published the *Creative Industries Mapping Document* (DCMS, 1998), representing their first attempt to quantify the economic and employment potential of the creative industries. Alongside this initiative, the National Advisory Committee on Creative and Cultural Education (NACCCE), reporting jointly to the Secretary for State for Education and Employment and the Secretary of State for Culture, Media and Sport, produced *All Our Futures: Creativity, Culture and Education* (NACCCE, 1999). The NACCCE report recommended that the key areas of industrial and educational policy be brought together in order to support the develop-ment of key corporations '*in the fields of communications, information, entertainment, science and technology*' (NACCCE, 1999: 19). These initiatives were to develop into a significant narrative which was to have, and continues to have, a profound effect on educational policy in the UK.

Initial estimates prepared by the DCMS in 1998 suggested that the cultural industries generated annual revenues of over £57 billion and employed more than 1.7 million people (NACCCE, 1999, pp.19-20). By 2014, these estimates had been upgraded to indicate that the Creative Industries, now a clearly defined subset of the Creative Economy, accounted for 5.2% of Gross Value Added (GVA for 2012) or £71.4 billion. Employment for the creative economy accounts for an estimated 2.55 million jobs, and the creative industries itself is estimated to account for 1.68 million jobs or 5.6% of the UK work-force (DCMS, 2014, p. 5). The economic strength of the creative industries has become such that in November 2014 a newly created non-Governmental organization, *The Creative Industries Federation* (CIF) has been created, with support from more than 220 companies including film, television, publishing, fashion and the arts. The organization is being promoted as an independent lobbying group that will represent the creative industries in the same way that the Confederation of British Industries (CBI) represents independent employers.

The relationship between higher education and the economy was cemented in 2009 when the Department for Business, Innovation and Skills incorporated higher education as part of its remit. Further reports such as *Higher Ambitions: The Future of Universities in a Knowledge Economy* (2013) aimed to build a '*consensus between individuals, government, and employers as to how our higher education system should be supported, adapted and expanded*' (BIS, 2013). The implication of the report was that major changes would be required to '*expand new types of higher education programmes that widen opportunities… to reflect the reality of the modern working lives*' (BIS, 2013, p. 6).

While policy shifts and the reorganization of government departments pointed towards a bringing together of education and industry, the picture emerging from publications such as the *Manifesto for the Creative Economy* (NESTA, 2013) provided a stark reminder of the disconnect between education and employment.

Academic Education

Evidence suggests that most universities haven't been producing the kind of talent that the creative industries demand. We see this in the poor employment outcomes of graduates from creative media specialist degrees evidenced in *Next Gen* (2012). Only 12 per cent of those graduating from games courses secured employment in the industry within six months of leaving university (Bakhshi et al. 2013, p. 103).

The implication of this report is that there is a potential disconnect between the skills used in education, and the skills demanded by employers that policy initiatives alone have failed to reconcile. In his reflections on the music industries, O'Hara points out that, '*There are two parallel worlds – one of a growing field of education and the other of an increasingly complex industry that largely ignores the existence of the education programs. There has not been much thought given to best practice in linking the courses to the as yet undeclared needs of the music industry*' (O'Hara. 2014, p 28).

PRACTICE

Drawing on a longitudinal study of creative graduates, Ball noted that '*45 per cent of graduates had worked on a freelance basis and around one-quarter had started a business during their early careers… Self-employment is a serious career entry strategy and feature of portfolio working, as well as reflecting the way in which work is organized in the creative sector – a predominantly contract economy*' (Ball *et al.*, 2010, p. 28).

Putting Freelance Practitioners at Central Focus

We have presented this extended contextual account and outlined some of the political, educational and philosophical narratives that have influenced our thinking. The UK account will, in some ways, mirror the experience of other countries whose governments will have developed their own response to the cultural industries and from this their own educational agendas (European Commission, 2006, 2008; World Economic Forum, 2009). For the UK, while policy is set centrally, it is for each university or higher education provider to determine their response to the work-ready agenda.

As a University, we are also concerned with the wider cultural economy and have a wide range of courses including film, game design, performing arts, art and design and music, as well as a range of courses in events management and related areas of tourism and hospitality. Our institutional response is, as follows most institutions in the university sector, centred around a number of institutional and school-based initiatives including careers services, boot camps, networking events, grant funding, business incubators, work placements, visiting industry professionals, work-placements, work-simulated assignments, and the employment of industry experienced academic staff.

The changing characteristics of the music industries over the past few years (Williamson, & Cloonan, 2007) underline an additional problem for developing a direct relationship between higher education courses and employment, a situation which is replicated in other areas of the creative and cultural industries. In addition, the agenda has been dominated by a discourse which has privileged the '*interaction between large organizations and SMEs*' (Culkin & Malick, 2011). However, this may be an inappropriate model for the cultural industries and for the music industry in particular, which has, according to Ball et al., seen '*a drift away from work in medium-sized enterprises to micro-businesses [which] is consistent with recent changes in the sector*' (Ball et al., 2010, p. 3).

Our concern here is for the freelance practitioner, whose existence can easily become lost in the focus on employment in larger organizations or small to medium enterprises. For the past three years we have established a research program which has focused on freelance practitioners working in the music industry with the aim of exploring the transition to employment in this field. We have used semi-structured interviews with a range of established industry professionals, recent alumni who have gained a foothold in the industry and current undergraduates who have expressed or demonstrated an interest in working professionally within the music industry.

The Apprenticeship Model

In our field study it became clear that many of the experienced professionals who entered the profession before 1980 did so through an apprenticeship scheme. The nature of this apprenticeship varied but for some, this was largely informal situational learning.

*'Probably for those first couple of months, as a tea boy/runner,
I was probably 9 to 5 office hours just to see was I reliable, capable of getting the tea,
getting the sandwiches, getting the coffee machine going every morning and doing whatever else was asked. By three months it was decided that I could be left on a session.'*

For some, the three months could be years (six was the most time spent as a runner)
but for those who went through this journey, this period was invaluable.

*'The longer you spend in watching people making decisions that
you really learn to hear inside music, your ear becomes naturally critical...In the same
way that a Navy admiral would make instant decisions with an educated and experienced insight, it's the same thing with making records but you learn that from just spending
a lot of time with people.'*

People skills emerged as an important theme as professionals discussed their early
experiences, including an awareness of their own skills and abilities:

*'There was no formal training it was 'dive straight in' and one of
the earliest lessons I learnt from that, which is a very important credo that I still hold
today was to not pretend you know something when you don't. If someone asks you and
you don't know how to do it, just say 'I'm sorry, I don't know'. I still do that now.'*

The apprenticeship model is one which addresses education from a situational viewpoint: apprentices are immersed in the world of work and it was seen as not only a
place to meet musicians but also to learn from them. Learning in this kind of situation
brings out a number of skills, many of which can be mapped onto what the Quality
Assurance Agency for Higher Education in UK refer to as an *'entrepreneurial mindset'*
(QAA, 2012, p. 13) which includes:

- aspects of personality and social identity
- personal ambition and goals
- personal confidence and resilience
- self-discipline and personal organisation
- understanding of one's own motivation
- ability to go beyond perceived limitations and achieve results
- tolerance of uncertainty, ambiguity, risk, and failure
- personal values: ethical, social and environmental awareness.

Developing the Entrepreneurial Mind-set

Developing the entrepreneurial mind-set might not, however, be straightforward as
one of our professional interviewees pointed out.

*'You can't make a valid comparison between apprenticeships and
formal education because they serve different purposes. On the educational end it's geared
towards the end result of the piece of paper you get, or specific goals in this module or that
project. If you're in a real-time studio situation you're talking about being in a commercial environment and everything that goes along with that.'*

This critical appraisal offered a specific industry perspective from which to view our courses and consider the strengths of the apprenticeship approach and what skills it develops in comparison to our present approach. We were also aware that the apprenticeship model did not offer all the answers. Although not specifically related to the cultural industry, Unwin's (2007) study of apprenticeships in England noted that while *'just over 50 per cent of apprentices achieve the prescribed qualifications, in some service sectors, achievement rates are staggeringly low: for example, 16 per cent in health and social care, 31 per cent in hospitality'* (2007: 118). There are no figures available from the music industry but we from our study, we might have to conclude that even at its height, the apprenticeship route is not necessarily a successful gateway to the music industry as an independent freelancer.

We undertook a further set of interviews but this time with students who completed a simulated industry experience at the university, where visiting freelance musicians work with students on a defined project over a two week period. Initial comments from the student group mirrored some of the comments from the professionals group and focused on the importance of social skills.

> *'I think [the most important skill] was people skills, pure people skills... you had to get to know someone quite quickly.... and you needed to have a relationship with the person you are working with... it makes it much more comfortable, a much more enjoyable place to work.'*

His master/apprentice setting created a different experience for the students. Working with other people foregrounded a different set of parameters to those normally found in a student-led recording experience. The students discussed their experience of the recording process noting that,

> *'...you have to keep the flow of the sessions.....when we do modules at 'uni', the flow doesn't necessarily matter....you are normally recording yourself or your friend, so you just get on with it.'*

When asked about the overall experience that the employability experience provided, one student put it succinctly by suggesting that,

> *'We learned more in the employability fortnight than we had learned on the course so far...even if it was only a simulated working environment...'*

The employability Fortnight we offered

The experience provided an opportunity for students to benefit from working in a simulated environment it is a limited experience. The activity would accord with O'Hara's suggestion that *'emphasis should be placed on opportunity formation'* linked to students developing *'social and interpersonal skills'* (O'Hara, 2014: 36). This kind of experiential learning seems to raise an understanding of the importance of social and interpersonal skills, but we would ask how well this awareness might prepare students for working at a professional's level.

PRACTICE

QAA guidelines on enterprise and employability suggest that students pass '*through the stages of enterprise awareness, entrepreneurial mind-set and entrepreneurial capability to achieve entrepreneurial effectiveness*' (QAA, 2012, p. 24). What we saw from the employability experience was the development of the awareness stage with some understanding of the mind-set required. Of the five students in the interview group, one in particular demonstrated '*entrepreneurial capability*' in the way he began to work with people, organize the schedule, and took responsibility for the recording process. One reason for this capability could have been that this student had been able to shadow a dubbing engineer working on a drama series for the BBC shortly before the employability experience. In addition to this experience, the same student was able to take part in the Joint Audio Media Education Support summer course (JAMES, 2013) where he was nominated as '*student of the week*'. These experiences provided a way to develop his entrepreneurial capability both inside and outside of the university environment and provided a positive range of experience for the student to launch his career as a freelance practitioner.

Using this model, we began to explore ways in which students who moved rapidly through the stages of awareness and demonstrated a strong mind-set and capability could be developed using aspects of the apprenticeship model. One such student that emerged was Christian, who was a student on our MSc Sound design course. Christian had quickly established himself as the '*go to*' person for anyone wanting sound on their film and it was clear that his mind-set and capability were of a highly developed. We approached a local post-production company using our industry contacts and provided an opportunity for Christian to shadow an experienced dubbing engineer, who was working on a post-production project for the BBC.

Christian undertook this role as a research component of his final project and his report focused on two significant areas of learning. The first was an understanding of the strict technical standards necessary for the delivery of television programmes to the EBU R128 standard. The second factor concerned what he called '*studio skills*' which were the '*interpersonal skills that are crucial when working with directors and producers, who spent a lot of time to make their vision [into] a television programme... In the end, it is a team working process, with the aim of creating a series that is great to watch, sonically enjoyable... and in terms of content an interesting and thrilling experience*' (Christian, 2014).

On completion of the shadowing experience, we were able to provide a live project from Ideas Tap, which our Film School uses as part of their strategy to support progression into the industry. Christian was given the role of sound designer for an animation project called *Arlene*[1] directed by London based animation studios, Sherbert.[2] Christian was able to put into practice all the skills and aptitudes acquired from his previous experience in the post-production environment to produce an excellent finished product. What was also very much in evidence was the professional approach he had in the dubbing meeting. His entrepreneurial effectiveness was demonstrated by the way he took the lead in organizing the necessary resources, schedules, managing

http://www.sherbet.co.uk/clips/235/arlene-13-08-14
http://www.sherbet.co.uk/

collaborators and ensuring all studio deadlines were met. This was all the more impressive because he was networking with a range of people while living at home at the European continent.

Reconciling Education and Industry

We are aware that our approach so far is very limited in the number of students who can take advantage of these opportunities but what we offer is more of a progression through the stages of *'awareness, mind-set, capability and effectiveness'*. Other students have benefited from this type of approach and have gone on to establish a freelance profile as a practitioner, with various degrees of success. However, not all students would be able to benefit from this direct experience in a freelance role and the step from *'awareness'* to *'capability'*. In addition, we would suggest that not all students would want such an opportunity. The capability to work in a freelance environment is something that comes from a particular mind-set and any mismatch could be problematic for student, freelance professional and the University. We are now in the process of developing new studio facilities that will act as intermediate spaces for those students who need more support to develop their capabilities prior to working in a freelance environment.

Reconciling the different needs of education and industry has been highlighted as a problematic existing, as they do, in separate worlds. Our approach here has been to find ways in which we can link the world of education and employment as a freelancer in a productive, positive and sustainable way. As educationalists, we are tasked with, amongst other things, *'creating learning environments that encourage entrepreneurial behaviour'* and *'exploiting opportunities for enhancing the student experience'* (QAA, 2012, p. 22).

If we were to effectively exploit learning opportunities by creating environments that encouraged entrepreneurial behaviours, what would that educational world look like? How can we reconcile the need for the compartmentalization of students into faculties, schools, year groups, courses and modules? The world of research, for which we are also responsible, embraces intra-, inter-, multi, and trans-disciplinary approaches which is generally seen as a positive step for research. Yet at the same time, research in the UK is categorized according to criteria from the Research Assessment Council which recognizes 36 categories of research including subjects such as Chemistry; Physics; Computer science and informatics; Philosophy; Art and design (history, practice and theory); Music, Drama, Dance and Performing Arts; Communication, Cultural and Media Studies.

Traditionally, education has, directly or indirectly, always prepared people for work. The challenge of the enterprise narrative as the *'engine fuelling innovation, employment generation and economic growth'* (World Economic Forum, 2009, p.6) has been to focus the range of activities in higher education; moving towards an employment-ready imperative.

In many ways, this narrative can be seen to be little more than a simplistic cause and effect model that fails to acknowledge the complexities of the employment environment. The freelance practitioner adds to this complexity, because it may take several years for someone to establish themselves in their professional world. In his discussion of

PRACTICE

contemporary theories of learning, Illeris (2003) suggests that to manage the complex functions of modern life, we need to consider how to combine the '*complex totality of traditional and up-to-date knowledge, orientation and overview... with professional and everyday life skills and a broad range of personal qualities such as flexibility, openness, independence, responsibility, creativity, etc. ... for learning theory and educational practice it is an evident challenge to develop a concept of learning that is able to... include the acquisition of the whole range of different competencies at stake*' (Illeris, 2003, p. 397).

Disrupting the higher Education Agenda

The combination of economic change, policy documentation and a more fragmented employment environment has already contributed to significant disruption to the educational agenda here in the UK. The impact of policy initiatives taken in the latter part of the 1990s are still working their way through the system. The current government has signalled its willingness to disrupt the higher education agenda through further policy changes and by merging higher education with business and enterprise departments. Documentation from advisory bodies, such as the HEFC and QAA, provide a framework to support these changes. However, the overall narrative linking higher education with economic generation and employment growth, may find it impossible to take into account the complexity of the working environment.

Further disruption has come from the students themselves. In their work on the experience economy, Pine and Gilmore argue that '*experiences should yield transformations... the individual partaking in the experience often wants something more lasting than memory... People enroll in... school because they want to affect their professional and financial well-being*' (Pine and Gilmore, 2014, p. 26). New courses that appear to directly address the needs of the cultural industries have been criticized as not fulfilling the promise of employment (Bakhshi et al. 2013). However, their comments do not take into account the difficulties of the freelance practitioner, who may take many years to establish a strong footing in the industry and for whom direct entry into the freelance profession takes place over a timeframe that cannot be captured by statistics alone.

Stronger narratives may be required to frame the experience of the freelance practitioner and his or her progress after graduation. Our example here is only one of several that provide both empirical and anecdotal information to inform our educational practice. Bögenhold, Heinonen and Akola's (2014) recent discussion of the '*myth*' of entrepreneurship provides an interesting critique of the entrepreneurial narrative by alerting us to the complexities inherent in preparing for employment as a freelance practitioner. We might use this approach to critique the myth of the academic discipline and ask if the complex, dynamically changing and increasingly fragmented world of the cultural industries is met by an equally complex and dynamically driven transformative curriculum experience.

PRACTICE

About the Authors

Dr Robert Davis is Senior Lecturer at Leeds Beckett University teaching across undergraduate degrees in Music Performance and post graduate programs in Music Production and Music for Film.

References

Acs, Z., Szerb, L., and Autio, E. 2014. **Global Entrepreneurship and Development Index 2014.** Washington, US: The Global Entrepreneurship and Development Institute.

Ashton, D. (2010). Productive passions and everyday pedagogies: Exploring the industry-ready agenda in higher education. In **Art, Design & Communication in Higher Education** 9 (1), 41–56.

Bakhshi, H., Hargreaves, I., & Mateos-Garcia, J. (2013). *A Manifesto for the Creative Economy.* London: Nesta. p. 103.

Ball, L., Pollard, E., Stanley, N., & Oakley, J. (2010). *Creative Career Stories.* Retrieved from: http://www.employment-studies.co.uk/pdflibrary/477.pdf

BIS. 2013. *Higher Ambitions: The Future of Universities in a Knowledge Economy* (Executive Summary). Dept. Business, Innovation and Skills. Retrieved from: http://www.creativeindustriesfederation.com/about/

Borgenhold, D, Heinonen, J., and Akola E. (2014) 'Entrepreneurship and Independent professionals: Social and Economic Logics. In: *International Advances in Economic Research* 20, 295-310

Chell, E. (2008) *The entrepreneurial personality.* Routledge, East Sussex.

Christian. 2014. 'The Benefits of Industry Input on Educational Experience' (Unpublished MSc Project Report), Leeds Beckett University, UK.

Culkin, N. and Mallick, S. (2011). 'Producing work-ready graduates: The role of the entrepreneurial university'. In: *The Market Research Society* 53 (1), 347-368, DOI: 10.2501/IJMR-53-3-347-368

DCMS. (1998). *Creative Industries Mapping Document.* Retrieved from: http://www.culture.gov.uk/Reference_library/Publications/archive_1998/Creative_Industries_Mapping_Document_1998.htm

DCMS. (2014). *Creative Industries Economic Estimates.* Retrieved from: https://www.gov.uk/government/uploads/ system/uploads/attachment_data/file/271008/Creative_Industries_Economic_Estimates_-_January_2014.pdf

Draper, P. (2008), 'Music two-point-zero: music, technology and digital independence'. In: *Journal of Music, Technology and Education* 1 (2), 137–152, doi: 10.1386/jmte.1.2 and 3.137/1

Draper, P. (2007), *Students Doing the Driving: How Undergraduates Use ICT to 21st Century.* Proceedings of the NACTMUS National Conference, Brisbane 29. June–1 July 2007. Retrieved from: http://www98.griffith.edu.au/dspace/handle/10072/18446

European Commission. (2006). *Implementing the Community Lisbon Programme: Fostering Entrepreneurial Mindsets Through Education and Learning.* Retrieved from: http://eurlex.europa.eu/LexUriServ/LexUriServ.do?uri=COM:2006:0033:FIN:en:PDF

European Commission. (2008). *Entrepreneurship in Higher Education, Especially in Non-Business Studies: Report of the Expert Group*, Retrieved from: http://ec.europa.eu/enterprise/policies/sme/files/support_measures/training_education/entr_highed_en.pdf

Hesmondhalgh, D., & Pratt, A. C. (2005). Cultural industries and cultural policy. In: *International journal of cultural policy.* 11 (1). 1-14. DOI: 10.1080/10286630500067598

Ideastap (2015) *Ideastap.* Retrieved from: http://www.ideastap.com/

Illeris, K. (2003). Towards a contemporary and comprehensive theory of learning. In: *International Journal of Lifelong Education.* 22(4), 396-406. DOI: 10.1080/0260137032000094814

PRACTICE

Robert gained his PhD in popular musicology from Montréal University. He has worked as a freelance practitioner in education and received two Creative Arts Research Awards funded by the UK Arts Council to explore creativity in the curriculum. His work in higher education has resulted in the development of a number of courses in music that look to develop new models for students to develop their potential for working in the wider music industries. He is currently working on a number of cross-faculty initiatives to develop the profile of the freelance creative entrepreneur within the University.
—
R.W.Davis@leedsbeckett.ac.uk

Julia Calver MA PGCE BA(HONS) is Senior Lecturer of Events Management at UK Centre for Events Management (UKCEM) at Leeds Beckett University. Within her role she is Level 6 Leader and Faculty Champion for Student Enterprise. UKCEM manages the region's Yorkshire Event Network with a membership of over 600 businesses related to the events sector. This is an area she is particularly keen to develop. Prior to joining the academic team Julia was Manager of the Creative Industries Sector Group for the West Yorkshire Lifelong Learning Network following ten years developing strategic partnerships between the cultural and education sectors at Arts Council England. This involved managing lottery funding and supporting creative business development.

She is currently in the completion stages of her doctoral research investigating university collaborations with the creative sector.

—

j.calver@leedsbeckett.ac.uk

Dr Steve Parker is Head of Research and a Principal Lecturer in Music Technology and Production at Leeds Beckett University. He joined the University after many years working in the music and recording industries. Parker's research takes a critical approach to the tensions that exist between higher education and the music industry by comparing contemporary approaches with the apprenticeship system of the past. Using interviews with industry professionals, current students and recent graduates who have achieved some success in the industry, his research explores the myths and contradictions of the apprenticeship-training model with changes in the contemporary professional environment.

—

S.L.Parker@leedsbeckett.ac.uk

JAMES. 2013. **Gus Dudgeon Foundation JAMES Summer Course**, 2013. Retrieved from: http://www.jamesonline.org.uk/gdf2013.html

National Advisory Committee on Creative and Cultural Education. (1999). **All Our Futures: Creativity, Culture and Education.** London: Department of Culture Media and Sport. Retrieved from: http://sirkenrobinson.com/pdf/allourfutures.pdf

Next Gen, Retrieved from: http://www.nesta.org.uk/sites/default/files/next_gen_wv.pdf

O'Hara, B. (2014). 'Creativity, Innovation and Entrepreneurship in Music Business Education'. In: **International Journal of Music Business Research** 3/2, pp. 28-59. Retrieved from: https://musicbusinessresearch.files.wordpress.com/2012/04/volume-3-no-2-october-2014_ohara_end.pdf

ONS. (2013). **Graduates in the UK Labour Market 2013**. ONS. Retrieved from: http://www.ons.gov.uk/ons/rel/lmac/graduates-in-the-labour-market/2013/rpt---graduates-in-the-uk-labour-market-2013.html

Pine, J. and Gilmore, J. 2014. 'A leader's guide to innovation in the experience economy'> In: **Strategy and Leadership** 42/1 pp24-29 proceedings of Music in Australian Tertiary Institutions

QAA. 2012. **Enterprise and entrepreneurship education: Guidance for UK higher education providers.** Retrieved from: http://www.qaa.ac.uk/en/Publications/Documents/enterprise-entrepreneurship-guidance.pdf

REF. (2015). **REF 2013: Units of Assessment.** Retrieved from: http://www.ref.ac.uk/panels/unitsofassessment/

Sherbert. (2015). **Sherbert.** Retrieved from: http://www.sherbet.co.uk

Unwin, L. (2007). English apprenticeship from past to present: The challenges and consequences of rampant 'community' diversity. In J. Hughes, N. Jewson and L. Unwin, (Eds.), In: **Communities of Practice: Critical Perspectives.** London: Routledge.

World Economic Forum (2009) Educating the Next Wave of Entrepreneurs: **Unlocking entrepreneurial capabilities to meet the global challenges of the 21st Century**. Report of the Global Education Initiative, Switzerland. Retrieved from: http://www.weforum.org/reports/educating-next-wave-entrepreneurs

Williamson, J. & Cloonan, M. (2007) 'Rethinking the music industry'. In: **Popular Music**, vol. 26, 2, pp. 305-322.

PRACTICE

Rosa Perez Monclus
Roberta Comunian
Nick Wilson

RISING TO THE KINGS' CULTURAL CHALLENGE TEACHING AND LEARNING CULTURAL ENTREPRENEURSHIP THROUGH A PROJECT-BASED COMPETITION

PRACTICE

Abstract

This article reflects on extra-curricular opportunities that creative graduates voluntarily engage with when studying cultural entrepreneurship and enhancing their profile. It highlights the role of universities in creating platforms for graduates to avail themselves of such learning beyond their specific degree.

In particular, we use as a case-study the Kings' College Challenge (KCC) - a university-wide project-based competition, established by the Kings' Cultural Institute at Kings' College London in 2012. The KCC was developed in collaboration with leading arts and cultural organisations in London, including the Royal Opera House, Royal Shakespeare Company, Southbank Centre and V&A Museum. It required students to think of an innovative entrepreneurial proposition in response to a key challenge being faced in the creative and cultural sector. In keeping with this model of engagement with project-based work, the students with the winning proposal were offered as prize; a paid internship with a leading cultural organisation.

We look at the rationale of the competition, its structure, and the opportunities it offers from an entrepreneurial teaching and learning perspective. By talking to the people who launched and managed it, and the students, both participants and winners. The article highlights the clear potential of the competition format in enhancing entrepreneurial skills, whilst revealing insights as to the kind of conditions that influence students' approaches towards and thinking about cultural entrepreneurship more generally.

Introduction

The situation that young graduates face today is starkly different from that of previous generations. Until the 1990s being in possession of a higher education (HE) qualification opened the path towards a stable professional career, whereas today such prospects appear to be long gone (Brown et al, 2011). Such an uncertain context further deteriorates for creative graduates confronted with lower salary levels and poorer career outlooks in comparison with non-creative graduates (Comunian et al, 2010). Students are conscious of the circumstances they will encounter as young professionals, and consequently they increasingly demand an HE experience that facilitates the connection with *'real life'* situations. Sometimes through work placement programs, more space for applied learning, or a greater attention to the generation of transferable skills across a variety of work environments, such as communication skills or teamwork competences (Wilson & Stokes, 2006; Rae, 2010). The particular role of universities, in creating platforms for graduates to avail themselves of such learning beyond their specific degree, is highlighted as of central importance in subsequent career development.

Entrepreneurship Education in Creative
and Cultural Industries

In the last two decades, entrepreneurship education has been progressively incorporated into Higher Education (HE), with a central aim being easing the progression of students into the labour market - either as independent professionals or through the establishment of new ventures (Matlay and Carey, 2007). Early approaches to the field sought inspiration from models taught in business schools. However, criticism regarding the somewhat constrained understanding of both the entrepreneurial figure and the pedagogical approach (Kirby, 2004) soon appeared, as entrepreneurship education was expanded across academic domains. A limited conceptualisation of the overall entrepreneurial field, its multiple forms and conditions of operation (Shane, 2003; Gibb, 2005) as well as the lack of an agreed definition over fundamental concepts, such as entrepreneur or entrepreneurship (Gartner, 2007, Stokes & Wilson, 2010), raised important questions regarding how entrepreneurship should be approached by universities (Wilson and Stokes, 2006). Such questions are of particular relevance in the context of arts and culture, where, on the one hand, it is common to encounter a reluctance to engage with such terminology at all. And, on the other hand, one finds self-employment and the artisans' micro-business are strongly characteristic organisational forms (Rae, 2012). It is of paramount importance, therefore, to resolve and then to articulate clearly just what is to be gained from incorporating entrepreneurship programs within Arts and Humanities (A&H). Faculties, and indeed what these should be comprised of.

According to Bilton (2007) a cultural entrepreneur is capable of effectively managing the whole of the value chain rather than limiting their role to the production of art and culture. As Anderson and Jack observe *'teaching entrepreneurship needs to produce a combination of the creative talents of the artist, the skills and ability of the artisan, yet include the applied knowledge of the technician with the know-what of the professional'* (Anderson and Jack, 2008, p. 260). In keeping with these views, we emphasise the composite nature of the entrepreneurial act and personality (Ellmeier, 2003). One, that needs to be adaptive to different domains and importantly, evolves over time. Entrepreneurial activity, and its teaching, demands special attention across (at least) two complementary dimensions, which we describe in terms of disposition and process.

First, according to Gibb (2005) an entrepreneurial *'disposition'* is comprised of those behaviours, attributes, skills and values required to successfully navigate complex environments and articulate action. These represent a compendium of attitudes and capacities that while extending across it, transcend the business domain. As noted by Oakley (2014) cultural entrepreneurship has never fully adapted to the mainstream myth of the entrepreneur motivated by economic pursuit. Rather, self-employment is often a forced option in front of the lack of secure employment. Along this line, it is claimed that the entrepreneurial paradigm offers a set of transposable abilities useful in a multiplicity of contexts, ranging from traditional business ventures to radical activism or social endeavours (Rae, 2010; Oakley, 2014). We consider it axiomatic that entrepreneurial programs in HE should aim to develop these multi-functional capacities, allowing students to successfully act within multiple grounded realities.

PRACTICE

Second, Wilson and Stokes (2006) propose an approach to entrepreneurial education that is not only contextual but also processual. Entrepreneurship can be approached as an interactive process of learning and doing within particular social spaces (Wenger, 2000). From the very initial stage of ideas generation, to the specific knowledge required to overcome particular problems in the day to day operation of an organisation, specialist management of tasks and managing collective knowledge effectively are key to any entrepreneurial activity (Becker & Murphy, 1992; Wilson, 2009). According to Rae (2012), students in A&H tend to be naturally inclined towards the creation stage, which potentially limits their capacity to deal with problems and issues arising down the value chain. Equally, he notes how successful creative ventures often require time and space to learn through iteration. As such, identifying, testing and developing tailored solutions that will stand the test of time, rather than short term 'creative' solutions, are elements that need to be taken into account when teaching programs of cultural entrepreneurship. However, as organizational structures, career paths and working patterns – particularly in the art sector - are continuously adjusting and being redefined, it is important also that tools for entrepreneurship reflect these conditions. In this sense, static tools that are often privileged in entrepreneurial programs, such as developing a business plan, are potentially of limited help.

Constructing spaces, within a university setting where students are invited to confront real life challenges, is a way to expose them to situations that they will need to face in their upcoming professional careers. Competitions, especially in the US, have been used as an attempt to model these future scenarios. Their success varies greatly in relationship to their design and expected aims. In business schools, business plan competitions are a common practice (Shane, 2003). Arguably, however, they appear to be more successful in teaching how to comply with the parameters that render the exercise theoretically attractive to the panel of investors, rather than providing a solid base for developing sustainable ventures (Gailly & Fayolle, 2006). In the domain of engineering and computer science, team work in a competitive framework is an established tradition, as in the case of robotics competitions (Manseur, 2000). Over time, these programs have expanded their reach into international competitions, often enjoying participation from key industry players (Heil et al, 2004). In many universities such competitions have progressed from activities at the margin of the curriculum, to be included as optional modules (Grimes & Seng, 2008). From these basis, competitions have been expanded to wider academic disciplines, e.g. geography (Chalkley and Gibson, 2009), yet they appear to remain relatively rare in the specific context of A&H. It might also be observed that Gibb (2005), while listing competitions among the pedagogical tools available to develop entrepreneurial behaviours and skills, does not review them in terms of their usefulness or adequacy.

For all these reasons we have been encouraged to undertake our particular study of the contributions and limitations of the Kings' Cultural Challenge, a relatively high profile example of such a competitive learning space in the cultural sector.

Kings' Cultural Challenge: a case Study of Entrepreneurial Education

Before discussing the findings of the research project, it is important to provide some background to KCCs' structure, remit and development, since its establishment in 2012. The Cultural Institute (CI) at Kings' College was launched with the remit to 'connect

(left margin: PRACTICE)

*the College with practitioners, producers, policy makers and participants across arts and
culture, creating space where conventions are challenged and original perspectives emerge.*
One of the strategic aims, around which the Institutes' program of activity is organized,
is focused on 'enhancing the academic and student experience through teaching, learning
and research through cultural connections, in collaborative teaching, research and learning'.
The development of the KCC responded directly to the perceived need to create opportunities for teaching and learning in this area beyond the College and in partnership
with cultural organisations. As the Director of the Institute explains: *'It was about students*
responding to real world challenges, and really it was about harnessing the creativity of
the Colleges' 24,000 students to respond to very real life challenges in the cultural sector'
(interview with the Director).

This framework moves beyond the classic consideration of students as passive receivers of
knowledge, and inherently recognizes them as subjects capable of providing valuable
answers. The *'prize'* for students was the opportunity to undertake a paid internship
with one of the Challenges' external partners – drawn from a selection of prestigious
London-based cultural organisations (including the Royal Opera House, the Victoria
and Albert Museum and others). For their part, the partners benefit from the challenge
in two ways *'they get a high calibre student doing an internship with their organization;*
but they also get the thinking from the students around issues they are grappling with
everyday' (interview with the Director). The KCC aims to support the students with
workshops focused on ideas-development, project planning and presentation skills.
For the CI this reflects their objective to *'create spaces in which people can incubate,*
develop thinking and [...] their ideas in collaboration' (interview with the Director).

For the purposes of this article – while the KCC also represents an interesting platform
for knowledge exchange between Higher Education and the creative and cultural sector –
we focus primarily on the experience and learning of the participating students, as it
relates to cultural entrepreneurship. Specifically, we have structured our findings
around three key themes that emerged in the qualitative interviews:

- The motivation and engagement for learning beyond the curriculum
- Entrepreneurial disposition versus entrepreneurial learning
- The value and nature of learning outside the curriculum.

Exploring Motivation and Engagement beyond the Curriculum

All the participants highlighted the importance of the prize, a paid internship in
one of Londons' leading cultural organizations, as a key motivation to take part in the
KCC. Notwithstanding the growing and very legitimate unease concerning the level
of structural inequality associated with unpaid internship in the arts and cultural
sector, internships are now widely recognized strategies for stepping into a desired
career path in the London arts' scene. All participants came across as highly career
driven, and some expressed their concerns around the difficulty of entering this job
market without having built up an adequate network of relationships, especially those
coming from outside London. However, the internship was not seen solely in instrumental terms. Participants talked about working for one of these organizations
as a *'dream job'*, showing a strong emotional connection with such institutions.
'I saw that all the institutions involved where institutions that I would have loved to have

PRACTICE

an internship [with] or work [for], I have somehow been related to [them] emotionally.' (Interviewee 1). *'I was really keen on getting work experience, especially work experience in London, because I moved from abroad and I saw that they were handing out internships as a prize'* (Interviewee 3).

Participants were aware of the highly competitive nature of the KCC given the limited number of internships. Consequently, they also found value in participating as an opportunity to show engagement, acquire further experience or grasp new opportunities. In this respect, KCC was seen very much as a learning experience providing an opportunity to expand knowledge beyond a degree program and build bridges with *'real life'* in preparation for the future. *'When we had a presentation on the Challenge I found it very interesting not only because of the reward, but the whole experience'.* (Interviewee 1). *I didn't expect to win so I obviously wanted to learn through the process [...] I just wanted to show that I was interested as well in taking up the opportunity* (Interviewee 4).

Students expressed the understandable anxiety, that getting involved in such an extra-curricular program in the first place might have a negative impact on their formal studies. Unfortunately, the research was not able to capture just how many were put off from entering the Challenge, but one would suppose that many students, however capable and interested *'in theory'*, would have fallen into this category. Classic entrepreneurial trait theory would emphasise the need for a risk-taking personality, but we would suggest that it is also legitimate to posit a more pragmatic, even calculated, career-oriented disposition, as being a central driver for those that did decide to take part.

Entrepreneurial Disposition vs Entrepreneurial Learning

A central observation was that the majority of participants was already active, and tended to engage in extra-curricular activities, within Kings' and outside; some even managed their own businesses. There was a conscious intention to use the KCC to either test or take those interests and dispositions further (into the industry; outside their comfort zone), or to use it as an opportunity to differentiate themselves from their peers: *'I have always run my own business [...] I have always been aware of the money side and financials* (Interviewee 5). *I do a lot of extra-curricular things that are outside Kings' College, attending events that have cultural speakers and help network with cultural partners'* (Interviewee 3).

One participant from a non-arts department seems to suggest her willingness to engage in entrepreneurial activities like KCC as a goal in itself, rather than moved by a particular field of interest: *'[Its'] what fuels people to create and I think thats' what everybody needs; we will need new things and we will need new ideas'* (Interviewee 2).

It is important to consider whether these kind of approaches are the result of an *'entrepreneurial disposition'* (which the literature has tended to suggest is more often located outside A&H departments), or whether for certain students we can see the interiorization (and possibly the acritical acceptance) of a narrative of the importance of entrepreneurial and innovative behaviours. Therefore, it seems important to critically consider how the entrepreneurial behaviour is contextualized with a career path in the arts sector, rather than considering it as a goal in itself.

PRACTICE

To reiterate, KCC does not operate as a platform to launch a student participants' prior idea or project. This being the case, the KCC represents a one-off opportunity to apply entrepreneurial skills and knowledge to a '*new*' context. In this sense, experiential learning complements and enhances the standard academic learning at Kings' College. For example, remaining at a broad level of transferrable skills, the opportunity to practice and refine ones' presentation skills was clearly highly valued, especially in terms of building up self-confidence: '*I think the pitching workshop is the best for me, learning wise. I don't really like public speaking so it was really good for me to go into a workshop and kind of fine tune that*' (Interviewee 4). '*...and suddenly I am in charge and I need to make all the decisions - which was a bit scary at the beginning - but definitely I felt because I have done this kind of work experience before that I kind of know what is expected of me so I wasn't afraid to take that responsibility, while, for instance, two years ago I wouldn't have done it. [...] It made me more confident*' (Interviewee 3).

In general, the research supports the widely discussed importance of self efficacy (McGee et al, 2009), and entrepreneurial intention (see Dhose and Walter, 2012) in the development of young nascent entrepreneurs (Pruett et al, 2009; Edwards and Muir, 2012). However, we could find no clear indication that KCC works as a catalyst towards practicing entrepreneurship, with some participants stating the intension to undertake further studies or to look for a permanent position in a cultural institution rather than, for example, running a business. The organisers of the Challenge themselves acknowledged the potential tension between promoting an entrepreneurial mind-set and interning in a cultural organization. For example: '*I think students just need to get a foot in the door because they just need to start getting experience somewhere, and an internship always works for that; and if you need to be creative and entrepreneurial for that it doesn't really matter that is not necessarily needed for an internship, because its' going to be needed later*' (Interview with director).

Learning outside the Curriculum

Several participants described the nature of the process as a holistic learning experience that provides the opportunity to learn beyond a one-off essay. In this sense, they highlight the potential benefit of developing a disposition that places real life circumstances and constraints at the centre of their thinking and practice, with associated positive impact in terms of self-responsibility and dedication. There was an acknowledgement that the competition provides the opportunity to use academic skills transversally. For example, traditional research skills were thought as important to raise the level of the KCC project presented by the student: '*In the Challenge I gave in my proposal [...] and it was 'all me', talking with somebody, me getting feedback properly; it was different because I was continuously working on something for a whole year, a lot more fine-tuned. You use different skills as well because you have to be business-minded rather that analytical; it was just a different set of skills that I had to develop but they do kind of link.*' (Interviewee 4).

Participants place a high importance on originality and creativity as a key factor to win the competition. Yet, they are aware that originality is a necessary but insufficient condition if the idea is not transposable to reality and vice versa. In this respect, the opportunity to get feedback from external partners was considered a hugely valuable learning opportunity. For the participants this involved learning through a relational process of selection, trimming, re-working and re-framing as they turned ideas into

PRACTICE

feasible projects: '*At first it was a crazy, random, far-fetched idea. Then I got selected to the first stage, and then I had a meeting with people from the KCI and one of the partners [...] They gave me this little brief so I could reduce my idea [...] [now] I understand what they were looking for, what is the type of project my client is looking for, and then come with ideas, very concrete ideas trying to approach that request; but yeah, I say I learnt that from the KCC.*' (Interviewee 1). '*I love the creative process more than the actual practical process, I focused on coming up with an idea and then I just tried to make the budget work. But I think the workshops were useful in that they did teach us some things about events management that I still come across in my work now.*' (Interviewee 3). '*I was quite nervous about coming up with big ideas, but yeah, at first I felt that I had to really impress them, because I had to come up with these ideas all by myself; but then I gradually learnt that [...] they wouldn't hold it against me and it was actually great to work with people and to learn about things; it was intimidating at first, and I kind of got over it and learned more.*' (Interviewee 4).

Conclusions

Through researching the KCC we have been able to reflect on student learning outside the traditional activities that have been associated with cultural entrepreneurship. The findings suggest that this kind of competitive entrepreneurial learning experience represents a useful addition to the curriculum. Following Gibbs (2005), we can see that the competition provides a compelling context in which to develop key supporting *entrepreneurial behaviours*, including risk taking and a willingness to engage with new content and contacts. And foster *entrepreneurial attributes*, such as self-efficacy, building up confidence, and learning new transferrable skills, e.g. presentation or negotiation skills. Whilst also re-defining and re-confirming individual values in reference; for example, to students' independence, work-ethos and sense of belonging to the cultural sector.

Those we interviewed recognised the value of the experience as a unique '*holistic*' opportunity, within oftentimes-fragmented programs. Here they found a given space to move from the creative idea stage through to '*the pitch*' in an organized manner. It is hard not to find value in this, especially if one agrees with the Director of the CIs' contention that '*anyone wanting a career in the arts sector needs to be entrepreneurial [...] The way it works is you get out there and you do stuff.*'

However, as the KCC enters its third year, we feel that there are a number of recommendations that might help KCC and others, wanting to establish this kind of competition as part of a wider portfolio of cultural entrepreneurship learning opportunities in their institutions.

1.   Firstly, one apparent limitation is that this type of opportunity remains self-selective in nature. It is very evident from our finding that the KCC encourages and empowers students who are *already* motivated and, indeed, entrepreneurial to move '*up a gear*' in their practice; more could and arguably should be done to empower students who do not have this attitude (often for lack of experience, issues of confidence or cultural barriers). One thing to consider is the carefully and appealingly packaged publication of case-studies, where students can read about how it *is* possible to meet the often demanding requirements of a university degree, whilst engaging in such a competition.

2. Secondly, there is a problematic boundary in competition-type of work between encouraging and enabling collaboration and networking, while protecting students' individual contributions and copyright – especially when the prize is an individual internship. '*Collaborative*' learning needs to happen with partners and experts here, rather than amongst peers, because of the individualistic nature of the format, compared with other competitions which are structured around groups' participation. Group competitions are another interesting format, which can encourage team-building skills, but individuals contributions are often hard to assess and evaluation.

3. Finally, it seems particularly important, in these competitive environments, to provide careful and valuable feedback to all participants - especially those that do not '*win*'. A failure to win might give rise to the unwitting consequence of increased insecurity, as students feel that not only their ideas, but also their skills and personality have fallen short. This final point reminds us that the possibility of failing is, of course, central to the very process of creativity and entrepreneurship in any context, including learning in HE (Jackson et al, 2006). Furthermore, the development of entrepreneurial learning is always culturally specific (see Giacomin et al, 2011). Some societies have a more tolerant and open attitude to failure than others. In an increasingly competitive context of globalisation where students come (to London in this case) to study from many countries and backgrounds, this represents a very real '*challenge*', all of its own, one to be pursued in and out of the classroom.

About the Authors

*Rosa Perez-Monclus
MA BBA is a PhD researcher
at the Department of Culture,
Media & Creative Industries,
King's College London.
Earlier she received a BA
in Humanities, Cultural
Management, and a BBA
at the Universitat Oberta
de Catalunya, Spain.*

*Rosa is interested in cultural
policy and cultural and
political economy.
More specifically, her work
examines financial inter-
mediation for the cultural
and creative sector from
a policy perspective.*

*maria_rosa.perez_monclus
@kcl.ac.uk*

*Dr Roberta Comunian is
Lecturer in Creative and
Cultural Industries at
the Department of Culture,
Media and Creative
Industries at King's College
London.*

References

Anderson, A. R, & Jack, S. L. (2008). Role typologies for enterprising education: the professional artisan? In: *Journal of Small Business and Enterprise Development*, 15(2), 259-273.

Becker, G.S. and Murphy, K.M. (1992). The division of labour, coordination costs, and knowledge. In: *The Quarterly Journal of Economics*, November, CVII, 4.

Bilton, C. (2007). *Management and creativity: From creative industries to creative management*. Blackwell Publishing.

Blossfeld, H. P, Klijzing, E, Mills, M, & Kurz, K. (Eds.). (2006). *Globalization, uncertainty and youth in society: The losers in a globalizing world*. Routledge.

Brown, P, Lauder, H, & Ashton, D. (2010). *The global auction: The broken promises of education, jobs, and incomes*. Oxford University Press.

Chalkley, B, & Gibson, K. (2009). Enterprise education in Geography: the case of the Plymouth Dragons. In: *Planet*, (21), 43-46.

Comunian, R, Faggian, A, & Li, Q. C. (2010). Unrewarded careers in the creative class: The strange case of bohemian graduates. In: *Regional Science*, 89(2), 389-410.

Dohse, D, Walter, S. G. (2012). Knowledge context and entrepreneurial intentions among students. In: *Small Business Economics*, 39, 877-895.

Edwards, L. J, Muir, E. J. (2012). Evaluating enterprise education: why do it? In: *Education+Training*, 54(4), 278-290.

PRACTICE

Ellmeier, A. (2003), Cultural entrepreneurialism: on the changing relationship between the arts, culture and employment, In: *International Journal of Cultural Policy*, Vol. 9 No. 1, pp. 3-16.

Gailly, B, & Fayolle, A. (2006). Can you teach entrepreneurs to write their business plan? An empirical evaluation of business plan competitions. In: *International Entrepreneurship Education: Issues and Newness*, 133-154.

Gartner, W. B. (2007). Is There an Elephant in Entrepreneurship? Blind Assumptions in Theory Development. In: *Entrepreneurship* (pp. 229-242). Springer Berlin Heidelberg.

Giacomin, O, Janssen, F, Pruett, M, Shinnar, R. S, Llopis, F, Toney, B. (2011). Entrepreneurial intentions, motivations and barriers: differences among American, Asian and European students. In: *International Entrepreneurship & Management Journal*, 7, 219-238.

Gibb, A. (2002). In pursuit of a new 'enterprise' and 'entrepreneurship' paradigm for learning: creative destruction, new values, new ways of doing things and new combinations of knowledge. In: *International Journal of Management Reviews*, 4(3), 233-269.

Gibb, A. (2005). *Towards the Entrepreneurial University. Entrepreneurship education as a lever for change*. National Council for Graduate Entrepreneurship. Policy article, 3, 1-46.

Grimes, J, & Seng, J. (2008, October). Robotics competition: Providing structure, flexibility, and an extensive learning experience. In: *Frontiers in Education Conference*, 2008. FIE 2008. 38th Annual (pp. F4C-9). IEEE.

Heil, M. R, Fornaro, R. J, Green, N. D, Maness, J. W, & Webb IV, W. H. (2004, October). On becoming a winning student team: placing third in an international design competition. In: *Frontiers in Education*, 2004. FIE 2004. 34th Annual (pp. F4G-1). IEEE.

Jackson, N, Oliver, M, Shaw, M. and Wisdom, J. (2006). *Developing Creativity in Higher Education*. Abingdon: Routledge.

Kirby, D. A. (2004). Entrepreneurship education: can business schools meet the challenge? In: *Education+ training*, 46(8/9), 510-519.

Manseur, R. (2000). Hardware competitions in engineering education. In: *Frontiers in Education Conference*, 2000. FIE 2000. 30th Annual (Vol. 2, pp. F3C-5). IEEE.

Matlay, H, & Carey, C. (2007). Entrepreneurship education in the UK: a longitudinal perspective. In: *Journal of Small Business and Enterprise Development*, 14(2), 252-263.

McGee, J. E, Peterson, M, Mueller, S. L, Sequeira, J. M. (2009). Entrepreneurial self- efficacy: refining the measure. In: *Entrepreneurship: Theory and Practice*, 33(4), 965-988.

Oakley, K. (2014). Good work? Rethinking cultural entrepreneurship. In: *Handbook of Management and Creativity*, 145.

Pruett, M, Shinnar, R, Toney, B, Lopis, F, Fox, J. (2009). Explaining entrepreneurial intentions of university students: a cross-cultural study. In: *International Journal of Entrepreneurial Behaviour & Research*, 15(6), 571-594.

PRACTICE

Roberta Comunian joined the Department of CMCI at King's College London in September 2012. Previously she was Creative Industries Research Associate at the School of Arts, University of Kent and lecturer in Human Geography at the University of Southampton.

—

Her work focuses on the relationship between arts, cultural regeneration projects and the cultural and creative industries. She has recently worked on the connections between Higher Education and the Creative Economy and has published extensively on the career opportunities and patterns of creative graduates in the UK.

—

Roberta.Comunian@kcl.ac.uk

Dr Nick Wilson is Senior Lecturer in Cultural & Creative Industries and Program Director of the MA Arts & Cultural Management at the Department of Culture, Media and Creative Industries, King's College London. He was previously Principal Lecturer in Small Business Management and Entrepreneurship at Kingston University, and Course Director of the Program of Master's courses in the Creative Industries & the Creative Economy. Currently he is lead researcher on the integrated Get Creative research project for the BBC. Nick's research and teaching focuses on everyday social creativity, cultural management, the sociology of creativity and the creative economy.

—

nick.wilson@kcl.ac.uk

Rae, D. (2010). Universities and enterprise education: responding to the challenges of the new era, In: *Journal of Small Business and Enterprise Development*, 17 (4), 591 - 606

Rae, D. (2012). Action learning in new creative ventures. In: *International Journal of Entrepreneurial Behaviour & Research*, 18(5), 603-623.

Shane, S. (2003), *A General Theory of Entrepreneurship: The Individual-Opportunity*. Nexus, Cheltenham: Edward Elgar.

Stokes, D. and Wilson, N. (2010). *Small business management & entrepreneurship*, London: CENGAGE.

Shattock, M. (2005). European universities for entrepreneurship: Their role in the Europe of knowledge the theoretical context. In: *Higher Education Management and Policy*, 17(3), 13.

Wenger, E. (2000). Communities of practice and social learning systems. In: *Organization,* 7(2), 225-246.

Wilson, N. C, & Stokes, D. (2005). Managing creativity and innovations: The challenge for cultural entrepreneurs. In: *Journal of Small Business and Enterprise Development*, 12(3), 366-378.

Wilson, N, & Stokes, D. (2006). *Entrepreneurship education· The road less travelled*. National Council for Graduate Entrepreneurship Working Article, 24.

Wilson, N. (2009). Learning to manage creativity: An occupational hazard for the UKs' creative industries. In: *Creative Industries Journal*, 2(2).: 179-190.

PRACTICE

Karla Penna
Jorge Tinoco
Elisabeth Taylor

NEW TEACHING AND LEARNING APPROACHES TO CULTURAL ENTREPRENEURSHIP FOR HERITAGE CONSERVATION TRAINING PROGRAMS IN BRAZIL

Abstract

In this chapter we discuss innovative teaching and learning approaches to cultural entrepreneurship for training in conservation and preservation of cultural heritage. We investigate training programs established at world heritage sites in Latin America, with a particular focus on a postgraduate program developed by the Centre for Advanced Studies in Integrated Conservation (CECI) in Brazil. Whilst a number of training programs have been operating worldwide during the past four decades, new demands arising from a rapidly changing world continue to challenge experts and educators alike to find new, effective ways to deal with contemporary educational issues in response to global change.

Introduction

The voices cry out ever louder. What began as a hum is now palpable and tangible. Concepts such as soft power, empowerment, shared management, managerial behaviour, and participatory approaches, are no longer merely words with subjective meanings, not normally part of the field of theoretical knowledge; with no known strategies for their practical application in cultural heritage preservation. Worldwide, there is growing recognition that to train professionals in these new holistic competencies is essential to the development of policies, the effective implementation of political programs and to conservation work.

Training programs now focus on the teaching of how to develop and implement cultural projects, but also on how professionals can contribute to changing scenarios present in developing countries. Contemporary cultural entrepreneurship thus demands new levels of thinking and planning, as well as flexible, new attitudes amongst professionals who must consider legal, economic, political, sociocultural, and managerial context-related factors before making decisions. These new attitudes are critical to the operation and sustainability of projects in the heritage conservation market. The purpose of this chapter is to analyse critically the current preservation scenario focusing on an example from Brazil, and to highlight the importance of cultural entrepreneurship as a tool to aid in reconceptualising existing training programs based on new teaching/learning approaches. These include, among others, sustainable strategies, transformative education, and local identity reinforcement and cultural meanings. All of these teaching and learning approaches have been employed to improve CECIs' (the Centre for Advanced Studies in Integrated Conservation) course curricula in light of social and cultural sensitivities. CECI is situated in Olinda, Brazil.

Given increased global demands for entrepreneurship training, CECI broadened the curriculum of its postgraduate course '*Management of Conservation Works and Cultural Heritage Restoration*' which it had been offering since 2007 by including a cultural entrepreneurship unit. Over time, the course had undergone several reviews, based, at first, on critical insights offered by research findings (Penna and Tinoco).

Conservation education

The concept of conservation education in cultural heritage has evolved continually throughout recent decades, along with the definition of the skills and knowledge required in conservation (Cather, 2000). Over this period, the United Nations Educational, Scientific, and Cultural Organization (UNESCO) and the International Council on Monuments and Sites (ICOMOS) have made dozens of international recommendations since the Athens Charter (1931). These have attempted exhaustively to adjust aims, methods, concepts, and approaches to modern social dynamics and, more recently, to local cultural contexts and resources.

It is our understanding that conservation education has the daunting task of '*preparing professionals so that they can identify issues, use a holistic approach, critically analyse and solve problems, plan, develop, implement, and manage strategic solutions, take into consideration local cultural pluralism, respect the contribution at all levels of other professionals involved in conservation/preservation initiatives, and have a flexible yet pragmatic approach based on cultural consciousness, sound judgment, and an understanding of the communitys' needs*' (ICOMOS, 2003). It not only sounds impossible for any single human to absorb this knowledge all at once. From our perspective, it truly seems unfeasible: training may not provide all the knowledge needed, however it is essential for alerting professionals that '*being*' a conservationist goes beyond a set of technical abilities. Moreover, it is about respecting the historical and cultural meanings of societies not just about buildings – it is effectively about people.

Cultural heritage sites are created by societies and reflect the varied social, cultural, and economic conditions of different periods of the past. Work on such sites, therefore, requires interdisciplinary, multidimensional education that includes sensitization and training of the various actors participating in protecting and conserving a specific cultural heritage site (ICCROM, 2010). Standards, principles, and ethical practices in conservation education are relative and not universal. Conservationists thus must respect local cultural contexts and promote integrate management attitudes with contemporary social, cultural, and economic goals.

Recognizing that sustainable development relies on culturally oriented strategies, Zancheti (2014) has identified three main challenges faced by preservation educators:

(1) a shift in the disciplines' empirical paradigm from scientific objectives to a postmodern, cultural approach;
(2) decision-making processes that involve many stakeholders and that search for a balance between new and traditional knowledge, techniques, and materials in diverse cultural contexts;
(3) the renewed emphasis on a conservation ethic for professional practice.

In addition, cultural heritage is both tangible and intangible. It is simultaneously linked to identity and based on shared appreciation. It considers not only historical traditions but also contemporary expressions of the new social and cultural practices required by contemporary life styles (Lakerveld & Gussen, 2009). Moreover, since culture and heritage are part of peoples' daily lives, an important issue is to establish: what is heritage actually? Who defines heritage within the new context? (Zancheti, 2014)

PRACTICE

Entrepreneurship: An expected, necessary Attitude

Because cultural heritage is broad, complex, and multiform, its management demands both a comprehensive understanding of the spirit of places (ICOMOS, 2008) and a new perspective taken by conservation professionals. To undertake successful heritage preservation projects, and policies, cultural preservation professionals are called upon not only to intervene in material restoration but also to deal with the pluralistic political, economic, and sociocultural contexts of historical sites. Entrepreneurship has been identified as the engine of successful cultural projects. An entrepreneurial attitude defines the success or failure of many cases. For this reason, entrepreneurship seems essential to be included in heritage education as a vital part of competency-based learning. Consequently, learning becomes a journey of discoveries and initiatives in dealing with things and people (Lakerveld & Gussen, 2009).

Entrepreneurship is a necessary quality for those who are aware that, currently, implementing projects of any kind is impossible without innovation, the courage to take risks, and a holistic approach to identifying, seizing, or creating opportunities. More than a skill, an entrepreneurial attitude is to believe that one can accomplish projects and lead teams towards common goals seeking to change current situations where many societies are plagued by extensive economic contrasts. In this case, the project goals often include sustainable development of favourable economic conditions, improvement of peoples' quality of life and socio-environmental conditions. In addition, entrepreneurship ought to be viewed as a combination of technical expertise, knowledge of appropriate legal frameworks, entrepreneurial behaviour and the ability to persuade and attract others — also known as '*soft power*' (Nye, 2004).

The Role of Cultural Educators

Who are (or who should be) the educators of cultural entrepreneurs? Delors, c.s. explained in the report '*Learning: The Treasure Within*' (1996), that education should, in fact, convey — in a solid and effective way — more and more knowledge and evolutionary know-how adapted to cognitively developed societies, as these are the foundation of future skills. At the same time, educators should find and mark references that prevent people from being submerged by more or less ephemeral information waves that invade public and private spaces and should orientate people in developing individual and collective projects.

Education is responsible for providing maps of a complex, constantly agitated world and, at the same time, for enabling the compass needed to navigate through it. Educators, therefore, are responsible not only for efficiently facilitating knowledge construction, but also for teaching students to use this knowledge appropriately in their field. Successful learning relies on successful teaching. For educators, it is their technical and methodological capacity, and thus the ability to have a flexible yet pragmatic approach, based on cultural consciousness and respect for cultural diversity and its meanings, that ideally penetrates all their practical work. Educators' creative and critical-analytical capacities are based on proper education and training, sound judgment, and a sense of understanding of the community' needs (ICOMOS, 1993). Equally, the community of learners must be considered - the students for whom courses are intended. For the purpose of undertaking a course of cultural entrepreneurship, it is recommended that a student has

PRACTICE

(at least) basic-knowledge levels of fundamental disciplines (in our case, Portuguese and mathematics), interest in learning, and natural skills that can be developed and improved during the courses.

We believe that the main role of educators, whatever the area of human knowledge, is to show students various ways to be, to see, to look at, and to know about observable and knowable '*objects*' and concepts. Education has the potential to lead individuals to awaken, to feel empowered, and to develop what educators refer to as resilience – the ability to bounce back from adverse conditions which is essential to adapt to changes.

Cultural Entrepreneurship and CECI Conservation Training

Until the early 2000s no training course or specialization in conservation and restoration existed in Brazil to prepare professionals in management practices and execution of construction projects. This was a time when across the country many restoration and revitalization projects were undertaken thanks to the newly created Programa Monumenta/Inter-American Development Bank (BID) of the federal government. This program overseen by the Ministry of Culture and the BID innovated preservation processes by combining restoration and preservation of historical heritage with economic and social development.

To bridge this gap in practical knowledge of Cultural Heritage Restoration a postgraduate program titled '*Management of Conservation Works and Cultural Heritage Restoration*' was created in 2003. This program was directed at professionals engaged in maintenance, preservation, and restoration of built heritage. Since its conception the program has been conducted through distance-education-mode using technology in a virtual classroom environment. Regular classes are organized in module-form. Virtual and practical aspects are combined through technical visits and study tours to cities with conservation and restoration projects. This provides students with ample opportunities to observe and evaluate on-site problems and situations previously presented to them during on-line lectures. The program aims at training professionals in conservation management practices fit for work on projects involving buildings of high cultural value.

The programs' broad curriculum scope affords the trainees with tools and knowledge needed to manage, implement, supervise, and monitor conservation and restoration projects and maintenance services. Each unit seeks to enhance progressively students' professional potential by helping them improve their human, technical, and conceptual skills. Popular demand as evidenced by increasing participant numbers for this program throughout its 14 years of existence attests to its success (from 13 bapplicants isn 2003, until 76 in 2015).

The demand for speed generated by contemporary lifestyles, has resulted in the fact that knowledge constructed through traditional master-apprentice relationships has become rare or virtually non-existent, which, in our view, affects the quality of teaching and learning in the training of new conservation professionals. Consequently, since its first year of existence in 2003, the CECI program has aimed at recovering at least in part the traditional, one-on-one approach to transferring knowledge. It encourages direct, extensive academic experiences, as well as contact between artisans and professionals, thereby ensuring a healthy theory-practice mix of knowledge construction.

In training, know-how is developed through continuous, progressively deeper inter-actions between students, instructors, academics, and experienced practitioners. Pedagogically, this ensures the rapid maturation of learning capabilities through student-master interactions.

CECIs' pedagogical methods are continuously revised and remain open to innovation, new concepts, and alignment with local and international discussions. Procedures and practices follow these basic features:

a) significant value is given to the accumulated experience that each person brings or acquires in the training process.
b) knowledge and power load associated with decision-makers and workers are demystified.
c) involvement, commitment, and responsibility of students in interdisciplinary relationships through which knowledge is transmitted.

An important issue, that the CECI program has had to deal with repeatedly, is that some artisans and professionals with only below elementary education levels, have limited access to the program. This fact creates a large gap between top-level technicians responsible for conservation within restoration projects, and some of the artisans who possess knowledge of traditional techniques and procedures. The ensuing lack of dia-logue between 'those who think and make decisions' and 'those who do and know their stuff' effectively discourages a healthy dialectical relationship between 'knowing' and 'doing'. This theory/practice gap reportedly directly affects the quality of some projects which can be verified during technical education visits and study tours when students and lecturers visiting construction projects witness first-hand barely - or badly - finished works every year.

Of course it has to be said that a few days in the field when they are in direct contact with construction sites will not give students all the information they will need in their future professional activities. However, the practice of bringing together theoreticians and practitioners has proven to be an indispensable component of the program allowing direct 'dialogues' between master artisans and apprentices. It is a way to encourage a paradigm shift among architects and engineers as well as teachers and artisans. The former group discovered that workers have much practical knowledge and wisdom, the latter have the opportunity to develop a desire for joining in the 'doing' and 'knowing.'

The Relationship with the Job Market
From its seventh year of existence onward, CECI added opportunities for students to participate actively in the job market of built heritage conservation positions to the management program by including a cultural entrepreneurship unit in the curriculum. With the help of experts, students now construct scenarios for work-ing initiatives by developing conservation plans for specific restoration/revitalization projects. This progressive vision of professional specialization has the strategic pur-pose of meeting a market need for technical mastery and for developing interpersonal skills in demand in contemporary societies.

PRACTICE

The idea using entrepreneurship as a tool is to stimulate innovation and add holistic understanding of what cultural heritage management requires. In Brazil, people tend to seek job stability even when this means low salaries. One of the main dreams of any professional is to become a civil servant, a career move subject to a variety of increasingly competitive tendering processes due to the perceived stability offered in these jobs. The incessant search for this elusive, professional '*El Dorado*' has been a relevant factor in delays for graduates seeking to enter the job market. Professional training programs in architecture and engineering do not include everything the job market has to offer in their core curricula or even in their elective units, nor do they exploit all the wider possibilities that each individuals' talents may provide. This is aimed at showing students that being an entrepreneur is not a gift from heaven but instead knowledge acquired by making an effort.

A conservationist-planner-manager should know his or her personal skills and improve these abilities to make opportunities appear. This is what entrepreneurship is for. Skills such as, critical thinking, problem solving, holistic viewing, entrepreneurial behaviour, and leadership are now recognized worldwide in academic and professional circles as fundamental to the formation of new citizen-professional fields. In reality, the survival prospects of these professionals depend on self-direction, innovation, creativity, measured risk taking, and adaptability which are important for increased employability (OECD, 2010).

How can teaching and learning Cultural Entrepreneurship be improved with new Approaches?

'...few [educators] have reflected critically on their role as agents of enculturation of their own students into a Western modern worldview societies. Most are predisposed to reforming established teaching and learning practices in their schools and universities from within existing curricular structures, rather than seeking to reconceptualise their societys' educational goals. Why is this? The answer lies in the invisible part of the political spectrum where hidden assumptions govern beliefs about the purpose of schooling, giving rise to an uncritical belief in a 'one-size-fits-all' curriculum for modernising societies worldwide' (Taylor, 2013, p 169).

Often, the problems of day-to-day life consume educators so intensely that they forget the importance of their role in the social and cultural education of their students. New cultural entrepreneurship teaching and learning methods need to be based on a more integral, comprehensive paradigm of education (Albert, Bernecker, Perez, Thakur & Nairen, 2007). Education for preservation concerns not only students, but also the knowledge and synergy generated between teachers, students, technicians, managers, professionals, businesspersons, academics, politicians, and local community interaction. All actors need to '*teach*,' '*learn*,' and '*behave*' within this new paradigm.

However, choosing to work within this new paradigm is not really an option (yet) in Brazils' education system, whether for elementary, secondary, or higher education. Reportedly, to our knowledge, Brazilian education tends to define students using pre-established, closed '*truths*,' rules, and concepts. This approach categorizes each person through '*preconceptions*.' On the other hand, most people find it easier and more comfortable to accept dogma already recognized as fact by the majority (Freire, 2003). Because of this, it is quite easy to manipulate the '*intelligent*' (i.e., educated

PRACTICE

by academia) minority and oppress the majority of the population (i.e., poor people with restricted access to education and other basic services), by using partial reasoning to induce perceptions and tangible sensations.

Educators' view of the world has changed from universal to singular approaches (i.e, from absolutism to relativism), where beliefs and reality can be modelled and understood through separate sets of parameters (i.e. postmodernism) and where educators recognize their worlds' complexity and dynamism, as well as the variety in its species and cultures.

In this context, Jack Mezirows' (1991) theory of transformative learning has been implemented over the last 20 years to a variety of adult education contexts such as workplaces, communities, and in higher education. Recently, others have added to it theories of wisdom, culture, consciousness, society, feminism, globalization, spirituality, sustainability, and so on, to generate an attractive aesthetic, ethical, and spiritual perspective on educations' role. This helps create a more just, peaceful, diverse and sustainable world (Taylor, 2013). According to Elias (1997), transformative learning is the expansion of consciousness through the basic transformation of worldview and specific capabilities of *BEING*. Transformative learning is facilitated through processes consciously directed by the individual learner as to how to access and enjoy the symbolic contents of the unconscious underlying assumptions and critical analysis.

The challenge for heritage education is to develop high quality cultural entrepreneurship through key competencies, such as social and civic conscientiousness, cultural awareness and appropriation, and the following themes (Lakerveld & Gussen, 2009, pp 18-19):

1. **Meaningful contexts**: students learn to respect local values and practices, as educators look for meaningful contexts in which students can experience the relevance and meaning of competencies acquired in a natural way.
2. **Multidisciplinary approach**: competencies are holistic and, consequently, the pedagogical approach needs to be holistic and integrative as well.
3. **Constructive learning**: learning is conceived as a process of constructing ones' knowledge in interaction with ones' environment, rather than as a process of absorbing pre-arranged knowledge.
4. **Co-operative, interactive learning**: educators help learners develop and construct their own knowledge and seek ways to make optimal use of other peoples' competencies in their learning itinerary. Cooperation and interaction are both domains of learning, as well as vehicles of learning in other domains. This requires an open approach in which education includes dialogues between learners and educators about needs, goals, choices, and expectations.
5. **Discovery learning**: open learning processes require learning that can be characterized as active discovery, as opposed to receptive learning. This means not only that course content should be made available and accessible but also that the way of acquiring this knowledge or these competences is more than a process of being provided information. Learning should always be embedded in a discovery-based approach.

PRACTICE

6. **Reflective learning**: competency-based learning requires an emphasis on learning processes. By reflecting on ones' own needs, approach, progress, results, and motivations, students develop learning competencies/strategies in a process of '*learning to learn*.'

7. **Personal learning**: in competence-oriented theories, learning is conceived as a process of constructing ones' own personal knowledge and competencies. Knowledge, strategies, and information only become meaningful if they become an integral part of ones' body of knowledge and competencies. In education, this implies that students need to be able to identify with contexts, people, interests, and situations that are part of the learning domains in question.

Active learning in realistic situations, in which students have a distinct and valuable role, makes the learning process a worthwhile event with outcomes that will prove useful in many other contexts. The process that leads to the acquisition of competencies involves three basic elements: motivation, experience, and reflection. Furthermore, both educators and students familiarize themselves with the following transformative learning qualities (Taylor, 2013):

a. **Cultural-self knowing**: to more fully understand ones' worldview (or way of knowing, being, and valuing), especially values, ideals, emotions, premises, and frames of reference residing in the subconscious - and connected to the collective unconscious - which underlie habits of mind, constitute cultural/individual identity, and govern social inter/actions

b. **Relational knowing**: to understand and appreciate the value of reconnecting with the natural world and with culturally different others' ways of knowing, being, and valuing in the world

c. **Critical knowing**: to understand how economic and organizational power has historically structured sociocultural reality—especially, class, race, gender, and the conventional scientific worldview—and thus governs (i.e., controls, restricts, limits, and distorts) identities and relationships with the natural world and with culturally different others

d. **Visionary and ethical knowing**: to envision through idealization, imagination, and dialogue with culturally different others what a better world this could/should be

e. **Agency knowing**: to realize that contributing to making the world a better place is feasible, desirable, and necessary and that one has the capacity and commitment to do so.

PRACTICE

Words of Caution and Reassurance

Transformation is dependent on the individuals' construction of knowledge. Moreover, this knowledge has to be viable i.e. it has to fit within the pre-existing knowledge, values, and lifeworld of an individual for it to make a difference. Learning from a constructivist point of view is always an active process that fully involves the individual unlike the passive knowledge transfer envisioned by behaviourist' approaches.

Transformative education is by definition firmly grounded in the critical constructivist paradigm which puts the onus of learning – in this case, transformation - into the hands of the learner. '*If Mezirow was right and changes of our attitudes and values are the result of transformative learning then this means that transformative learning is dependent on our ability for critical self-reflection*' (Taylor, 2009, p. 358). Consequently, the transformative educator is a facilitator of learning, who offers a wide range of learning opportunities that allow individuals to transform themselves. Transformative learning theory originates in constructivist adult learning theory which tends to view adults as competent, self-directed learners who continuously make decisions regarding their own learning (von Glasersfeld, 1990, 1995; Mezirow, 1991; Taylor, 2009).

We envisage that transformative curricula indeed have the potential to greatly enhance heritage preservation training programs, due to the emphasis on the combination of active theoretical and practical knowledge construction, professional integrity through values, development of resilience and a holistic awareness of social and cultural factors impacting their work.

References

Albert, M.; Bernecker, R.; Perez; D.; Thakur, N. and Nairen, Z. (Eds.) (2007). *Training strategies for world heritage management*. Germany: Deutsche UNESCO-Kommission.

Cassar, M. (2002). *Education and training needs for the conservation and protection of cultural heritage: Is it the case of 'one size fits all'?* Workshop 2, 5th EC Conference, Cultural Heritage Research: a Pan-European Challenge. Cracow: European Commission.

Cather, S. (2000). The dillema of education conservation. Comité International de la Formation (CIF). *The Getty Conservation Institute (GCI)*. Newsletter 15.1. Retrieved 12 February 2010 from: http://www.getty.edu/conservation/publications_resources/newsletters/15_1/feature1_3.html

Centre for Advanced Studies in Integrated Conservation - *CECI website*. Retrieved from: http://ceci-br.org/ceci/en/treinamento/cursos/restauro-cursos/gestao-de-restauro.html

Delors, J., Al Mufti, I., Amagi, I., Carneiro, R., Chung, F., Geremek, B., Gorham, W., Kornhauser, A. Manley, M., Quero, M., Savané, M., Singh, K., Stavenhagen, R., Suhr, M. And Nanzhao, Z. (1996). *Learning: The Treasure Within*. Paris: UNESCO. Jacques Delors, *Chairman*

Elias, D. (1997). Its' time to change our minds: An introduction to transformative learning. In: *ReVision*, 20 (1), pp 2-6.

Frederickson, B. L. (2009). *Positivity*. New York: Three Rivers.

Freire, P. 36.ª ed. 2003; 1.ª ed. 1970. *Pedagogia do Oprimido*. Rio de Janeiro: Edições Paz e Terra.

ICCROM (International Centre for the Study of the Preservation & Restoration of Cultural Property) (2010). Training strategy in the conservation of cultural sites (revision). Document prepared by ICCROM in consultation with UNESCO, the World Heritage Centre and the Physical Heritage Division, and ICOMOS. Retrieved 08 October 2010 from: http://cif.icomos.org/pdf_docs/Documents%20on%20line/Training%20strategy%201995.pdf.

International Council on Monuments and Sites – ICOMOS. (2003). *Guidelines on education and training in the conservation of monuments, ensembles and sites.* Retrieved 05 March 2013, from: http://cif.icomos.org/pdf_docs/Documents%20on%20line/GUIDELINES%20FOR%20EDUCATION%20AND%20TRAINING%20IN%20THE%20CONSERVATION.pdf.

About the Authors

Karla Penna MA is architect, urban planner and cultural heritage manager. She is an associate professor for the Centre for Advanced Studies in Integrated Conservation (CECI, Brazil) and a PhD candidate of Murdoch University's Scholl of Education (Perth, Australia). She has also been a preservationist for 17 years in Latin American countries, her work focuses on developing strategic plans to promote economic and sociocultural inclusion, and on training professionals for managing cultural projects and carrying out preservation policies in UNESCO's World Heritage cities.
—
karla.nunespenna @hotmail.com

Prof Jorge Tinoco is architect and urban planner, specialized in conservation and restoration of historical monuments and construction work management. He is the former director of the Cultural Heritage Department in Pernambuco and the former Secretary of Planning in Olinda, Brazil. He is currently the Associate Director and Professor for the Centre for Advanced Studies in Integrated Conservation (CECI, Olinda, Brazil)

—

prof.jorgetinoco@gmail.com

Dr Elisabeth Taylor is an adjunct senior lecturer at Murdoch University's School of Education, specialized in educational research focusing on social and cultural aspects of education, including girls' education, Aboriginal education and education for sustainability. Whilst she appreciates the value of quantitative approaches for appropriate research purposes she prefers naturalistic research methodologies such as ethnography, phenomenology and grounded theory approaches. Much of her research is embedded in critical constructivist and social constructionist research paradigms.

—

l.taylor@murdoch.edu.au

International Council on Monuments and Sites – ICOMOS (2008). *Quebec declaration on the preservation of the spirit of the place.* Retrieved from: http://www.international.icomos.org/quebec 2008.

International Council on Monuments and Sites - ICOMOS (2013). *The Burra Charter*. Retrieved from: http://australia.icomos.org/wp-content/uploads/The-Burra-Charter-2013-Adopted-31.10.2013.pdf.

Lakerveld, J. and Gussen, I. (Eds) (2009). *Acquedut: Acquiring key competences through heritage education*. Bilzen, Germany: Lies Kerkhofs.

Mezirow, J. (1991). *Transformative Dimensions of Adult Learning*. San Francisco, CA: Jossey-Bass.

Miranda, M. (1998). Inteligência e Contemporaneidade. *Trabalho e Educação*, Belo Horizonte, v. 4, p. 63-75. Retrieved 21 December 2014 from: http://www.propp.ufms.br/ppgedu/geppe/artigo8.htm.

Nye, J. (2004). *Soft Power: The means to success in world politics*. New York: Public Affairs.

Penna, K. (2014). *Empreendedorismo Cultural.* (Cultural Entrepreneurship). Olinda-BR: CECI - Centre of Integrated Preservation Advanced Studies /UFPE.

Organisation for Economic Co-operation and Development - OECD (2010), Main findings from local case studies and policy recommendations. In OECD. *Key policy issues in entrepreneurship and SME development*. OECD. Retrieved 12 September 2014 from: http://www.oecd.org/site/cfecpr/42203294.pdf.

Taylor, E. (2009). *'Adding zest' to science education: Transforming the culture of science classrooms through ethical dilemma story pedagogy*. Saarbrücken, Germany:VDM.

Von Glasersfeld, E. (1990). An exposition of constructivism: Why some like it radical. In R. B. Davis, C. A. Maher & N. Noddings (Eds.), *Constructivist views on the teaching and learning of mathematics* (pp. 19-29). Reston, VA: The National Council of Teachers of Mathematics.

Von Glasersfeld, E. (1995). A constructivist approach to teaching. In: L. P. Steffe & J. Gale (Eds.), *Constructivism in education* (pp. 3-15). Hillsdale, NJ: Lawrence Erlbaum Associates Publishers.

Zancheti, S. (2014). Challenges and dilemmas in heritage conservation. In: Stiefel, B. And Wells, J. (Eds) *Preservation education: Sharing best practices and common ground* (pp 83-96). Hanover: University Press of New England.

PRACTICE

Stephen B. Preece

APPLYING LEAN START-UP METHODOLOGY TO CULTURAL ENTREPRENEURSHIP

Abstract

Lean start-up methodology has transformed the entrepreneurship education field in recent years (Blank, 2013). With its emphasis on up-front iterating and testing of new venture ideas, using a business model canvas (Osterwalder & Pigneur, 2010) - as opposed to developing expansive, front-end business plans - entrepreneurship education has been revitalized into a major thrust for university educators and students alike (Morris, Kuratko, & Pryor, 2014). Traditional entrepreneurship methods emphasized a rational and linear approach to entrepreneurial formation (Read, Sarasvathy, Dew, Wiltbank & Ohlsson, 2011), often assuming start-up companies were just small versions of larger, more established firms (Blank, 2013). Based on research in recent years, principles from lean start-up has brought greater alignment between how skilled entrepreneurs function in real life, in contrast to how the process has been taught over the decades since the mid-20th century (Sarasvathy, 2001).

Despite roots in Silicon Valley (dominated by engineers and software developers), lean start-up principles have been successfully applied to multiple fields and disciplines, generating a methodology that can provide guidance to new ventures across sectors and industries (George & Bock, 2012), holding promise for the field of arts entrepreneurship. Nevertheless, the unique challenges associated with new arts ventures arguably require special consideration in the application of lean start-up principles for them to be successfully applied (Colbert, Nantel, Bilodeau & Rich, 2001).

The tension for artists is that lean start-up assumes the product/service which is offered to the audience/consumer is negotiable and should be adjusted to suit the tastes of the receiver. As will be discussed, this flies in the face of the essential facets of artistic vision and creation. The contention here is that much of the lean start-up process can still be applied to the situation of arts entrepreneurship, while still keeping the artistic vision intact.

Lean Start-up and Arts Entrepreneurship

A fundamental principle in arts management is that such organizations are mission-driven, where the defining '*product*' is in the hands of the artists, as opposed to the marketing manager. As such, arts managers necessarily seek out audiences (i.e., consumers) who are attracted to the art product, as opposed to developing a product that audiences are most likely to desire (Colbert, 2003). This emphasis, which includes not abandoning artistic vision for market considerations, has been identified as a defining difference between arts marketing and mainstream marketing (Colbert et al., 2001; Wilson & Stokes, 2004).

PRACTICE

At first glance, this appears fundamentally at odds with lean start-up methodologies where the prevailing mantra is to seek consumer input early, adapting the product as needed based on research, and thereby avoiding the production of something that is ultimately unwanted in the marketplace (Blank, 2013). While this initial principle of adapting product to consumer preferences is hardly compatible with artistic vision, the contention of this paper is that many of the lean start-up principles can still apply—and are in fact all the more essential—meanwhile leaving the ethic and practice of artistic autonomy intact.

We argue that emergent arts organizations must identify the core artistic principles that shape and guide their essential offerings, and deem these elements as being non-negotiable. However, when considering variables beyond these elements, the principles of lean start-up and the attendant search for an appropriate business model, all hallmarks of lean start-up methodologies, should be enlisted. Essential principles such as: minimum viable product, pivoting, failing fast, and continuous learning, are all relevant to business model development (Blank, 2013), and thereby can aid in seeking the most effective way the artistic offering can be presented to the public.

For the arts to thrive in the foreseeable future, creative or even radical innovations around business models to accompany artistic ventures will help purge unnecessary and outdated practices to keep up with contemporary and evolving tastes, lifestyle choices, funding models, and marketing norms. Lean start-up methods offer substantial promise for helping meet those ends.

In broad strokes, lean start-up methodology encourages three major processes, prior to actually building a new venture (Osterwalder, Pigneur, Bernarda & Smith, 2014)[1]:

1. evaluate problem-solution fit
2. test product-market fit
3. formulate business model

In order to illustrate each of these principles, a fictitious case study will be introduced here.

Case Example: Chamber Music Society

The example of a starting a chamber music society will be used to help illustrate the lean start-up concepts being introduced.

Imagine an arts entrepreneur interested in starting a chamber music society. As a gifted youth, Mary chose medicine over music for her profession, though now in mid-life as an established physician, she would like to revisit her other passion by presenting high-end, professional chamber music in an intimate setting. Her motives include realizing beautiful music in her life, contributing to her community, and interacting with interesting people (artists and audiences). Her vision includes presenting traditional chamber groups such as string quartets, duos with various instruments (e.g., piano & violin), piano trios/quartets/quintets, some solo performances, as well as other various chamber configurations.

PRACTICE

---

[1] Lean startup tools and methods can also be applied within existing companies
(see Osterwalder, Pigneur, Bernarda & Smith, 2014)

Mary has high standards and a well-tuned ear such that she is only interested in music of a high level of professional quality. She envisions traditional classical chamber music (e.g., Beethoven, Haydn, Schubert) comprising roughly half of the music on offer, more adventurous moderns (e.g., Bartok, Shostakovich, Britten) making up the next quarter, with the last quarter comprised of new music by living composers.

With this artistic vision, Mary presents a chamber music offering similar to what might be found in a variety of other urban settings (though program weightings and emphases may vary). Numerous unknowns exist at this point including where this offering might take place, how much it would cost, when performances would run, target audience, etc. Once the core vision has been established, the recommendation is to hold off on determining some of these points to address the first important step, that being value proposition development.

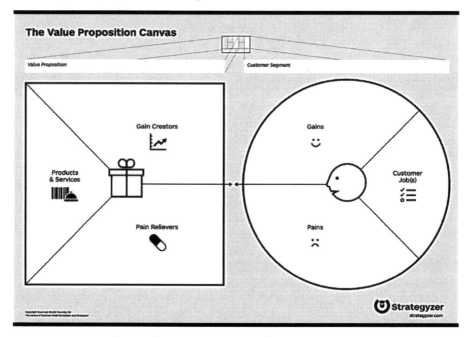

Figure 1 The Value Proposition Canvas. Retrieved from: Strategyzer.com

Building the Business Model

Herewith we will treat the different business model aspects.

Problem-Solution Fit consists of two sides: Value Proposition on the left, and Customer Segment on the right (Osterwalder, Pigneur, Bernarda & Smith, 2014) (figure 1). The Value Proposition has three components, including a list of all the products and services the value proposition is built around, the gain creators which increase positive elements, and the pain relievers which remove negative elements in customer lives through the product/service. The corresponding customer profile includes the desired customer jobs, as well as the reduction in pains and increase in gains customers would like to realize as their jobs are met.

Value Map. Given the artistic emphasis on artistic vision preceding the marketing challenge, it makes most sense to elaborate on Mary's vision by fleshing out the value map starting with products and services.

We have already indicated that live, classical chamber music performance is at the core with a number of other key characteristics including: high professional quality; mix of traditional, adventurous and new music; intimate setting (good acoustics, close audience proximity), mix of formats (e.g., solo, duo, trio, quartet), all presented with some kind of regularity (nested within a repeatable season).

In our fictitious example, audience gain creators associated with this offering could include such elements as: delight associated with fine music performance; catharsis within the artistic flow; reward for working hard in the rest of life's endeavours; education around art music; a refined social setting in which to engage friends; a sense of artistic community; interaction between audience and artist.

Similarly, pain relievers might include: regret for wasted time; disappointment with quality of the offering; feeling of being overcharged; worry about inappropriate programming taste. Mary's offering is hypothesized to increase gains as articulated, and reduce or eliminate pains.

Customer Segment. We now flip to the right hand side of the Value Proposition equation and consider customer segment (figure 1). The first point is to define customer jobs. When attending a chamber music performance the customer is looking for some combination of: entertainment; relaxation and stress relief; education; variety/tradition; stimulation, etc.

For our purposes, customer gains associated with attending a chamber music performance could include such elements as: excitement and anticipation for the event, status and cultural standing in the community, topics for conversation, and hedonic pleasure, among others.

Similarly, customer pains associated with attending a chamber music performance include: cost of admittance, difficulty of parking, risk of disappointment in the program, rude fellow audience members, sold out performance, and conflicting events at the same time, among others. Mary's challenge would be to investigate customer segments that match her offering.

The arts entrepreneur achieves problem-solution fit through evidence suggesting there are large enough customer segments where the jobs, pains, and gains sought (customer profile) sufficiently match the characteristics, gain providers, and pain relievers on offer (see Figure 1 for the Value Map). It should be recognized that problem-solution fit often varies as customers experience the offering under different conditions/contexts. For example, experiencing chamber music on a romantic outing, would likely differ from experiencing chamber music with family and friends, or with children.

PRACTICE

The challenge, therefore, is to investigate the possible customer segments that would provide a value proposition match. With our chamber music example, the following customer segments could be hypothesized. Initially, serious music lovers could be identified, possibly including people who experienced such music offerings as children, people who play (or have played) instruments, and people who self-identify as classical music lovers. With that as a first cut, further identifying potential audience members could include life-stage variables, for example the following three groupings: young professionals on a date; mid-life parents exposing their children to cultural activities; and retirees looking for meaningful leisure events. While valuing classical music in common, each of these three groups would have varying jobs, pains, and gains to address for fit to occur, often with varying priorities. For example, cost pain could vary substantially for each of the three groups, as could risk of disappointment in the program and concert logistics (e.g., seating and parking).

For an in-depth investigation into the different customer segments with respect to the chamber music offering, identifying the possibility of problem-solution fit, is the first step in the process. Here the entrepreneur enters the world of their customers (i.e., potential audience members) to fully understand their desire to have jobs completed, pains removed, and gains achieved. To do this, numerous creative options exist to help the entrepreneur understand audience segments, gaining empathy by assuming a variety of possible roles including: data detective, journalist, anthropologist, impersonator, co-creator, and scientist (Osterwalder, et al, 2014). Assuming characteristics from these types of roles enables unique insights for each segment, allowing deeper understanding into their life patterns, priorities, and preferences.

In summary, the Value Map is analogous to the essence of the artistic vision. The arts entrepreneur then must investigate potential Customer Profiles that match up with the Value Map. Adequate convergence results in Problem-Solution fit, thus progressing to the next step.

Product-Market Fit

Once problem-solution fit has been investigated with a defendable value proposition aligning with a sufficient number of customer segments, the arts entrepreneur can confidently move on to product-market fit. Here is where evidence is gathered that audiences are actually willing to pay for and/or attend events that are being proposed (as opposed to responding to interviews or surveys, which can be unreliable). In this case actual arts experiences are proposed or presented to experiment with actual up-take.

For our chamber music example, the most direct option is to actually hold an event performance and observe the uptake amongst the proposed target markets. Gathering data from such an event, investigating customer/audience uptake is key to help shape and guide future decision-making. As much as possible, specific information around participation amongst specific customer segments will help validate hypotheses around the kinds of audience members that will be attracted to such an event.

Actually holding events is probably the most direct and obvious way to gauge product-market fit. However, a number of other options are also available to help gain information about customer intentions, preferences, and practices. A variety of prototyping techniques can help gain early insight into product-market fit. The concept of minimum viable product, seeks to establish some kind of base-line offering that potential customers can respond to. An example might be to develop a simple website that would include video of a chamber music performance, with a description of an offering (perhaps even a series), asking people to at least sign up to receive more information, or more aggressively to look for pre-payment for a concert or series.

With minimum viable product approaches, it's possible to experiment with variables amongst different target groups. Things such as pricing, timing, location, program, and so on, can be manipulated to look for variation in uptake amongst different audience groups. In this stage, the goal is insight towards the broader objective. The arts-entrepreneur can expect substantial '*failure*' of ideas, guesses, or hypotheses around how potential audiences are anticipated to behave. If produced cheaply and without substantial investment, these experiments yield insights that help move the finished product towards a stable, repeatable and sustainable offering.

In summary, Product-Market fit seeks to test the proposed Value Proposition using data from actual experiments to validate hypotheses around how audience members will behave. The key here is to get some kind of support data for these postulations. In the event they are not supported, this can be considered progress (despite the initial feeling of failure) as it enables the entrepreneur to regroup and rethink their position, and then test again. Such data will ultimately provide confidence to stay motivated and move further with the idea towards a fully- fledged business model.

Business Model Formation

With sufficient evidence for product-market fit, the arts entrepreneur can confidently move towards business model formation. While value-proposition fit presents the starting point, business model options can often make or break the viability of the overall entrepreneurial venture. This is particularly the case for arts organizations where so much depends on a broader set of community stakeholders who can contribute to arts venture viability.

PRACTICE

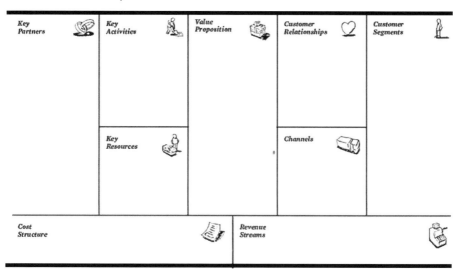

Figure 2 The Business Model Canvas. Retrieved from: Strategyzer.com

At the business model stage, value proposition is placed within the broader organizational context including an articulation of key activities & resources, spelling out customer channels & relationships, considering partnerships, and finally, weighing cost and revenue streams (Figure 2). Some question the Business Model Canvas for its lack of unique conceptual contribution (Eppler & Hoffmann, 2012). Nevertheless, the value of the canvas lies in the ability of the entrepreneur to conceptualize the entire start-up puzzle and consider its interconnected pieces (Blank, 2013), as well as consider the essential relationships that will enable sustainability.

Arts organizations occupy an important place in society, contributing to the communal fabric. As such, it is critical to embed the organization as much as possible into community. This impacts the shape of business models on a number of fronts. For example, in many cases key resources can be donated for free or provided at a reduced cost, given the socially generative status of the arts organization. Similarly, partnerships can often be formed with the intent of piggy-backing on the goodwill that arts groups generate.

Early stage arts organizations also need to choose wisely the key activities they choose to take on, always delegating any activity they possibly can as a way of simplifying their operations and potentially reducing cost, stress and complexity (Preece, 2005). Integrating with partners and other stakeholders can have a dual benefit, firstly relieving the organization from a particular set of tasks, but also having the benefit of involving more people in the activities of the venture; an added benefit can be the ability to draw on outside expertise, specialized to the task.

Customer relationships will depend on individual customer segments, and may vary substantially by age and the degree to which audience members are technologically oriented (i.e., 'digital natives'). Many arts organizations are utilizing technology to animate their offerings and creatively engage people through digital platforms. Similarly, social media marketing and promotion can piggy back on established networks creating widespread reach with relatively little cost or effort. Regardless of the vehicle (web, digital, physical or otherwise), when it comes to relationships, arts organizations need to be sure to weigh heavily on the side of differentiating their products based on the joy they bring into people's lives (i.e., creating delight) and doing so through exceptional programming, but also maintaining that sense of both anticipation and memory around the offerings (Preece & Johnson, 2011).

Channels deserve special consideration, with particular care taken on determining the best possible venue for the artistic offering. Venues represent so much to the offering, forming the context and functioning as the face to the audience. It can represent production values, convenience, sight lines, comfort, and so many other things, ultimately becoming the artistic home for the art.

Finally, both costs and revenue streams need to be projected and balanced with respect to proposed offerings. Once overall business model components have been considered, it's possible to assign related revenue and cost numbers to each, resulting in a *pro forma* income statement projection. This spreadsheet provides connecting logic for the overall model, indicating areas where fixed and variable revenues and expenses may interact. If inflows and outflows are substantially out of balance, consideration of radical alterations to the original business model may be necessary. Less dramatic imbalances will necessarily require more iterative considerations.

Building our Case

An example of business model design for a chamber music society could be as follows. Starting from scratch (in the absence of major start-up funding), the initial goal would be to look to community players to contribute essential resources to the cause. Such resources might include website development, poster & flier design, legal & accounting assistance, and so on. Aside from being time intensive for the entrepreneur, this element of community engagement through contributed resources both provides the services sought, but also—or perhaps more importantly—builds a foundation of excitement and anticipation for the emerging arts venture in the community. In short, building on the excitement of a chamber music society, people from the community will pitch in to help get the venture running.

As an example, recognizing mutual interests, the local symphony, public schools, and conservatories, could all see possibilities for cross-promotion, and providing links to music lovers. As for channels, it might be possible to present in a church for little or no rent, if the interests of the congregation were simultaneously met, with little cost to them. The benefits of a shared space would greatly enhance the viability through simplicity and cost savings. Finally, financial projections would need to assess the possibilities for paying artists of the calibre desired. With the prospect of ticket revenues not covering artist costs, the arts organization needs to recognize the opportunity of capitalizing on community benefit and look to narrow the funding gap with grants and sponsorships. Initial financial projections will necessarily require creative juggling of: various operational options, financial resources, mutually-beneficial partnerships.

Summing up, in arts start-up mode, business models typically need to be radically evaluated and improvised, to piece together a venture puzzle that has a chance at viability. With the confidence coming from a rigorous Value Proposition evaluation, and evidence indicating Product-Market fit, creatively building the appropriate business model context around the artistic offering is a critical step towards launch and viability into the future.

Key Points within the Start-up Process

This paper demonstrates the power of lean start-up methodology for new venture creation in the arts sector. Recognizing the inherent characteristics of arts organizations, lean methods—including value propositions, problem-solution fit, product-market fit, and business model creation—are adapted to the unique challenges of these organizations. Recognizing these important variables, the arts entrepreneur is then able to utilize the substantial benefits associated with lean start-up. This next section reiterates some of the key points in this process, while also discussing important supplemental principles.

PRACTICE

a. **Establish the Core**

Artistic vision is paramount for arts organizations. Defining a clear sense of purpose, identity, and reputation provides unequivocal signals for stakeholders to attach to and bond with. In this process it is also important to delineate boundary definitions for what is the core, recognizing negotiable and non-negotiable actions, activities and associations that accompany those definitions. This provides two important areas of consideration. The first is to define where the greatest core strength comes from and being sure to give that the proper attention and resources necessary to achieve the most important aims. The second is to signal non-core areas of flexibility, compromise and creativity.

b. **Stay Flexible and Experiment**

As arts organizations adapt to contemporary audience preferences, funding structures, and granting patterns, it's possible to engage in radical creativity when it comes to presenting the arts using lean start-up and business model canvas approaches—without 'selling out' or compromising the 'core'. Such actions will arguably be necessary to keep arts organizations viable for contemporary audiences and contexts. In contrast, many arts groups have the danger of falling into patterns of presentation that may have persisted over time, confusing them as being essential, while in fact not being part of the core offering. Missing this point keeps established institutions stuck in the past, while newer, more nimble start-ups re-think, re-envision, and re-vitalize arts presentation.

c. **Community Goodwill**

A key component for staying vital is recognizing the value of the arts to our communities and then exercising on that value. A variety of stakeholders are thoroughly invested in the success and well-being of arts in our midst; lean start-up and business model canvas methods help facilitate this engagement. Allowing them into the flexible and negotiable operations of emerging arts organizations enables opportunities for investment, engagement, excitement, anticipation and pride as the arts venture takes root and grows. Not making these overtures risks isolation, limited resources, and detachment—characteristics that will ultimately result in unsustainable art into the future.

d. **Non-linear Progression**

The new venture creation model has been presented as a linear, subsequently progressive process. While there are good reasons to suggest a disciplined progression through this process, the reality is that new arts ventures will progress in a much more organic and sometimes chaotic fashion, potentially moving back and forth between stages. This is very much in line with the more realistic assumptions inherent in lean start-up methodologies (Blank, 2013). The most important consideration is to not skip essential steps as short cuts to disciplined implementation.

Conclusion

The overarching message of this essay is that lean start-up methods, while needing adaptation, are very appropriate - if not essential - to the processes surrounding arts entrepreneurship. While some would argue lean start-up does not belong in the arts in that it would corrupt the principle of artistic integrity, this paper shows that perspective to be narrow and not valid once important adaptations are made. Further research will be necessary to validate this claim, and this will be possible as more arts entrepreneurs are exposed to the relatively new principles of lean start-up methodologies. Issues to be on the look-out for will be how flexible arts managers can be, once the core values and mission are established. Too often arts administrators confuse long-standing patterns ('*the way we have always done things*') with what is actually essential about the art and how it is presented and received.

This essay also holds substantial promise for arts entrepreneurship education. The adapted approach to lean start-up means that educators and students in arts entrepreneurship will be able to participate in evidence-based, new venture creation activity which has seen exceptional growth across campuses virtually across the world. It is important to find this common ground in order for arts entrepreneurs to benefit from the broader practice of new venture creation, whenever it is appropriate. To conclude, lean start-up methodology holds great promise for nascent arts organizations. Adapting lean principles to the unique challenges inherent in cultural offerings provides a viability framework that can greatly improve the potential for longer-term viability, while also enabling adherence to core artistic vision.

About the Author

Dr Stephen B. Preece has taught Strategic Management and International Strategy at the School of Business & Economics since 1993. His research focuses on cultural industries, in particular the management of performing arts organizations (dance, music, theatre, opera). Dr Preece's research projects have focused on sponsorships, audience patterns, partnerships, governance and new media. He does consulting in the area of strategic planning and analysis within the culture sector. Dr. Preece has published a number of articles in journals such as: Journal of Business Venturing, Long Range Planning, Journal of Small Business Management, International Executive, Canadian Public Administration, and International Journal of Arts Management.

—

spreece@wlu.ca

References

Blank, S. (2013). Why the lean start-up changes everything. In: *Harvard Business Review*, 91(5), 63-72.

Colbert, F. (2003). Entrepreneurship and leadership in marketing the arts. In: *International Journal of Arts Management,* 6(1): 30-39.

Colbert, F., J. Nantel, S. Bilodeau and J.D. Rich (2001). In: *Marketing Culture and the Arts*, 2nd ed. Montreal: Presses HEC (1st ed. 1994).

Eppler, M. J., & Hoffmann, F. (2012). Does method matter? An experiment on collaborative business model idea generation in teams. In: *Innovation, 14*(3), 388-403.

George, G. & Bock, A (2012). *Models of Opportunity: How Entrepreneurs Design Firms to Achieve the Unexpected*. New York: Cambridge University Press.

Morris, N. M., Kuratko, D. F., & Pryor, C. G. (2014). Building Blocks for the Development of University-Wide Entrepreneurship. In: *Entrepreneurship Research Journal, 4*(1), 45-68.

Osterwalder, A., & Pigneur, Y. (2010). *Business Model Generation: A Handbook For Visionaries, Game Changers, And Challengers*. Hoboken, New Jersey: Wiley.

Osterwalder, A. Pigneur, Y., Bernarda, G. & Smith, A. (2014). *Value Proposition Design*. Hoboken, New Jersey: John Wiley & Sons.

Preece, S. (2005). 'The Performing Arts Value Chain'. In: *International Journal of Arts Management.* 8(1): 21-32.

Preece, S. & Johnson, J. W. (2011). Web Strategies and the Performing Arts: An Answer to Difficult Brands? In: *International Journal of Arts Management.* 14(1): 19-31.

Read, S., Sarasvathy, S., Dew, N., Wiltbank, R., Ohlsson, A. (2011). *Effectual Entrepreneurship.* New York: Routledge.

Sarasvathy, S. D. (2001). Causation and effectuation: Toward a theoretical shift from economic inevitability to entrepreneurial contingency. In: *Academy of management Review, 26*(2), 243-263.

Wilson, N. C., & Stokes, D. (2004). Laments and serenades: relationship marketing and legitimation strategies for the cultural entrepreneur. In: *Qualitative Market Research: An International Journal, 7*(3), 218-227.

PRACTICE

Guillermo Olivares Concha

PROFESSIONAL SHORT-TERM TRAINING FOR CULTURAL ENTREPRENEURS IN VALDIVIA, CHILE INNOVUSS PROGRAM

Abstract

In 2012 started the work of the Creative Industries Node, an entrepreneurial support project funded by the National Agency for Entrepreneurship and Innovation (*CORFO*) in Chile and run by the Universidad San Sebastian Business School in the city of Valdivia, in the Southern part of Chile.

This project began with a gap diagnostic which pointed at the lack of business management skills and knowledge within the creative industries. Creative businesses and cultural entrepreneurs show a sub-optimal conduct within their projects, which limits their ability to promote both innovation and development.

Based on this analysis, sectorial needs and requirements have been identified. An intensive training program for professional cultural entrepreneurship has been developed, called *Innovuss*. It covers four training modules: creativity and innovation, business modelling, marketing, and oral communication; aimed to strengthen the business development of the participants through a one-month process.

This paper presents this community based training program, focussing on sectorial innovation for active creative entrepreneurs in the Southern region of Chile.

Introduction

'The creative and cultural industries constitute one of the fastest-growing sectors globally. The sector is forecast to play a bigger role in coming years. If the countries of the Americas are to achieve a balanced, high-growth economy, it is vital that the key strengths of businesses in the creative sector are nurtured' (Inter American Development Bank, 2013, p. 3).

According to the Organization for the Economic Co-operation and Development (OECD) both creativity and culture can be regarded as relevant factors in development at a personal level, but especially at a societal level. *'They are a driving force for economic growth, are at the core of 'glocal' competitiveness in the knowledge society and shape territories and local economies in a way which is both innovative and creative'* (OECD, 2005).

The international body affirms that the ability to bring to the forefront and spread values and references offered by cultural activities can make an outstanding support in development processes. This contribution makes possible that individual and communities plan their future, design new initiatives and collaborate in finding solutions (OECD, 2005).

PRACTICE

Dos Santos (2008) has set an important emphasis for mid-income countries like Chile. The Brazilian expert notes that poverty has remained as an important and unsolved matter in developing countries, especially in those depending on commodities. In spite of the efforts made to redefine industrial strategies in this type of countries, they lack of productive diversification. It is difficult to build a feasible development based on local realities and scarcities in labour, infrastructure and investment.

The Planning Context

In 2007-2008, the *Región de los Ríos*[1] started a process to define its development strategy towards 2019. The objective of this planning tool is to generate the conditions and the environment to foster prosperity in the region by improving quality of life to its inhabitants. The creative economy, which is assessed at a national scale, is seen as an emergent sector with an incipient development but a considerable potential of growth with a medium-sized state effort to achieve competiveness (CNCA, 2014).

The region capital, Valdivia[2], located 800 kilometres south of Santiago, the national capital, has developed a strong identity as a university and cultural pole in the south of the country. It holds the Universidad Austral, one of the top five universities in the country, and is also hosts the most important film festival in Chile and is headquarters of important events on classic music, jazz, theatre, dance, rock, etc. This identity, has been developed from the touristic tradition founded on its heritage, the *Mapuche*[3]. The Mapuche were of the most important first nations in Chile; they consis of Spanish and German immigrants, and of course Chileans, which surpassed the regional frontiers, generating an image of cultural capital in the southern region of the country.

In 2013, the national arts council (CNCA) conducted a national mapping study on creative industries, oriented to assess the state of the art and its overall behaviour in the whole country. This mapping process, based on a multidimensional analysis (labour, education, infrastructure and public funding) also provided data on the regional activities. The *Region de Los Ríos* is part of those regions that hold less labour, less infrastructure, less economic activity and less creative education supply (CNCA, 2013).

A regional mapping conducted earlier in 2011 provided information about the creative economic activity in the region, as a first attempt to describe the creative contribution to local economy. Among the data collected, the research concluded that the creative economic activity in the region accounted for 0,3% of the regional total sales. In labour, however, 5,9% of national employment corresponds to creative workers and, at a regional scale, this figure is even higher (6,1%).

PRACTICE

---

[1] *The Región de los Rios is one of the 15 administrative divisions in which Chili is divided. It was created in 2007 and it counts 369.000 inhabitants.*

[2] *The city of Valdivia has 140000 inhabitants*

[3] *Mapuche means People of the Land in mapudungun, the mapuche language. This indigenous group currently lives in central-south Chile and south-western Argentina,*

Creative Labour	Total Labour	Creative Labour	Employment Rate
Regional (Los Rios)	8228	134071	6.1%
National	409406	6914037	5.9%
Concentration rate in the region	2.0%	0.7%	

Table 1 Comparative chart on creative and total labor rates at a regional and national scale (2011) Source: CNCA

At the regional level, the local mapping study observed that creative labour has been mainly performed by university graduates (IDEE, 2011). In contrast, the region has scarce educational offerings in creative professions. To a certain extent, this apparent contradiction is due to the positive image of especially its capital Valdivia; conditions that appeal to creative talent and labour. Several surveys include the city among the best places to live/study/visit in the country.[4]

Within this context, a competitiveness program on creative industries is initiated. In order to foster the local creative sector as an economic pillar in regional development, a baseline study is executed. One of the most important findings is the need to improve the managerial skills and innovation management in the creative sector. Based on this analysis, *CORFO* funded a project aimed to deliver technologic transferences of innovative solutions and managerial tools to improve competitiveness and, as a consequence, to improve the development of cultural and creative businesses and projects. This project called *Nodo de Industrias Creativas* (Creative Industries Node), commenced in 2012. Its intention is to improve the result of cultural and creative businesses by means of training, counselling and support in an initial group of 20 entrepreneurs.

Fundamentals
One of the main findings in the research of creative and cultural entrepreneurship is that entrepreneurs show a lack of skills in management and business-aspects (Power and Jansson, 2006).

In Chile and, to a great extent in Valdivia, cultural entrepreneurs' lack of abilities obstructs the economical results. In general terms, creative entrepreneurs exhibit some generic notions about '*free trade agreements*' or '*world heritages' condition*', however this knowledge is not regarded as opportunities in terms of arts practice or business (Santiago Consultores, 2006). This assessment on cultural entrepreneurs in Chile states confirms the lack of skills to visualise the business or economic dimension in their disciplines, a lack of a clear marketing strategy, and few links to private entities to obtain sponsorship. In addition, a lack of professionalism and abilities to manage resources can be noted, especially in business and project design. During the design of the project on creative industries in Valdivia (Dalberg consultancy, 2009) a '*gaps map*' is created, sketching a possible favourable environment for cultural and creative entrepreneurship. Among the four main gaps, the study pointed at the development of talent in managerial and business skills.

---

[4] *E.g, a survey called Barometro Imagen Ciudad, conducted by Vision Humana (2014) ranked the city in 4th place among the best Chilean cities to live. The Urban Quality of Life Index 2014 (Intermediate Cities) ranked the city 5th in the country*

PRACTICE

Design, Validation and Implementation

With this context in mind, we started to define a training program in cultural entrepreneurship. As previously indicated, the project *Creative Industries Node* began its work in 2012. The program started with a group of 20 entrepreneurs from micro-companies[5], committed to participate in a training plan on managerial and innovation skills.

At the beginning, the project-team designed and implemented a technology audit, whose aim is to know the level of business development and internal organization in the projects and entrepreneurs participants. This activity provided a significant amount of information to perform both an individual and a collective diagnostic that allowed the project to visualize the most important gaps. If one applies the entrepreneur equation proposed by Drucaroff (2006) to this diagnostic, the outcome is that the weakest stages in the development in cultural and creative entrepreneurship are both analysis and strategy, especially in innovation management. The audit revealed that creative entrepreneurs often connected directly their creativity to action with no analysis and strategy to prevent or minimize mistakes and failures.

CREATIVITY $+$ **ANALYSIS** $+$ **STRATEGY** $+$ **ACTION**

Figure 1 Entrepreneurship Equation. Source: Drucaroff (2006)

The project provided an individual counselling service to participants, offering an additional possibility to identify the main concerns and issues for their business development. A part of the project team offered support and advice on business model design and marketing, allowing to confirm the need to improve managerial skills, as well as those related to innovation and marketing.

Based on the information provided via the technological audits and counsel meetings, the team evaluated the results and designed a program oriented to deliver intensive short term training on current entrepreneurship methodologies, in order to improve the existing cultural and creative projects, the innovation processes, and the analytical skills regarding the current state of their business.

The design is summited to a double validation filter. First, *CORFO*, the funding body, evaluated the results obtained from the different audits. It resulted in a designated plan to teach entrepreneurship techniques to creative entrepreneurs. It validated the program as a micro incubator for cultural and creative projects; emphasizing the support of business ideas as a concrete way to help entrepreneurs to grow. The second filter is executed by the creative entrepreneurs involved. The program is summited to the participants' approval.

[5] *According to the technological audit these original participants originated from several sectors; design, music, crafts, software, architecture.*

PRACTICE

The Structure of the Program

The program, called *Creative Project Acceleration Program*, branded as *Innovuss*[6], is planned to support creative businesses from the initial stage of idea. Due to the tight schedule of the participants - mainly entrepreneurs and independents workers, who have not enough time available to attend extended class modules - the program is designed as an intensive and focalized generation and acceleration of new creative businesses (Olivares et all, 2014). It holds a series of 4 short modules, a collaborative workshop and a permanent support by the staff-team. This training program aims to improve the participants' skills, and train them to prepare new projects, to market them and to pitch them before customers, investors and/or public funding bodies. Originally, the program is designed to be implemented a short period of time. However, due to the interest of entrepreneurs and the lack of learning opportunities in creative methodologies, the team developed a second and a third version, adding the number of participants to 75 per session, over 3,5 times the original numbers planned.

When implemented, the program started with a call for entries of business ideas through an online form inviting entrepreneurs to propose projects to be assessed by the team. After a review, much-promising application were followed-up by a personal interview, aimed to evaluate the entrepreneurial skills. When admitted, the short term training in creative entrepreneurship followed. The applications process allowed the receipt of business ideas from different sector such as design, visual arts, music, traditional gastronomy, cultural tourism, software, communications and publishing, crafts, architecture and cultural management. During the one-month training, the participants took part of a series of teaching modules with experts in every field, completed with a number of counselling sessions.

After a number of trial sessions the program *Innovuss* included different phases:

1. Module 1: Design Thinking
2. Module 2: Business Model Generation
3. Module 3: Marketing
4. Module 4: Elevator Pitch

The course starts with **Design Thinking;** '*a discipline that uses the designer's sensibility and methods to match people's needs with what is technologically feasible and what a viable business strategy can convert into customer value and market opportunity*' (Brown, 2008, p. 86). This workshop offers innovative techniques to develop creativity in finding solution to customers' problems. Frequently, within the cultural and creative professions the focus is inside oriented; '*our*' or '*my*' work, with not much attention focussed on audiences or customers. This workshop promotes a change in the point of view in the process of designing products/services.

This workshop iss presented to applicants as a tool to create value in developing goods, services and creative experiences. It is thought as a technological transference, whose objective is to help entrepreneurs to create new projects by generating innovative ideas, research strategies, design process, and also by fostering them to think out of

PRACTICE

---

[6] *The name emerges by combining the word Innovation and an acronym for Universidad San Sebastian, USS.*

the box. The aim of this module is to offer a new perspective to design new products or services in cultural context, with a special focus on - current or eventually future-needs and wishes in cultural consumption. It is commonly assumed that creative sector is permanently creative; however the findings in the technologic audit contrast with this extended view, especially when creative work become a daily routine. This module delivers tools to facilitate the innovation process in every project to generate new creative services or cultural goods

The second module offered is **Business Model Generation** (Osterwalder and Pigneur, 2010), which is a tool where one can find all the aspects involved in a business, even in a non-profit cultural project. In words of the authors 'a business model describes the rationale of how an organization creates, delivers, and captures value' (Osterwalder and Pigneur, 2010). This is a tool that offers a simplified way to describe visually a business, especially to those with no training in management. It is also a method to add value to a project, by means of visualizing what the customers segments are, and what the proposition values have to be delivered to these segments. It offers a visual method, easier to handle by those entrepreneurs in cultural and creative industries. In a one-sheet diagram, participants define all main factors involved in their businesses. In addition, it offers a proper and professional advisory, improving the concepts by visualizing new factors that have remained out of sight.

The third module is **Marketing.** Yet, it is not offered in the traditional meaning of advertising a product and services for sale. In the words of the creative consultant David Parrish, it is 'about designing your business with markets in mind. Strategic marketing focuses on choosing the right customers to buy your products, before you start to do any selling' (Parrish, 2014, p. xi). The aim of this module, paraphrasing Parrish, is a complex and integrated process oriented to go in depth into the knowledge of the business, to evaluate its position in a market occupied by competitive actors and make connections with the appropriate customers. 'Strategic marketing is the vital matter of making the right products, selecting the best customers, and then managing the relationship with those selected customers. It's about aligning your whole business to the changing needs of the most important customers' (Parrish, 2014).

The program ended with a module on the **Elevator Pitch.** Participants deliver appropriate business presentations before investors, partners, funding bodies and/or customers. Presenting ones' work is identified as a competitive gap, identifying a lack of clarity and synthesis in expressing the core elements of ones' projects. One is in need of a clear expression of creative aspirations to endeavour a new project, more than a viable business model. In this way, this workshop is regarded as a tool to strengthen the business model design in a way to make clear all the main elements involved, facilitating the process of communicating to external audiences. This workshop is designed in a two-part module. The first one is related to redesign the narrative of the business, and the second one is geared to rehearse and perform this new narrative via a test-and-error approach. The module helps participants to define and arrange a sort of a script in which is defined 'what to say', trained to manage the body and voice, as an actor rehearsing a role to play.

PRACTICE

Concluding, as a transversal work, the project provided a collaborative workshop called *Minga*[7] *Creativa*, in which a group of entrepreneurs were oriented to visualize problems at a local scale (i.e. Urban issues) providing ideas to solve them by interchanging their different points of views. The purpose is to generate a networking opportunity, but also a chance to share knowledge and experiences with other entrepreneurs, providing them the occasion to create ideas by constructing collaboratively new ones based upon the ideas of others. This workshop has also been designed as an application period of all the other modules, by using the learnt techniques to identify problems and to try finding solutions by means of thinking out of the box and trying to define a proposition value to users or customers.

As a summary, the program includes four modules, a final workshop and the counselling services, all aimed to achieve and improve the required innovative skills, to support entrepreneurs in the process to build a business, and to perform properly before the investors or sponsors.

Public Funding

Following the general cultural entrepreneurship projects, Chile created an annual schedule for public funding for private initiatives in business and culture, offering seed capital that are open to a public application. The core of this funding is to help entrepreneurs to start or develop a business or, in other cases, to fund a cultural or creative project (mostly oriented to the film industry). In advanced stages of the applications process, the public funding bodies (CORFO, SERCOTEC[8], CNCA[9], c.s), require to present the business model, a pitch and/or the distribution policy.

During the validation process, CORFO expressed its interest in generate a series of initiatives to be presented to funding bodies to create new entrepreneurial projects in cultural and creative industries. In this way, one of the additional objectives of the program *Innovuss* is to prepare and support entrepreneurs to apply for public funding in order to bring the idea to life as a new business-venture.

PRACTICE

---

[7] *Minga is the name of a traditional cultural practice in the South of Chile, where local communities work in coordination and collaboration to support their members to harvest, to make apple cider, and, especially, to literally move houses across the sea and fields to a new location. This physical relocation process has become a communal celebration.*

[8] *Sercotec is the Spanish acronym for Cooperation and Technical Support Service, a public agency oriented to support and fund SME's and micro-companies.*

[9] *CNCA is the Spanish acronym for Arts and Culture National Council, equivalent to a Ministry of Culture.*

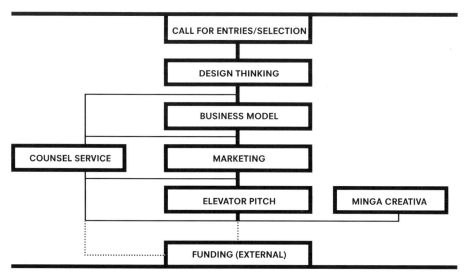

Figure 2 *Innovuss* program diagram

Results

In order to measure the impact of the program in the community, a qualitative survey post-evaluation has been developed. Based on the survey developed, entrepreneurs stated that their knowledge of their own business improved by means of considering new variables, analysing factors that previously remained ignored to them, such as customer needs or value to be delivered (see for a comparison Chris Brown, 2008).

Another relevant outcome is that entrepreneurs were eager to use the learnt methodologies in their business-activities, with the purpose to improve management and innovation in order to become more competitive.

A third remarkable element in the analysis is that entrepreneurs have developed a positive attitude towards sharing their experiences with colleagues. Exchanging one other's experiences is regarded as a lesson to all the participants, and also seen as a constructive feedback from others. The collaborative work used to be a tradition in the history of Chile. However in business and even in arts, individualism has played an important role. In this sense, this project attempts to recover part of this traditional grass-root practice.

Another positive result can be identified in the field of funding. Despite the fact that it is not mandatory to apply for funding, it is considered to be a success indicator for the project. The success-rate in applying to public subsidies, dedicated to start a cultural business or to create a creative project, is considered to be very positive. During the program 12 projects supported by *Innovuss* applied for public funding, with a rate of approval of 75%, equivalent to 9 approved projects. These figures cannot be compared to any other information, because it is the first edition. However, according to the funding body, teaching entrepreneurship techniques to cultural practitioners with an applied experience in fund-raising (public or private) is seen as a positive improvement. This opinion is confirmed by the entrepreneurs themselves, who expressed their opinion about the program. It has been meaningful in terms of helping them to analyse and

PRACTICE

plan their business-strategy to business. The counsel provided, made them feel sure about a business idea; the support made them feel accompanied in the adventure of creating a creative business.

References

Anderson, C. (October 2004). *The Long Tail*. Wired 12.10

Brown, T. (June 2008). Design Thinking. In: *Harvard Business Review*, 84.

CNCA (Consejo Nacional de la Cultura y las Artes). (2014*) Mapeo de las industrias creativas en Chile*. Cultura Publicaciones. Santiago de Chile

CNCA (Consejo Nacional de la Cultura y las Artes). (2013) *Caracterización y Análisis Regional de las Industrias Creativas. Región de Los Ríos*. Retrieved from: www.observatoriocultural.gob.cl. Sección Observatorio Cultural. Publicado: Noviembre, 2013.

Dalberg Consulting. (September 2009). *Programa de Mejoramiento de la Competitividad de las Industrias Creativas*. Valdivia. Chile

Dos Santos-Duisenberg, Edna. (2008). Creative economy: is it a feasible development option? In: *Creative economy : as a development strategy : a view of developing countries* (52 - 73). Sao Paulo, Brazil: Itaú Cultural.

Drucaroff, Sergio. (2006). *Caja de Herramientas: Módulos de formación para emprendedores culturales, Laboratorio de Industrias Culturales*. Buenos Aires: Laboratorio de Industrias Culturales.

IADB (Inter American Development Bank). (2013). *The economic impact of the creative industries*. Oxford Economics/British Council/

IDEE Consultores. (2011). *Mapeo Industrias Creativas Región de Los Ríos*. Informe Final.

OECD (Organisation for Economic Co-Operation and Development). (2005). *Culture and local development*. OECD Publishing

Olivares, G., Cabezas, M., Mena, F. y Matamala. S. (2014). *Región Creativa. Experiencia del Nodo de Industrias Creativas en la Región de Los Ríos* (2011-2013). Valdivia: Universidad San Sebastián.

Osterwalder, A. y Pigneur, Y. (2010). *Business Model Generation*. New Jersey: John Wiley & Sons, Inc.

Parrish, D. (2014). *Chase One Rabbit: strategic marketing for business success*. Wordscapes. Liverpool. UK.

Pratt, A. C. . (2009). Policy Transfer and the Field of the Cultural and Creative Industries: What Can Be Learned from Europe? In: *En Creative economies, creative cities : AsianEuropean perspectives*, editado por L Kong y J O'Connor. Heidelberg: Springer, 2009.

Santiago Consultores (November 2006). *Consultoría para elaborar diagnósticos y propuestas regionales para el fomento del sector cultural*. Informe Final, Sintesis y Propuestas. Santiago de Chile.

Wilson, G. (November 2012). *The history of the Elevator Speech*. Retrieved from: http://www.the-confidant.info/2012/the-history-of-the-elevator-speech/

About the author

Guillermo Olivares Concha MA BA holds a BA degree in Journalism and Communications from Universidad Austral de Chile (Valdivia). He also holds a MA degree in Cultural and Creative Industries from King's College London (UK). He has also run several projects in cultural entrepreneurship in Chile.

He is currently Coordinator of the Regional Strategic Program "Valdivia Creativa", funded by Corfo. He is also a regular invited panellist to seminars and national conferences on the subject, and permanent columnist of the cultural content portal.

guillermo@valdiviacreativa.cl

PRACTICE

Elonahas Lubytė

PEST-CONTROL TRAINING ENVIRONMENT OBSERVATION AND ASSESSMENT OF ARTISTS-TO-BE IN LITHUANIA

Abstract

Referring to the case study of Lithuania (a post-Soviet Baltic country), this article discusses the teaching of social science disciplines in a university-type art school (Vilnius Academy of Arts). The article focusses on the possibilities of applying the method of PEST (political, economic, social, technological) macro-environmental research, when training the skills of environment observation and assessment of artists-to-be. It supports them in making renewal-promoting (innovative) decisions in the presence of the experienced changes, and supports the development of culture and creative industries.

The author of the publication makes use of the theoretical insights from the disciplines of management (Milena Dragićević-Šešić, Peter F. Drucker), marketing (Philip Kotler) and political science (Elemer Hankiss, Ronald Inglehart). The article starts with a description of the changes that are taking place in Lithuania (the PEST environment) during the transition from a planned economy to market relations. While referring to the case analysis of the Vilnius Academy of Arts (Lithuania), a three-step method (concentration of attention, problematic approach and practical application) of practical tasks is presented. This supports training the abilities of observation and assessment of the environment (political, economic, social, and technological) of artists-to-be.

Introduction

Culture management and marketing are the youngest disciplines of social sciences in institutions of higher education in the post-Soviet space. The collapse of the Berlin wall, the disintegration of the Soviet Union, and the regaining of Lithuania's independence in the late 20th century prompted rapid changes (transition from a centrally planned to market economy, integration into NATO and the European Union). In the context of these changes society faces a need to understand the logic of the course and management of these processes. It is also important for artists-to-be who seek international recognition.

While moving from ideological regulation (censorship) of the Soviet period to the freedom and variety of creative expression, one has to identify his or her worldview values and justify creative solutions. For that purpose it is necessary to know, observe, and critically assess the changes that take place in the environment.

Post-industrial knowledge and service society is characterised by a growing belief in creative economy and its potential to drive economic growth and promote development. It provides empirical evidence that creative industries are among the most dynamic emerging sectors in world trade.

PRACTICE

However, in the discussions of politicians and academicians analysing the entrepreneurial dimension of culture and the development of creative industries, insufficient attention is paid to artists who produce creative products and services, and to the training of their abilities to adapt to the rapid development of culture and creative industries.

Theoretical Approach

While seeking to strengthen the students' abilities of self-realization, in theoretical classes we look for an answer to one fundamental question, which is of key importance to each creator: *What does it mean to be an artist today?* Referring to the theoretical insights of Peter F. Drucker, the attention is drawn to the fact that an artist living and creating in post-industrial information society today is a knowledge worker rather than manual labourer, and his creative resources generate added value. In the art world, it is new ideas that first manifest themselves as an alternative rejected by the majority.

However, in the long run it becomes recognized and commercially attractive. '*Today a knowledge worker, who is independent of politicians, government, and economic crises, must be his own master, and must learn when and how to change. He is mobile and free to choose, being the sole master of his own 'means of production' – knowledge and skills'. Until now, 'changes are still thought of as death or taxes: they should be postponed as long as possible, and they are not considered as something desirable*' (Drucker, 2004).

The Hungarian political scientist Elemer Hankiss confirms that people regard changes with distrust. Discussing the response of Central and East Europeans to the recently experienced changes, the author refers to the state of *the great regression, 'when people are unable to cope with themselves or the world, and as a defence they revert to a chronologically earlier (e.g. childlike) state of mind or behaviour. [..] One of the symptoms of this regression is the larval reflex: many [people], in their state of alarm, have shut themselves up, crawled into their shell, clammed up; they have no wish to see or hear what is going on around them, and having dismissed the outside world [..]. The snail reflex is a somewhat milder form of this type of regression. Many of our fellow citizens have become supersensitive, cautiously sticking their heads out of their shells only every now and again, only to pull back in alarm, touchily and huffily, into the dark, steamy warmth of the shell'* (Hankiss, 2007).

The Social Dimension

Speaking in terms of management, changes are a social process, in which an individual plays the leading role. Its success is determined by an individual's knowledge, his understanding what and why should be changed, his wish and will to change, and his skills and abilities showing him how to make changes.

As the ideological regulation of the Soviet period is giving way to a democratic variety of views, the issue of the values of world outlook of creators is becoming very important. Within '*the Soviet society beyond classes, in which the property is single and belongs to all, as well as full social equality*' (Marshal, 1994), the diversity of different values based on diversity of interests was not recognized. It must be noted that this can be seen as a contradiction to human nature; different people have different needs, interests, values; and/or different world-views expressing their desires. When developing the present emerging liberal market in Lithuania, the relations go beyond monolithic ideological nature, at presence, touching *'existing and potential buyers of the product or service as a whole'* (Kotler, 2003).

Having carried out a quantitative survey of the values of the world population, the political analyst Ronald Inglehart (2007) distinguishes two dimensions of changes marking the transition from *Traditional/Secular-rational* values to of *Survival/ Self-expression* values. While looking for a comprehensive measurement of all major areas of human concern, major areas of human concern, from religion to politics to economic and social life have to be identified. The two dimensions mentioned (*Traditional/Secular-rational* and *Survival/Self-expression*) explain more than 70 per cent of the cross-national variance in a factor analysis of ten indicators – and each of these dimensions is strongly correlated with scores of other important orientations.

The Traditional/Secular-rational values dimension reflects the contrast between societies in which religion is very important, and those in which it is not. A wide range of other orientations are closely linked with this dimension. Societies near the traditional pole emphasize the importance of parent-child ties and deference to authority, along with absolute standards and traditional family values, and reject divorce, abortion, euthanasia, and suicide. These societies have high levels of national pride, and a nationalistic outlook.

Societies with Secular-rational values have the opposite preferences on all of these topics. The second major dimension of cross-cultural variation is linked with the transition from industrial society to post-industrial societies-which brings a polarization between Survival and Self-expression values.

Ronald Inglehart found evidence that orientations have shifted from *Traditional* toward *Secular-rational* values in almost all industrial societies. Yet, modernization is not linear. When a society has completed industrialization and starts becoming a knowledge society, it moves in a new direction, from *Survival* values toward increasing emphasis on *Self-expression* values.

A central component of this emerging dimension involves the polarization between *Materialist* and *Post-materialist* values, reflecting a cultural shift that is emerging among generations who have grown up taking survival for granted. The *Self-expression* values give high priority to environmental protection, tolerance of diversity and rising demands for participation in decision-making in economic and political life. These values also reflect mass polarization over tolerance of outgroups, including foreigners, gays and lesbians and gender equality.

> *'The shift from Survival values to Self-expression values also includes a shift in child-rearing values, from emphasis on hard work toward emphasis on imagination and tolerance as important values to teach a child. And it goes with a rising sense of subjective well-being that is conducive to an atmosphere of tolerance, trust and political moderation. Finally, societies that rank high on Self-expression values also tend to rank high on interpersonal trust. This produces a culture of trust and tolerance, in which people place a relatively high value on individual freedom and Self-expression, and have activist political orientations'*
> *(Inglehart, 2008).*

PRACTICE

In the survey *Eurobarometer 69*, carried out by the European Commission in 2008, the EU countries were compared according to the number of *Materialists*, *Post-materialists* and individuals of mixed world outlook. The obtained results made Lithuania stand out. If in the entire European Union post-materialists comprise approximately 9 percent; in Lithuania their number is mere 3 percent (i.c. Sweden 23 percent, the Netherlands 20 percent; Denmark 16 percent).

This small proportion of *Post-materialists* and the exaggerated emphasis on material things is typical of young economies, the countries that did not enjoy long-term material welfare and riches passed from generation to generation.[1] These kinds of society's attitudes should be related with the model of cultural policy of national emancipation;

> *'This is typical of former colonies and is applied in many post-Soviet East European countries (including Lithuania – E. L.). Its basic feature is the establishment and development of national cultural traditions, which had been suppressed by colonization or occupation. This often leads to the 'seclusion' of culture and nationalism, even chauvinism, when all art of the period of occupation is discarded, and the culture of the minorities, as well as the already existing or emerging alternative and experimental art is ignored. In many of these countries an opposition is formed between a European-minded minority (national elite) and the majority of the population living in the environment of traditional culture: it gives rise to new conflicts between the elite cultural model oriented to the universal cultural values, and the populist model oriented to national values'*
> *(Dragićević-Šešić, 1998).*

PRACTICE

Central and Eastern Europe, now entering a new phase of its history, *'unites 15 countries lying between Russia on the East and Germany and Italy on the West, – a territory in between Estonia and Greece, with the population of ca. 160 million people, 15 small and medium-sized nations, who lived under occupation from 150 to 1000 years. [..] This zone [..], with the history rich in bloody catastrophes and a very melancholic present [..], is the youngest and most vital part of the Christian West Europe'*
(Pakštas, 2003).

Lithuania is a transit corridor between the East (Russia) and the West (Europe). In this scattered territory, open to influences from both sides, with the pressures and pulls of different centres, the development of modernity in the 20th and 21st centuries was determined by the unique system of viewpoints. In this space, influenced by rather contradictory factors, a lifestyle open to influences and changes has developed, adjusting to diverse and sometimes mutually exclusive factors. Its distinctive feature is *change*; however, not via alternatives, but rather through obeying the rules of the big centres, e.g. the *adaptive development of art and culture*, when new Western expressions emerge here, not in their original shape, but sometimes with some delay caused by historical circumstances.

[1] *Incidentally, friendship is very important to a statistical EU citizen. 27 per cent of the people who participated in the survey confirmed it. However, only 13 per cent of Lithuanians associate the feeling of happiness with friendship.*

Late Modernisation

With regard to this, Lithuania is a phenomenon of late modernisation. The Soviet occupation, for half a century, unnaturally stopped the development which had been initiated in the 20ᵗʰ century interwar period as a process of synchronisation with West European processes of modernisation. '*Now, over a very brief period of history, Lithuania continues experiencing the societal and political pressures of the kind which took place over long segments of history in European and American processes of civilisation*'
(Donskis, 1993).

The environment is changing faster than the need to analyse and critically assess the reasons, the course and the outcomes of the changes. One of the reasons why in Lithuania there are not strong traditions of societal activism, is the fact that over history, for a long time, vertical ties dominated, those between *a master and a serf.* Lithuanians were peasants, whereas a civil society is a feature of urban rather than rural origins. The revival in public life that coincided with the first period of independence, in Soviet times became vertical again. A person communicated with a clerk '*like a boor asking for mercy, but not a citizen demanding that his rights be respected [..] Therefore, the second national renaissance came to [..] a nation [..] hardly in possession of public capital and civic solidarity*'
(Girnius, 1999).

The liberated nation became scattered, and its citizens, especially, those in the creative field, focused on striving for individual goals. This held back the development of conditions for shaping up an actual and decentralised rather than an officially (legally) organised system of decision-making in arts management, encouraging the determined cooperation between the state and the public and private sectors. In the environment of rapid changes, society became fragmented into supporters of renewal, and supporters of traditional values (old organisational structures). A tension emerged between the following societal groups: on one hand, those open to change and future-driven, and, on the other hand, those romanticising the past; otherwise put, between followers of established and followers of new methods of management and administration.

The artist's Mission

Some envision the artist's mission as exclusive, deserving the special attention of the state, forgetting what during the Soviet era guaranteed the well-being of obedient artists, and long for *bygone times*. Others, supporters of a liberal and free market, oppose the exclusiveness of the creative activities of artists. Among the younger generation are some who accept *the lessons* of *Las Vegas*. They fulfil the needs of the consumer society, and also those who confront them and - following the leftist intelligentsia of the West - take a critical stance towards the new post-Soviet capitalism, or focus on the opportunities for alternative creative expression, criticising the institutional powers of art organisations.

This means that in a small and economically vulnerable country, we are dealing with the fact that the inherited centralised system of art development coordination has been changing very slowly, mostly without upsetting the former organisational and value system. Just as in the late Soviet era, *façade* or *festival culture* priorities are in favour, emphasising ephemeral events with public exposure, rather than revamping the art management system.

PRACTICE

The development of art has still been supported by the state, and at the same time there are organisations funded through project-based schemes delegating experts to the expert boards of the Ministry of Culture, making decisions on overall funding redistribution. By this, the state hardly encourages productive competition between the private and the state sectors; moreover, it shelters unequal conditions, thus obstructing the process of decentralisation. Subsequently, the communities of creative workers maintaining controversial viewpoints, along with private, state and public art organisations, in the context of changes but with limited centralised restructured state funds, have taken the position of *self-defence*, deterring the dynamics of renewal.

Setting Priorities

Within the actual development, art management manifests itself in the collaboration of three elements, the artist, the art organisation and the public. There appears a reciprocal relationship between all links in the art management system. Hence, *art* (works of art and services) circulates in the environment not as a product of physical evidence (food, clothes, warmth, safety), but rather as a product, or service, responding to the individual societal and cultural needs of the human kind. It can be seen as the functions of *education, representation* (belonging) or *the economy*.

Yet, in the artwork (services) market, two segments of art can be identified: *visual* (alternative, official recognition, commercial success) and *utilitarian/applied* (single, limited circulation, mass circulation) *art*.

The access of the artworks (services) to the public (the customer) is guaranteed by various art organisations (academic art institutions, museums, travelling exhibitions, art galleries, art auctions and the creative industries sector, such as advertising, publishing and other enterprises). In the course of the transition, the activities of Lithuanian art management are influenced by the external (local, European, global) political, economic, social and technological environment.

a.   *Political* changes in Lithuania can be associated with its transition from a centralised (totally dependent on Moscow), one-party (ideologically politicised) country towards one with a democratic system, tolerating a diverse political and *Weltanschauung*-driven civil and community creed, encouraging private (business) and public (voluntary activity) initiatives, openness and international cooperation.

b.   *Economic* changes can be seen in the light of the transition from a centralised towards a decentralised system of culture and art development support (*arm's length bodies*), e.g. regulating taxes, encouraging citizens.

The Law on Charity and Sponsorship allows the transfer of 2 per cent of a person's income tax to non-profit organisations, and business and public bodies that support the development of art and culture. This decentralisation of the state subsidy system leads to a redistribution of funds. As a consequence some of the public spending, with the consultancy of independent expert commissions, should be restructured via project-based funding. State support for artists can be decentralised through *project funding*. Artists can claim funds, by representing an organisation which serves as a protector of the foreseen project implementation. This kind of *artist support* offers

PRACTICE

them national and government prizes, pensions and grants in two categories. In addition
it creates the possible *acquisition of artworks*, conducted by national, state, institutional and municipal museums.

c.   *Social* changes can be seen in relation to the unrestricted freedom of the artist's
     creative self- expression, and the determination by the public as to which artistic
     event should be preferred, and on whether to do support it, if at all. There are laws
     determining the status of the creative artist, and preserving his or her authorial
     rights in Lithuania.

However, in reality, the situation of a free artist is rather complicated. It can hardly be
mitigated, even by the favourable tax rates on creative (authorial) agreements, adopted by
the State Tax Inspectorate (from 1990 to 2002 - 13 per cent, from 2003-2008 - 15 per cent
and from 2009 – 27 per cent). No provision has been created to make it possible
to accumulate some of the funds for an old-age pension or health insurance while
deducting those amounts. In addition, the unbalanced renewal of the economy, which has
failed to enable the development of a middle class. As a consequence one can identify
the polarisation between the centre (city) and the periphery (the regions), the unstable
economic state of the country's citizens, increasing emigration and the low birth
rate, etc. do not encourage the consumption of cultural services for non-primary or
non-subsistence needs.

Herewith, art organisations and the lower end of the media take insufficient care of
the development of public needs. Narrow demand, especially for pure art, along with
the erratic adaptation by creative artists to the challenges brought about by the changes,
boosts the pressures of *self-defence* among members of the artistic community and
art organisations.

d.   *Technological* changes can be associated with the development of new products,
     services and technologies. New information technologies modify the means of
     expression of artists, art organisations and public communication (for instance,
     web portals of artists or art organisations, e-commerce, simplified international
     cooperation procedures, the digitalisation of the collections in museums, etc).
     Information technologies have also become an instrument of new creative move-
     ments (new media art), substantially shifting forms of artwork event organisation
     and presentation (for instance, white cubes in museums are replaced by black or
     dimmed-out space, or hardly transportable three-dimensional artwork is substi-
     tuted by the CD format).

Analysis of Practical Tasks

To encourage the students to apply the acquired knowledge in practice and train their
abilities of environment observation and assessment, a *three-step method* (concentration
of attention, problematic approach and practical application) of tasks collating with
the material taught in theoretical lectures is used.

PRACTICE

First Step – Concentration of Attention

It is a practical task introducing the PEST research method; analysing political, economic, social, technological changes. It is performed in classroom, and the students are divided into four teams. Each team is given a task to name the factors of the positive and negative (+ and -) impact of one of the four segments of environment. Their presentations are discussed in classroom.

Before carrying out the task, two figures are discussed. The 1st figure: 'Portrait of the Artist' (2007) imaged by Helen Blejerman introduces to the students the channels of interaction with the outer world (macro environment; government, university, media, etc.). The 2nd figure is the PEST scheme of the Lithuanian cultural field compiled by the student Andrius Dubinas (2010), which presents the key concepts of the task to the students.

PRACTICE

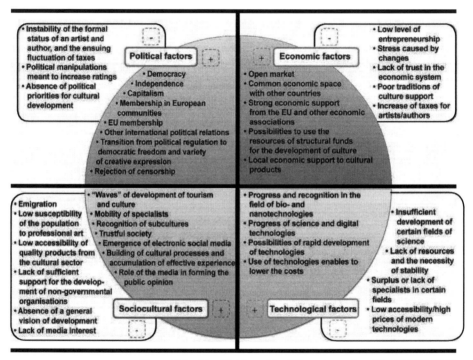

Figure 1 Andrius Dubinas The Lithuanian cultural field PEST 2010

Second step – Problematic Approach

Here we offer an individual task, during which the students, acquainted with the texts by the theorists discussed in lectures, have to write a two- or three-page essay relating their approaches with the local PEST issues. The most interesting projects of the students' homework are presented and discussed in classroom.

A comparison of remarks by the Hungarian political scientist Elemer Hankiss about the state of the *great regression* (*larval reflex, snail reflex*), are juxtaposed with the descriptions of insect life by the 19th century French entomologist Jean Henry Fabre, and confronted with the thoughts by the lecturer of the Chair of Photography and Media Art of the Vilnius Academy of Arts (entomologist Andrius Surgailis). It discusses the similarities of social insects and artistic communities. Can the hierarchical model of social insects and an anthill (queen ant, guards, worker ants, scout ants) be applied to an artistic community?

Third Step – Practical Application

Either the individual student or a students'-team, when preparing a plan of commercial or non-profit art project, have to perform the PEST analysis of the environment of the conceived project. The results of this analyses are presented and discussed in the classroom. An example; we did a futuristic project of military industry, created in preparation for World War IV '*Stones and Sticks*'.[2] The students' task is to set up '*the commercial sale of stones and sticks of different size, weight, form, and surface texture, with the aim to arm the country while protecting safe environment and preparing for future wars.*'

The student has distinguished the following PEST factors that play a part in the project:

Political:
- There are a lot of wars, terrorism, and uncertainty. Intimidated people are making preparations for the future. They collect ammunition, thus causing a threat to others who will have to defend themselves;
- We don't know which weapons people are going to use in World War III, but in World War IV it is definitely going to be stones and sticks.

Economical:
- While expecting a great deal from the future, people will get ready to face it by investing in a possibility to survive. Or they will take care of their children, so that the latter would not have to buy weapons.

Socio-cultural:
- Everyone in Lithuania is still waiting for manna from heaven. In the United States of America gun sales have increased by 70 %, and sales of general ammunition by 140 % in the last ten years;
- An investment in the future will venerate the past.

Technological:
- If a citizen does not have a licence to carry a gun, he can always pretend that he is only holding a stone or a stick in his hand.

The PEST of the project presented by the student reveals his ability to assess the environment in a matter-of-fact, critical and self-ironic way. Could it mean that as a lecturer I have succeeded in focusing his attention on the observation and assessment of the outer environment!?

Conclusion

The theoretical insights and research by the political analyst Ronald Inglehart draw attention to the fact that the modernisation processes taking place in Lithuania in the late 20th – early 21st century testify to an uneven (intermittent) and belated transition.

PRACTICE

---

[2] *This project was done by the master student of the Chair of Painting of the Vilnius Academy of Arts Algimantas Černiauskas (a task for the autumn semester of the school year of 2010).*

It is moving from agrarian/industrial society to a post-industrial knowledge and service society. In the process, the value orientations have become polarised between the large majority of materialists and the minority of post-materialists.

That is why, with the aim to increase the number of citizens adhering to the post-materialist values, a teacher of social sciences disciplines at a university-type art school must train the students' skills of environment observation and assessment. It would help them to make renewal-promoting (innovative), decisions in the presence of the experienced changes, and promote the development of culture and creative industries.

References

DONSKIS, L. (1993). Kultūrinė situacija: Vakarai ir Lietuva. II. In: *Metmenys*. 65, 114- 121

DRAGIĆEVIĆ ŠEŠIĆ, M. (1998). *Kultūros vadybos įvadas*. Kultūros aktualijos. 5/7, 16

DRUCKER, P.F. (2004). *Valdymo iššūkiai XXI amžiuje (Management Challenges for the 21st Century)*. Tallinn: Goldratt Baltic Network.

EUROBAROMETRAS 69 (2008). Visuomenės nuomonė Europos sąjungoje. 2008 m. pavasaris. In: Šalies *ataskaita (TNS Opinion & Social)*. Lietuva: Europos Komisijos atstovybė Lietuvoje

GIRNIUS, K. (1999). Pilietinė visuomenė Lietuvoje. In: *Naujasis* Židinys-Aidai. 11/12, 589-590

HANKISS, E. (2007). *Virsmas ar Virsmai?* Vidurio Rytų Europos transformacija 1989-2007 m. (Transition or Transitions? The transformation of eastern central Europe 1989-2007). In: *Kultūros barai*. 10, 19-24

INGELHART, R. (2007). *The World Values Survey Cultural Map of the* World http://www.worldvaluessurvey.org/wvs/articles/folder_published/article_base_56 KOTLER, P (2003). Rinkodaros principai. Kaunas: Poligrafiaj ir informatika

MARSHAL, G. (1994). *The concise Oxford dictionary of Sociology*. Oxford: Oxford Universyty Press.

PAKŠTAS, K. (2003). *Kultūra. Civilizacija. Geopolitika*. Vilnius: Pasviręs pasaulis.

PARKIN, M. (2001). *Tales for Coaching. Using stories and metaphors with individuals and small groups*. Great Britain: Kogan Page Limited.

About the author

Prof Dr Elonahas Lubytė is Art critic, Curator of Lithuanian contemporary sculpture in the Lithuanian Art Museum, and Lecturer at the UNESCO Chair for Culture Management and Culture Policy of Vilnius Academy of Fine Arts, Member of AICA (Lithuanian branch).

Since 2003, Elonahas Lubytė has been teaching the subject of Basic Management for Artists for master students of the Vilnius Academy of Arts. Since 2005 it has been supplemented by Basic Marketing for Artists. Since 2006 – she teaches Basic Entrepreneurship for bachelor students.
—
lelona@email.lt

Isaac Bongani Mahlangu

PRODUCT DEVELOPMENT TRAINING AS A TOOL FOR EMPOWERMENT IN CRAFTS A FOCUS ON TRAINING INITIATIVES IN POTTERY FACTORIES IN THE NORTH WEST PROVINCE

Abstract

A significant number of initiatives have been undertaken by the South African government to address key challenges such as inequality, migration, geographic segregation, unemployment, sluggish economic growth and poor education issues. Poor education, poverty and geographic segregation significantly hinder the chances of attaining formal qualification therefore reducing chances of formal employment for those within marginalized communities.

With the growing need for entrepreneurial development, the craft sector has been identified as one of eight key priority sectors to grow the economy and create employment. The crafts sector is a sector dominated by women and thus makes them visible producers in the value chain. The indigenous knowledge transfer and the general low cost of some raw materials and the potential of entering into existing local markets are characteristics that have stimulated the identification of crafts production, as stated in this article, as a potentially valuable vehicle of job creation.

Introduction

A noteworthy number of initiatives have been undertaken by the South African government to address key challenges such as inequality, migration, geographic segregation, unemployment, sluggish economic growth and poor education issues. Poor education, poverty and geographic segregation significantly hinder the chances of attaining formal qualification therefore reducing chances of formal employment for those within marginalised communities. Historically, '*discriminatory expenditure on education...*' (Bond, 2006: 3) facilitated inequality in education and this is identified to be an ongoing challenge, a legacy of apartheid, which the Department of Education continues to struggle with, '*a bloated administrative infrastructure that included the parallel operations of White, Coloured, Indian, urban Black, and then Bantustan education system...*' (De Kock, Bethlehem & Laden, 2004: 214).

The National Development Plan (2011) envisages that to eliminate poverty and inequality, society and the state need to engage in the impact of gender inequality that ultimately indicates that the life challenges of women are generally worse than those of men. The plan envisages that by 2030; '*the economy should be close to full employment; equip people with the skills they need; ensure that ownership of production is less concentrated and more diverse (where black people and women own a significant share of productive assets); and be able to grow rapidly, providing the resources to pay for investment in human and physical capital*'. (NDP, 2011: 10). With the growing need for entrepreneurial development aimed at reducing poverty and unemployment, the South African government has identified the craft sector as one of eight key priority sectors to grow the economy and create employment.

The Importance of the Creative Industries

The value of crafts is, on the one hand, that it is an occupation dominated by women and thus makes them visible producers in the value chain. On the other hand craft production is possible even at the most remote of areas. Craft production has the potential to encourage community engagement, participation and enhance economic vitality as it is in many poor communities an indigenous practice carried over from generation to generation. This indigenous knowledge transfer and the general low cost of some raw materials and the potential of entering into existing local markets are characteristics that have stimulated the identification of crafts production, in this research, as a potentially valuable vehicle of job creation. The Creative Industries Sector Report (2007) reveals that the tourism and décor markets show significant and continuing growth; with annual rates more than twice that of services industries, and more than four times that of manufacturing in the Organisation for Economic Cooperation and Development (OECD) countries. Domestic South African creative industries markets have indicated significant growth of between 3-4% (Joffe & Newton, 2007: 38). It is anticipated that the industry will continue growing particularly because of the rising middle class with disposable income. With the promise of growth in both international and domestic markets, these findings shed light on the importance of the creative industries as a potential economic industry to help alleviate poverty and create jobs.

Crafts production in marginalised communities has a long standing history. Yet, unskilled jobs are much sought after by the poor (Elsenburg, 2005:32). Partly, because there is often a greater number of job seekers than available jobs, particularly for those considered unskilled. Most of the growing markets indicated above are concentrated and generally exclude the marginalised communities. There are three types of producers identified by the Gauteng Craft Strategic framework (2008). We have the producer enterprises which make up to 30% and are established entities having been stable over time. Then there is a 30-40% of young micro-enterprises, with the potential to grow and create employment, and in addition a survivalist category, making up between 30-40%. The stand-alone category is that of the designer maker and presents a very different profile; that is, of significant stability and exhibits an employment rate of approximately 8 people per enterprise as oppose to the 1 or 2 people employed in the other three categories respectively. This stability is a result of benefits from high end domestic and export markets from earlier market expansion strategies implemented in South Africa.

Context for the Research and Case Study

Irivwieri (2009) anticipates that, should the manufacturing and services sectors fail to grow, the rate of unemployment could become unmanageable. With the anticipated consistent growth of the creative industries pointed out by the DTI (2005), and the low requirements of entry into the crafts production generally identified by the poor, the South African government has *recently taken an explicit step forward in optimising the contribution of craft as a powerful engine of economic growth and promoting development in a globalising world* (Rhodes, 2011:3). As such, the mainly informal craft *'projects'* have undergone transformation towards becoming businesses aimed at addressing some of governments key priorities, specifically poverty alleviation,

(side margin) PRACTICE

women empowerment, black economic empowerment, support towards the development of the '*marginalised economy*' and the development of SMMEs. This has enabled
small business development and local beneficiation of products and access to mineral
raw materials.

Minteks' Timbita Ceramic Incubator

Minteks' Timbita Ceramic Incubator, hereinafter called Timbita, under the Small Scale
Mining and Beneficiation Programme hereinafter called SSMB, serves as an example
of initiatives taken by the government. These initiatives are aimed at using crafts for
socio-economic gains of marginalised communities. The programme integrates traditional
craft skills with technology and contemporary pottery making techniques, enabling
access to resources, financial capital and craft skills development.

Mintek has played a significant role in providing product development training (to fulfil
the requirements for an NQF 2 level qualification). It offers market support to ensure
sustainable livelihoods for poor rural communities, beneficiating from the programme
that examines opportunities for rural areas without '*more exciting minerals such as gold
and diamond in their immediate areas*' (SSMB brochure, 2013). It concentrates on seeking alternative minerals that exist in the area which are often clay and sand. It recognises
that these resources can be harnessed for the benefit of the local communities enabling
them to make sealable craft products.[1]

In the North West province, in partnership with the Department of Educations'
(NWDE) Adult Basic Education and Training directorate, within a decade Timbita has
helped set up eight pottery factories, the highest number in one province. This trans-
lates to a total of 86 learners graduating and receiving certificates in NQF level 2 Craft
Production (Minteks' Annual Report, 2011: 33) in the North West province alone. Of
the eight factories set up in the North West, only four still operate today and despite
the promise of enabling the factories to '*compete favourably in mass and export markets*'
(Minteks' Annual Report, 2003: 32), none of the factories have gained entry or sustained
participation in markets beyond their local communities. The factories still in operation are made up of members with disability disorders, with the exception of one,
consisting of members without disabilities.

The Central research Question

The central research question therefore investigates whether training offered by Timbita
has led to the empowerment of the beneficiaries, understood in terms of the beneficiaries'
ability to earn income in the long term, and their ability to independently integrate
concepts, ideas and actions to sustain their livelihoods economically.

Using a qualitative research approach and three methods of collating data that are
semi-structured interviews, a case study as well as a focus group discussion gathering
data from Timbita as well as the factory identified in the case study. By combining
these three methods of data collection, the research overcame the bias of constructed
data often associated with semi-structure interviews and, instead experience to some

PRACTICE

---

[1] *The development of skills, meaningful jobs using local mineral resources and incorporating
technology is a government priority embedded in the NDP vision 2030.*

extent, the *'everyday life brought into being'* into the thoughts and practices of the participants. In order to analyse and interpret the data, the research combined both thematic analyses and an inductive approach.

The data was measured against, on the one hand, the South African Qualifications Authoritys' (SAQA) benchmark of competency requirements for obtaining a level 2 NQF qualification. And on the other, Risattis' (2007) concept of craftsmanship which stresses three main areas: the quality of thought in the making of crafts objects/design which enables innovation and diversification, technical manual skills/dexterity, and the creative technical manual skills involved in the process of selecting the relevant material to support the form and function. This offers a comprehensive approach that takes into account factors such as size, weight, shape and form/the practicality laws.

1. First, the research traced how needs where assessed and beneficiaries selected for the Timbita programme. Have the beneficiaries been exposed to crafts before, what technical skill do they have and has it been improved by the training? At the end of the programme were the beneficiaries able to independently design and manufacture products?
2. Secondly, as an extension to assessing the beneficiaries ability to design and manufacture products, the research also took cognisance of inspiration drawn from local culture and indigenous knowledge as a basis for design, decoration and in the process of making.
3. Thirdly, to measure the socio-economic impact Timbita has had on the beneficiating communities, we have looked at sales reports as well as the diversity of markets penetrated in line with the quality of product produced and their relevance to market. We also took cognisance of the beneficiaries' ability to identify potential markets, network and participate independently from Timbitas' intervention in markets outside their locality.
4. Fourthly, we identified the contribution Timbita has had in attracting partnering institutions and other stakeholders to help diversify expertise, reduce duplication and channel resources in a manner that insures continuity to a point of the beneficiaries' self-reliance and sustainability.
5. Lastly, we have investigated whether or not this initiative has grown and created new jobs. The research reveals how many people have received employment since the inception of Semphete initiative (see further) and how many have left, as well as factors driving these movements.

From these assessments, the research was able to answer these five key questions:

a. Since the training, where the members able to innovate and independently develop new and/enhance existing products for a specific target market?
b. Are their products relevant to the particular markets they produce for, and are they able to follow through orders?
c. Were the beneficiaries able to expand from their initial point which is market penetration and expand drawing from the three expansion strategies explained by Goodwin (2005) to be product development, market development and diversification?
d. Have these factories created new jobs or have they collapsed. Are they still dependent on government support, if so then to what extent?
e. Are they able to sustain the livelihoods of the beneficiaries?

Introduction of the Case Study

The research investigates one main case that has received training from Timbita and
a supporting case that offers a different training perspective. The case partly includes
academic training as well as undergoing self-initiated mentoring. For the main case
study we chose Semphete pottery, and L'estrange pottery as a comparative case.
Semphete was trained by Timbita and has had neither any prior academic background,
nor any direct interactions with consumer markets outside the province of the North
West. On the other hand, L'estrange has had some academic training in Sculpting, and
has travelled abroad always directly interacting with consumer market until the relocation
of the business to the North West province. In the past, L'estrange pottery flourished
growing economically, with products consumed all over the world and employing over
5 people at various stages prior to relocating to the North West.

The research has identified three central issues that have affected Timbitas' quest for
empowering marginalised communities:

1.   Timbitas' own organisational structure and trainers (how this directed the selection
     of beneficiaries and partnering organisations)

2.   The training programme content on product and product development

3.   The training programme content on marketing and market access.

Taken from the literature, drawing from Bradshaw (2006), we identified the strategy
adopted by Timbita; the type of poverty, and how they address them. These range from
deficiencies to cumulative and cyclical interdependencies (See; Bradshaw, 2006).
We also identified which of Ifes' (1996) perspectives of allowing people to take power
into their own hands Timbita chose, for developing the content of the training programme,
and how indigenous knowledge and western training methods were integrated to
enable beneficiaries access to exercising choice in the conceptualizing, developing and
production processes of products. In the context of Timbitas' trainers we took cognisance
of the potential power the trainers can exercise over the beneficiaries and how this
power may be wrongfully used to manipulate or control the situation.

Findings

In essence, we questioned if Timbita does not simply use empowerment, job creation and
economic development as nice sounding buzzwords, designed to enable sustain funding
for unsustainable projects. We have found that Timbita has chosen a comprehensive
strategic approach, establishing a training and marketing division to coexists with the
research and development division. This comprehensive approach enables the beneficiaries' access to infrastructure, resources, production training and access to markets.
Benefits which would have not been accessible to the beneficiaries to claim on their own.
Hence, the comprehensive strategy/concept has yielded positive results in enabling the
beneficiaries access to resources, needed to generate well-being as well as claiming
ownership of production resources. However, in the context of strategic assessment
discussed by Blakely (1979) which looks at techniques or approaches applied by a particular agency, we have found that there is a lack of integration between the various
divisions within Timbita. This lack of integration has led to fragmented planning and
needs assessments of beneficiaries. We concluded that the strategic approach adopted

PRACTICE

by Timbita is that of identifying Geographic Segregation as a cause of poverty, suggesting that by simply redistributing productive resources, people would be able to get themselves out of poverty, irrespective of the skills needed to generate human capital. This approach has thus not facilitated the process of encouraging the development of indigenous knowledge, nor has it enhanced the skills for crafters to utilize the technology which is at their disposal. The planning and implementation has not been an indigenous process that *'...builds on the skills, strengths and ideas of people living in poverty-on their asset'* but rather it has *'treated them as empty receptacles of charity'* (Green, 2008: 7). This approach perpetuates dependency where handouts tend to become expected as a norm.

Timbita has therefore failed to *'look at individual situations and community resources as mutually dependent...'* (Bradshaw, 2006: 14) and identify the importance of establishing partnerships with local organisations/aid agencies. This might have insured continuity and growth. Instead, four of the eight potteries have ceased operation.

One may easily relate these challenges to a lack of or limited funding. However Timbita, being responsible for the proposal, had the power to request sufficient funds. In the context of Semphete, approximately 46% (R144 000) was used for the provision of stipends to the ten members making up Semphete. The remaining sum was utilized for the purchase of resources, raw material, marketing material, the training logistics and the management fee paid to Timbita. The training was carried out in three months with two-week intervals between each session of the training, meaning that the beneficiaries did not receive training for SAQAs' recommended 720 core hours for obtaining an NQF level 2 certificate.

Training & Product Discussions

Drawing from Cohen (1988) & Markwick (2001), crafts products may be broadly categorised into three main categories:

- Sacred crafts product – retain their original characteristics and meaning. However, their purchase is constrained as a result of some level of understanding towards their function as they often possess a strong symbolism element.
- Touristy crafts products – are sacred crafts products which have evolved by generally growing smaller in size and thus enable ease of carrying and convenience. Cohen (1988) & Markwick (2001) further identify that these products retain some kind of characteristics which are relevant to tourism destinations.
- Secular crafts products – are entirely new products without any specific relation to the culture of their local producers. They are developed in response to opportunities presented by the market.

The first two can be associated with cultural entrepreneurship, as they draw to some extent from cultural and indigenous content. However, we have found that Semphete, like many of the Timbita trained potteries, has produced products that cannot be categorised in any of the three categories. In other words, beneficiaries produce these multiples not because these generate significant economic benefits or profit, but simply because they were not trained to understand and implement product development stages.

PRACTICE

Therefore, they are unable to see the possibility in the raw material and they lack *'the foundation for development into areas of craft...'* SAQA. In other words, they remain excluded from what DAC identifies as *'a colourful, diverse and vibrant craft sector'*.

The beneficiaries' lack of skill is no means due to the trainers' failure to transfer skills. We have found that the trainers from Timbita have very little disadvantage in the context of the ability to carry out the training. They (all 3) have gained financial security through employment, have been empowered through skills development programmes. Timbita has afforded them - and are still practicing – art; they remain within the industry they are passionate about. What has acted as a significant barrier towards them, carrying out the training and empower beneficiaries, has manifested from the programme content as well as the fragmentation between divisions, specifically training and marketing.

Trying to fulfil their targets in maximising production within a limited time frame, the trainers are forced into compromising basic pottery skills training. They are expected to teach the learners how to reproduce a prescribed design. A design issued to them by the marketing division, which then means the trainers are excluded in the process of trends and product research. Timbita has thus not managed to enable the beneficiaries the opportunity to *'compete favourably in mass and export markets'* (Minteks' Annual Report, 2003). The approach has been one that prioritizes maximising production and overlooked the importance of training the beneficiaries.

The Concept of Market Expansion Strategies

The Department of Environmental Affairs and Tourism (2002) warned against premature market expansion strategies, stating that market and financial feasibility assessments need to be conducted prior to *'raising expectations and exposing the community or local entrepreneurs to risk'*.

As discussed above, direct export has yielded little success for crafts markets. The economic impact has been one that is beneficial to the elite design businesses. National markets such as Decorex S.A., the Design Indaba Expo and SARCDA, have benefited some of the more established businesses. To a lesser extent, a number of survivalist businesses in partnership with some supporting aid agencies have benefitted. Most of the survivalist businesses however rely on local markets.

Tirthankar (1993: 3-5 cited in Greyling, 2003: 170) makes an example of a situation in India where rural and low skilled producers rejected striving to compete with industrial production, where *'...craftsmen survived the competition, not by making the same products cheaper, but by making new and different products'*. Looking at Goodwins' (2005) concept of market expansion and comparing between Semphete and L'estrange, we have found that:

- Semphete produces for the 3 lower categories of consumer markets because of a lack of design capacity and in-depth knowledge of expanding their target market. However, Semphete continues to survive, because the business is located within its market. Here, brand affiliations from the community are formed from longstanding community bonds. Further benefits to their location is lower transport costs (if any), lower marketing cost and accessibility.

PRACTICE

- Although their products lack creativity or cultural significant, yhe community takes pride and supports Semphete, because they are the only local pottery producer in much of the district. The pride developed from supporting local businesses, coupled with low cost of products, means that these consumers are able to afford purchasing the goods. Hence, Semphetes' products are best described as import substitutes – products made cheaper than imports, or - in Semphetes' case – with lower travelling costs (Norsker & Danisch 1991).
- L'estrange produces for the cosmopolitan and affluent markets. This business, while operating in Johannesburg, had managed to create a niche and interact directly with its market. Exposure to academic training meant networking opportunities that helped position the business with like-minded creatives, in a variety of disciplines such as architects, designers, other potters and business people.
- Relocating to the North West compromised the networking opportunities, and affected the visibility of the business to its markets. The North West province is dominated by the lower 3 markets. Transportation costs and transaction costs have now become challenging, taking into account the scale of the products this business produces. As Lestrange pointed out, the move to North West also meant that the business had to, for the first time, invest in marketing which is a costly exercise.

Reflections on the Case

Training is considered in this research as a tool for empowerment. It is no longer enough to rely on product designs and techniques passed on from one generation to another, without any professional intervention. This often poses a challenge; desperate communities find themselves in a *'build and they will come'* situation (Department for Environmental Affairs Tourism, 2002: 23). Traditionally, low quality, poorly finished and common products are manufactured. This often forces crafters, who flood the markets with similar products, to compete at sub-minimal price, disregarding the entire production and distribution cost for the sake of generating some income. This therefore does not give empowerment; not having the ability and resources to make decisions about and improving ones' own living conditions, and promotes the development of meaningful jobs (Ife, 1995).

We have stated that beneficiaries remain vulnerable to the erratic market environment, and cannot access markets beyond their immediate locality. In this case, mainly because of a training programme that has weak content, lacks indigenous organisational support, and financial limitations that dictate the duration of the training, irrespective of reaching the intended empowerment goal. The process of making requires extensive thinking and planning; it takes into account Indigenous Knowledge Systems culture, industry, conscious choice in raw material selection, and its relationship to (environmental) issues (Charny (2011). These processes are related to demand-factors; product ranges that span from products manufactured by the poor for the poor, to products made for luxury high end decor markets, driven by trend and desire over basic necessity.

The direct consequences of this lack of expertise is the failure of the beneficiaries to expand in any of market expansion strategies (Hiroyukis 2011). Instead the beneficiating factories, if they survive, remain stagnant in a low risk/low benefit environment, where they sell existing products and compete at price point. This subsequently means that the beneficiaries rely on other forms of income such as government grants. Hence, they are not empowered and remain welfare dependent. It is therefore important that training is constantly analysed, so as to keep it relevant to contemporary markets within the context of craftsmanship. Training need not be limited to refining the skill of product making (workmanship) in the sense that communities are given ready-made designs to manufacture. In this way they will be oblivious to key areas, fundamental for empowering self-reliance such as design, research and product development (craftsmanship). Products designs and techniques passed on from generation to generation, without any professional intervention, often pose a challenge were desperate communities find themselves in a *'build and they will come'* situation (Department for Environmental Affairs and Tourism, 2002: 23). In this way, low quality, poor finishing and common products are manufactured. This often forces crafters - who flood the markets with similar products - to compete at price points, disregarding the total cost of production and distribution.

About the author

Isaac Bongani Mahlangu MA BA is a freelance artist, researcher and facilitator. He is Philosophy of Community Arts trainee facilitator, at the Sibikwa Arts Centre (Gauteng Organization of Community Arts and Culture Centres (GOMACC). He has been Assistant Director, Product Development at the North West Craft and Design Institute in Pretoria (SA). In 2014 he received a Masters Degree in Arts and Culture Management at the WITS University of Witwatersrand, Johannesburg, South Africa.

mahlangu.bongani @yahoo.com

References

Blackely, E. J. (1979). *Community development research: concepts, issues and strategies*. New York: University of California.

Bond, P. (2006). *Looting Africa: The economics of Exploitation*. South Africa: Africa World Press and the University of KwaZulu-Natal Press.

Bradshaw, T. K. (2006). *Theories of Poverty and Anti-Poverty Programs in Community Development*. Human and Community Development Department, University of California.

Charny, D. (2011). *Power of making: The importance of being skilled*. London: V & A Publishing and the Craft Council.

Cohen, E. (1988). Authenticity and Commoditization in Tourism. In: *Annals of tourism research* 15: 371-386.

Cultural Industries Growth Strategy (1998). *The South African Craft Industry* prepared by BDM Consulting for the Cultural Industry Growth Strategy commissioned by the then DACST

Customised Sector Programme for Craft (2006). *Sector Development Strategy: Beyond Planning to Action* prepared by the Department of Trade and industry. Retrieved from: http://ccdi.org.za/research/Customised%20Sector%20 Programme%20for%20Craft.pdf [accessed 14th March 2013]

De Kock, L. Bethlehem, L. & Laden, S. (2004). *South Africa in the global imaginary*. Pretoria. Unisa Press.

Denzin, N. K. & Lincoln, Y S. (2000). *Handbook of qualitative research: second edition*. Thousand Oaks, CA. SAGE.

Department for Environmental Affairs & Tourism (2002). *Responsible tourism manual for South Africa*. Retrieved from: http://www.info.gov.za/ view/DownloadFileAction?id=164725 [accessed 11th April 2013]

Department of Sport, Arts, Culture and Recreation (2008). *Craft Strategic Framework*. Retrieved from: http://www.sacr.gpg.gov.za/SACRDocuments/ Strategies/Craft%2520Strategic%2520 Framework.pdf

PRACTICE

Department of Trade and Industry (2005). *Sector Development Strategy: Customised Sector Programmes for Craft.* Retrieved from: http://www.ccdı.org.za/research-and-publications/Sector/Programme/for/Craft.pdf. [Accessed 10th October 2014]

Elsenburg, N. (2005). *A profile of the North West province: demographics, poverty, inequality and unemployment.* South Africa. Retrieved from: http://www.elsenburg.com/provide/documents/BP2005_1_6%20Demographics%20NW.pdf [accessed 25th June 2013]

Goodwin, H. (2005). *Tourism and Local Economic Development.* Unpublished MSc Course Lecture, Tourism in less developed countries handout on 24th February, 2005. Guildford: University of Surrey.

Green, D. (2008). *From poverty to power, how active citizens and effective states can change the world.* South Africa: Oxfam international.

Grobler, A. T. (2005). *Product development for community-craft projects in Mpumalanga.* M. Dissertation, Tshwane, TUT.

Hatch, G. Becker, P. & Van Zyl, M. (2011). *The dynamic African Consumer Market: Exploring growth opportunities in Sub-Saharan Africa.* Accenture South Africa. Retrieved from: www.accenture.com

Hiroyuki, Y. (2011). *The value of craft products development for pro-poor tourism growth in Bhaktapur, Nepal.* Retrieved from: http://www.techmonitor.net/tm/images/5/5a/TM_Feb2009.pdf [accessed 11th May 2013]

Ife, J. (1996). *Community development: creating community alternatives-vision, analysis and practice.* Australia: Longman Malaysia, GPS.

Irivwieri, G. O. (2009). *Arts and crafts as springboard for sustainable development and industrialization in Nigeria.* Nigeria: Delta State University, Abraka.

Joffe, A. & Newton, M. (2007).*The creative industries in South Africa*: Sector studies research project. Commissioned by the Department of Labour. Retrieved from: http://www.labour.gov.za/downloads/documents/research-documents/Creative%20Industries_DoL_Report.pdf [accessed 17th February 2013]

Markwick, M. C. (2001). Tourism and the development of handicraft production in the Maltese Islands. In: *Tourism Geographies* 3(1): 29-51.

Mintek Annual Report and Financial Statements (2003). Retrieved from: http://www.mintek.co.za/wp-content/uploads/2003/11/AR2003_complete.pdf. [Accessed 20th May 2013]

Mintek Annual Report and Financial Statements (2011). Retrieved from: http://www.mintek.co.za/wp-content/uploads/2011/11/mintek-ar-2011.pdf. [Accessed 14th March 2013]

Mintek Small Scale Mining and Beneficiation (2012). *Timbita Ceramic Incubator.* Retrieved from: http://www.mintek.co.za/wp-content/uploads/2012/10/Revised-Timbita-Brochure.pdf. [Accessed 10th March 2013]

National Planning Commission (2011). *National Development Plan Vision for 2030*: The Presidency. RP270/11. South Africa. Retrieved from: http://www.npconline.co.za/medialib/downloads/home/NPC%20National%20Develop ment%20Plan%20Vision%202030%20-lo-res.pdf [accessed 24th March 2013]

PRACTICE

Norsker, H. & Danisch, J. (1991). *Forming techniques for the self-reliant potter.* Federal Republic of Germany. Deutsches Zentrum fur Entwicklungstechnologien.

Africa Department of environmental Affairs and Tourism. South Africa (2002). *Responsible Tourism Manual for South.* Retrieved from: http://www.gauteng.net/campaigns/uploads/gallery/Tourism_RT_Responsible_Touris m_Manual.pdf [accessed 31st March 2014]

Rhodes, S. (2011). *Beyond 'Nourishing the Soul of a Nation': craft in the context of South Africa.* PhD dissertation. University of the Arts London. Retrieved from: http://makingfutures.plymouthart.ac.uk/journalvol2/pdf/Rhodes_Sarah.pdf [accessed 13th April 2014]

Risatti, H. (2007). *A theory of craft; function and aesthetic expression.* The United States of America. The University of North Carolina Press.

Woodhouse, P. (2002). *Natural Resource Management and Chronic Poverty in Sub- Saharan Africa: an overview paper.* Institute for Development Policy and Management: Manchester.

PRACTICE

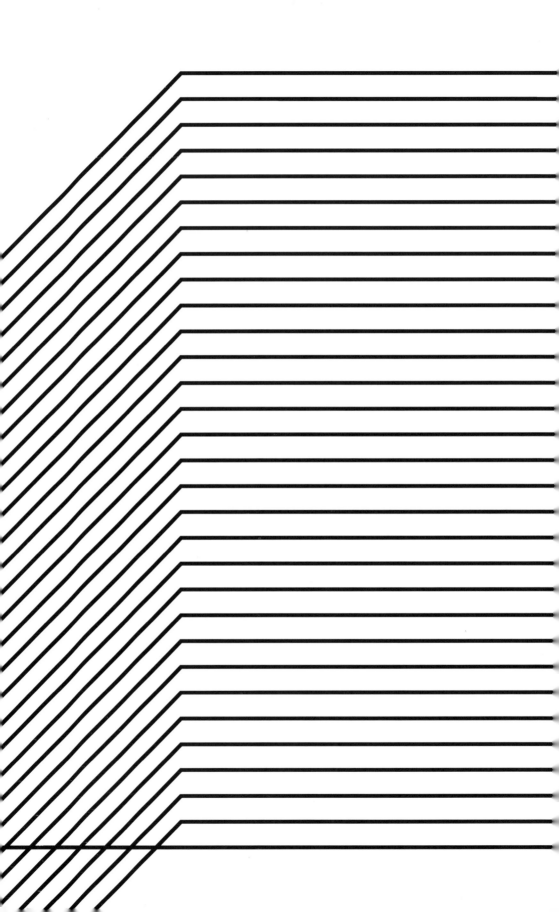

EXPANDING THE
GLOBAL VISION

SHAPING STRATEGIES AND BUILDING CREATIVE CAPACITIES THE PERSPECTIVE OF THE UNITED NATIONS

Abstract

The creative economy has been playing a catalytic role by dealing with the interface among arts, culture, technology, social innovation and business. At the global level the United Nations have played an active role in driving the creative economy discourse.

The United Nations Conference on Trade and Development - UNCTAD had a proactive role in sensitizing governments and promoting international policy to assist countries to enhance their creative economy. Promoting development through creativity has been the motto of some bold and far-reaching initiatives put forward by UNCTAD.

Education is a fundamental right. Knowledge and access to information and communication are at the core of human progress and well-being. The United Nations Institute for Training and Research *UNITAR* through its *Creative Economy Initiative* is taking on the quest for capacity-building for the UN Member States. In the present knowledge-based era, UNITAR is offering learning and training to develop skills and creative capacities in support to the post-2015 development agenda.

Introduction

Now-a-days, in every corner of the world there are countless creative environments and cultural events reminding us that the creative economy became an integral part of our daily life. The creative economy is a high-growth sector that relies on creative ideas, knowledge, skills and the ability to seize new opportunities. There are more evidence-based studies showing that the creative economy is actually driving economic growth, trade, employment and social cohesion in many parts of the world (Dos Santos-Duisenberg, 2010). At the political level governments in all continents, are realizing that the cultural and creative sectors are fundamental for advancing prosperity, inclusiveness and sustainability.

Recently, the creative economy has been playing a catalytic role by dealing with the interface among arts, culture, technology, social innovation and business. Obviously, this vibrant sector is not a panacea to solve all the systemic problems of our society. Expectations around the spill-overs of the creative economy are probably too high, but undoubtedly if the right mix of policies and institutions will be in place, the creative economy is able to foster socio-economic transformation while promoting culture and human development. Strategies focusing on the creative economy are being implemented as a pragmatic way to revitalize not only economic growth and the cultural and social life of cities, but also have been used as an attractive path offering new prospects for the youth, particularly in the post-crisis period. (Dos Santos-Duisenberg, 2013).

Creative thinkers and doers from various fields are indeed the source of creativity, innovation and vision that the contemporary world so desperately need for facing the challenges of the 21st century. Yet, creative talents and cultural assets are necessary but not sufficient conditions to unlock the full potential of this dynamic sector. While cross-cutting mechanisms and concerted policy actions should be articulated, it is crucial to attract investments and financing, to stimulate creative entrepreneurship and trade, as well as to nurture creative capacities among the new generation.

In this context, the United Nations Organization has been drawing the attention of the international community to the fact that the creative economy represents a positive-sum game for developed and developing countries (UNCTAD, 2004). However, policies should be shaped and human capacities need to be harnessed, in order to strengthen the creative economy for development gains.

The role of the United Nations in the Creative Economy Debate

In general, people recognize the value of the UN Charter, but is unaware of the full spectrum of the functions and activities executed by the United Nations Organization. The great majority is more familiar with the main political mission of the United Nations which is the maintenance of international peace and security, but somehow overlook the complexity of the UN efforts at the humanitarian and socio-economic development areas.

In the year 2000, a series of world conferences convened by the United Nations about the environment, human rights, population, the advancement of women and other international issues culminated in the Millennium Summit - the largest ever gathering of world leaders[1] - which adopted an ambitious declaration setting a course for humankind in the new century. The '*Millennium Declaration*' identified eight major goals that needed to be addressed globally so that to promote higher standards of living, employment, health, education and conditions of economic and social progress and development for the world population. The so-called *Millennium Development Goals* (MDGs) set specific targets to be reached by 2015, expressing the international community's commitment to the global development agenda.

It was in this international policy framework highly influenced by the Millennium Declaration that the creative economy emerged in the turn of the century. A series of policy instruments was articulated by the United Nations bodies to assist developing countries in the process of achievement of the MDGs. Among the decisions taken at the multilateral level at the beginning of the third millennium, some had particular relevance to the creative economy:

(i) The Program of Action for the Least Developed Countries[2] for the Decade 2001-2010;
(ii) The São Paulo Consensus adopted in 2004 at the Eleventh Session of the United Nations Conference on Trade and Development - UNCTAD XI, the first UN mandate introducing the creative economy into the international economic development agenda;

---

[1] *Governments from 192 Member States of the United Nations unanimously adopted the Millennium Declaration at the United Nations General Assembly in 2000.*

[2] *Least Developed Countries (LDCs) is a category that includes the 48 poorest or underdeveloped countries that have a per capita income extremely low*

(iii) The Declaration of Principles and the Plan of Action of the World Summit on the Information Society; and

(iv) The UNESCO Convention on the Protection and Promotion of the Diversity of Cultural Expressions.

Moreover, the World Trade Organization launched in 2001 the Doha Development Round of trade negotiations, and the World Intellectual Property Organization introduced its Development Agenda to address the concerns of developing countries in the area of intellectual property rights. All these multilateral processes had in common the fact that development was placed at the heart of their concerns and actions (UNCTAD, 2008).

Growing Interest towards the Creative Industries

Against this background, UNCTAD had a proactive role in sensitizing governments and promoting international policy to assist developing countries to enhance their creative industries, and hence their creative economy. In discharging its mandates, UNCTAD built synergy among relevant United Nations institutions with a view to explore complementarities and promote concerted and more effective international actions in the area of the creative economy. In this spirit, the United Nations Multi-Agency Informal Group on Creative Industries[3] was set up in 2004, bringing together six relevant UN bodies, namely: United Nations Conference on Trade and Development (UNCTAD); United Nations Development Program (UNDP), through its South-South Unit; the United Nations Education, Science and Culture Organization (UNESCO), the World Intellectual Property Organization (WIPO); International Labour Organization (ILO); and the International Trade Centre (ITC). The main outcome of the work of this group and a good example of inter-agency cooperation was the preparation of the first Creative Economy Report (2008) the *Creative Economy Report 2008: The challenge of assessing the creative economy - towards informed policymaking* - prepared under the guidance of UNCTAD, bringing together contributions from five collaborating UN agencies. The group also helped to align the development dimension of the creative economy by examining its economic, technological, trade, cultural, educational, labour and intellectual property aspects.

Later, other UN agencies such as the United Nations Industrial Development Organization (UNIDO), the United Nations Regional Economic Commissions, the United Nations Environment Program - UNEP and more recently the United Nations Institute for Training and Research - UNITAR also recognized the growing importance of the creative economy to promote socio-economic transformation. These UN bodies are designing projects in their respective areas of competence.

Today, the so-called Post-2015 Development Agenda is the process led by the United Nations to define the future global development framework, including a new global partnership, as an innovative vision for the sake of humanity. The intention is to move from vision to action, and inspire a new generation to believe that a better world is within its reach. Along these lines, the role of the UN in areas such as the creative economy is also moving from theory to practice. From 2000 to 2014 emphasis was in

XTRADUCTION

---

[3] *The Group set-up by the Secretary General of UNCTAD, Rubens Ricupero, was Chaired by Edna dos Santos-Duisenberg, Chief, Creative Economy Programme of UNCTAD from 2004 to 2012. This Group maintained regular dialogue and convened meetings in Geneva twice a year.*

conceptualizing and analysing the creative economy, sharing a vision and sensitizing governments. For the years beyond 2015, focus will be on concrete actions, including the promotion of learning activities to empower creative people, while enhancing knowledge, building skills and forging partnerships.

The Development Dimension of the Creative Economy

The infinite cultural and artistic heritage of the developing world such as music-making, painting, dance, handicrafts, fashion, cultural festivities are often economically disregarded and considered priceless..., but in reality they offer a major opportunity for economic growth, revenue, jobs and social inclusion. Worldwide the creative economy, driven by a rapidly growing multi-billion-dollar business generated by creative industries, is a field in which developing nations have enormous potential.

The vast deposit of cultural and creative expressions of developing countries usually ignored, should be better nurtured (UNCTAD, 2004). Countries should take better advantage of the pool of their creative talents for advancing development. Evidence-based research presented at the UN Creative Economy Report 2008, pointed that due to its multidisciplinary nature the creative economy engender a multitude of spill-overs that contributed towards the achievement of at least six out of the eight MDG goals.

At the local level, the creative economy has a positive impact on the growth of small and family business, providing possibilities not only for income generation but also for helping community regeneration, thus contributing to poverty reduction. The creative process also provides opportunities for women and pro-poor projects particularly in rural areas. Creation of art crafts (pottery, basket weavers, wood carvers etc.) and fashion products (clothing, embroiderers, leather works, silk weavers, jewellery etc.) are important creative activities for many female artisans. Arts and other cultural and creative activities have proven to be helpful for engaging marginalized young people from disadvantaged areas who otherwise would be unemployed and perhaps at risk of antisocial behaviour (UNCTAD, 2010).

Creativity in the Knowledge-based Era

Education is a fundamental right. Knowledge and access to information and communication are at the core of human progress and well-being. The main inputs for the creative economy are intellectual capital and creativity (Dos Santos-Duisenberg, 2005). Having creativity as the main driver, the creative economy turns around products and services bearing creative content, cultural and economic values and market objectives.[4]

The creative economy deals with the interface between economy, culture, technology and social aspects, gathering both traditional and leading edge activities. At the heart of the creative economy are the creative industries, which combines heritage, the arts, media, design and creative services like architecture, advertising and new media products etc. In the knowledge-based era, creative services have been growing faster than more conventional services. The creative economy in all regions of the world continues to expand at impressive levels. The prospects for the coming years is optimistic, reflecting

XTRADUCTION

---

[4] UNCTAD definition (2005), adopted in the UN Creative Economy Reports

the new lifestyle of the contemporary society which is increasingly associated with creativity, connectivity, style, status, brands as well as with cultural experiences, co-creations, social media and virtual networking embedded around the creative economy.

According to UNCTAD, the creative economy is the most dynamic sector of the world economy. The world demand for creative goods and services has grown sharply. The creative sector was also more resilient during the economic downturn resulting from the financial crisis of 2008. World trade of creative products more than doubled in a decade, reaching US$ 624 billion in 2011[5]. While developed countries had a predominant role in global markets, exports of creative goods from developing countries had an annual growth rate of 12% in the period from 2008 to 2011. A remarkable growth has been noticeable particularly in Asia, mainly due to the explosion of production and trade of creative products from China. In Africa, the Nigeria film industry generates about US 900 million annually and is the second largest employer in the country involving over a million people[6]. Other amazing examples are the TV soap-operas from Brazil and Mexico, and the pop music and video-games from the Republic of Korea.

Moreover, creativity, connectivity and innovation are transforming our attitudes and the way we live. The reach of the digital revolution, especially the widespread use of mobile phones combined with the growing impact of social networks, have contributed to unlocking marketing and distribution channels for music, digital animation, films, news, advertising etc., thereby expanding the economic benefits of the creative economy. Today, many creative professionals are making their living from trading their ideas. Many creative products are now digitalized and thus subject to entirely new business models that requires new institutions and regulatory regimes.

Creative Economy: a development Opportunity and a Policy Challenge

As mentioned earlier, the creative economy discourse was introduced into the international economic and development agenda in early 2000's. By now, governments started to realize that creativity and cultural assets are pivotal for economic and social development, since they are drivers of innovation, jobs, trade and inclusiveness, even during the turbulent times of economic crisis.

Many governments in developing and developed countries alike, are identifying the creative sectors as priority in their national development strategies. Consequently, policies are being designed to promote the creative economies as a feasible option to help out recovery and prosperity. More recently, the creative industry was recognized as potential enabler for sustainable development and an important element of the post-2015 development agenda (ECOSOC, 2013).

The creative economy has a powerful transformative force. Nevertheless, most developing countries are not yet able to utilize fully their creative capacities to leapfrog into this booming sector. The main constraints are policies weakness and lack of knowledge

XTRADUCTION

---

[5] *Retrieved from: UNCTAD Global Data Base on Creative Economy: www.unctad.org/creative-economy*

[6] *UN Creative Economy Report - 2010 (UNCTAD-UNDP), Nollywood: a creative response (pg 250)*

and skills. The opportunities provided by the creative economy are unmatched and need to be unlocked. The challenge is to build the capacities needed to explore the wide range of opportunities the creative sector can offer.

UNITAR's Creative Economy Initiative

The United Nations Institute for Training and Research (UNITAR) has the mission to deliver innovative training and conduct research on knowledge systems to increase the capacity of its beneficiaries to respond to global challenges. In recent years, UNITAR expanded its outreach covering virtually all Member States of the United Nations. It enhanced the quality of its programs and increased the use of new technologies for learning. Furthermore, UNITAR embarked upon a major reform for positioning the Institute to make significant contributions to address emerging training and capacity development needs.

Against this scenario, UNITAR as the UN umbrella for research and training, designed its Creative Economy Initiative proposing a series of capacity-building activities to the UN Member States. The objective is to develop a learning approach to enhance knowledge, build skills and develop capacities to harness the potential of the creative economy to promote inclusive socio-economic transformations[7].

The Knowledge Systems Innovation (KSI) section coordinates actions to support innovation in the design of UNITAR's learning and training products. In carrying out its activities, the session makes intensive use of digital tools with a view to develop new learning approaches and training methodologies. This was the rationale for the design in 2013 of UNITAR's initiative entitled *Creative Economy: Developing Capacities for Inclusive Socioeconomic Transformations*.

Despite the proliferation of projects around the creative economy, the overall impact of these activities remains fragmented. Thus, UNITAR decided to enlarge the offering of learning products with the aim to provide better services to its beneficiaries. The intention is to facilitate synergy and add value to the relevant work of key actors within and outside the UN system. As result, UNITAR is proactively seeking partnerships to materialize its Creative Economy Initiative.

UNITAR has expertise on how best to deliver adult training, how best to capture and retain knowledge and professional learning. The work of the Institute is useful to other partners and the entire United Nations system, in its drive towards a more integrated delivery framework.

I. Objectives and Expected Results

UNITAR Creative Economy Initiative was designed to help governments to advance socio-economic change. Governments will be encouraged to address national and international bottlenecks. The purpose is to assist not only policymakers and creative entrepreneurs but also independent artists and professionals engaged in the day-to-day business of the creative economy, with a view to assess their real needs and identify areas requiring policy interventions and concrete initiatives by the private sector.

[5] *UNITAR Creative Economy Initiative : www.unitar.org/ksi*

The intention is also to stimulate, educate and train a new generation of creative professionals and cultural entrepreneurs including youth and women involved in creative business.

Another goal is to facilitate good governance principles across the creative sectors and better interactions between producers, distributors, creative workers and retailers. This is likely to facilitate co-creations and better relations among artists and artisans from the informal sector, SMEs, public cultural institutions and the corporate sectors. Activities will benefit a broad range of stakeholders working through open and participatory processes.

The Initiative will promote culture and creativity, while improving human capacities for creating, producing and marketing creative goods and services. These activities are expected to increase opportunities for collaboration and partnerships, including between the public and private sectors.

II. Methodology

UNITAR will act as a knowledge broker, facilitating learning, and knowledge exchange, development of skills and sharing of best practices, information and business tactics. Learning tools will enable learners to collaborate and aggregate knowledge and to evaluate information from various sources, grasp its meaning and enrich its contents. The CE Initiative will include face-to-face workshops and on-line courses combining three main principles:

- *Knowledge*: mastery of creative economy policies to enable innovative approaches to shape creative economy policies, through a better understanding of local and international issues and market trends in the sector.
- *Skills:* development of advanced skills and the ability to translate knowledge into effective execution, including through creative entrepreneurship, arts management, and the use of ICT tools to facilitate the creation and distribution of creative content.
- *Attitudes:* through the awareness of the cross-cutting aspects of the creative economy to support a shared vision that creates value, while promoting cultural diversity and sustainability.

XTRADUCTION

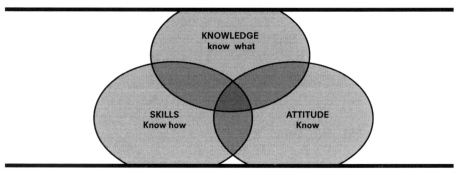

Figure 1: Main Principles UNITAR Learning Processes (Dos Santos, 2013)

UNITAR is offering its expertise on methodological approaches. Learning will be anchored on experience-based, dynamic processes and will take place in groups or communities, through actions and interactions. Activities will include hands-on and collaborative processes. Modern interactive tools will be used for facilitating knowledge-sharing and local partnerships.

III. Quality Assurance Framework

Learning materials will be supported by quality assurance and certification. The e-learning courses will be aligned with international standards for capacity-building (ECBCheck). Courses will be composed by modules and toolkits. An international quality certificate will be provided for participants who successfully complete all the activities and assessments.

The *Quality Assurance Framework* was developed for strengthening the quality of UNITAR products and services, and validating UNITAR training products and services through relevant certification[8]. It also provides a platform for sharing experiences and lessons on quality review. The framework has three main elements:

a. the quality Assurance Committee;
b. a set of standards and guidelines; and
c. a self-assessment and review process.

IV. Proposed Activities

The UNITAR approach is developed around the idea that knowledge is contextual and co-created by stakeholders taking into account the needs, constraints and specificities of target countries and communities. A set of customized learning products will be developed around five components:

1. **Transformative Dialogues on Creative Economy**
    These dialogues will create the space for extensive conversations, providing opportunities for the various actors to grasp the issues associated with creative economy, so as to favour innovative approaches that appreciate and understand the dynamics of the sector. This activity will focus on : (i) providing the conditions and adequate methodological approaches for cross-sector and multi-actor dialogues to facilitate knowledge and experience sharing; (ii) improving interactions among major actors to inspire and promote initiatives that incorporate the socio-economic development dimension of culture and creativity; and (iii) promoting cooperation to facilitate partnerships and joint endeavours.
2. **Transformative Development Strategies**
    Policy-makers will be empowered to design transformative development strategies to integrate creative economy into national development plans and execute the policies and regulations needed to nurture the sector. The purpose will be: (i) creating an environment where policymakers can broadly reflect on national strategies taking into account its cross-sector and multi-agent nature; (ii) facilitating the articulation of a coalition among creative economy's sectors and actors with a view to develop a shared vision; (iii) designing concerted and coherent strategies and participatory action plans; and (iv) developing leadership skills to enable policymakers to deal with competing priorities and country conditions.

---

[8] *UNITAR Quality Assurance Framework, August 2014*

3. **Creativity & Creative Economy**

   Participants will be sensitized about the value of culture and creativity, and its contribution to a culture of innovation such as entrepreneurship, tolerance of failure, creative thinking curiosity, ability to deal with uncertainties and thoughtful risk-taking. This on-line course will promote understanding on the creative and innovative capacities of societies.

4. **Creative Entrepreneurship**

   This on-line course will develop skills on creative entrepreneurship and equip creative professionals to establish and nurture their business (micro and or/SMEs). The aim is to stimulate creative movers and shakers to develop new insights and become more creative and productive. It will particularly target youth and women with potential entrepreneurship capacities. Participants will be expected to articulate their own sustainable creative business.

5. **Open Knowledge & Digital Storytelling Platform**

   This virtual platform will tap on crowdsourcing methodologies to collect, aggregate and disseminate knowledge on creative economy. As a crowd powered platform, it will enable access to information (documents, reports, studies, national publications, statistics, stories etc) for its practical use. The UN portal will facilitate dissemination of experiences, success stories, good practices and case studies through digital storytelling (content directly contributed by creative professionals). The content will cover practical, real-time narratives, as well as academic and journalistic contributions.

V. Financing and Implementation

UNITAR is a project-based organization supported by voluntary contributions from governments, intergovernmental organizations, and other non-governmental sources such as foundations and private sector. The Institute has been seeking for donors and strategic partners for funding this initiative, which may be entirely or partially funded through allotments earmarked for selected activities.

A pilot phase is envisaged to start in 2015-2016. Countries that have identified creative economy as a priority in their national development plans, may be selected for a pilot phase. In subsequent years, following an evaluation of the pilot phase, the number of beneficiary countries is expected to increase, subject to the availability of resources. The learning activities will be adapted to the realities of each beneficiary.

UNITAR is proactively seeking partnerships with governments, academics and institutions as well as public and private entities for making this challenging project operational in the near future.

XTRADUCTION

References

UNCTAD/UNDP (2008). *Creative Economy Report – 2008, The challenge of assessing the creative economy: towards informed policy-making*, Geneva/New York

UNCTAD/UNDP (2010). *Creative Economy Report – 2010, Creative economy: A feasible development option, Geneva/New York*. Retrieved from: www.unctad.org/creative-economy

About the Author

Edna dos Santos - Duisenberg is Policy Advisor and Associate Expert, United Nations Institute for Training and Research - UNITAR; Founder and Former Chief, Creative Economy Programme, United Nations Conference on Trade and Development- UNCTAD.

*Edna is an Economist,
who became a world
reference for her
pioneering work on research
and analysis about
the creative economy and
its development dimension.
Ms. dos Santos developed
an international career of
nearly 30 years at
the United Nations in
Geneva. In 2004,
she founded and became
Chief of the Creative
Economy Programme of
the United Nations
Conference on Trade and
Development – UNCTAD.
She directed the research
and is the main
co-author of the UN Creative
Economy Reports of 2008
and 2010. She also set-up
the UNCTAD's Global
Database on Creative
Economy providing world
trade statistics for
creative products.
Her work was instrumental
to shape the policy and
the research agenda around
the creative economy.
She articulated intergovernmental policy debates and
promoted synergy,
partnerships and networking
among governments,
practitioners and academia.
At present, Edna dos Santos-
Duisenberg is
Vice-President of
the International Federation
of Multimedia Associations
- FIAM. She collaborates
with universities in different
regions of the world,
gives lectures and has
a number of published
articles. As an international
consultant, she provides
advisory services to
governments and institutions.*

—

creative.edna@gmail.com

—

edna.duisenberg@unitar.org

UNCTAD (2004). *Secretary-General's high-level panel on the creative economy and industries for development.* (TD(XII)/BP/4) Geneva.

United Nations (2003). *Encyclopaedia of the United Nations and International Agreements* - Volume 1. A-F, New York - Edited by A. Mango

United Nations (2013). *Report of the High-Level Panel of Eminent Persons on the Post-2015 Development Agenda*, New York

UNITAR (2013). *Creative Economy: Developing Capacities for Inclusive Socioeconomic Transformations*, Geneva. Retrieved from: www.unitar.org/ksi

UNITAR (2014). *Quality Assurance Framework*

Dos Santos-Duisenberg E. (2014). Cultural and Creative Industries, Knowledge Institutions and the Urban Environment, preface book; in: A. Schramme, R. Kooyman (Ed). *Beyond Frames.* EBURON Delft

Dos Santos-Duisenberg E.(2009). The creative economy: beyond economics. Article published in: *After the Crunch*, London, Creative Commons. Retrieved from: www.creative-economy.org.uk

Dos Santos-Duisenberg E. (2009) - Expanding trade flows of creative goods and services. In: *Trade Negotiations Insights*, Issue 1, Volume 8, Brussels. Retrieved from: www.acp-eu-trade.org/tni

XTRADUCTION

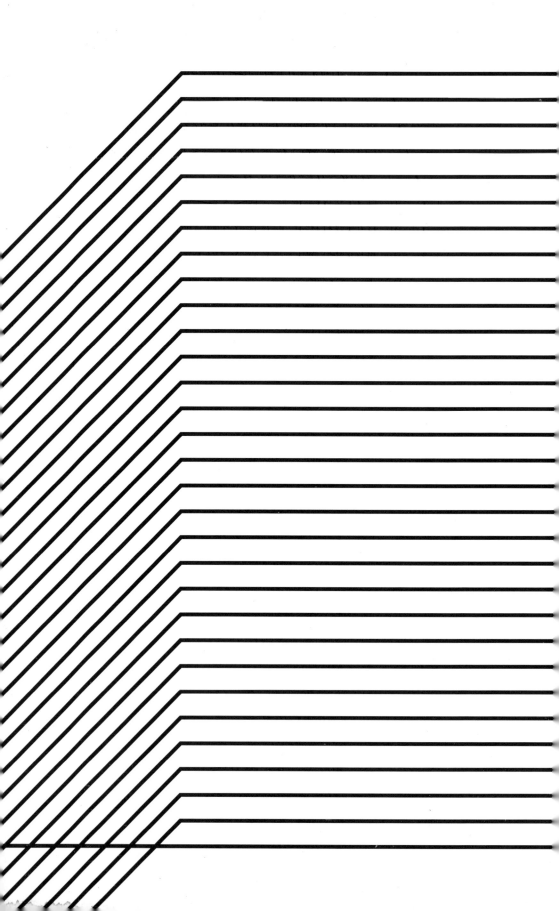